Toward a
Theory of Historical Narrative

Toward a Theory of Historical Narrative

A Case Study in Perso-Islamicate Historiography

Marilyn Robinson Waldman

Ohio State University Press: Columbus

Library of Congress Cataloguing in Publication Data

Waldman, Marilyn Robinson
Toward a theory of historical narrative.
Bibliography: p.
Includes index.
1. Bayhaqī, Abū al-Fazl Muhammad ibn Husayn, 996 (ca.)–1077. Tārīkh-i Bayhaqī. 2. Iran—Historiography. I. Title.
DS288.7.B33W34 955'.007'2 79-886
ISBN 0-8142-0297-7

For my parents, who
taught me to value learning

Contents

Acknowledgments xi

Note on Transliteration xiii

Note on the Islāmic Calendar xiv

1 Toward a Mode of Criticism for Premodern Islamicate Historical Narratives 3

2 The Life and Times of Abū'l-Fażl al-Bayhaqī 27

3 The Method of the Secretary as Historian: An Analysis of the Structure and Contents of *Ta'rīkh-i Bayhaqī* 51

4 The Pattern in Bayhaqī's Carpet: An Analysis of the Themes of *Ta'rīkh-i Bayhaqī* 79

5 History and Language: The Style of *Ta'rīkh-i Bayhaqī* 109

6 Bayhaqī's Place in Persian and Islamicate Cultural History 121

7 *Ta'rīkh-i Bayhaqī* in the Light of Speech Act Theory 131

Appendixes 143

Glossary 199

Bibliography 205

Index 211

Maps

1 The Dār al-Islām circa 1050 28

2 The Break-up of the Caliphate, Showing the Independent Dynasties 29

3 The Extent of the Ghaznavid Empire circa 1030 32

Acknowledgments

The inspiration for this study came from my teacher and friend, the late Marshall Hodgson of the University of Chicago, who made his students want to understand the human meaning of the cultural works of other civilizations. Thanks to the sympathy of Professors William H. McNeill, Heshmat Moayyad, Reuben Smith, and John Woods, I was able to continue my pursuit of this goal after Marshall Hodgson's death. To my classmate at the University of Chicago, Guity Nash'at Mirdamad, my thanks for opening up the treasures of Persian historiography for me.

This work has also benefited immeasurably from those patient listeners—my colleagues and students at the Ohio State University—who have made many suggestions that have broadened and deepened my vision. Without the help of Mrs. Clara Goldslager and her Inter-library Loan staff at the Ohio State University, it would have been impossible for me to complete this work.

My husband and daughter, who have often had to allow me to be with them in name only as I toiled at this labor, expect none but deserve the best of thanks. May their patience and compassion have been justified.

Note on Transliteration

The system of transliteration of Persian words (including Arabic words in Persian) used in this work follows the Library of Congress Persian Romanization system except in the following five cases:

ĥ instead of ḥ
ŝ instead of ṣ
z̈ instead of z̤
t̂ instead of ṭ
ẑ instead of ẓ

A few Persian words and names that have common Anglicized forms have not been changed, e.g., Tehran, Said Nafisi, Turkestan.

Where Arabic words appear in Arabic, the Library of Congress Arabic Romanization system has been used, except in the following five cases:

ĥ instead of ḥ
ŝ instead of ṣ
d̂ instead of ḍ
t̂ instead of ṭ
ẑ instead of ẓ

Note on the Islamic Calendar

The Islāmic calendar has twelve lunar months and a total of 354 or 355 days:

Muharram	30 days	Rajab	30 days
Safar	29	Sha'bān	29
Rabī^{c}ah I	30	Ramadhān	30
Rabī^{c}ah II	29	Shawwāl	29
Jumādah I	30	Dhū'l-Qa'dah	30
Jumādah II	29	Dhū'l-Hijjah	29*

For every thirty years, thirty-one lunar years elapse. The first Muslim year is considered by Muslims to have been 16 July 622 of the Common Era (C.E.), when the founder of the Muslim community, Muḥammad, emigrated from his native town of Mecca. This emigration was called the *hijrah,* so a year of the Muslim calendar is referred to as A.H., after the *hijrah.* The entire system of dating is called *hijrī* dating.

This work frequently retains the system of double dating, for example, fourth/tenth century; 1393/1973; 7 Shawwāl 421/8 October 1030; the first date given is the *hijrī*, the last the Common Era. Sometimes the *hijrī* year may be linked to two C.E. years, for example, 1387/1967–68, because the Muslim year 1387 ran from 11 April 1967 to 31 March 1968. This double-dating system is retained primarily because the *hijrī* years communicate as much or more than the Common Era ones for many Islāmicists.

*Thirty in leap year.

Toward a
Theory of Historical Narrative

1

Toward a Mode of Criticism for Premodern Islamicate Historical Narratives

"It is easy to cut to pieces a dead elephant." —Yoruba Proverb

INTRODUCTION

However suggestive previous studies of the rhetoric of formal historical writing may have been, they have not forced today's historians to view or to use historical narratives from the past in new and different ways.[1] Professional historians, however much they may try to weigh the importance of the styles, precommitments, and world views of the authors on whose narratives they depend, still look upon formal historical compositions essentially as a filter through which to view past "reality," their true focus.

In the field of Islamicate history, where scholars have tended to use historical narratives almost exclusively as unstructured, uninterpretive mines of factual information, the handling of sources has been particularly problematic.[2] The criteria of validity for the facts obtained from historical narratives are largely external; rarely are they related to the internal dynamics of the work from which the facts have been taken or to the interaction of the author's mind with the material he has presented, matters that have long been important in European and American historiography.[3] Systematic methods and categories of analysis through which such questions could be approached are virtually nonexistent. The usefulness of facts mined from historical writings is thus reduced and the relevance of the whole source to the history of ideas entirely neglected.[4] Instead of asking what a premodern Muslim author was trying to do as a historian and how he accomplished his goals, the scholar of Islamicate history has usually been content to ask what information the source provides that can be useful in solving *his own* problems.

This study challenges the status quo in Islamicate historiography through attempting a multifaceted analysis of a single text, in this case a major Islamicate historical narrative and a pivotal work in the history of new Persian (post-tenth-century) language and culture—the Ghaznavid period *Ta'rīkh-i Bayhaqī*.[5] A brief survey of the fields of Ghaznavid and Islamicate historiography as they exist now and as they are beginning to change will demonstrate the need for such a study and its problems in such a way as to point to possible solutions.

GHAZNAVID HISTORIOGRAPHY

The study of Ghaznavid history and historians is not yet well-developed. The Ghaznavids have only recently begun to attract serious and critical scholarly attention[6] for at least two reasons: (1) scholars have tended to view them as less important than the better-known Saljūqs, for whom they paved the way, and consequently only the heroics of their most famous member Maĥmūd have merited much attention;[7] (2) the sources for Ghaznavid history are in Arabic and Persian, often difficult to read and scattered over a broad spectrum of genres; and though many have been published and/or translated for some time, updated critical editions and translations in Western languages are only now beginning to appear.[8]

A thorough historiographical study of any or all of the primary sources for Ghaznavid history is yet to be undertaken. Although there are useful remarks in the introductions to two basic works, a few scattered articles and general surveys of Irānian historiography, and a new anthology of papers presented at a colloquium on one of the most famous Ghaznavid historians and subject of this study, Abū'l-Fažl-i Bayhaqī (ca. 966–1077), these works are not free from the problems described in the introduction to this chapter.[9] Among them there are no works that aim to analyze the total structure and pattern of any single Ghaznavid historical text, though there are many that evaluate the reliability or particular aspects of a given history.

In addition to exposing pitfalls in writing about individual historians, Ghaznavid historiography has shown the dangers of using historical sources as pools of facts and quotations. For example, even a careful and excellent scholar of the Ghaznavids like Clifford Bosworth, with many good insights into the views behind the works he quotes from, has often quoted out of context, including an assertion that has been contradicted on a preceding page of the original source, or quoting half of an assertion without the other half that would give it a different connotation.[10]

ISLAMICATE HISTORIOGRAPHY

The double problem of superficial analysis of the sources themselves and of uncritical use of them for writing history has also characterized Islamicate historiography as a whole. There are a number of general works, both books and articles, on Islamicate historical writing or a section of it, but they tend to be marred by an overconcentration on Arab as opposed to Persian and Turkish historians and on earlier rather than later ones; by categorization of types and schools of historical writing based on a very small sample of writers, not all of whom have been systematically studied; and by attention mainly to those aspects of historical writings that are thought to be useful in establishing the validity of factual information.[11]

Interest in intensive studies of individual Muslim historians has been rare. Of the forty-one articles in a recent anthology on Islamicate historiography, only four are on individual authors, and two of those are mostly on the sources the authors used.[12] In journal articles on individual historians, one historian—Ibn Khaldūn (1332–1406)—is overwhelmingly preferred; and in his case, as in that of other historians, usually only one aspect of his work is extracted for study.[13]

The preference for Ibn Khaldūn is symptomatic of the presentist or modernist tendency already discussed in the preceding section on Ghaznavid historiography. Much "internal" analysis in Islamicate historiography has tended to pick out those authors or elements most relevant to modern times; in the case of Ibn Khaldūn, it has even been argued that he was a precursor of nineteenth-century European sociology.

The preference for Ibn Khaldūn is also symptomatic of the fact that textual analysis of Muslim scholars has been reserved largely for systematic thinkers, like philosophers and theologians; or for literature; or for the Qur'ān.[14] In the many articles on Ibn Khaldūn, it is his philosophy rather than his history that has attracted the most attention.

There are a number of partial exceptions to these deficiencies in Islamicate historiography. Among them are three book-length analyses of individual historians: published studies on Ibn Miskawayh (d. 1030), Ibn Khaldūn (d. 1406), and Mas^{c}ūdī (d. 956).[15] These are only partial exceptions because, first of all, the historians in question have an explicitly philosophical orientation toward history that lends itself to critical analysis, whereas most Muslim historians do not.[16] Second, the book on Ibn Khaldūn, which analyzes only his introduction not his history, goes to a certain point in its analysis, with excellent insights about what issues interested Ibn Khaldūn and how he handled certain themes, but does not aim to explain why he has handled things the way he has or to achieve a total unifying vision of his work. The study of Ibn Miskawayh is fascinating, but tends to evaluate Ibn Miskawayh's historical ideas and writings in terms of his philosophical system, not as works in their own right.

FRESH STARTS

The glimmerings of a good beginning are to be found rather in a number of unrelated articles and books, particularly in a pioneering but poorly disseminated article by Marshall Hodgson and in the lengthy introductions that accompany some of the more recent critical editions and translations of historical works. It would appear that since the translator or editor needs to give every word equal consideration rather than to mine for facts, he is often led to an over-all understanding of what the author is saying and trying to do.[17] One article on Mamlūk historiography has clearly set a new standard for critical handling of evidence, and has skillfully used comparisons among a number of accounts and between historical and biographical literature to explore the usefulness of formal historical writings. But the author is still limited in his ability to determine what can be used from the sources by his failure to employ textual criticism of them.[18]

THE NATURE OF ISLAMICATE HISTORICAL WRITING

Role of Context

Scattered and unsystematic as this new activity has been, it has suggested a number of features apparently common to Islamicate historical narratives and also desiderata for their analysis that can provide a backdrop to any methodological discussion. First of all, just as has been assumed in European and American historiography, so in Islamicate: formal histories, whether contemporary with the periods they describe or not, can be assumed to be pervaded by the views of the author and his age on writing history, on the meaning of history in general, and on the particular history that is the subject of the work. Since one would expect histories written on the same subject(s) to vary significantly from author to author, from place to place, and from time to time, an analysis of the structure and content of a work can add to an understanding of the values that lie behind it.

In Western historiography it has become axiomatic that the understanding and use of formal historical writings, both their facts and interpretations, must be controlled by a knowledge of the way in which their content has been influenced by the values of their authors, so much so that warnings to that effect are included in rudimentary form in freshman manuals.[19] There are even studies to demonstrate this phenomenon in the works of Western historians of Islām, but few on Muslim historians themselves.[20]

Because of the interaction between author's values and historical composition, it is here assumed that it is impossible for a researcher reading a text to keep his textual analysis "unpolluted" by contextual factors; it is even assumed that the separation of text and context is undesirable. In this regard, any method appropriate to Islamicate historical narratives will have to diverge from the method of textual criticism employed by certain philosophers, for example by Mahdi in his study of Ibn Khaldūn, perhaps because of certain differences between philosophical and historical writing. Mahdi explains his approach this way:

> The basic methodological approach of the following study adopts certain aspects of the traditional method of philosophic commentary. The object of this method is to ascertain the *deliberate intention* of the author instead of seeking to explain his meaning as the product of his psychological or social conditions. It concentrates on the text of the author and preserves its integrity. And its exclusive aim is the elucidation of what the author says and the way he says it. It does not challenge the possibility that a reader may have a deeper knowledge of the subject matter than the author he is reading. But it assumes that the reader can never know what the author deliberately meant to say better than the author himself, and that the full understanding of what the author intended to say must precede interpretations based on principles other than those accepted by the author.[21]

On the contrary, in Islamicate historical writing (1) there seems to be much unconscious patterning, particularly in a work based on any kind of oral tradition, which has meaning beyond the deliberate intention of the author; (2) in a historical work the deliberate intention of an author can be in fact misread or inaccessible without reference to his intellectual, social, and psychological conditions; and (3) applying principles or analytic vocabulary other than that accepted by the author is unavoidable and may enhance rather than do violence to his meaning, as long as the *conclusions* reached through them are not anachronistic or presentistic.

There is more to a full understanding of an older historical work than ascertaining the deliberate intention of the author. Pre-modern Muslim historians were more often than not unsystematic thinkers; they expressed many of their attitudes below the level of deliberate intention. And the recognition of unconscious patterning can come only from as wide as possible an awareness of the author and his intellectual milieu.

Furthermore, even ascertaining the deliberate intention of an author can depend upon knowing some aspect of the context in which the work was written. For example, suppose that one man writes a set of personal confessions in an original way. A century later, by which time the pattern he used has become stylized, someone else writes one because it is fashionable to do so, or uses this pattern not because it is fashionable to write confessions but because this pattern is standard among men wanting to write confessions for more serious reasons. Or suppose that an old and a young man say the same things about women or about death, but because of the difference in their ages do not have the same deliberate intention. Or, again, suppose that a bureaucrat and an army man write the same things about war, one from hearsay and the other from experience. How is one to ascertain deliberate intention in such cases, and in many others, without reference to certain intellectual, psychological, and social conditions?

But then the question arises, Can this assumption of non-deliberate meaning and can this application of "principles [of explanation] other than those accepted by the author" be reconciled with an expressed desire to understand an author in his own terms and to maintain the integrity of his work? The answer in the strictest sense is "no"; some distortion is inevitable in this type of analysis, even when one adheres to the use of principles accepted by the author.[22] However, the use of principles or of an analytic vocabulary not accepted by, or unknown to, an author does not necessarily lead to anachronistic conclusions. Sometimes, for example, the principles that in an esoteric work would have led a reader to an understanding of the author's deliberate intention have been lost to a modern scholar, who must then devise a new method to uncover them. A scholar working on Persian historiography of the Ghaznavid and Saljūq periods has illustrated how a modern method or "principle," communications theory, can be used precisely to understand the deliberate intention of certain historical writers.[23] Or, to give an example of another type of problem, it is acceptable to consider an author's social position relevant to understanding the significance of his views on wealth (even though he might not have made the connection) as long as one does not cast one's conclusions in terms of a social class structure or a theory of social class inapplicable to that author's time. In these ways, "principles other than those accepted by the author" may actually serve as bridges of communication between one age and another.

What Mahdi opposes is the historicist approach to textual criticism, one that views an entire work as simply a product of something outside the control of the author, for example, the age in which he lives or the intellectual influence on him. Any method developed here should also oppose an exclusively historicist approach. In fact, it should add a corollary—that it is very dangerous to assume *a priori* what would be the "typical" effect of a given contextual circumstance and then to read a text from that point of view. This corollary is particularly useful in Islamicate historiography, where the scarcity of evidence tempts one to evaluate a thinker according to what one would expect from a typical bureaucrat, a religious scholar, a man of a particular age, or whatever other category the author in question might belong to.

Nevertheless, the very study of historical writings from other ages shows the modern scholar that one is a product of one's age, especially when working in history. The modern scholar is not exempt. It is better to acknowledge, understand, and control one's assumptions than to have them at work unconsciously. In some forms of literature that have become the object of textual criticism, like myth and folklore, scholars have looked for timeless themes. The theme a historian uses, however, is much more closely tied to the age in which he lives, just as the modern historian will inevitably express his understanding of a previous historian in the vocabulary of his age. To the extent that he can bring his values to the surface, his understanding of the past will be that much improved.

Didacticism

The second feature, related directly to the first, is that the degree to which moral values ordinarily control historical composition seems to have been especially great in premodern Islamicate society, where formal historical writing tended to be peculiarly didactic in intention and function. As Hodgson has argued for the two historians he studied, ''accuracy as to 'fact' was much less important than validity as to life-vision.''[24] ''Facts'' often served as the raw material of problem-solving, or at least of problem-raising. The reader must be prepared to assess whether the issues involved in the material selected for treatment fall into any pattern of repeating themes and motifs. The material can be expected to raise a set of problems distinct from those raised by other historians.

Cantor has argued in a slightly different way that the same is true for pre-eighteenth-century European historical writing. According to him the events described in it ''were made to conform to an image of reality that governed all social thought. . . . Historians did not argue from the particular to the general; rather they made particular events and people conform to the traditional types or patterns.''[25] Cantor goes on to add that, given this element of didactism, one would expect to find in a premodern history a large number of paradigms or typologies. From early Anglo-Saxon historiography, Barlow has supplied the example of the famous portrait of Edward the Confessor on his deathbed, which was in fact adapted from a text dealing with Saint Audemer.[26] In Islamicate historiography there is a similar tendency to fit the events of a reformer's life into the pattern of Muḥammad's career, regardless of whether the reformer had consciously done so himself. Related to this tendency is the tendency to mythologize the past, as in the image of the first four caliphs—the so-called Rāshidūn—that grew up gradually after the death of the last of them.

Despite the obvious presence of such typologies, paradigms, and myths and the need to be prepared to meet them, there are added complications in their use by Muslim historians that can serve to refine Cantor's argument. First of all, Cantor's concept of a single ''image of reality which governed all social thought'' needs to be altered for use in the Muslim context. Often, Muslim writers of any particular age had a number of conflicting but equally acceptable typologies available from which to choose. Or if there was one dominant typology, they might not share it. In using typologies and paradigms, Muslim writers also seem to have been more aware of what they were doing than the authors Cantor describes. Muslim historians may have felt obligated to make history conform to a particular pattern that most readers would and could accept; if they themselves did not completely accept it, they might then contradict it under the surface. For instance, in certain traditions of writing about kings, all kings must be shown to be *ḥalīm,* "forebearing," and *karīm,* "generous"; but perhaps not all have to be shown as *mutaḥawwiṭ,* "cautious," so that when one is, it may be a sign that the typology is being contradicted and that something particularly revealing is being said. Hidden critiques could even be built right into a given typology. Juvaynī (1226–83), a Muslim historian forced into the service of the Mongols, has been shown by his translator to have built criticism of the Mongols into his praise of them as great conquerors.[27]

Esotericism

The complex use of typologies that has just been described is related to a third aspect not only of Muslim historical writing but in this case of non-historical Muslim scholarship as well: Muslims writing history usually felt themselves, with or without immediate justification, to be under the constraints of what they called *taqiyyah,* dissimulation or complete concealment of one's true feelings not only from authorities but from most ordinary readers as well.[28] The discussion of the second feature held clues as to why this should be the case. The subject matter of Islamicate historical writings is primarily politico-religious. The conclusions reached through the study of Muslim history were very important to many different types of people: since from the beginning Muslim polity and society had been considered as manifestations of the divinely directed destiny of the Muslim community, reaching the "right" historical conclusions became essential. Not only rulers but also pious Muslim readers in general wanted the events of history to be shown to be on the right track. But because the ideal community was considered desirable and possible, the gap between the ideal and real that is always present took on particularly sharp significance. The explosive potential of historical writing lay in its ability to point out this gap, to reveal that whatever could be learned about elusive "historical reality" could contradict the ideals of the very pattern into which it was being pressed.

Not only political ideas could necessitate *taqiyyah.* A historian could also have attitudes about the very nature of the historical pursuit that could be offensive to certain pious readers. In general, the norms of a Muslim historian's audience seem to have been opposed to the obvious use of human reason to explain what could and should only be explained according to divine will. Many writers shared these norms and felt guilty about seeming to transgress them; other writers reject the audience's norms on this and other matters but felt compelled to pay lip service to them. It was also possible for a writer to be writing for the part of his audience that shared his values and have to conceal them from the authorities and the rest of the audience. For all these reasons Muslim histories on the surface often have an air of objectivity and equanimity that has misled many modern critics.[29] In addition, between the tenth and fifteenth centuries, the tendency to argue from the general to the particular was replaced or supplemented among some Muslim historians by argument from the particular to the general, thus allowing the study of historical "facts" to lead to general laws or patterns instead of reworking history always to fit a pattern. When and where this change took place, the explosive nature of historical studies came to be more clearly felt, and in turn often required even greater *taqiyyah.* In addition to all these causes of *taqiyyah,* there is the fact that a quality of esotericism pervaded much Muslim scholarship. The premodern Muslim audience had time to reflect and read between the lines, and at least some part of it was expected to. But it was always safer for an author to write on the surface for the widest possible audience and let those who would, read deeper.

There are numerous techniques or signs of dissimulation that can be looked for in the content of a work, among them symbolism, allegory, myth, anachronism, and ambiguous word usage. In the case of allegory, an anecdote from another time and place might be appended to a narrative account and to the perceptive reader say many things about that narrative account which are not said in the account itself. This reshaping of the narrative may in turn raise it to a symbolic or mythical level. Such a simultaneous conjunction of allegory, myth, and symbolism has been demonstrated in Holt's analysis of Jabartī's (Egyptian historian, early nineteenth century) *Introduction to the History of Ottoman Egypt.* Holt argues that Jabartī indicates the existence and significance of the themes he is exploring not by tracing them in detail but through the use of legendary anecdotes that played the part of parables[30] employing characters symbolic of the forces struggling for control of Egypt—forces that Jabartī has not chosen to make explicit in the narrative itself.

Such pressing of narrated events into symbolic and mythical shape is in turn also related to the tendency to didacticism described above. A comparable use of legend occurred when Shakespeare moved away from recent political subjects, which were too obvious, to mythical or ancient ones, like Troilus and Cressida and Julius Caesar—"dramas which spoke out freely on the political troubles of the British state under the guise of dealing only with the remote past."[31] In many cultures the evaluation of the distant past can be much safer than an open study of the present.

A type of anachronism very common in Muslim historical writing occurs in Ṭabarī's account of the death of ᶜUthmān (the third caliph, reigned 644–56), in which ᶜUthmān, about to be brutally assassinated (656), delivers an oration prophetically embodying all the wisdom of hindsight that Ṭabarī's generation (Ṭabarī died in 923) had garnered.[32]

It was also possible to use words with a number of different, sometimes almost opposite, shades of meaning. In this way a single word could communicate to different readers on different levels. Mahdi has demonstrated the wide ramifications and multiple levels in a single Arabic word in his analysis of Ibn Khaldūn's use of *"ᶜibar."*[33] An Arabic word like *ḥaqq,* which is used in significant statements in Abū'l-Fażl-i Bayhaqī's work, can range from "right" in the sense of a dynasty's right to exist, to "truth" meant either in the metaphysical sense or in the sense of the real truth behind the image, to "obligation," all the way to a mystical sense connected with a divine attribute. So when Bayhaqī says he will show the *"ḥaqq"* of the Ghaznavid dynasty, it can be a statement truly full of many levels of meaning.

Interpretation through Structure

Although there are numerous ways in which content signals dissimulation, the fourth feature is that in premodern Muslim historical writing, as perhaps in other premodern writings,[34] it is the structure of the work that often bears the brunt of communicating the author's values. Elements of structure—organization, pace, arrangement, focus, selection, repetition, juxtaposition, omission, and emphasis—can convey the attitudes of the author. The attitudes thus conveyed are often not found in, or reinforced by, any explicit declarations. Thus it often can be easy to suspect that an author is trying to communicate a point of view, but difficult to be sure what that point of view is.

An example of one structural sign, focus, is illustrated in the work of Ṭabarī (d. 923). An analysis of Ṭabarī's account of the Battle of Ṣiffīn (657), a pivotal battle in the early history of the Muslim community, shows that, unlike other contemporary historians, he focuses almost exclusively on the crises in the camp of one of the two protagonists, ᶜAlī, perhaps because Ṭabarī was himself sympathetic to the ᶜAlid cause, as has often been argued, or more likely because it was in ᶜAlī's camp that the problems of legitimacy that preoccupied Ṭabarī were most sharply delineated. This latter possibility is also connected with the discussion of didacticism in the second hypothesis.

The work of the subject of this study, Abū'l-Fażl-i Bayhaqī, provides a good example of the conflict between explicit and implicit values, or, put another way, of the juxtaposition of explicit declarations and a structural feature that reveals another set of values. Fairly early in his work, Bayhaqī explicitly states that it is God's ability, with which he has no business, to analyze the heart (*żamīr*); his job is just to tell what happened (*sukhan randan*): "God the powerful and mighty can know of the heart of his servants; I have no business with that; my job is just telling what happened."[35] But in his book there is a rather overwhelming emphasis on the analysis of what is in people's minds and hearts, though he frequently feels compelled to apologize for it, with the above and numerous other more routine pieties.[36]

Another example of arrangement and juxtaposition, also from Bayhaqī, provides an opportunity to define further what additional questions the textual critic would ask of Muslim historical materials. At one point Bayhaqī includes the text of an official letter that he copied, sent from King A to King B, describing a situation that has just been related orally to King A by one of his advisers.[37] The modern historian of Islām, interested in the letter for its information, would be very pleased and impressed to have such a document (a rarity in Muslim historical materials) and, after assuring himself it could reasonably be considered authentic (there is almost no way to *prove* that it is), would use it for its substance, for what it told about diplomatic relations between King A and King B, and for what could be inferred from it about chancery practice in that time and place. He might even assume that the account given in the letter was more trustworthy than the account given orally to King A in the first place.

Any textual critic, attentive to structural features, would be interested in these matters but would put them aside while he asked:

1. Is there any discrepancy between the oral account to King A and the letter to King B; and if so, what reasons could there be for it?
2. Why does the author include the text of the letter at that point when he has just told essentially the same story, especially if the accounts are different? Does he include it just because he has it or because he thinks it adds something?
3. In the latter case, what does this use of a document tell us about his views on historical evidence and how do these views compare with other historians of his day describing the same event? In the former case, has the letter been included to emphasize the author's credentials or simply to brag about his closeness to the sources?
4. How does the form of the letter compare with other comparable documents in the book, if any?

After answering such questions, the textual critic could then go back to questions he had left aside and be in a much better position to decide how to use the letter to answer them.

An example of the absence in explicit declarations of values communicated through structure can be found in Hodgson's study of Ṭabarī's method of historical composition.[38] Hodgson has shown that the pattern of Ṭabarī's seemingly careless arrangement of numerous different versions of a given event holds clues to Ṭabarī's own beliefs and favored interpretations that are never made explicit elsewhere.[39] Such structural analysis has made it possible to go far beyond, or below, the fruitless perspectives that have dominated scholarship on Ṭabarī, as exemplified in the following critique by Marin, one of his translators:

> His [Ṭabarī's] function as an annalist was not to interpret history but only to record it on the statements of his various authorities; there was little sorting or choosing of facts on the basis of their possible correctness [thus despite the fact that Marin soon goes on to make a point of the inexplicability of Ṭabarī's omissions]; and one will find no seasoned opinion or comment by Ṭabarī. . . .[40]

On the contrary, Hodgson has shown that Ṭabarī's "seasoned opinion or comment" is imbedded in the structure itself. The structure of even a telephone directory says a good deal about the values and character of the society that necessitated and produced it as well as about the function it is to serve. Ṭabarī's case also points up the fact that in certain styles of historical composition there was little room for overt value declarations; values had to be communicated in other ways.[41]

Genre

This last point leads directly into the fifth and final aspect, namely, that Muslim historical works, like other types of literature, tended to be written within the framework of set genres or styles, so that there were limits to be transcended if more than was ordinarily expected in a given genre was to be communicated. This is a problem closely related to that of typology and paradigm, except that the style and pattern of a genre encompass the entire work in which typologies and paradigm of content may play a large part.

The aesthetics of premodern Islamicate society fostered variations within a given form, more and more as time passed. Whenever approaching genre writing, there is obviously a necessity to separate what is *de rigeur* in terms of structure, content, and style—what is "stylized"—from what is spontaneous; and even when something is *de rigeur,* to evaluate any subtle variation from the norm. Obviously, expressions that are formulaic in a particular type of writing are to be taken differently from those that are not. A simple example is the almost habitual, routinized use of pious expressions; for example, "God have mercy on him!", for instance, after the names of the Prophet and members of his family, or after the names of revered caliphs. It would be the omission of such a pious exclamation, or the use of an unusual and ambiguous one, or the use of one in an unusual place, that would be telling. Even small things like pieties are important, despite the fact that translators consider them meaningless and often omit them entirely.

The existence of genre writing requires that the researcher be familiar with all the styles of writing relevant to the particular work he is studying and that he understand the stage represented by that work in the development of its genre. But since most Muslim thinkers were not so narrowly pigeonholed as modern thinkers often are and were often involved in a number of genres and traditions, this can be a difficult job indeed.

The problem of genre writing also gives new twists to the meaning of plagiarism. A famous example, and one that shows how easy it is for stylization to be overlooked, was the discovery that Ghazālī's (Muslim theologian, d. 1111) famous confession or autobiography, which had always seemed surprisingly personal, was actually constructed according to an established pattern for "personal" confessions.[42] This was not considered plagiarism in Ghazālī's day, even though he did not acknowledge his inspirer, and should not be evaluated as such.

Even the act of lifting whole sections from others' works without acknowledgement of any kind was not always considered plagiarism by the Muslims themselves, especially if the passages were so well known as not to need acknowledgement. It must also be remembered that among premodern Muslims scholarship was considered to consist of passing on existing knowledge intact and adding comments along the way. Lifting of whole passages from the tradition, which was the common possession of all scholars, was therefore frequent.

Even if such lifting was regarded by contemporaries as plagiarism (and this judgment seems to have been reserved for mediocre writers who had nothing of their own to offer), the modern researcher cannot automatically discount such material because the author's placement, use, and alteration of it, and also his reasons for not writing it himself, are still of interest; and he may still be a significant thinker. Such is the case with Rashīd al-dīn, a major Persian historian (1247–1318) of the early Mongol period, who felt obligated because of the genre he was adhering to, a type of universal history, to include certain material that he did not feel inclined, or able perhaps, to compose himself. A critic has written that Rashīd al-dīn's "brief chronological summary of universal history . . . is an epitome [it would be interesting to know how the two differ, since "epitome" implies neither paraphrase nor verbatim] of Ibnū'l Athīr [d. 1233], and the account of Sulṭān Maḥmūd [Ghaznavid ruler, r. 998–1030] is an unacknowledged verbatim copy of Jurbādhāqānī's translation of ᶜUtbī's *Kitābū'l Yamīnī*. It is a glaring instance of plagiarism in Oriental literature."[43] The critic is right about the facts but very possibly wrong in his interpretation of them. It is not clear that Rashīd al-dīn thought he was fooling anyone; if he could not fool his modern critic, could he have fooled his contemporaries? And there is still much that can be learned from his use of the "plagiarized" material.

Involved in the problem of genre writing is the problem of language and style. Muslim historical materials were part of the life of letters; and many historians were very conscious of style, more conscious of being "literary" than most modern historians. For example, Abū'l-Fażl Bayhaqī appears in surveys of Persian "literature" as well as in books about Persian historiography; and an historian of literature can well view his book solely in terms of its contribution to the development of Persian prose style. For example, the wealth of detail in Bayhaqī's work is simultaneously a new development in historical method and an innovation in terms of Persian prose style.[44] This means that the way in which some historical ideas are expressed can be guided by a desire to try to develop a particular language style and can take over from historiographical concerns.[45]

These then are five interrelated aspects of pre-modern Islamicate historical writings that have been suggested by the best studies of them: (1) that their historical vision is clearly related to the time and place in which the history was written, (2) that Muslim historical writings tended to be consciously didactic, (3) that Muslim historians often felt the need to dissimulate their preferences and values in the lessons they were teaching, (4) that structural features can communicate the author's values, and (5) that historical writing was subject to genre and stylistic limitation.

TOWARD A MODE OF CRITICISM

As rudimentary as these assumptions may seem to anyone who works extensively with literature and language, they have not been applied to formal historical writings in such a way as to make any meaningful difference in the way such writings are viewed or used. Historical narratives have always occupied an anomalous position for all types of critical theory, none of which has itself arrived at a valid understanding of "literature" as a body. Even at its best, conventional historiographical analysis, such as that described in the foregoing section or in standard manuals, has asked interesting questions but only unsystematically and only as preparation for using their "sources" in conventional ways.[46] True textual analysis, as critics today speak of it, has for conventional historiographers taken second place to more unfashionable "contextual" considerations, such as biography, milieu, intellectual traditions, and audience. Those who do focus on text rather than context—linguists, French structuralists, Russian formalists—focus either on ordinary language or on poetic language, into neither of which historical narrative seems comfortably to fit. The small number of attempts to apply this or that existing critical technique (and even critics who eschew history provide promising techniques) have not been followed up. The historiographer who adapts others' critical techniques is always cast in the role of a parasite living off the life of another body without ever becoming a welcome part of it.

For different reasons for different types of professionals, historical narrative is always problematic essentially because it is neither ordinary discourse nor is it literary or poetic discourse in today's usage; because it is presumed to be a special kind of language whose determining characteristic is its aim to be truthful—to reconstruct reality in a "factual" way, that is, to be free from fictivity to the extent that it is good history, and because its analysis seems to be unamenable to an exclusively textual focus.

Northrop Frye, whose work has so much possible relevance to the analysis of formal historical writing, explicitly excludes historical narrative by asserting that "literature" must ultimately focus on itself, not on things external to itself, be they events or the tastes of the audience; that literature does not describe or assert; that it is an "autonomous verbal structure," free from "the controlling aim of descriptive accuracy":[47]

> We should, perhaps, like to feel that the writer of a historical drama knew what the historical facts of his theme were, and that he would not alter them without good reason. But that such good reasons may exist in literature is not denied by anyone. They seem to exist only there: the historian selects his facts, but to suggest that he had manipulated them to produce a more symmetrical structure would be grounds for libel.[48]

Ironically, the one author who has aggressively tried, rather, to reconcile "literature" and "history," David Levin, has grounded his effort on a similar assigning to history of the property of "descriptive accuracy" in Frye's terms. "For this chapter, I should define *history* as the written record and interpretation that tried to describe human experience of the past as accurately as possible; *literature,* as any written language that expresses a serious effort to understand and evaluate human experience."[49]

Although Levin goes on to try to achieve a reconciliation, he does so while maintaining a desire to find no hostility between "literary effects and factual accuracy."[50] That is, for Levin, the property of accuracy must be shown to exist in spite of, or perhaps even because of, any "literary" qualities:

> Let us begin, then, with this premise: *In formal history the highest literary art is that combination of clear understanding and exposition which brings us closest to a just evaluation of the past now present to us.* Bad history can be written with grace and wit, but so long as it is "bad" its art cannot be consummate.
>
> Thus we reject the contradictory notion that a literary success may require or condone historical error. For if history is a literary art, the artistry deserves our attention only as it accepts the fundamental purpose of the *genre,* which is not, in Mr. Carr's condescending phrase, to tell stories and legends without significance or purpose but to communicate a just understanding of the past in relation to the present and the future.[51]

Levin's struggle, along with everything said so far in this chapter, points the way to the fundamental desideratum of a new method of analysis for formal historical writings, in this case Islamicate—a conceptual framework that transcends the view of historical narrative as a special kind of language possessing special properties, especially accurate description and relevance to things outside itself in order to provide a real place for historical narrative in an analytic class or category constructed according to entirely different principles.

The recent publication by Mary Louise Pratt of *Toward a Speech Act Theory of Literary Discourse* opens up such a possibility, though, ironically, never once does she herself make the leap from her own subject to its application to the analysis of historical narrative.[52] The key to Pratt's contribution to the study of historical writing is her construction of a new category of analysis that she calls "display texts." She does so out of her extended understanding of the implication of Labov's study of natural narrative.[53] Starting from a speech act theory background, Pratt argues that a whole series of hitherto unrelated "texts," for example, natural narrative, exclamations, some speeches, most "literature," belong to the same "speech situation," wherein the "speaker"

> is interested not only in reporting states of affairs, but in verbally displaying them, responding to them, evaluating them, and interpreting them. He creates and tables a verbal version of an experience ["real" or fictitious, that is] seeking his audience's imaginative, affective, and evaluative involvement and its support for his interpretation or its help in finding a better one.[54]

To arrive at this class of things, "whose primary point is thought-producing, representative or world-describing," Pratt has adapted from single-sentence-utterance analysis an important distinction crucial in overcoming the problematic nature of historical narrative—a distinction between the assertible, i.e, true and informative, and the tellable, i.e., the not obviously true, possessing "display-producing relevance."[55] I quote now at length from her elaboration of this distinction because it is essential to my decision to place the text under study into this class for purposes of analysis:

> Assertions whose relevance is tellability must represent states of affairs that are held to be unusual, contrary to expectation, or *otherwise problematic* [emphasis mine]; informing assertions may do so, but they do not have to, and it is not their point to do so. Both types are used to inform, but they inform for different reasons. In making an assertion whose relevance is tellability, a speaker is not only reporting but also verbally displaying a state of affairs, inviting his addressee(s) to join him in contemplating it, evaluating it, and responding to it. His point is to produce in his hearers not only belief but also an imaginative and affective involvement in the state of affairs he is representing and an evaluative stance toward it. He intends them to share his wonder, amusement, terror, or admiration of the event. Ultimately, it would seem, what he is after is an *interpretation* of the problematic event, an assignment of meaning and value supported by the consensus of himself and his hearers.
>
> Let me stress here that in distinguishing between tellability and assertibility, I am distinguishing not between two types of information, but between two uses of information. That is, I am not trying to distinguish between information or states of affairs which are in fact unexpected and those which are not. Rather, I

am distinguishing between information or states of affairs that are being verbally represented because they are felt to be unexpected and those that are being represented for some other reason.[56]

The advantages to seeing historical narrative in this light are enormous, for one is enabled to handle at the same time the twin problems of fact-fiction and text-context that have stymied analysis of historical texts. She addresses the fictivity issue directly in the following way: "As I have already suggested, the fiction/nonfiction distinction is neither as clear-cut nor as important as we might think [readers familiar with historical works will recall the number of different "pictures" that can be drawn with the same facts], at least not in the realm of the tellable. Our capacity for verbally displaying and evaluating experience and for finding pleasure in such displays applies equally to experience which is claimed to be real as to that which is not."[57]

In her handling of the issue of fictivity, Pratt implies her response to the problem of text and context, a response fundamental to the idea behind speech act theory. The state of affairs that any text displays must be viewed in terms of the context and conditions in which the text is produced and the principles by which readers "read," or cooperate with the author in receiving his message. For those readers who are still concerned that there must be a difference between an image of an event that actually occurred and one that occurred in the mind of the author, her response would probably be that the burden of proof would be on them to demonstrate this difference in terms of the way the text was composed and read, since all existing evidence seems to point away from the meaningfulness of such a distinction. Ironically, Frye and Levin, as quoted above, point the way to Pratt's conclusions but fail to take the last, crucial step: "The view that literary works are verbal displays designed to re-create, interpret, and evaluate experience is a familiar one to most literary scholars. The important point for the present argument is that this re-creative, interpretive activity is not unique to literature."[58]

The potential fit of Pratt's ideas to the needs of Islamicate historiographical analysis has by now become apparent. It becomes even clearer when she describes two fundamental features that one should expect from display texts—detachability and susceptibility to elaboration.[59] By detachability, she means partly that they "do not have to relate to the concrete, momentary concerns of the addressee. They are not primarily aimed at correcting the addressee's immediate knowledge or expectations of his surroundings. (As I suggested earlier, this is probably the reason we so easily tolerate exaggeration, embellishment, and fictionalizing in natural narrative.) The only hearer-based appropriateness condition for display texts is that the hearer be able to recognize and appreciate the tellability of what is being asserted."[60] Immediately the historian is reminded that many widely read and appreciated historical narratives have information not *needed* by their readers in any immediate sense of the word.

In her discussion of the susceptibility of display texts to elaboration, Pratt indirectly addresses the problem of repetitiveness in Islamicate historical texts, especially in those like Ṭabarī's that string together separate short narratives on the same event, by pointing out that the speaker of a display text can "pile detail upon detail, and can be blatantly repetitive, because he is understood to be enabling his audience to imagine and comprehend a state of affairs more fully and to savor it for a long time."[61]

Despite the fact that Pratt's approach to display texts seems to address the features previously described for Islamicate historical writings (and perhaps for any historical narratives), the obstacles to even beginning to apply it systematically are formidable. First of all, the whole enterprise hinges on being able to define the given speech situation correctly, which in itself involves discovering, through the determination of normative texts, the grammar of the maxims that govern their production and reception (or the appropriateness conditions in speech act terms) and of the meaning and parameters of acceptable deviance from them, deviance (or violation) through which the author communicates important messages to his audience. (Pratt herself relies on H. Paul Grice's formulations, which will be tested in the final chapter of this study.)[62] Since no one is yet able to be sure of these elements for Islamicate historical texts because we do not yet have normative texts established and because we are in fact text-dependent to talk about text production and reception, a case study like this one can but be a contribution to the beginnings of a speech act understanding and its implications for the utility of historical narratives for writing narrative history today.

Therefore, before any direct application of Pratt's conceptualization is attempted, the text under study will be analyzed from more conventional textual and contextual points of view (suggested by eclectic reading in historiographical and critical literature of all sorts), in this case biography, historical method, thematic patterns, structural features, language style, and historical place, in order to familiarize the reader with the text and to build up enough information to begin to talk about it in unconventional ways, that is, in terms of its possible place in the class of display texts. In this work contextual and textual analysis are assumed to be complementary, not mutually exclusive.

Before turning to the first chapter in the study of *Ta'rīkh-i Bayhaqī* itself, it is perhaps important to restate the goals of this study in the order of their importance. Without a doubt, its first and foremost aim is to contribute, in however halting and meager a way, to the methodology of the study of historical narrative and by extension of all "display texts," if only by encouraging other studies like this one. Beyond that, it is hoped that this analysis will encourage scholars to consider thinking about the historical narratives they use in new terms, to the extent that they begin to use them for new, probably more appropriate, purposes. With regard to the Persian historical text itself, one wishes to know, of course, the "thought processes" (i.e., motivations, intentions, biases, values, preferences, impact of cultural and educational heritage and author's life experiences, paradigms, models, attitudes toward the theory and practice of history as a genre) that resulted in, and guided, its production. Once these thought processes have been specified, the historian of course wishes to go further to evaluate the text's place in, and significance for, Persian and Islamicate intellectual and literary history and its valid uses in writing history today. Of course, it is assumed that unanalyzed sources cannot be used reliably at all. It remains to be seen, in light of this statement of goals and the way in which the format of the work has been described, whether questions that seem to interest a historian but not a speech act theorist can in fact be incorporated into a speech act understanding or must be added to it.

The inevitable tentativeness and eclecticism of any work like this one reflect the state of the field of Islamicate studies as a whole, not just Islamicate history and historiography. Oleg Grabar, in his recent book on the formation of Islamicate art, has also worked in a number of similar contexts and has described the nature of his investigation in terms equally applicable to this study: "What is presented here is an exercise in *Problemstellung,* in the setting up of categories of learning and investigation through which a series of fundamental questions may be answered."[63]

Such an approach is as novel in Islamicate historical criticism as it is in Islamicate art criticism, and Grabar also says that the conclusions of any such study are not carved in stone and often cannot even be formulated in a definite fashion. As Grabar writes, and as is hoped in this study, it is possible and useful to "define the limits of our knowledge and the questions which require further investigation."

1. For example, Peter Gay, *Style in History* (New York: Basic Books, 1974); Hayden White, *Metahistory* (Baltimore: John Hopkins University Press, 1973); David Levin, *In Defense of Historical Literature* (New York: Hill and Wang, 1967); and John Clive, *Macaulay: The Shaping of the Historian* (New York: Alfred A. Knopf, 1973). Note that even in European and American historiography such works are relatively rare.

2. "Islamicate" is a new term coined by Marshall G. S. Hodgson, *The Venture of Islam* (Chicago: University of Chicago Press, 1974), 1:57ff., to distinguish products of the civilization that came to be associated with the faith of Islām from things having to do directly and specifically with that faith itself, for which he reserved the older term, "Islāmic."

3. There is by no means complete agreement on the procedure to be followed in establishing such reliability; but the criteria that seem to be employed include the author's proximity to the events he describes, the "reliability" of the sources he uses, his care with dating and placing, the fullness of his account as compared with other historians, his "professional credentials," and so on. Often, once the "overall" reliability and authenticity of a source has been established, it is common for a historian to use any information supplied by the source wherever needed, unless

there is a special reason for not using it on some particular point. Usually this use is made without reference to the place of that piece of data in the work as a whole.

4. Marshall G. S. Hodgson, "Two Pre-Modern Muslim Historians: Pitfalls and Opportunities in Presenting them to Moderns," in *Towards World Community,* ed. John Nef, World Academy of Arts and Sciences Publications, vol. 5 (The Hague: Dr. W. Junk N. V. Publishers, 1968), p. 64, labels this tendency "reductivism." But whereas Hodgson was concerned mainly with the potential disservice to the historical works themselves, I am concerned as well with the criteria for establishing the validity of the facts "mined" from them. A number of historians in different fields have begun to comment on the difficulties of using formal historical narratives to write narrative history. In Islamicate history, see K. Allin Luther, "Bayhaqī and the Later Seljūq Historians: Some Comparative Remarks," in Mashhad University, Faculty of Letters and Humanities, *Yādnāmah-yi Abū'l-Fażl-i Bayhaqī* (Mashhad: Mashhad University Press, 1350/1971), pp. 14–33; Donald P. Little, "The Historical and Historiographical Significance of the Detention of Ibn Taymiyya," *International Journal of Middle Eastern Studies,* 4 (July 1973): 311–27; and Peter Hardy, *Historians of Medieval India* (London: Luzac and Company, 1960).

5. The Ghaznavids were a Turkish Muslim dynasty centered in eastern Irān, Afghānistān, and later in India from 962 to 1186. This work was produced by a chancery worker at their court in Ghazna in the first half of the fifth/eleventh century.

6. Most notable are three works, two of which remain unpublished: Clifford Edmund Bosworth, *The Ghaznavids; Their Empire in Afghanistan and Eastern Iran 944:1040* (Edinburgh: Edinburgh University Press, 1963); R. Gelpke, "Sultan Mas^{c}ud I. von Gazna" Ph.D. diss., University of Basel, 1957); and Yūsuf ^{c}Abbās Hashmī, "Political, Cultural and Administrative History under the Latter Ghaznavids" (Ph.D. diss., University of Hamburg, 1956).

7. Biographies of Maĥmūd, who impressed the Muslim world by his raids into India and gained the image of a religious fanatic in the West, go back a long way; not all of them are critical: M. Melon, *Mahmoud le Gasnevide* (Paris: n.p., 1732); Muĥammad Ĥabīb, *Sultan Mahmud of Ghaznine,* 2d ed. (Aligarh: Cosmopolitan Publishers, 1951); Muhammad Nazim, *The Life and Times of Sulṫān Maĥmūd of Ghazna* (Cambridge: At the University Press, 1931).

8. See Bosworth, *The Ghaznavids,* pp. 7–26, 308–22; and W. Barthold, *Turkestan Down to the Mongol Invasion,* E. J. W. Gibb Memorial Series, vol. 5, n.s., 3d ed. (London: Luzac and Company Ltd., 1968), pp. 1–37, 528–38, for thorough essays on sources and for bibliographies. Only one of the primary sources has been recently translated into "European" languages, in this case Turkish and Russian (see note 49 below, chapter 2). Most translations date from the end of the nineteenth and beginning of the twentieth century and are in need of revision, as is evident from the corrective work of S. H. Hodīvālā, *Studies in Indo-Muslim History; A Critical Commentary on Elliot and Dowson's History of India as told by its own Historians,* 2 vols. (Bombay: n.p., 1939).

9. The two basic works are Bosworth, *The Ghaznavids,* pp. 7–26; and Barthold, *Turkestan,* pp. 1–37. In addition to superficial articles on Bayhaqī in the first and second editions of the *Encyclopedia of Islam,* as well as short articles on a few other Ghaznavid historians, there is a suggestive but all too brief article by the doyen of Persian studies, Mujtaba Minovi, "The Persian Historian Bayhaqī," in *Historians of the Middle East,* ed. Bernard Lewis and Peter M. Holt, Historical Writings on the Peoples of Asia (London: Oxford University Press, 1962), pp. 138–40. There are also brief but perceptive remarks in the "Introduction" to Hashmī, "Political, Cultural and Administrative History," pp. 1–5. Also see informative articles on Persian historiography by Bertold Spuler, "The Evolution of Persian Historiography," in *Historians of the Middle East,* pp. 126–32; and "Die historische und geographische Literatur in persischer Sprache," in *Handbuch der Orientalistik,* vol. 4: *Iranistik,* ed. Bertold Spuler (Leiden: E. J. Brill, 1968), pp. 100–67; and A. H. Zarrīnkūb, *History of Persia in the Islāmic Period* (Tehran: n.p., 1965), "Introduction;" all of which contain some material on the Ghaznavid period. The anthology about Bayhaqī, the result of a meeting held to celebrate his 1,000th birthday, is Mashhad University, *Yādnāmah-yi Abū'l-Fażl-i Bayhaqī.* One paper presented at the conference was printed not in the anthology but rather in a journal: ^{c}Abbās Zaryāb Khū'ī, "Ta'rīkh-i nigārī-yi Bayhaqī," *Revue de la Faculté des Lettres et Sciences Humaines de Meched,* 4 (1972): 760–71.

10. Bosworth, *The Ghaznavids,* pp. 50 and 63, quoting Abū'l-Fażl-i Bayhaqī, *Ta'rīkh-i Bayhaqī,* ed. Qāsim Ghanī and ᶜAlī Akbar Fayyaż (Tehran: Bank Millī Press, 1324/1945), pp. 101 and 92 respectively. This work uses this edition and the 1350/1971 edition of Fayyaż (Mashhad; Mashhad University Press), hereinafter referred to as *TB*, and provides pagination for each, respectively. Bertold Spuler, "Ghaznawids," *Encyclopedia of Islam,* 2d ed., 2:1053, specifically calls *Ta'rīkh-i Bayhaqī* "a mine of information on cultural and diplomatic matters and the technique of government," and uses it as such.

11. Most notable general works are H. A. R. Gibb, "Tarikh," *Encyclopedia of Islam Supplement,* pp. 233–45; David S. Margoliouth, *Lectures on Arab Historians* (Calcutta: University of Calcutta Press, 1930); Franz Rosenthal, *A History of Muslim Historiography* (Leiden: E. J. Brill, 1952); and *Historians of the Middle East,* ed. Lewis and Holt, which has tried to overcome the bias for earlier historians and for historians writing in Arabic.

12. Lewis and Holt, *Historians of the Middle East.*

13. See the sections on historiography in the *Index Islamicus,* a reference guide to periodical publications on Islām, in which Ibn Khaldūn merits separate sections almost as long as the sections for all other historians put together. See also the forty-two-page bilbiography, "Ibn Khaldunia," in Walter J. Fischel, *Ibn Khaldūn in Egypt* (Berkeley: University of California Press, 1967), pp. 167–212.

14. The classic work in Islāmic philosophy is Muhsin Mahdi, *Ibn Khaldūn's Philosophy of History: A Study in the Philosophic Foundation of the Science of Culture* (Chicago: University of Chicago Press, 1957). On Ibn Khaldūn as sociologist, see Howard P. Becker and Harry Elmer Barnes, *Social Thought from Lore to Science* (Washington, D.C.: Harren Press, 1952, pp. 266–79; and Don Martindale, *The Nature and Types of Sociological Theory* (Boston: Houghton Mifflin Co., 1960), pp. 132–33. See also the interesting books by Albert Hourani, *Arabic Thought in the Liberal Age* (London: Oxford University Press, 1970); Mia I. Gerhardt, *The Art of Storytelling; A Literary Study of the Thousand and One Nights* (Leiden: E. J. Brill, 1963); and Toshihiko Izutsu, *Ethico-Religious Concepts in the Qur'ān* (Montreal: McGill University Press, 1966), which is the revised edition of *The Structure of Ethical Terms in the Koran; A Study in Semantics* (Tokyo: Keio Institute of Philological Studies, 1959), for various other styles or modes of textual criticism.

15. Mohammed Arkoun, *Contribution à l'étude de l'humanisme arabe au IVᵉ/Xᵉ siècle: Miskawayh Philosophe et Historien,* Etudes Musulmanes, vol. 12 (Paris: Librairie Philosophique J. Vrin, 1970); Fischel, *Ibn Khaldūn;* and Tarif Khalidi, *Islamic Historiography* (Albany: State University of New York Press, 1975). There is also a study on Ibn Qutaybah, but his historical writing is only peripherally interesting to its author: Isĥāq Mūsa Huseini, *The Life and Works of Ibn Qutayba* (Beirut: American Press, 1950).

16. Arkoun himself has commented on the disjunction between Ibn Miskawayh's philosophical and historical writing (*Contribution à l'étude de l'humanisme arabe,* pp. 329 ff.), finding the former easier to structure. Many students of Ibn Khaldūn would argue that even though he has written a systematic introduction to the philosophy of history, his own historical writing is careless and structureless, probably because the "structure" of historical material is more elusive than, and different from, that of philosophy.

17. Five articles and three books stand out as original ways of looking at Islamicate historical writings: Hodgson, "Two Pre-Modern Muslim Historians"; Luther, "Bayhaqī and the Later Seljūq Historians"; Little, "The Historical and Historiographical Significance of the Detention of Ibn Taymiyya"; Peter M. Holt, "Al-Jabartī's Introduction to the History of Ottoman Egypt," *Bulletin of the School of Oriental and African Studies* 25 (1962): 38–51; Ullrich Haarmann, "Auflösung und Bewahrung der Klassischen Formen Arabische Geschichts-schreibung in der Zeit der Mamluken," *Zeitschrift der Morgenlandisches Gesellschaft,* 121 (1971): 46–60; Hardy, Historians; Donald Little, *Introduction to Mamluk Historiography* (Wiesbaden: F. Steiner, 1970); and Ullrich Haarmann, *Quellenstudien zur Früher Mamlukenzeit* (Freiburg im Breisgau: U. Schwarz, 1970). In addition, very interesting criticism is to be found in the introductions to Kritovoulos, *History of Mehmed the Conqueror,* trans. Charles T. Riggs (Princeton: Princeton University Press, 1954); Juvaynī, *The History of the World Conqueror (Ta'rīkh-i Jahāngushay),*

trans. J. A. Boyle (Manchester: Manchester University Press, 1958); and Balādhurī, *The Ansāb al-Ashrāf of al-Balādhurī (Kitāb Ansāb al-Ashrāf),* ed. and trans. S. D. Goitein (Jerusalem: ha-Hevrah le-hotsa'at sefarim 'al-yede ha-universitah ha'writ, 1936), vol. 5.

18. Little, "The Historical and Historiographical Significance of the Detention of Ibn Taymiyya."

19. Norman F. Cantor and Richard I. Schneider, *How to Study History* (New York: Thomas Y. Crowell, 1967).

20. Albert Hourani, "Islam and the Philosophers of History," *Middle Eastern Studies* 3 (1967): 206–68; J.-J. Waardenburg, *L'Islam dans le miròir de l'Occident* (Paris: Mouton, 1963).

21. Mahdi, *Ibn Khaldūn's Philosophy of History,* p. 11.

22. On the intentional fallacy, see Northrop Frye, *Anatomy of Criticism* (Princeton University Press, 1957), *passim.*

23. Luther, "Bayhaqī and the Later Seljūq Historians."

24. Hodgson, "Two Pre-Modern Muslim Historians," p. 62.

25. Cantor, *How to Study History,* p. 58.

26. Frank Barlow, *Edward the Confessor* (Berkeley: University of California Press, 1970), p. 128.

27. J. A. Boyle, "introduction," in Juvaynī, *History of the World Conqueror,* vol. 1, pp. xxx–xxxv.

28. Cultural anthropologists of the Middle East have commented on the presence of this attitude of mind and behavioral trait in Muslim society in general, up to the present day, and particularly in Iran. See for example, Gustav Thaiss, "Unity and Discord; The Symbol of Husayn in Iran," in Charles J. Adams, ed., *Iranian Civilization and Culture* (Montreal: Institute of Islamic Studies, McGill University, 1973), pp. 111–19.

29. See Little, "The Historical and Historiographical Significance of the Detention of Ibn Taymiyya," p. 319, who alludes to "the characteristic objectivity of Muslim historical writing in general: the equanimity with which anything but physical calamity or rank heresy is observed and reported." Also see H. A. R. Gibb, "Tarikh," in H. A. R. Gibb, *Studies on the Civilization of Islam,* ed. Stanford J. Shaw and William R. Polk (Boston: Beacon Press, 1962), pp. 120–21, where he assumes early histories, like that of Ṭabarī, to be free from political bias.

30. Holt, "Al-Jabartī's Introduction," pp. 50–51.

31. Anthony Burgess, "Permissiveness, with Misgivings," *New York Times Magazine,* 1 July 1973, p. 20.

32. Ṭabarī, "The Death of ᶜUthmān," in *Introduction to Islamic Civilization,* ed. and trans. Marshall G. S. Hodgson (Chicago: University of Chicago Press, 1964), 1 (revised): 34–36. (Mimeographed.)

33. Mahdi, *Ibn Khaldūn's Philosophy of History,* pp. 63 ff.

34. Compare William H. McNeill, "Herodotus and Thucydides: A Consideration of the Structure of their Histories" (M. A. thesis, University of Chicago, 1939).

35. *TB*, p. 61/68.

36. These pious expressions or disclaimers are also often used by Ṭabarī and others to fill in where the author cannot or will not comment.

37. *TB*, pp 78–84/88–97.

38. Ṭabarī's method involved collecting, choosing, and arranging various *ḥadīths*, authenticated stories about the Prophet and about the early history of the Muslim community, event by event, year by year.

39. Hodgson, "Two Pre-Modern Muslim Historians," pp. 55–58.

40. Elma Marin, "Introduction," in Ṭabarī, *Abū Jaᶜfar Muḥammad b. Jarīr al-Ṭabarī's The Reign of al- Muᶜtasim (833–842) (Ta'rīkh al-rusul wa'l-mulūk)*, trans. Elma Marin, American Oriental Series, vol. 35 (New Haven, Conn.: American Oriental Society, 1951), pp. xv-xvi.

41. For an interesting and new treatment of this problem, see K. Allin Luther, "The Literary Analysis of *Inshā'* Texts and Historical Works from the Saljūq and Mongol Periods," paper presented at Middle East Studies Association Annual Meeting, Los Angeles, 1976.

42. Hava Lazarus-Yafeh, lecture to Social Science 221 (Islamic Civilization 1), University of Chicago, 1966. See also her *Studies in al-Ghazālī* (Jerusalem: Magnus Press, 1975).

43. Nāzim, *The Life and Times,* p. 10.

44. Mālik al-Shu'arā' Bahār, *Sabk Shināsī* (Tehran: Khudkār Press, 1921/1942, 2:67 ff.

45. Compare Clive, *Macaulay,* p. 48, on Macaulay's early overuse of metaphor and simile.

46. E.g., Cantor, *How to Study History.*

47. Northrop Frye, *The Anatomy of Criticism* (Princeton: Princeton University Press, 1957), pp. 73–74.

48. Ibid., p. 75.

49. Levin, *In Defense,* p. viii.

50. Ibid., p. 3.

51. Ibid., pp. 5–6.

52. Mary Louise Pratt, *Toward a Speech Act Theory of Literary Discourse* (Bloomington, Ind.: Indiana University Press, 1977); thanks to Professor Michael Zwettler of the Arabic Program of the Ohio State University for making me aware of Pratt's work.

53. William Labov, *Language in the Inner City* (Philadelphia: University of Pennsylvania Press, 1972); and William Labov and Joshua Waletzky, "Narrative Analysis: Oral Versions of Personal Experience," in *Essays on the Verbal and Visual Arts: Proceedings of the 1966 Annual Spring Meeting of the American Ethnological Society* (Seattle: University of Washington Press, 1967).

54. Pratt, *Toward a Speech Act Theory,* p. 140.

55. Ibid., pp. 138–39.

56. Ibid., p. 136 and pp. 138–39.

57. Ibid., p. 143.

58. Ibid., p. 149.

59. Ibid., p. 143.

60. Ibid., pp. 144–45.

61. Ibid., p. 146.

62. Her reference is to H. Paul Grice, "Logic and Conversation" (William James Lectures, Harvard University, 1967), excerpted in Peter Cole and Jerry L. Morgan, eds., *Syntax and Semantics,* vol. 3: *Speech Acts* (New York: Academic Press, 1975).

63. Oleg Grabar, *The Formation of Islamic Art* (New Haven, Conn.: Yale University Press, 1973), p. xvii.

2

The Life and Times of Abū'l Fažl al-Bayhaqī

INTRODUCTION

The author of *Ta'rīkh-i Bayhaqī,* whose full name was Abū'l-Fažl Muĥammad ibn Ĥusayn al-Kātib ("secretary"; or in Persian, *al-Dabīr*) al-Bayhaqī,[1] included numerous personal names in his work but was oddly casual about the forms in which he wrote them. It would seem only fitting to call him by the shortened form he used for himself in his work, Bū'l Fažl; but to avoid confusion with the famous Mughal historian commonly known as Abū'l-Fažl, Abū'l-Fažl al-Bayhaqī will in this work be called by his common appellation, Bayhaqī. Factual information about Bayhaqī's life is meager—as much can be learned from the text of his history as from biographies about him—and what facts there are will be more meaningful if they can be evaluated in the context of the tenth-century eastern Irānian environment in which he was born.

POLITICAL BACKGROUND

The century at whose end Bayhaqī was born—the fourth/tenth—was a tumultuous one for most of the Dār al-Islām.[2] (See map 1.) Ever since the beginning of the ninth century, the centralized control of the caliph[3] at Bāghdād over the outlying provinces had been weakening. By the middle of the tenth century, independent local dynasties, sometimes giving nominal allegiance to the caliph and sometimes not, were ruling over Muslims in all but the heartlands of the caliphal empire. (See map 2.) Even there the caliph was at the mercy of a Persian dynasty, the Būyids, which had just recently

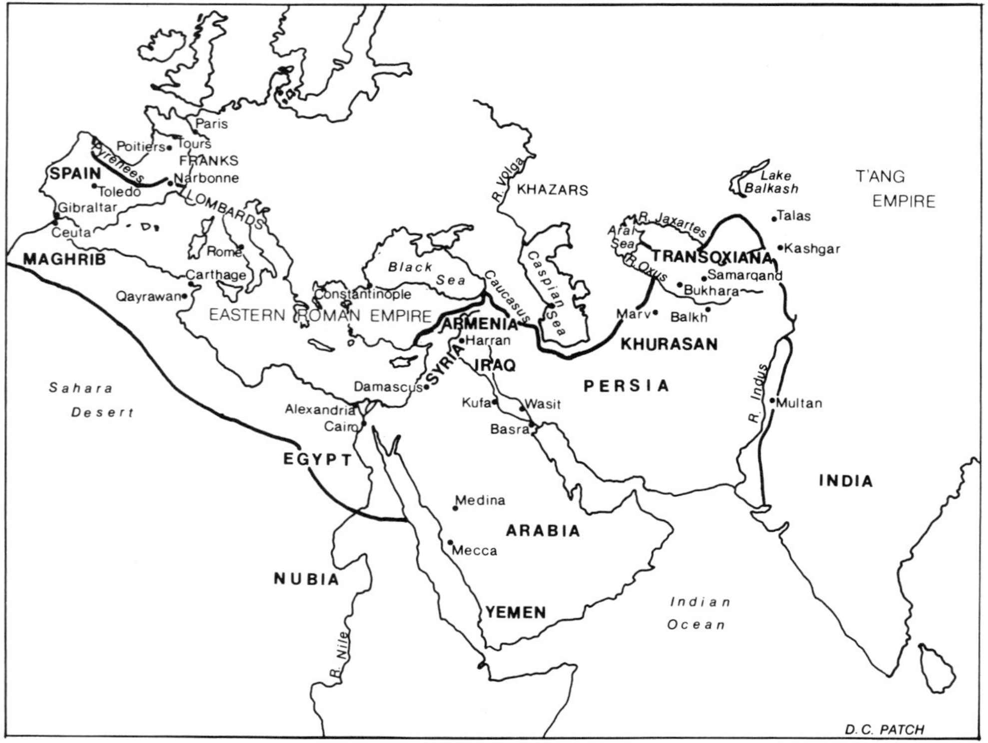

MAP ONE. The Dār al-Islām circa 1050. Adapted from J. J. Saunders, *A History of Medieval Islam* (New York: Barnes and Noble, 1965), pp. 78–79.

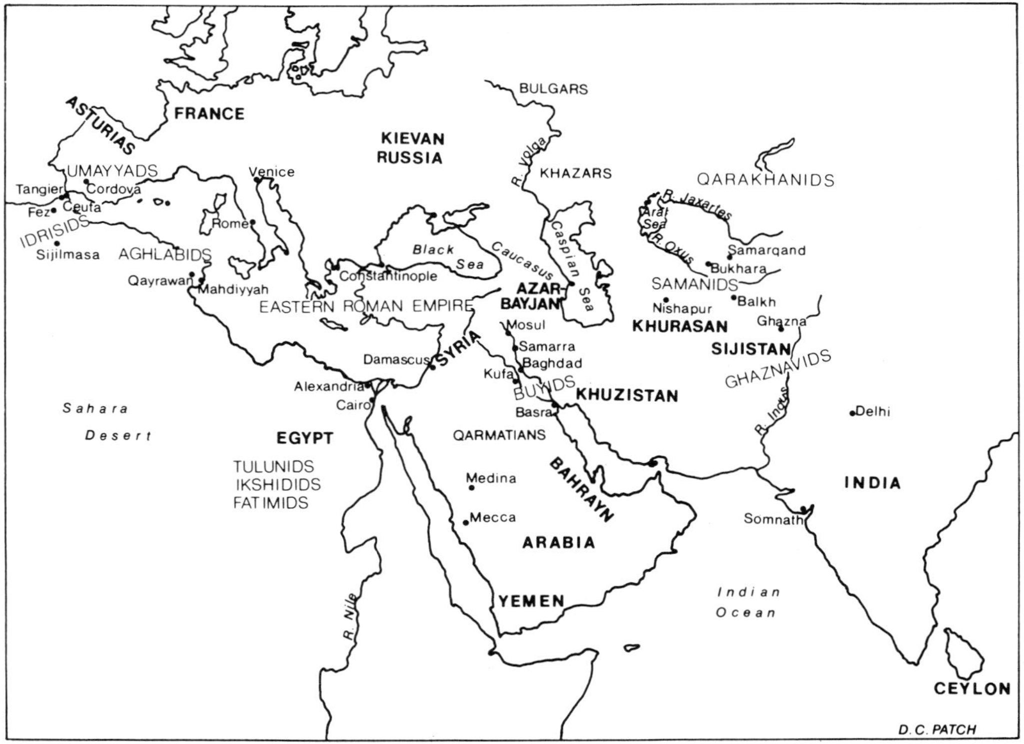

MAP TWO. The Break-up of the Caliphate, Showing the Independent Dynasties. Adapted from J. J. Saunders, *A History of Medieval Islam* (New York: Barnes and Noble, 1965), pp. 108–9.

extended its jurisdiction southwards from the Caspian Sea into Irāq and western Irān. To complicate matters further, the Buyids (932–1055), like many of these regional dynasties, belonged to a branch of the revolutionary politico-religious movement known as the Shīᶜah, which denied the legitimacy of the caliph at Bāghdād.[4]

In eastern Irān, and especially in Khurāsān province where Bayhaqī was born, this fluid political situation was even further complicated. The importance of Khurāsān province (see map 2) as a crossroads of trans-Asian trade and as a buffer against the nomads of the Central Asian steppes is well known.[5] It had also been a proving ground for a number of political and religious movements, including the Shīᶜah itself, since the early eighth century. In eastern Irān, including Khurāsān, some of the earliest defections from the caliphal empire had occurred. First the Ṭāhirids became an independent dynasty of governors in Khurāsān (820–72); then the Saffārids emerged (867–903) in Sijistān and eventually took Khurāsān from the Ṭāhirids; soon after the Sāmānids arose as a local dynasty in Transoxiana and eventually took Khurāsān from the Saffārids and extended into Ṭabaristān as well (874–999); and finally, toward the end of the tenth century, the Ghaznavids (962–1186) created an empire that was by far the largest of the four. It centered in Irān and Afghānistān, stretching westward to a common boundary with the Būyids, eastward across the Oxus River into Khvarazm, and southward into parts of northern India.

The Ghaznavids shared three new features with their original overlords the Sāmānids, and added a fourth feature of their own: (1) they were avidly Sunnī Muslim, that is, loyal to the majority of Muslims whose views on religion, history, and politics were not shared by the Shīᶜites, including their neighbors the Būyids; (2) they were culturally Persian, in the sense that they encouraged the revival of Persian language and culture; (3) they attempted to make their regional court a center for intellectual "stars" from all over the Dār al-Islām; and (4) unlike the previous dynasties of eastern Irān, they were ethnically Turkish, military men by occupation, originally of slave origin. The presence of slave Turkish soldiers in the armies of the eastern Muslim world had become steadily stronger since its beginning in the early ninth century. In eastern Irān from the tenth century on, the relationship between Turkish military origin and rulership and avid Sunnism became almost axiomatic; the rise of the Ghaznavids also took on an aspect of holy war *(jihād)* that was characteristic of all frontier regions of the Dār al-Islām, but particularly of the Central Asian marches, so much so that many supporters of the caliph in Bāghdād, and perhaps even the caliph himself, looked to them as possible liberators from Būyid overlordship.[6] Of all the frontier groups who held the title of *ghāzīs,* warriors who expanded the faith, the Ghaznavids most actively sought to merit it by their militancy.

The political history of the Ghaznavids themselves involves an early meteoric rise of a heroic military figure followed by a long slow decline, a pattern characteristic of many Muslim dynasties after the tenth century.[7] (See Appendix for the Ghaznavid dynastic tree.) The history of this dynasty also reflects many of the causes of political instability that had come into Islāmic government as the caliphate declined, namely, the role of Turkish military slaves, the failure to develop laws of succession, and the fostering of a dangerous atmosphere of political intrigue and factionalism at court.

The dynasty was founded about 977 by Sabuktigīn, a Turkish general and governor of the Sāmānids. Sabuktigīn's father-in-law, Alptigīn, had been a Turkish slave of the Sāmānid ruler ᶜAbd al-Mālik (r. 954–61) who had favored him with the command of the Sāmānid forces in Khurāsān. At the time of ᶜAbd al-Mālik's death, Alptigīn found himself supporting the wrong contender for the throne, withdrew to the town of Ghazna in the east (thus the name Ghaznavids), and reestablished himself as a local leader there.[8] Ten years later Sabuktigīn, Alptigīn's own slave and son-in-law, emerged as head of the Turks at Ghazna and began to extend Alptigīn's territories rapidly, using Ghazna as a base and *amīr* as his title.[9] By 994 he had become so powerful in the east that he too was "granted" the command of Khurāsān, this time by another Sāmānid ruler, Nūh II (r. 976–97). When both Sabuktigīn and Nūh II died in the same year, 997, Sabuktigīn was still a nominal vassal of Nūh but already more powerful than he.

It was one of Sabuktigīn's sons, Maḥmūd (r. 998–1030), whose reign brought the empire at Ghazna to an extent never again reached (see map 3). By the time of his accession, the Sāmānids had declined; and, after fighting off the heir-designate, his brother Ismāᶜīl, Maḥmūd was free to substitute for his father's nominal allegiance to them an equally nominal allegiance to the caliph at Bāghdād. Maḥmūd quickly extended his empire in all directions, to a common border with the Būyids in central Irān, to the Oxus River as a boundary with the Qarakhānids, and into northern India across the Indus River valley. Maḥmūd's conquests, which were really his personal creation, amounted to the largest Muslim empire since the caliphal empire had reached its fullest geographical extent at the beginning of the ninth century; but this huge empire failed to expand further and in fact began to contract after Maḥmūd's death.

To a large extent Maḥmūd's own succession arrangements contributed to the problems that plagued his successors.[10] In a series of decisions curiously analogous to those of the famous caliph Harūn al-Rashīd (r. 786–809), and even to those of Maḥmūd's own father, Maḥmūd changed his mind about the succession near the end of his life and turned from the son who was more capable and more popular with the army, Masᶜūd, to the one who was weaker in governing ability but more popular at court, Muḥammad.

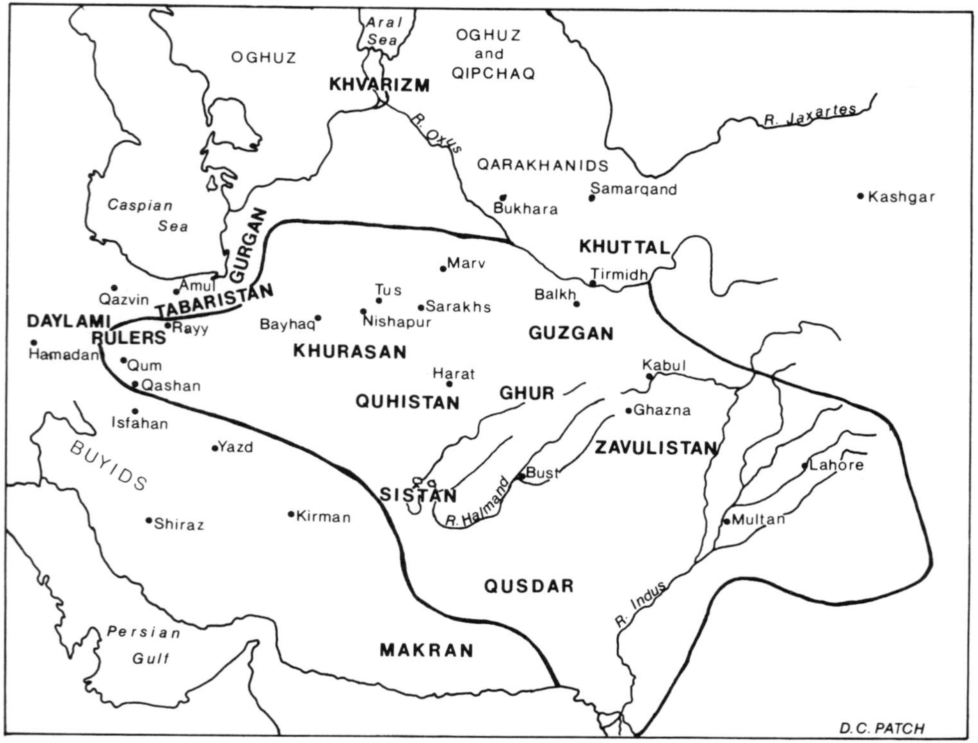

MAP THREE. The Extent of the Ghaznavid Empire circa 1030. Adapted from Clifford Edmund Bosworth, *The Ghaznavids* (Edinburgh: Edinburgh University Press, 1963), back cover foldout.

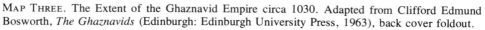

Muĥammad did succeed Maĥmūd in 1030, and ruled for only seven months, during which time his brother was constantly seeking the throne. Even after Mas^{c}ūd came to the throne, his brother having been blinded—some say by Mas^{c}ūd's own order—he was doomed to insecurity by the fact that many members of the court and bureaucracy had been loyal to his brother. Some of these Mas^{c}ūd liquidated, but he could not afford to do so with all.

A more serious source of insecurity came from his inability to deal successfully with a large body of nomads known as the Saljūqs who were at the time of his accession already beginning to come across the Oxus River from Central Asia to settle in Khurāsān province. Eventually Mas^{c}ūd lost all his Irānian territories to the Saljūqs as a result of a decisive defeat at their hands in 1040. Mas^{c}ūd himself was killed by a mutineer a year later.

After Mas^{c}ūd's death the kind of succession difficulties that had occurred at the death of Sabuktigīn and Maĥmūd recurred frequently. If Sabuktigīn is included in the count, only seven of the eighteen Ghaznavid *amīrs* came to the throne uncontested; this was to be a chronic problem for all Turkish dynasties in the Muslim world. In addition, the effects of the defeat at the hands of the Saljūqs were permanent: none of Mas^{c}ūd's successors was able to restore the lost Persian provinces; the Ghaznavids remained, to their end, a dynasty of Afghānistān and India.

From the region of Mas^{c}ūd's son and successor Mawdūd to the temporary displacement of the hereditary line by a usurper in 1052, no Ghaznavid ruler was able to regularize both internal and external situation simultaneously; and the dynasty was seriously weakened by succession crises. Mawdūd suffered no further geographical losses, but upon his death more internal quarrels over the throne broke out, resulting in the rapid succession of three rival candidates, Mawdūd's son Mas^{c}ūd II (only six years old and put up by a group of grandees), Mawdūd's brother, ^{c}Alī ibn Mas^{c}ūd, who was in turn overthrown by Mawdūd's uncle, ^{c}Abd al-Rashīd ibn Maĥmūd. This ^{c}Abd al-Rashīd was diplomatically successful in his three-year reign but failed to conciliate some of his enemies at court and in the army. One such enemy, a former slave of Mas^{c}ūd and now a military commander, Tughril, staged a coup against the royal family but was within a month himself dead at the hands of supporters of the hereditary dynasty.

The next three reigns seemed more hopeful. Tughril was replaced by a member of the hereditary line, Farrukhzād (r. 1052–59); both he and his brother and successor, Ibrāhīm, and Ibrāhīm's son and successor, Mas^{c}ūd III, managed to keep relative peace at court and to keep the Saljūqs, who were pressing on Ghazna's central territory, at bay. Ibrāhīm ruled for forty years, the longest reign of the dynasty. Ibrāhīm also replaced the title of *amīr* with the more well-known and exalted titles of *sult̂ān* on his coinage.

These three relatively peaceful though unproductive reigns ended in another brothers' war over the throne, with three sons of Mas^{c}ūd III succeeding each other fairly quickly. The third and most-famous son, Bahrām Shāh, managed to reign for thirty-nine years, but was in self-imposed exile in India during the last seven, during which time the Saljūqs made further inroads on Ghaznavid territory in the west.

During the rule of the last two Ghaznavid rulers, their territories contracted so at the hands of those who surrounded them that the empire eventually disappeared altogether. The capital itself was lost in 1163. For the last twenty-five years of their existence, the Ghaznavids were restricted to their Indian provinces, which were eventually lost to the Ghūrids, a dynasty of northeastern Irān.

In terms of political innovation and structure, the Ghaznavids represented the bare bones of a new form of statecraft among the Muslims that was to emerge first fully under the Saljūqs and to develop further under the Mongols and the Ottomans. This form of statecraft has been called by various names, such as the power state and the military patronage state,[11] in which the ideals of the Turkish or Mongol military rulers, be they slave or nomadic, were brought into uneasy coexistence with the Perso-Islāmicate form of statecraft that served the caliphs.

Until the time of the Ottomans, the theories that were worked out to justify these new systems almost completely avoided the issue of the spiritual legitimacy of the ruler, a quality that the caliphs had cultivated, and emphasized instead a legitimacy derived from the need of the subject population for security through the protection of military rulers. As had been the case since at least the beginning of the ᶜAbbāsid caliphate (750), the Persian bureaucracy provided continuity in times of political confusion, with prime ministers changing with much less frequency than rulers. The emergence of this new type of centralized state may even have raised the political status of the bureaucratic elements above that of the Persian gentry (*dihqān*s), who had been so important in the heyday of the caliphate.

The elaboration of the theory and practice of the new statecraft led to a spate of political writing during the next four centuries, ranging from formal systematic political theory to new variations on the old Persian tradition of "Mirrors for Princes"—books of counsel and advice for kings. The coming of these dynasties resulted in a general intellectual invigoration for eastern Irān, in which Irān and Irānians acquired a new role of leadership in the mainstream of Islāmic cultural life, in which they had always participated.

INTELLECTUAL MILIEU

A cultural history of Khurāsān province and its involvement in the wider cultural life of the Dār al-Islām is badly needed. As the study of Islāmic history widens, the pivotal position of Khurāsān, not simply commercially but also culturally, becomes clearer. Eastern Irān had been a hotbed of radical religiopolitical movements almost since the Islāmic conquest. Between the seventh and tenth centuries, Persian-speaking Muslims had come to participate extensively in the many intellectual endeavors that had arisen among the Muslims of the Islāmic heartlands, but always in the Arabic language. In fact, some of the exemplars of certain forms of Arabic scholarship, like the philosophers' philosopher Farābī (d. 950) and the historians' historian Ṭabarī (d. 923), were actually Persian culturally or literally. Even the independent dynasties that began to arise in eastern Irān after 800 were primarily involved in the Arabic culture of western Irān and Irāq, just as they were interconnected with the political life of those regions.[12] Not unexpectedly, the language of the chanceries of local Persian kings was Arabic throughout the tenth and much of the eleventh centuries.

With the rise of the Saffārids, Sāmānids, and Ghaznavids, a new cultural dimension began to appear; eastern Irān continued and accelerated its contribution to Islāmic culture as a whole, but began to do so in the Persian language and with Persian forms and ideas, Firdawsī being the figure whom the origins of this development are often tied.[13] It was also during the eleventh century that the affairs of the Ghaznavid chancery began to be conducted in Arabic and in Persian. The Sāmānids and Ghaznavids actively sought to attract the lights of Muslim intellectual life to their courts, to encourage the development of Persian, especially Persian poetry, and thus to add to the revitalization of Sunnī intellectual life at at time when Shīᶜism was spreading. Their policy was partly if not largely responsible for this new development of Persian language and literature.

As a background to Bayhaqī's work, it is useful to try to delineate the range of Muslim intellectual activity available in eastern Irān and, within that context, the cultural evolution of eastern Irān in the tenth century. For purposes of discussion it is useful to distinguish between sacred and profane studies. In the realm of sacred studies, it is clear that one of Khurāsān's intellectual capitals and the town in which Bayhaqī was educated, Nishāpūr, had been exposed prior to the tenth century to a wide variety of religious doctrines. These doctrines included important movements like Muᶜtazilism, a form of theological disputation based on the methods of argument of the Greek philosophers; but this was in retreat from the tenth century on. During and after the tenth century, Nishāpūr seems to have been providing a rather strict "orthodox" religious education. Such an education was necessary not only for men destined to become religious scholars but as a mark of social status for all men of good breeding, including government officials and servants.[14]

The basic religious studies were Qur'ān, Qur'ān commentary *(tafsīr),* and *ḥadīth,* the science of collecting and verifying sayings from and about the Prophet and his companions. In addition the religious education included law *(fiqh),* theology *(kalām),* and mysticism *(taṣawwuf).* Beginning in the tenth century, first Ĥanbalism and then Ash^{c}arism, two forms of fundamentalist theology, displaced the rationalist theological doctrine of the Mu^{c}tazilites, a school that had been of primary importance in ninth-century Nishāpūr. In law, competition raged between Ĥanafīs and Shāfi^{c}īs, with the Shāfi^{c}ī, a more recent and in some senses stricter school of law, becoming more important as time passed. It is interesting to note that from the tenth century on ŝūfism (Islāmic mysticism), often incorporating existing forms of extreme religious behavior like *zuhd* (asceticism) and *^{c}ibādah* (pietism), came to be more important as a doctrine and as a personal religious orientation.[15]

In addition to religious education, a wide range of "profane" pursuits and studies were open to tenth-century Persian men of learning.[16] Of particular popularity and influence at the courts of Irān were *shi^{c}r* (poetry) and *adab*. *Adab* was both the constellation of qualities that made up a genteel man and also the kind of literature that expressed and stimulated these qualities. As a literature, *adab* was a kind of *belles lettres* that included a wide variety of genteel study and prose writing, its material ranging from wisdom literature, much of it translated from pre-Islāmic Pahlavi and Sanskrit works; to collections of anecdotes, often historical, usually arranged according to ethical and moral qualities or faults; to animal fables; to a particular type of *adab* called "Mirrors for Princes," books written for the practical and ethical guidance of rulers, usually by their servants.[17]

This type of counseling material had begun to flower, particularly in eastern Irān, by the late tenth and early eleventh centuries. By then it was a rich, unsystematic mixture of the normative and the prescriptive—of old Persian stories, legends, and aphorisms from pre-Islāmic times, of general wisdom on the art and practice of governing, of stories from Islāmic times, all leavened by selected Islāmic or Islāmicized ethical dictates. Side by side with the "Mirrors for Princes" literature, there developed a more systematic political theory, parts of which were often incorporated into the "Mirrors" material and vice versa.

The "Mirrors for Princes" literature was not the only type of *adab* that was able to absorb elements from the folk tradition. Another form of prose, which combined the more sophisticated *adab* with folk literature, was the *maqāmāt*. This genre, which began to be popular in the tenth century, was comprised of a series of fictionalized sessions or discourses between a hero or central figure and others, detailing his adventures. *Maqāmāt* books were written in, and were popular reading in, Irān and Irāq, where the genre was brought to its pinnacle by Ĥarīrī (1054–1122) at the behest of a distinguished Persian statesman who later served a Saljūq *sulṫān*.[18]

In addition to *shi^{c}r* and *adab*, philosophy, medicine, and science were also encouraged by courts like the Ghaznavid and had become important throughout the Dār al-Islām, peaking in the tenth and eleventh centuries. Scientific figures like Bīrūnī (ca. 973–1048) worked at the Ghaznavid court. In their highest and most technical forms, these pursuits, by definition esoteric, involved a smaller personnel than *adab* or *shi*^{c}*r,* but they nevertheless had effects on a popularized level on a wide range of studies and people. For example, it became common for many "Mirrors for Princes" books to incorporate in simplified form some of the ideas of Galen, the primary ancient figure for Islamicate medical scholars. One such "Mirrors" book contains a whole chapter on Galen.[19] Astrology, too, was very popular. The rational sciences also had their effect on the development of a more scientific type of Islamicate geography and historiography, which subject constitutes the last major "profane" study to be discussed.

The evolution of Islāmic historiography from the seventh to the tenth century was very complex and not yet totally clear, but certain major strands can be identified. History seems to have begun among the Muslims as a pious activity, aimed at establishing the truth of Islām, and therefore often classed among the religious sciences. At first it focused on Mûhammad's life and activities. One early form of such historical interest was the *sīrah,* or biography of the Prophet, based on *ĥadīth*s about his life; the most well-known early biography is the *sīrah* of Ibn Isĥāq (d. ca. 768). The collecting and analyzing of these *ĥadīth*s themselves according to the strength of their chains or transmitters (*isnād*s) became a science in its own right, contributing not only to historical but also to legal studies. To buttress the study of *ĥadīth*s, another quasi-historical form, the *t̂abaqāt,* biographical dictionaries arranged according to generations since Muhammad's time, arose. The early historians were often primarily *ĥadīth* scholars *(muĥaddith*s*).*

In addition to the *sīrah* form, another early type of historical material was the *maghāzī* literature, unconnected stories about Mûhammad's military campaigns, modeled upon the accounts of pre-Islāmic Arab tribal raids and wars. Eventually these unconnected stories came to be worked into a connected narrative like that of Balādhurī (d. 892), who wrote one of the earliest accounts of the Arab conquests. Such connected or continuous narratives branched out further from histories of the conquests to histories of Islām or of the entire world, usually arranged in annalistic fashion and based on the *ĥadīth* method, as exemplified by T̂abarī (d. 923). Often, too, these works were called "universal histories." Occasionally, the scope of such "universal" histories was truly universal; more often the universal history merely provided a brief background for the deeper study of the history of Islām.

The growing study of Greek philosophy among the Muslims began to encourage, at least by the late ninth century, a more critical historical method and a more serious type of universal history, often written by geographers and often including a large amount of geographical observation, as in the works of Ya^c^qūbī (fl. 895) and Mas^c^ūdī (fl. 956). It is even possible that geography *(jughrafiyyah)* should be itself included as a quasi-historical genre, like biography. Even when the focus of these tenth-century works was not universal, the method might be consciously rational and "scientific" as in the works of the Būyid annalistic historian and philosopher Ibn Miskawayh (d. 1030), and the famous man of all professions Bīrūnī (973–1048).

During the tenth century, a number of changes began to take place in Muslim historiography, partly because of the impact of philosophical studies, but also because of the transfer of historical writing from the hands of religious scholars to those of government officials and bureaucrats. During the tenth century, Islāmic historiography began to be secularized, not only in terms of personnel, but also in terms of motivation and content. All these changes are relevant to a study of Bayhaqī.

The change in the personnel of historical studies had consequences in the areas of motivation and content.[20] Because he combined some philosophical ideas with the ideal of the *adab* tradition so influential on men of government, the new type of historian tended to seek historical knowledge for its own sake or for the morals to be derived from it, rather than for a pious religious purpose. The reliance on "verified" *ĥadīth*s was replaced often by a preference for government sources and contacts and gossip. This did not mean, as has often been argued by modern scholars, that standards of accuracy were consciously sacrificed.[21] On the contrary, some of the new historians claimed the older *ĥadīth* method was only pseudo-scientific and not critical enough of the substance of its reports.

In terms of form and focus, city, provincial, and dynastic histories became more common than before. Histories of Islām became less frequent. Likewise, the affairs of the court and ruler became the exclusive subject of many of these histories, whereas the earlier histories written by religious scholars tended to have a wider scope. Much more material from the *adab* tradition came to be incorporated into the historical narrative. Piously motivated historical activity continued nevertheless, especially in the field of biographical literature, which expanded after the tenth century. In Irān itself historical studies and interest in the mainstream of the Islamicate historiographical tradition expanded from the tenth century on. It was during the tenth century that a prime minister of the Sāmānids, Bal^c^amī, made an abridged Persian translation of Ṭabarī's *History of Prophets and Kings*. Moreover, Irān began to develop its own historical tradition, particularly in the form of dynastic, city, and provincial histories. It was into this creative intellectual environment, one with a number of new trends, particularly in historical studies, that Bayhaqī was born.

BAYHAQĪ'S BIOGRAPHY AND THE SOURCES OF BIOGRAPHICAL INFORMATION

There are two basic sources for Bayhaqī's biography: (1) two entries in a biographical history of Bayhaq, a district in Khurāsān near Nishāpūr, completed by Ibn Funduq in 563/1168; and (2) the text of Bayhaqī's work itself.[22] Even when the two are combined, the facts they yield about Bayhaqī are few; and what is more, within each there are contradictions. If Bayhaqī's history is read sensitively, it provides more information than does the biography, if not about dates and places, then about personality and motivation.

To begin at the beginning, Bayhaqī's birthdate is not firm. It is not mentioned at all by Ibn Funduq, but is mentioned indirectly by Bayhaqī in his history. At one point he says that he was sixteen years old in 402/1011–12; at another, that he was fifteen in the year 400/1009–10.[23] Thus his birthdate is usually given in secondary sources as 385–86/995–96, a year or two after Sabuktigīn of Ghazna was given control of Khurāsān by the Sāmānid ruler. Bayhaqī's birthplace is given by Ibn Funduq as Harisābād, a village in the district of Bayhaq near Nishāpūr. Nothing is known of his family, though he mentions his father in the text and calls him "my father the *khvājah,*"[24] perhaps implying that his father too was in government service.[25] It is clear from a number of references in the text that Bayhaqī spent much of his youth and adolescence in Nishāpūr, where presumably he was educated, as would be expected for someone from Bayhaq.

More is known about Bayhaqī's life from the time of his being apprenticed as *dabīr* ("secretary" in Persian; Arabic, *kātib*) in the Dīvān-i Risālat, Bureau of the Chancery, of the government of Maĥmūd of Ghazna. It is in this role that he is best remembered by his biographer, so much so that Ibn Funduq mentions his career as *dabīr* before he mentions his birthplace. In fact, Ibn Funduq's entire biographical entry focuses on Bayhaqī's career as *dabīr* and writer.

It is odd, then, that the date of his entry into the service of Maĥmūd is never mentioned. The time given by the modern scholar Nafisi, forty-six years of age, which would have been in 431–32/1040–41, is clearly too late since at that time Maĥmūd was already dead. Nafisi is relying on a place in the history at which Bayhaqī mentions the date of 451 and says he has been in the service of the Ghaznavids twenty years, which would place the beginning of his apprenticeship in 431/1040, the same year in which Bayhaqī's long-time master at the chancery died![26] This is clearly an error on Nafisi's part. What is more, in other places in the history Bayhaqī mentions that he was in the service of Maĥmūd when Maĥmūd made his expedition to the Indian shrine of Somnath (416/1025), when Bayhaqī would have been thirty. Clearly, Minovi's suggested age of about twenty for Bayhaqī's entry into the government service is more reasonable, in terms of the evidence and in terms of logic, young manhood rather than middle age being a predictable time for entry into apprenticeship.[27]

From approximately 416/1025 to approximately 441/1048, when Bayhaqī left office for good, he was a secretary in the chancery of six successive Ghaznavid *amīrs*, spending most of his time in Ghazna itself, though he also traveled with the *amīrs*.[28] For most of that time (to 431/1040), he worked under the guidance of the famous head of the early Ghaznavid chancery, Bū Naṣr-i Mushkān. Although Ibn Funduq alludes to this master only once, he is a key figure in Bayhaqī's history, and there are numerous indications of the deep and lasting impression made on Bayhaqī by his apprenticeship under this man. Throughout his history Bayhaqī calls Bū Naṣr *ustādam,* "my teacher"; he revered, and was impressed by, him, tolerating, even admiring, in Bū Naṣr behavior that he denounced in others. There is also evidence that Bayhaqī formed his views of court politics under Bū Naṣr's tutelage, internalizing Bū Naṣr's own labels and interpretations and employing them in his work.

Bū Naṣr is known to have upheld a high standard of chancery practice and routine.[29] He and his apprentices were very proud of what they deemed to be their superiority, especially in the preparation of state documents and royal correspondence, Bayhaqī's specialty.[30] In his history Bayhaqī takes every opportunity to evaluate men he is discussing according to their skill at *dabīrī;* and a number are found wanting, good at everything else but at *dabīrī,* simply *piyādah* (literally, "pedestrian," in the modern meaning of "ordinary").[31] Not even the *amīr* Masᶜūd himself escaped a rating on this score; his superior skill at *dabīrī* was one attribute that seems truly to have impressed Bayhaqī.

The reasons for this snobbishness are tied up in the role and heritage of the *dabīr*. Being a *dabīr* had been a very special way of life since pre-Islāmic times; thousands of years before Bayhaqī, the *dabīrs* had been distinguished, along with the priestly class, by their possession of literacy.[32] The great empires of Irān, including the caliphal empire, had depended on the Persian bureaucracy, and the Ghaznavid empire was no exception.

Dabīrī was not simply a nine-to-five job in the modern jargon; it was rather a style of thinking and acting, based on years of education and cultivation. *Dabīrs* spent much of their time at the palace, living there or nearby; their apprenticeship in the arts of *dabīrī* was a long one; all their work was done in a special section of the palace; much of their socializing, during and after hours, seems to have been done with other palace officials.

To the holder of the office of *dabīr* accrued a much higher status in society than would be associated with a civil servant or bureaucrat in modern states. The *dabīr*'s success in the bureaucracy depended on his facility in Arabic and Persian style, including his conciseness of expression, the niceties of his turns of phrase, and the accuracy of his technical vocabulary. There was some tendency for *dabīr*ship to run in particular families, as may have been the case with Bayhaqī. In short, *dabīrī* was an art, and a very important one in the Ghaznavid empire, in which experience counted more than anything else. Bayhaqī says he was passed over as Bū Naṣr's successor because of his relative youth and inexperience: he was then forty-five years old, twenty-five of them spent in government service.[33]

The bureau in which Bayhaqī worked, the *Dīvān-i Risālat,* Bureau of the Chancery, was a very important organ of the central government. There was a close relationship between the chancery and the intelligence system. The Bureau of the Chancery was so important that its major officials and its records accompanied the Ghaznavid *sulṭān* on campaign; its tent was set up as close to the *sulṭān's* tent as possible. Its head—the *Ṣāḥib-i dīvān*—was on a par with the *vazīr*, or prime minister. The *Ṣāḥib-i dīvān* supervised a large number of well-paid *dabīrs*, one of whom was always on duty, night and day. Bayhaqī's particular duties were the copying of texts of diplomatic correspondence of all kinds—treaties, letters, decrees—most of which were composed by the *Ṣāḥib-i Dīvān* himself. The copying of diplomatic correspondence was considered a more responsible job than that of copying internal texts.

Bayhaqī says in his history that he was busy at least as early as the first part of Mas^{c}ūd's reign collecting stories, keeping a diary of notable daily occurrences, and making secret copies of documents he was charged with copying, all with a view to writing a history of the Ghaznavid dynasty someday. During this time he also must have done some amount of history reading, judging from the references in his work, though it is not clear whether he read serious histories or historical material in the *adab* tradition.

Nishāpūr during Bayhaqī's childhood had been transformed by the activities of Sabuktigīn. Bayhaqī had been impressed, as had probably many young men in Nishāpūr, by the deeds of Maḥmūd and the exploits of the crown prince Mas^{c}ūd. After entering the chancery, he came to feel it was his desire and duty to write about the dynasty. As was discussed in the section above on intellectual milieu, the writing of dynastic histories had become popular in Irān; Bayhaqī also felt he had something to add to ordinary accounts because he was so close to the sources of official information.

He did not, however, move beyond collection to composition until some time after he had left official life. Shortly after the accession of ^{c}Abd al-Rashīd (441/1049), Bayhaqī fell into some sort of political difficulty and ended up dismissed, imprisoned, and with all his properties confiscated. Bayhaqī himself in his history is vague about his experience.[34] Ibn Funduq is both vague and contradictory about his affair, which seems to have been a source of embarrasment and is worth exploring. In the beginning of his account, Ibn Funduq avoids the crucial period from the end of Mawdūd's reign (1048) to the end of Farrukhzād's (1059), saying,

> . . . Abū'l-Fażl [Bayhaqī] . . . was a *dabīr* of Sulṭān [an anachronistic usage on Ibn Funduq's part] Maḥmūd . . . of Sulṭān Muḥammad . . . of Sulṭān Mas^cūd . . . of Sulṭān Mawdūd [d. 1048] . . . and then a *dabīr* of Sulṭān Farrukhzād [d. 1059, with three reigns intervening]; when the reign of Sulṭān Farrukhzād ended, *he* [i. e., Bayhaqī] *chose retirement* and became occupied in composing [italics supplied].[35]

Thus if one reads no further, one would, as is characteristic in much Islāmic scholarship, miss important complications that appear later in this same entry where Ibn Funduq goes on to say:

> . . . And on account of the dowry of his wife the *qāżī* [judge of the religious law] ordered him confined in Ghazna and after that [what follows indicates that the above occurred during the reign of ^cAbd al-Rashīd, 440–44/1049–52] Tughril who was a runaway *(gurīkhtah)* slave of the dynasty captured the kindgom and killed ^cAbd al-Rashīd and sent the servants of the king to the fortress and one among them was Bū'l-Fażl, who was sent from the *qāżī*'s prison to confinement in the fortress [1052]. . . . After a little while the time came when Tughril was killed at the hands of Nūshtigīn Zubīndār [a general loyal to the dynasty], and the time of his ascendancy was not more than five to seven days, and the kingdom [once again] fell to the hereditary line [literally, to the descendants of Maḥmūd]. . . . And Bū'l-Fażl died in 470 [1077].[36]

Ibn Funduq does not mention that Bayhaqī was apparently still a *dabīr* from Mas^cūd's death into the reign of ^cAbd al-Rashīd, during which time he was a deputy of Bū Naṣr's successor, the powerful Bū Sahl Zawzanī, and possibly head of the chancery himself. On the other hand, Ibn Funduq claims Bayhaqī *was* a *dabīr* of Farrukhzād, for which there is no evidence in Bayhaqī's work. Although there are in Bayhaqī's history a number of references to Farrukhzād, including his death, at which time Bayhaqī was exclusively engaged in writing,[37] there are no references to serving in Farrukhzād's administration.

As to the cause of Bayhaqī's arrest and imprisonment in ^cAbd al-Rashīd's reign, Ibn Funduq uses the phrase "on account of the dowry of his wife," apparently the pretext used for Bayhaqī's arrest; but Bayhaqī's several allusions to his debacle in his history indicate the causes were more serious—that he had made political enemies after Mas^cūd's death and that they managed to unseat him during ^cAbd al-Rashīd's reign, which was filled with court intrigue. One such enemy was Bū Sahl Zawzanī, Bū Naṣr's successor, for whom Bayhaqī had been passed over. Both Bū Naṣr and Bayhaqī disliked, nay despised, Bū Sahl, for reasons not entirely clear. One of the reasons seems to have been that Bū Sahl transgressed the norms of gentlemanly behavior at court and in government. It was also the case that he had made his mark before the reign of Mas^cūd as head of the Dīvān-i ^cArż, the bureau that supervised pay and support of the army; this connection with the military may have had the effect of alienating him from the "men of the pen" like Bū Naṣr and Bayhaqī. It is also possible that his experience in *dabīrī* was less than that of Bū Naṣr.

Perhaps after Bū Naŝr's death in 431/1039 Bayhaqī had gradually taken over the former's pivotal role in the intrigues of the court and had ended up on the wrong side of an intrigue during ᶜAbd al-Rashīd's confused reign. In his history the one result of his imprisonment he most laments was that not only his property but most of his notes and document copies were confiscated. He implies that they contained revealing political information, commenting several times that he could really "tell all" if he had all his papers. Whether the information in the papers was considered dangerous by enemies like Bū Sahl and thus related to Bayhaqī's imprisonment is unknown.

Finally, Ibn Funduq implies that Bayhaqī remained a *dabīr* through Farrukhzād's reign and then "chose retirement" and began to compose. Here Ibn Funduq must be mistaken, perhaps intentionally, because it is irrefutable from the text of Bayhaqī's history that he was already composing from the middle of Farrukhzād's reign (448/1056); and it seems that he was already in retirement, a retirement he cannot really be said to have "chosen," when Farrukhzād died.

One further minor point of Ibn Funduq's account should be noted. He plays down the seriousness of Tughril's usurpation. First of all, Tughril was not a fugitive slave but a former slave of Masᶜūd I who had become a military commander and had the support of at least some of the dignitaries of the court. Second, the time between Tughril's murder of ᶜAbd al-Rashīd and his own death is usually given as not five to seven days but a little more than a month.[38] Ibn Funduq's handling of this point is relevant in that it further shows the tendency to play down embarrasing events, which is evident in his handling of Bayhaqī's fall from grace.

Thus the period of Bayhaqī's life from 440/1048 to 451/1059 is still confused, but it is not at all unlikely that he may have fallen on the wrong side of one of the unending series of court intrigues that had plagued the dynasty since its inception. It is also not clear whether he returned temporarily to government life after Tughril was replaced by Farrukhzād, a descendant of Masᶜūd (444/1052), but it seems unlikely since at that time he was already close to sixty years of age. It is clear from his history that during Farrukhzād's reign he maintained close contact with the officials at court.[39]

The nature of Bayhaqī's life between the end of Farrukhzād's reign, when Bayhaqī was still involved in narrating Masᶜūd's reign, and the death date of 470/1077 given by Ibn Funduq, is totally unknown, except that Ibn Funduq and others have claimed that Bayhaqī managed to bring his work up to or through the reign of Farrukhzād. His history, in addition to the major biographical facts discussed here, also provides a large number of small details—what letters he wrote, what ceremonies he witnessed, what conversations he overheard (eavesdropped?), what trips he made, what people he talked with, what thoughts he had—all of which build up a picture of a man whose total waking hours were spent in the concerns of office. Were Bayhaqī to appear in a miniature of the Ghaznavid court, he would be standing in an upper-story window, off in the corner of the frame, taking in the whole scene, more than a bit nosy, and as the Persians say, "biting the index finger in anticipation."[40] Specific aspects of his personality derived from this information have been left to emerge in the course of the discussions of his work in chapters 3 and 4. For now it is enough to say that though he does not include himself as a major character in the events he describes, ironically his personality and life come through strongly in his work, a general description of which follows.

BAYHAQĪ'S WORK

Descriptions of Bayhaqī's writings have varied so much that it is necessary to describe as completely as possible what he seems to have written and what remains of it before fitting it into the pattern of his life. Bayhaqī appears to have written three distinct works all in Persian.

1. A collection of anecdotes and documents called *Maqāmāt-i Abū Naŝr-i Mushkān,* the title of which indicates that it was biographical in nature, containing anecdotes illustrating Abū Naŝr's character, style, and wisdom. Ibn Funduq does not mention this work at all, but Bayhaqī mentions it in his history and implies that it has been composed for some time (i.e., before the 450s/1060s), perhaps while Bayhaqī was still in government service.[41] The work has not survived intact, but a larger number of passages, as they were quoted in later Muslim works, have been collected and printed.[42]
2. A work on chancery practice called *Zīnat al-kuttāb* [The art of secretaries], mentioned only by Ibn Funduq, who calls it "unique in its treatment of that art (*fann*)."[43] Manuals on secretarial practice constituted a minor genre in medieval Islām. Ibn al-Muqaffā', whose works were known to Bayhaqī, wrote one for the early ᶜAbbāsid caliphs (late second/eighth century).[44] Later the genre became more common, particularly in certain Turkish dynasties, with authors like Qalqashandī under the Mamlūks in Egypt. Nothing, however, survives from Bayhaqī's manual. Bosworth has argued that one passage quoted by Ibn Funduq may be from *Zīnat al-Kuttāb,* but it is equally possible that this passage comes from Bayhaqī's history of the Ghaznavids, which Ibn Funduq has just quoted.[45]
3. A history of the Ghaznavid dynasty in approximately thirty volumes, arranged annalistically within reigns, from the founder Sabuktigīn down to or through Farrukhzād. The whole book as well as its individual parts have gone under a number of different names.[46] Although Bayhaqī indicates that he began in earnest with Sabuktigīn, it has been argued

from an ambiguous sentence in his history of the reign of Mas^cūd that the serious account did not begin until the events of the year 409/1018, during Maḥmūd's reign, the early Ghaznavid years having been covered by a lost work by Bayhaqī's friend Maḥmūd Varrāq.[47] It has further been argued that the four and one-half volumes Bayhaqī says he devoted to the dynasty before Mas^cūd would not have been enough for him to have treated the earliest parts in depth.

This argument is necessary because all that remains of the thirty volumes are the end of the fifth, the entire sixth, seventh, eighth, and ninth, and the beginning of the tenth. One scholar has argued that parts of even these volumes are missing because there are gaps in the narrative; but this is not necessarily a justified inference.[48] The time period covered in what survives is the reign of Mas^cūd (421–32/1030–41) up to about the middle of the last year. When printed in a single volume, the length of this material is about 700 pages. It is usually called *Ta'rīkh-i Bayhaqī* or *Ta'rīkh-i Mas^cūdī*. In light of the fact that the work, though about Mas^cūd, is so much a product of Bayhaqī's own vision and personality, the former designation seems more appropriate and will be used here.

There have been five printed editions of these volumes; one partial translation into English; and three full translations, into Arabic, Russian, and Turkish. The page references in this work come from the 1945–53 edition by Ghanī and Fayyāż, the edition usually preferred, and from Fayyāż's 1971 edition.[49] Because Bayhaqī's narrative gives information and detail absent in other contemporary accounts, his work has been relied on heavily as a source for Ghaznavid history, both by medieval Muslim and by modern scholars.[50] However, no critical book-length study of *Ta'rīkh-i Bayhaqī* has ever been undertaken. There are three contemporary histories that cover some of the same material as *Ta'rīkh-i Bayhaqī*, namely, Gardīzī's *Zayn al-akhbār* in Persian, published during the reign of ^cAbd al-Rashīd (1050–53); an anonymous history of Sīstān province, *Ta'rīkh-i Sīstān* in Persian, which ends in 1056; and ^cUtbī's *Kitāb al-yamīnī* in Arabic (^cUtbī died in 1036 or 1039–40); *Ta'rīkh-i Bayhaqī* will be compared with these and others where relevant. ^cUtbī was clearly known to, and used by, Bayhaqī; the other two possibly so.[51]

It appears that Bayhaqī gave each set of volumes relevant to a single reign an epithet, e.g., those on Maḥmūd he called *Ta'rīkh-i Yamīnī* after his honorific title Yamīn al-Dawlah ("right hand of the state"); those on Sabuktigīn, *Ta'rīkh-i Nāṣirī*, after his title Nāṣir al-Dīn ("conqueror of the religion"); and so on. Whether what is now known as *Ta'rīkh-i Mas^cūdī* was ever called, by extension, *Ta'rīkh-i Shihābī,* after Mas^cūd's honorific title Shihāb al-Dawlah ("meteor of the state"), is not known. Bayhaqī refers to the entire work as *Ta'rīkh-i 'Āl-i Sabuktigīn* [History of the family of Sabuktigīn], and to the material on Maḥmūd as *Ta'rīkh-i Yamīnī;* but he never has occasion to refer to the material on Mas^cūd by title. Bayhaqī's volume divisions were apparently made according to length considerations, not according to substantive coherence.

Nothing survives of the volumes after the tenth, even in the form of quotations from later works. What survives of the volumes before the fifth survives in the form of quotations from later works; these have been collected, but amount to only about sixty pages, many of them duplicates of each other.[52] These quotations occur in works written up to the fifteenth century, but already when Ibn Funduq was writing in the middle of the sixth/twelfth century, he had never seen all thirty volumes though he believed they had been written. Because *Ta'rīkh-i Bayhaqī* represents such a small part of Bayhaqī's total plan, many conclusions about it can be only tentative. And this is not the first time an Islāmicist is confronted with a small fraction of a work conceived and written on a larger scale. On the other hand, Bayhaqī did to a certain extent view each reign as a discreet unit, and many conclusions that do not involve knowing the whole work can be safely drawn.

Bayhaqī's books were apparently published privately, as were many books in his day. Presumably an author, unless himself rich, would need a rich patron; often, of course, the ruler himself might be the most active publisher. But not all books were published at royal behest; and whether they were or not, they were not necessarily published at court. They could be published there, or privately, or at a special bookseller's market. The copying of books to be published and circulated was not limited to court or palace scribes either; there were also free-lance scribes as well as markets or shops of scribes. It would seem that not many copies were made of Bayhaqī's history, for most of its volumes went out of circulation quickly.

The first half of *Ta'rīkh-i Bayhaqī* was, according to the dates given by Bayhaqī in the text, written between 448/1056 and 451/1059, during the reign of Farrukhzād,[53] the last half after Farrukhzād's death. At that point Bayhaqī had outlived nine Ghaznavid *amīrs* and had served most of them. In a phrase he himself liked, Bayhaqī was by that time a man who *garm u sard chashīd,* who had experienced the hot and cold, that is, the ups and downs of life. He was also writing at a time when stability seemed to be returning to the descendants of Mas^cūd after the interval of the usurper Tughril.

The materials Bayhaqī used has been collected over a period of thirty years; much of what he described had happened at least twenty-five years before. These are important facts to remember in analyzing the work, which was begun when Bayhaqī was sixty-two. Partly because of his age, Bayhaqī felt that the first seven or eight volumes had gone too slowly, that he must curb his tendency to prolixity and speed up the pace of the writing, which he did.

There is no single comprehensive statement of Bayhaqī's motivations for writing the work; what can be discovered by putting together all references, explicit and implicit, is that his motivations were complex and that over time new motivations were added to old. He clearly states that he had at first, as a younger man, felt a *duty* to recall and record the deeds of the great dynasty he had served, though the context of these remarks usually seems to require them. He adds secondarily that he hopes the work will be a memorial to his name, of which he was very conscious.[54] Elsewhere he explains that he, a lesser light of the dynasty, is taking up the task because men more qualified are too busy running the state to write history, though this statement has the ring of consciously false modesty.[55] As his ideas and his experiences grew, he seemed to feel that he had things to tell that others might not be able to or wish to tell; and he seemed to want to interpret the past in new ways, in his own way, rather than just narrate dry facts.[56] Of course, there may have been explicit declarations of motivation and intent in the earlier lost volumes.

Although Bayhaqī does make occasional explicit remarks about his motivations, he does not directly describe the audience at which he is aiming the work. That is not to say that he does not mention his audience; on the contrary, he repeatedly addresses them, maintaining continuous contact with them, as his readers (*khvānandigān*), among whom there are wise men (*khiradmandān)* whom he is especially interested in reaching. It would be hard to imagine a Muslim historian who explains himself and what he is doing more frequently to his readers.

There are implicit indications that his immediate audience was a restricted one, though he hoped for the work to be meaningful to a general audience for generations to come after his own time. There is, first of all, no indication that the book was written at the behest of any Ghaznavid ruler; yet Bayhaqī clearly felt the need to appear loyal to the dynasty. He clearly states that the audience is both kings and not kings.[57] He wanted the book to be useful to kings, and indeed there is much didactic material from "Mirrors for Princes" literature in it; but he seemed to be aiming rather at those who served the king at the highest level, people who would already be familiar with most of the events of Mas^{c}ūd's reign and with recent local history, like that of the Sāmānids, but not with wider Islāmic history, like that of the caliphate. If one can use as a measure what Bayhaqī explains and what he does not explain, it is clear that the audience is expected to know the titles, offices, and history of the Ghaznavid dynasty, but not their counterparts in caliphal history. Not only does he need to explain famous events from caliphal history in detail; he rewrites them in a vocabulary understandable to a Ghaznavid government official, giving, for example, anachronistic Turkish titles to caliphal offices. Neither, it follows, does he expect his audience to be well-read in the history of times before the Sāmānids and Ghaznavids; he is constantly trying to impress his audience with his having read books about other histories. The audience is also not expected to be familiar with any form of historical writing other than the dry chronicle, and Bayhaqī is constantly explaining why he is deviating from that form.

The vision of a man of government writing from official sources is one that accords well with the earlier treatment of the development of Islamicate historiography up to the tenth century. But this is not all that needs to be said about Bayhaqī's work. It is true that he spent most of his life at Ghazna, in the rarefied atmosphere of the court. Thus his immediate scope appears narrow, limited to the Ghaznavids as a dynasty and not even to the region in which they lived but rather to the affairs of court. But his intellectual background was broad, and he brought to his main purpose a wider historical awareness, just as he hoped that there would be universal themes in his work that could appeal to audiences outside Ghazna. As for each individual, Bayhaqī's synthesis is by definition unique within the limits of his cultural heritage, not simply another case of a government official writing history. It will be the job of the textual criticism in chapters 3, 4, and 5 to arrive at a vision of his accomplishment.

1. Abū'l-Ĥasan ᶜAlī ibn Zayd Bayhaqī, known as Ibn Funduq, *Ta'rīkh-i Bayhaq,* ed. Aĥmad Baymānyār, 2d ed. (Tehran: Islāmiyyah Press, 1385/1965), p. 20; also quoted in Said Nafisi, *Dar Pīrāmūn-i Ta'rīkh-i Bayhaqī* (Tehran: Furūghī Maĥfūz, 1342/1923), 1:7.

2. Dār al-Islām (literally in Arabic "Abode of Islām) was a phrase used by Muslims themselves to describe the area of the world ruled over, and lived in, by Muslims. The complementary phrase was Dār al-ĥarb (literally "Abode of War"), that area surrounding the Dār al-Islām in which war against the infidels was justified in order to bring them into the Dār al-Islām.

3. Caliph (in Arabic, *khalīfah*) was the title used by the rulers of the Muslim empire from Muĥammad's death in 632 down to the Mongol conquest of Bāghdād in 1258, when the office was terminated there, to be continued in Cairo until 1517.

4. Other Shīᶜite dynasties included the Fâtimids in North Africa and Egypt (909–1171), the Idrīsids in the Maghrib (788–985), the Hamdānids in northern Syria (929–1003), and the Zaydīs in Yemen (893–1300).

5. See Bertold Spuler, "Trade in the Eastern Islamic Countries in the Early Centuries," in *Islam and the Trade of Asia,* ed. D. S. Richards, Papers on Islamic History, vol. 2 (Philadelphia: University of Pennsylvania Press, 1970), pp. 11–20.

6. H. A. R. Gibb, "Al-Mawardī's Theory of the Caliphate," in H. A. R. Gibb, *Studies on the Civilization of Islam,* ed. Stanford J. Shaw and William P. Polk (Boston: Beacon Press, 1962), p. 152.

7. See Bertold Spuler, "Ghaznawids," *Encyclopedia of Islam,* 2d ed., 2:1050–53, for a brief summary of their political history. Also Stanley Lane-Poole, *The Mohammedan Dynasties* (New York: Frederick Ungar Publishing Co., 1966), pp. 285–90.

8. The date of 956 given for this event by Spuler, "Ghaznawids," p. 1050, seems too early.

9. *Amīr,* the title used by the caliphs for their provincial governors, became in this period the most common title for the heads of semiautonomous regional dynasties. Later, in the reign of Ibrāhīm (1059–99), the Ghaznavids officially changed their title to *sulṭān,* a more exalted word also to be used by most independent dynasties thereafter, for example, the Saljūqs and Ottomans.

10. No Muslim dynasty ever developed a binding law of succession. Since the reign of the fifth caliph, Muᶜāwiyyah (661–80), the caliphs had tried to employ the rule of primogeniture where

possible. Among the Turkish dynasties, most of which were tribal in origin, no such policy was acceptable; and it was common for brothers, uncles, cousins, sons, nephews, and so on, to be involved in a contest for each succession.

11. Clifford Edmund Bosworth, *The Ghaznavids: Their Empire in Afghanistan and Eastern Iran, 994:1040* (Edinburgh: Edinburgh University Press, 1963), p. 63 and passim, uses the term "power state." For the use of the phrase "military patronage state," see Marshall G. S. Hodgson, *The Venture of Islam* (Chicago: University of Chicago Press, 1974), vol. 2, bk. 4.

12. For example, See Clifford Edmund Bosworth, "The Ṭāhirids and Arabic Culture," *Journal of Semitic Studies* 14 (1969): 45–77.

13. See S. M. Stern, "Yaᶜqūb the Coppersmith and Persian National Sentiment," in *Iran and Islam in Memory of the Late Vladimir Minorsky,* ed. Clifford Edmund Bosworth (Edinburgh: Edinburgh University Press, 1971), pp. 535–56. Stern argues that the origins of this development preceded Firdawsī by almost a century.

14. See Richard W. Bulliet, *The Patricians of Nishāpūr: A Study in Medieval Islāmic Social History* (Cambridge: Harvard University Press, 1972), pp. 47 ff.

15. Ibid., pp. 42–44. See also Vladimir Minorsky, "Persia: Religion and History," in *Iranica: Twenty Articles,* Publications of the University of Tehran, vol. 775 (Tehran: University of Tehran Press, 1964), pp. 242–59.

16. For a good summary of them, see Edward G. Browne, *A Literary History of Persia* (Cambridge: Cambridge University Press, 1951), vol. 2, chap. 2.

17. See E. I. J. Rosenthal, *Political Thought in Medieval Islam: An Introductory Outline* (Cambridge: Cambridge University Press, 1962), pp. 67–83; and F. R. C. Bagley, "Introduction," in Ghazālī, *Ghazālī's Book of Counsel for Kings (Naṣīḥat al-mulūk),* trans. F. R. C. Bagley (London: Oxford University Press, 1964), pp. ix–lxxiv, for excellent summaries of this genre.

18. See Reynold Nicholson, *A Literary History of the Arabs* (Cambridge: Cambridge University Press, 1969), p. 329.

19. See Kay Kāᶜūs ibn Iskandar, *A Mirror for Princes (Qābūsnāme),* trans. Reuben Levy (New York: E. P. Dutton and Co., 1951), chap. 33.

20. See H. A. R. Gibb, "Tarīkh," in *Studies on the Civilization of Islam,* pp. 118 ff., for a fuller treatment.

21. See ibid., p. 121.

22. Ibn Funduq, *Ta'rīkh-i Bayhaq,* pp. 20 and 175–78. For secondary treatments of Bayhaqī, see W. Barthold, "Baihakī," *Encyclopedia of Islam,* 1:752–73; Said Nafisi, "Bayhakī," *Encyclopedia of Islam,* 2d ed., 1:1130–31; and Mujtaba Minovi, "The Persian Historian Bayhaqī," in *Historians of the Middle East,* ed. Bernard Lewis and Peter M. Holt, Historical Writings on the Peoples of Asia (London: Oxford University Press, 1962), pp. 138–40.

23. *TB*, pp. 209/264 and 359/458 respectively.

24. *Khvājah* was an honorific title for minister of state and teacher.

25. *TB*, p. 242/314.

26. Nafisi, "Bayhaki," p. 1130.

27. Minovi, "The Persian Historian Bayhaqī," p. 138.

28. Typically in the early stages of Turkish and Mongol dynasties, the capital was where the ruler was. The early Ghaznavid *amīrs,* like the early Saljūq, Mongol, and Ottoman rulers, took an entire bureaucracy with them on long trips or campaigns, and not simply an auxiliary force but the leading officials. It was in this capacity that Bayhaqī traveled with Maḥmūd and Masᶜūd.

29. See Mālik al-Shuᶜarā' Bahār, *Sabk Shināsī* (Tehran: Khudkār Press, 1321/1942), 2:66 ff.

30. *TB*, pp. 77–78/88–89, 147–48/178–80.

31. Ibid., pp. 144/175 and 272/357. There are suggestions in these evaluations that, contrary to current scholarly opinion, being a good *dabīr* and being a good *abīb* were not synonomous. See also M. Carter, "The Kātib in Fact and Fiction," *Abr-Nahrain,* 11 (1971): 42–55.

32. Browne, *Literary History of Persia,* 1:8–9.

33. *TB*, p. 600/800.

34. *TB*, pp. 601–2/800–802.

35. Ibn Funduq, *Ta'rīkh-i Bayhaq,* p. 175.

36. Ibid., p. 178.

37. *TB*, p. 426/550.

38. Spuler, "Ghaznawids," p. 1052.

39. E.g., *TB*, p. 242/314. Nafisi, "Bayhakī," p. 1130, asserts that Bayhaqī was made head of the chancery at the beginning of ^{c}Abd al-Rashīd's reign, but offers no evidence for the assertion. W. Barthold, *Turkestan down to the Mongol Invasion,* E. J. W. Gibb Memorial Series, n.s., vol. 5, 3d ed. (London: Luzac and Co., Ltd., 1968), p. 23, mistakenly puts the imprisonment before ^{c}Abd al-Rashīd's. reign.

40. See *TB*, p. 251/328.

41. E.g., *TB*, pp. 109/130, 154/188.

42. Nafisi, *Dar Pīrāmūn-i,* 1:94 ff., and all of vol. 2.

43. Ibn Funduq, *Ta'rīkh-i Bayhaq,* p. 175.

44. Nicholson, *A Literary History,* p. 346.

45. Bosworth, *The Ghaznavids,* pp. 64–65, quoting from Ibn Funduq, *Ta'rīkh-i Bayhaq,* pp. 176–77.

46. Nafisi, *Dar Pīrāmūn-i,* 1:v.

47. *TB*, pp. 261–62/342–43.

48. Nafisi, "Bayhakī," p. 1131.

49. The five printed editions are, in order of appearance, *The Ta'rikh-i Baihakī . . .* , ed. W. H. Morley, Bibliotheca Indica, vol. 59 (Calcutta: Asiatic Society of Bengal, 1862); *Ta'rīkh-i Bayhaqī*, ed. Said Nafisi (Tehran: n.p., 1305–7/1887–89) (lithographed edition cited in Nafisi, "Bayhakī," p. 1131); *Ta'rīkh-i Bayhaqī*, ed. Said Nafisi, 3 vols. (Tehran: n.p., 1365–73/1945–53); *Ta'rīkh-i Bayhaqī,* ed. Qāsim Ghanī and ^{c}Alī Akbar Fayyāż (Mashhad: Mashhad University Press, 1391/1971). A partial translation, of the material relating to India, can be found in Sir H. M. Elliot and J. Dowson, *The History of India as Told by Its Own Historians,* vol. 2: *The Muhammadan Period* (London: n.p., 1869). The full translations are, in order of publication, *Ta'rīkh al-Bayhaqī,* trans. Sādiq Nash'at and Yahyā' al-Khashāb (Cairo: Dār al-T̂ibā^{c}ah al-Ĥadīthah, 1350/1960); *Istoriia Mas^{c}ūda*, trans. A. K. Arends, Pamiatniki pis'mennosti vostoka, vol. 22 (Moscow: Nauka, 1969); Necati Lugal has also done a translation into Turkish on which no bibliographical information is available. According to Fayyāż's introduction to his 1971 edition, there are numerous manuscripts of *Ta'rīkh-i Bayhaqī* in Irān, London, Leningrad, Paris, and India, but only one or two that are reliable.

50. For example, Y. A. Hashmi, "Society and Religion under the Ghaznavids," *Journal of the Pakistan Historical Society* 6 (October 1958): 254–68, is largely a collection of paraphrases and quotations from Bayhaqī.

51. See Ibn Funduq, *Ta'rīkh-i Bayhaq,* p. 176.

52. Nafisi, *Dar Pīrāmūn-i,* 1:1–72.

53. *TB*, p. 76/86, where Bayhaqī says he took down a report from a friend in 455, seven years after beginning "this work." There is, of course, the possibility that "this work" referred to the entire work; all that can be said is that the reign of Mas^{c}ūd was begun at least as early as 448.

54. Ibid., pp. 666–67/903–6. See also Appendix B, selection 12.

55. Ibid., p. 108/128–29.

56. Ibid., pp. 98-99/114-16. See also Appendix B, selection 2.

57. E.g., ibid., p. 106/126.

3

The Method of the Secretary as Historian: An Analysis of the Structure and Contents of *Ta'rīkh-i Bayhaqī*

INTRODUCTION

As would be expected from the description of Bayhaqī's intellectual milieu in chapter 2, his history is a blend of a number of elements, all held together by his own presence, vision, and interests. This blend arose from the interaction of Bayhaqī's experience, personality, and intellect with the complex cultural and political life of eastern Irān in the tenth and eleventh centuries.

Bayhaqī's method as a historian combined a secretary's standards of composition and attitudes toward the value of history with the secular and philosophical trends in Islāmicate historiography described in the preceding chapter. His materials, drawn from a variety of historical and nonhistorical sources, he put together in a conscious though not rigid structure and with certain standards in mind. It is through an analysis of the structure of his work and the function of the various materials in it, as well as through an examination of his explicit declarations about historiography, that his method is to be uncovered.[1]

STRUCTURE AS A CONDITION OF HISTORICAL COMPOSITION

Bayhaqī has himself indicated that it is not misguided to consider the over-all structure of his work first. Throughout his work he is in continuous communication with his readers about the order in which he puts his materials, the space he assigns to them, and his reasons for including them. Phrases like "I will discuss that in its proper place," "I have already discussed that in another place," "I put this here so you will understand it when I refer to it afterward,'' and ''I put that in Volume V and will put this in Volume VII'' abound and indicate that Bayhaqī had a sense of order as he wrote and a degree of foresight as to what he would write.[2] The book appears to have been written straight through.

Furthermore, Bayhaqī is concerned that readers not think any part of the work, whether related to the main subject or not, irrelevant. This insistence that everything in the book is there for a reason has an important implication for discovering the sources of his views about history, namely, that he may have been familiar with some of the philosophical historians of the tenth century. One can certainly find the insistence on the importance of structure in philosophically inspired histories of the same era. A famous, albeit extreme, example of the sacredness of structure occurs in the opening of Mas^{c}ūdī's (fl. 332/943) *Meadows of Gold;* and Mas^{c}ūdī himself was self-consciously innovative in this regard. After describing how carefully he has put his work together, he goes on to say: ''Whosoever changes in any way its meaning, removes one of its foundations, corrupts the lustre of one paragraph, or makes any change or alteration, selection, or extract; and whoever ascribes it to another author, may he feel the wrath of God!''[3] Such statements about structure occur not only in encyclopedic historians like Mas^{c}ūdī but also in narrative dynastic historians, like Khalīfah ibn Khayyât (end third/ninth century) and Ibn Miskawayh (fourth/tenth century), as well as in a book from the Būyid period that Bayhaqī himself used and quoted from, *Kitāb al-Tājī* (begun 371/981) of Abū Isĥāq al-Ŝābī. This al-Ŝābī may have been the real mentor of the more famous Būyid historian Ibn Miskawayh.[4]

Although Bayhaqī seems to have had in mind the topics he wanted to treat before he began writing, he did not commit himself rigidly to them in the way that a truly philosophical historian like Mas^{c}ūdī did. He was prepared to eliminate planned or desired topics if he could not find the information on time, or to add a new one if new sources became available, as was the case with the last chapter of Khvārazm.[5] Furthermore, for a historian like Mas^{c}ūdī, the chapter headings reflected a vision of what topics must be treated, chosen beforehand and clung to. Bayhaqī's chapter headings are not a good guide to the contents of his work; one must add to them extensively to understand the topics Bayhaqī treated.

What is more, not being a scholar or professional historian, Bayhaqī, where Mas^{c}ūdī was arrogant and self-assured, was apologetic and defensive about most aspects of his method including structure. Yet he was determined that his book have a structure even though aware that it deviated from ''other'' histories, histories that unfortunately he neglects to name. Immediately before beginning his ''theoretical'' introduction to the reign of Mas^{c}ūd (literally, *khuṭbah,* ''sermon''; such discursi and theoretical introductions were also common in philosophical historians), he wrote:

> My desire is not to explain to the people of this era [i.e., the reign of Farrukhzād, 1052–59] the affairs of Sulṭān Mas^{c}ūd . . . , because they have observed him and have become informed about his greatness and courage and singular ability in all tools of government. Rather my desire is to write a history-foundation [*payah*] and erect an exalted structure [*banā'*] such that the memory of it will last till the end of time. And success in completing that I hope for from the Eternal Presence, and God is the friend of success.[6]

THE BASIC STRUCTURAL FEATURE: NARRATIVE AND INTERPOLATION

The basic feature of the structure of *Ta'rīkh-i Bayhaqī,* as can be seen throughout the work, is that Bayhaqī interrupts the central annalistic narrative of the reign of Mas^{c}ūd frequently, almost regularly, with poetic selections and historical anecdotes from other times and places. These interpolations are of varying length, from a sentence or a paragraph to four or five pages. (There are also flashbacks to pre-Mas^{c}ūd Ghaznavid history, but these are essentially part of the narrative and will be treated as such.) The rate at which these materials occur is, on average, every twenty pages. This pattern seems to have been quite conscious on Bayhaqī's part; he saw his own structure as a continuous narrative interrupted by other types of material. The usual pattern for the inclusion of an interpolation consists of a defense for including the interruption, a promise to get back to the narrative once the interruption is finished, the interpolation itself, then a phrase like "Aknūn bisar-i ta'rīkh bāz shavam" ("Now I resume the history proper") perhaps along with another apology.[7]

At least by the time he reached Mas^{c}ūd's reign (it would be nice to have the structure of volumes 1–5), Bayhaqī had found a purely narrative framework unsatisfactory for at least two reasons that emerge from an analysis of structure and of his explicit statements. First, it made his favored flashback technique awkward: he did not like having to put all of a year's events into a year, as was common in Muslim annalistic form, if some of them would be more relevant later as background. To solve this problem simply by repeating himself was also unsatisfactory. For example, when he begins the reign of Mas^{c}ūd, he wants to set it against the background of his youth and the relevant events in Maḥmūd's reign.[8] He says that he dealt with some of Mas^{c}ūd's youth where it "belonged" in the annalistic framework, i.e., in Maḥmūd's years, but saved some to use as background at the beginning of Mas^{c}ūd's reign. Another example is a long flashback to the history of several generations of a prominent Nishāpūr family of judges, included in order to explain in depth Mas^{c}ūd's appointment of one of them as a diplomatic courier.[9]

This use of flashback, and the attendant feature of keeping many subplots going throughout the work, tends to reinforce the sense of total planned structure. The effect of these features is to make it difficult to read the history bit by bit; in order to make sense of much of it, it is necessary to read it from its beginning. These aspects of content and structure are supported by a stylistic device—the use of ambiguous personal pronouns whose referents are to be found several pages back in place of the use of proper names, which would have made the story easier to follow.

Bayhaqī gives the second reason for the alteration and expansion of the annalistic form explicitly: a purely annalistic form, and the contents and topics usually treated in it, leads to dryness:

> Although these stories [in this case, stories about a vassal of Mas^c^ūd] are far from the history [proper], how often in some histories one reads that such-and-such king send such-and-such commander to such-and-such battle and that on such-and-such day they made war or peace and this one beat that one or that one beat this one and they [the authors] passed on [to other things], but I have put in place whatever is necessary [*vājib*].[10]

How often, indeed, the modern historian will say. This is another instance in which Bayhaqī was self-consciously innovative.

The breakdown of the annalistic form that occurred in the works of many tenth- and eleventh-century historians is reflected in the pattern of Bayhaqī's chapter headings, few of which contain references to years. Nor is every year introduced by a heading: the early headings, as is usual in the Persian historiography of this period, are written in Arabic, in a quasi-technical vocabulary commonly used in historical chapter headings. Historical writing in Persian was only just beginning to develop in Bayhaqī's time—in fact, he was one of its originators—and the influence of Arabic forms was very strong. But though the first group of chapter heads are in Arabic, the next are in Persian, the next in Arabic, and the next mixed—half Arabic, half Persian in the same titles—after which the various types alternate randomly, symbolic of the fact that Bayhaqī found himself moving away from the historical forms with which he was familiar.

From what is known at present, one must consider Bayhaqī's structure, and his elaboration of materials within it, unusual if not unique for Persian historiography. The comparison of the sources, uses, contents, and standards of evidence of the narrative and interpolated material that now follows will further elucidate the nature of Bayhaqī's historical method and the richness of his creation.

NARRATIVE

The Sources and Their Use

Bayhaqī preferred as sources for the reign of Mas^c^ūd those contemporary with the events described: (1) official documents, as copied by him, and (2) eyewitness accounts, preferably his own, either remembered or recorded in a diary or notes. Most of the sources he used for the history of Mas^c^ūd's reign he seems to have supplied himself, more often from eyewitness accounts than from documents. A systematic count has not yet been made, though one is planned by this author; but it is possible that accounts given orally to him may actually slightly outnumber those he supplied himself. In addition to a large number of oral accounts given him by Bū Naŝr-i Mushkān, and a smaller number by a variety of other court personnel, Bayhaqī has included a long account, perhaps written for him rather than orally transmitted, by his friend ^{c}Abd al-Ghaffār on Mas^{c}ūd's early life, and an account of Munjuq's death from the Qāżī Abū'l-Muẑaffar. The use of other *books* for the reign of Mas^{c}ūd is infrequent: a small amount of material from a historical account of the Ghaznavids, and apparently of eastern Irān as a whole, written by a friend Maĥmūd Varrāq, whose work has been lost; and material from the Qāżī Abū'l-Alā Ŝā^{c}id *Mukhtaŝar Ŝā^{c}idī,* a contemporary book on law and legal figures of Nishāpūr.[11] In addition, Bayhaqī also refers several times to materials from earlier volumes of his history and from the *Maqāmāt.* In the earlier volumes Bayhaqī had used ^{c}Utbī's *Ta'rīkh al-Yamīnī,* though to what extent is not known. It is not mentioned in *Ta'rīkh-i Bayhaqī;* but since ^{c}Utbī did not cover Mas^{c}ūd's reign, the only use for it would have been for flashbacks to Maĥmūd.

The preference for, and reliance on, sources close to court and official life, and by extension a concentration on court affairs, was a characteristic of many if not most histories written by secretaries in the tenth and eleventh centuries.[12] But Bayhaqī is unusual in his feeling for the use of documents. The inclusion of documents is a rarity in Islāmic historiography as a whole. Scholars have shown most "documents" included by historians before Bayhaqī's time to have been anachronisms. Bayhaqī himself apologized for including lengthy documents, asking his readers not to find fault with him and explaining to them how important the documents were. Furthermore, his own inclusion of documents was limited by two other facts. (1) Many of his document copies were confiscated when he was imprisoned; he laments their loss and in fact says, "If my papers and [document] copies had not ended up destroyed, this history would have been of an entirely different cast [literally, *lawn,* "color"]."[13] Elsewhere he writes:

> The correspondence with the court of the Caliph, with the Khāns of Turkestan, and with the lesser rulers was done in my hand. I had all the copies, but these were deliberately destroyed. Alas, and many times alas, that these gardens of paradise are not still here, because if they were, this history would become singular [*nādir*]. I do not give up hope that by the mercy of God the papers will again be found by me so that all will be written.[14]

So it is important to know that *Ta'rīkh-i Bayhaqī* is not Bayhaqī's ideal form of history. (2) Bayhaqī purposely excluded some documents on the grounds that they were too long for historical reading and belonged more in the *Maqāmāt* where he had put them. Bayhaqī did not, then, include just any document, but only documents that were absolutely vital as proof and that were deemed palatable to the reader.[15]

If Bayhaqī did not manage to use documents to the extent he wanted, he used diary and eyewitness material extensively. However, it is clear that Bayhaqī's method was not simply to reproduce his diary or to turn his book into a set of memoirs, as some have called it.[16] Rather, he fitted events presumably recorded in notes or diary, or remembered, into a structure bigger than that which the diary or notes alone could flesh out.

The first reason for this hypothesis is that in volume the diary-type material accounts for no more than half of the book. It is true that the daily, sometimes hourly, pace that characterizes the treatment of many events reminds the reader of a diary. It is interesting, however, that this *''rūz-bi-rūz''* (''day-to-day'') treatment, which so impressed Ibn Funduq when he wrote Bayhaqī's biography, does not predominate in the book as a whole.[17]

Bayhaqī seems to have used the notes and diary extensively for events on which they were good, and in these cases he gives many precise dates. But the precise dates that characterize the accounts drawn from the diary are often entirely absent elsewhere, sometimes replaced by vague dating like ''when Maḥmūd and Mas^cūd left x together for y,'' as if the audience would know or perhaps remember the date from earlier in the book, or as if the precise date did not matter. Even in close day-to-day accounts, the days of the week are often mixed up, or two contradictory dates for the same event may be given.[18] In one place the news of the Caliph al-Qādir (r. 381–422/991–1031) is said to have arrived at Ghazna several days earlier than the date usually given for the death itself.[19] Finally, when Bayhaqī is using events to illustrate a point or to represent a period, he makes no attempt to put them in sequential order.

On events on which Bayhaqī's memory was faulty or on which the diary was either destroyed or inadequate, he had to use other materials, particularly oral testimonies from associates. Although Bayhaqī does not appear to have changed the substance of these accounts, for instance, censoring embarrassing remarks or providing dates, he has apparently rewritten them in his style.

Second, the pace of the narrative varies greatly. The most striking aspect of pace is that the first half of the book covers a four-year period (421–424/1030–32), whereas the last half covers more than twice that (424–32/1032–40). During the first half of the book, Bayhaqī was already concerned with his slowness and tendency to prolixity; at one point he remarks in exasperation that he has already written too long, is impatient to finish, and has decided not to wait any longer for material to turn up on a particular point.[20]

The real turning point seems to have come with the death of Farrukhzād (451/1059). This event managed to interrupt Bayhaqī's narration of an event that had happened in 425/1033 and to cause him to pause to eulogize Farrukhzād in uncharacteristically flowery language and to reflect on his death.[21] Bayhaqī was no doubt aware that at that point he had outlived nine

Ghaznavid *amīrs*. This curious interplay between the historian's present and past time has the unfortunate effect of breaking down the sense of involvement that Bayhaqī has tried to build for the reader. Then, too, the pace of what was written after Farrukhzād's death became much more rapid as day-to-day and hour-by-hour accounts became by necessity much less frequent.[22]

Any consideration of this change in pace must take into account Bayhaqī's own age and personal perception of it. Farrukhzād's death must have further stimulated the fear of not finishing, which Bayhaqī expresses throughout *Ta'rīkh-i Bayhaqī* and which probably became even more intense in the later volumes. At approximately age sixty-five, after more than four years of work (how much more is not known), Bayhaqī had arrived only at the fourth year of Mas^{c}ūd's reign. He had covered only two-and-one-half reigns and still had five reigns to go. There is, of course, always an outside possibility that more material was available on the earlier years, or that Bayhaqī was simply more interested in them; but the pressures of time and age, which communicate themselves in numerous other ways throughout the work, seem a more likely explanation.

Standards of Evidence and Presentation

In his handling of all this material, Bayhaqī was guided by high standards of accuracy and fullness, the two of which he saw as related. This is not to say necessarily that he achieved accuracy, but that he thought he could, or at least that he thought he should. In the case of eyewitness accounts, when the source was not himself, he insisted that the reporter have an exceptionally good repuation and a strong claim to know what he was talking about. If the claim of the reporter was not patent, Bayhaqī would spend a long time in the text building it up. Sometimes the kind of material gained from oral testimony, however, has the quality of sheer, unevaluated gossip; sometimes the sources of oral testimony are not given.[23] The pattern seems to be that when material is important, Bayhaqī is sure to show the source to be reputable; for trivial material, he deems the critical evaluation of the sources not so important.

The reputation of a source alone was not adequate to justify using him unless his account met other standards. These standards, which Bayhaqī applied to his own accounts as well, are connected with a not-well-defined notion that truthfulness is somehow related to fullness of detail and the presence of fine points *(nuktah)*. Bayhaqī never makes this relationship explicit, but it can be inferred from a number of examples. For instance, in one place Bayhaqī says that he preferred an account because it was the most truthful, and then goes on to say that this account had a fine point not already familiar to him.[24]

The insistence on accuracy and fullness of detail is given a theoretical justification by Bayhaqī in one of his two *khuṭbahs* (literally, "sermons," in the meaning of philosophical or theoretical statements).[25] This theoretical statement on method and evidence, like the declaration on structure quoted earlier in this chapter, resembles arguments made by philosophical historians of the tenth and eleventh centuries like Mas^{c}ūdī and Ibn Miskawayh. Like Bayhaqī's other *khuṭbah*, which is on government rather than on historical method, it is heavily laced with philosophical terminology not characteristic of the bulk of the work. It was common for historians at the beginning of the philosophical history movement, especially those not thoroughly schooled in philosophical ideas, to argue in a philosophical manner in theoretical passages or discursi, but not to be overtly philosophical in their history per se, or particularly at ease with philosophical reasoning.

At the beginning of the *khuṭbah* on history, Bayhaqī, in philosophical fashion, analyzes the way in which the human mind can separate true from false so that he can go on to relate this faculty to the ability to judge historical evidence: ". . . The eyes and ears are the look-outs and spies of the heart and mind. . . ."[26] As he proceeds to discuss the searching out of true historical knowledge, Bayhaqī is the sedentary, urbane man. He rejects for himself the method used by other "careful" historians; perhaps he has in mind justifying his being different from the traveler-historian Bīrūnī, from whom he is about to quote a long passage:

> Now, you can either learn about past history the hard way, by travelling around the world, enduring all sorts of hardships and searching out the historical information you want, or you can study reliable [*mu^{c}tamid*] books, and furnish yourself with accurate information from them.[27]

Bayhaqī then goes on to distinguish between the only two types of information about past history: ". . . One must either hear it from someone or read it in a book. And the condition is that the speaker be trustworthy and truthful and also intelligence should testify that that report is true."[28] This distinction will be important to remember when it is demonstrated below that Bayhaqī did not apply the same standards to books as he did to eyewitness or oral accounts. The insistence on intelligent analysis of the content of an account and not just the reputation of its source may contain an implicit critique of the *ḥadīth* method common to many Muslim historians, in which the reputation of the source or, rather, chain of sources was the sole determinant of its reliability.

In a criticism that reminds one of Ibn Khaldūn, who wrote much later (in the eighth/fourteenth century), Bayhaqī then goes on to argue against the acceptance of superstition, myth, and legend by historians. This denunciation may explain why his history is surprisingly lacking in mythical themes or characters from pre-Islāmic Persia, themes and characters that had begun to invade the works of numerous other Muslim historians and poets of the period.[29] Bayhaqī writes, having just praised the intelligence of the wise:

> But . . . most ordinary [*ammah*] people are such that they like the impossible and the absurd better, like stories of demons and fairies, and ogres of the desert and mountain and ocean, so that when a fool makes a scene and a crowd of similar ones gathers round, he says, "In such-and-such ocean I saw an island, and five hundred of us landed on that island. We baked bread and set up our pots. When the fire had become hot, and its heat reached the ground, the ground moved. We looked closely and it was a fish. . . . " and other types of superstitions like this which bring sleep when read to ignorant people at night.[30]

Bayhaqī goes on to say that though only a small number of people seek the truth and know it when they read it, he has decided to report in his history what he has seen or what is accurate and comes from a reliable source. Bayhaqī does not seem to have taken seriously the possibility that even what one has seen one may not be able to relate in an accurate fashion. In his attitude toward truth and superstition, Bayhaqī differs from much of the *adab* tradition that accepted marvels and superstitions. Rationalist movements, like the Mu^{c}tazilites and the philosophical historians, many of whom were also Mu^{c}tazilites, also played down or rejected these same elements. Although Bayhaqī himself seems to have belonged to one of the anti-Mu^{c}tazilite schools of Nishāpūr, and in fact condemns the Mu^{c}tazilites to hell in his work, Mu^{c}tazilism had been pervasive in Nishāpūr in the century before his birth.[31] It is interesting to find in a Mu^{c}tazilite judge, historian, and *adīb* of Baghdād like Tanūkhī (329–84/940–94), similar denunciations of superstition and an equally suspicious attitude toward miracles. There is no way to make a direct connection between Tanūkhī and Bayhaqī, but it is clear (as will be demonstrated below) that Bayhaqī had read some of the works of the early Buyid period. Tanūkhī himself died a year or two before Bayhaqī's birth, so his very popular works would have already been circulating by the time Bayhaqī was a young man.

Furthermore, the two men are similar not only in their attitude toward superstition but in several other ways as well. In the introduction to his collection of anecdotes, Tanūkhī says he had included certain material "such as may provide the intelligent person who has a taste for learning, when they strike his ear and are assimilated by his mind, with such moral lessons, such mental and sensuous delicacy, as may save him the trouble of going to experience or picking up the like from man's life. . . . ",[32] remarks that bear obvious similarity to those quoted above from Bayhaqī. Tanūkhī also says that he relied on personal knowledge of events or reliable oral accounts, avoiding what was in other books. a preference similar to Bayhaqī's.[33] To give a final example, trifling but intriguing, Tanūkhī uses an image also used, but in a slightly different way, by Bayhaqī. Tanūkhī says, "I hope that there may be a market for my collection and that the result of my labours, and the physical exertion of putting down in writing, may not be wasted. It would be something, if it only proved better than blank paper. . . . "[34] In one place Bayhaqī writes, "Whatever is written on paper may be better than the paper [itself]. . . . "[35] Although any connection is only circumstantial, and though Bayhaqī may not have known Tanūkhī in particular but rather other authors of the same school, it is worth keeping open the possibility of his having been influenced by Mu^{c}tazilite ideas, if only mediated by the ideas of philosophical historians.

The comparison with Tanūkhī also leads into Bayhaqī's final justification for length and fullness of detail. The *khuṭbah* does not fully contain this justification; it must be put together from a large number of individual references. Both Tanūkhī and Bayhaqī, as well as other historians of their day, believed that there were moral values and lessons to be derived from history. Statements about the moral values of history are to be found in most philosophically oriented works of the tenth century, particularly during the Buyid period in Irāq, where the movement was centered. Tanūkhī justifies his collection of historical anecdotes (begun in 361/971) in the following way:

> . . . [I will provide] such matter as will train him [the intelligent man] for this world and the next, teach him the consequences of well-doing and ill-doing, how actions must ultimately turn out, how a republic should be administered, what mistakes he should avoid, so as neither to be involved in nor plunge into the like. With this before him he will not need to spend his life in experiments, nor await the results which the years will reveal.[36]

Bayhaqī, however, carried this notion, which was common to the *adab* tradition, a step further. Whereas writers of *adab* tended to prefer short pithy historical anecdotes, or to choose anecdotes that proved some preconceived notion, Bayhaqī argued that any historical account, no matter how long, could confer a moral benefit on the reader. In fact, he seems to think that length adds to the moral benefit; but he also seems to think that his readers are not used to drawing moral benefits from anything but short, pithy, to-the-point anecdotes, and is consequently always explaining that just because the stories are long does not mean they do not have a moral benefit.[37]

Bayhaqī does not communicate his notion of the moral benefits of history in such lengthy declarations as Tanūkhī's, but rather uses a series of open-ended words to convey his sentiment. Some of the words he most uses are found also in works of *adab,* words like *favā'id* ("morals" [of a story]; also "uses" or "benefits"), *gharā'ib* ("strange things," "wonders"), *navādir* ("curiosities," "rarities"), *ārāstah* ("adornment"), and *^{c}ajā'ib* ("wonders").

There is another word, though, that may have a more serious connotation, the word that became so important in the work of Ibn Khaldūn, namely *^{c}ibrah.* Although there does not seem to be a systematic difference between the cases where Bayhaqī uses *^{c}ibrah* and the cases in which he uses the other words, there is some indication that his use of the word is similar to Ibn Khaldūn's use.[38] Bayhaqī seems to have had in mind that for intelligent people, his *khiradmandān* whom he addresses so frequently, there is the possibility of going beyond the "externals" of history to what one can understand of the nature of the historical process itself. This sense of esotericism is particularly strong in Bayhaqī's application of *ᶜibrah* to the use of interpolated material, to be discussed below.

One is ultimately led to ask whether the search for moral values in history is compatible with an insistence on accuracy. In Bayhaqī's case the answer is not clear-cut. Basically in his handling of the material on Masᶜūd's reign, Bayhaqī tries to balance a serious interest in the "reality" of history with its moral values. He does not seem to be interested exclusively in moral values, nor does he seem to be forcing history into moral patterns the way some works of *adab* do. Rather, he selects incidents that interest him or that he feels are important, tells about them in detail, and then draws morals from them. He does, however, tend to tell the stories so that they lead to a point; but the question of how much accuracy he has sacrificed, either in his terms or in others', is unanswerable at this time.

There is another series of words connected with Bayhaqī's method and standards of evidence. These are words that allude to certain features he considers to be the customs or rules of history. This author's research has not yet shown where or whether Bayhaqī derived these seemingly technical terms: *qāᶜidah* ("basis," "rule"), *qānūn* ("rule," "law," "custom"; also used synonymously with *qāᶜidah*), *rasm* ("custom," "mode"; used most frequently), and *shart̂* ("necessary condition"; used synonymously with *rasm*, *shart̂* is also a legal term).[39]

If one summarizes the historical practices with which these words are connected, they are, first and foremost, completeness and fullness of accounts, no matter how long they turn out to be; then the recording of illustrious (*bā nām*) deeds; and, finally, not being able to show friendship for all. It would appear that Bayhaqī uses these seemingly technical terms as justifications for things he wants to do anyway, rather than that they represent any organized body of rules.

This predilection for fullness, for every possible type of detail, for length, and for elaboration, as justified in the above ways, was strong in Bayhaqī; but it needs further discussion and analysis because Bayhaqī is also continually apologizing for being lengthy,[40] explaining that there are a number of reasons for giving so much detail,[41] one of which is that he does not want readers to think he has shortened anything.[42] It is as though shortening would mean he is hiding something. And he has earlier declared that he plans "to give this history as fully as I could, to go around every corner and angle, so as to leave nothing hidden.''[43] Often he exhorts the readers to be patient, assuring them that if they will bear with him they will not find fault with his lengthy treatment. This fear of doing something that could cause his readers to find fault or say unworthy things troubled Bayhaqī frequently.[44]

Surely the theoretical justifications discussed above are not sufficient to explain the use of a technique that necessitated so many apologies. There could be a number of additional reasons for Bayhaqī's insistence on detail in the face of possibly negative reader reaction. The easiest is that Bayhaqī was naturally prolix or garrulous, had the detail available, and, like a college freshman doing a term paper, could not bear to leave out any fruit of hard and long research, or that he was an old man out of work who had plenty of time to write.

These simple explanations are, however, unsatisfactory on a number of grounds. First of all, in general the details he includes are, though not always absolutely necessary, usually relevant and useful for proving a point or building up an argument or image. According to Bayhaqī he has even left out detail that he considered not germaine. Bayhaqī must have known that other histories written on the same subject and at the same time, like ᶜUtbī's, with which he was familiar, were less detailed. Even the version of Ṭabarī that Balᶜamī had translated into Persian had been abridged. Bayhaqī obviously knew he would be bucking audience resistance. It meant enough to him to do so because in this regard, as in others, he was consciously innovative and determined to lead his audience's taste rather than be led by it. Although Bayhaqī was prolix and gossipy by nature, he also seems to have been seriously interested in detail for what it could add to an understanding of any given situation and for the sense of ''telling all'' it could create. In places he explicitly compared himself with other histories of the Ghaznavids that did not tell enough.[45]

There may also be a sense in which the inclusion of so much ''inside'' detail is an attempt to establish Bayhaqī's authenticity or reliability as a historian of the Ghaznavid dynasty. As has already been shown in chapter 2, he makes it clear that he knows there are greater men who could make more of a claim to ''hit the mark'' in their account of the dynasty, but they are too busy running the state to be interested in history. Throughout his work there runs the theme of the not-so-great man, the civil servant, who is proud to have been near the great and who in fact feels that only his knowledge and understanding allow him to comment; without this knowledge he realizes that he would be considered too ordinary (*piyādah*) to write the history of the great.

It is interesting that the Ghaznavids did not have an official historian, at least one whose work is known today, and in general do not seem to have encouraged historical writing as much as they did other forms of scholarship.

It is possible that this relative dearth of Ghaznavid histories came about because the Ghaznavid rulers used the extensive presence of court poets to record historical deeds in an almost legendary form; for example, Maĥmūd's expedition to the Indian shrine of Somnath was extolled and immortalized in a poem by Farrukhī. More valuable material may be embedded in the poetry of the era than in the formal histories, though it has not been fully exploited. The lack of an organized historical tradition at Ghazna makes it even clearer why Bayhaqī, not a professional scholar, emerging as a historian of the dynasty, with no clear model to follow, would have been defensive and would have felt it necessary to defend his authenticity.

The question still remains one of whether the detail is included more because Bayhaqī really thought it important for its substance or for some reason extraneous to its content, for example, just because he had it or to prove his authenticity. His book, after all, is inordinately lengthy, far longer than any similar work. Any firm decision on this matter would obviously affect the way in which the mass of detail is to be evaluated, both for its validity and for what it tells about Bayhaqī as a historian. In general, the detail is not trivial and adds to the narrative, giving it a greater sense of reality; Bayhaqī must have taken its purpose seriously to have gone against what he felt to be audience preference for shorter accounts.

Contents

The narrative material in *Ta'rīkh-i Bayhaqī* begins with the last days of Amīr Muĥammad's reign, including an unusual amount of material on Mas^{c}ūd's affairs during this period, then soon (after ninety-five pages) begins Mas^{c}ūd's reign proper, with a long flashback to his life before his accession, up to the beginning of the last year of his reign (432/1040). There are a number of striking features about the focus, scope, selectivity, and emphasis of the contents of this material. The first is that they reflect Bayhaqī's interest in building up a picture of Mas^{c}ūd, whether at Ghazna or not, as administrator and diplomat rather than as military, cultural, or religious leader, the three qualities that Bayhaqī seems to have stressed about Maĥmūd.[46] In particular Mas^{c}ūd's involvement in letter-writing and chancery matters is examined in detail. Most accounts of interviews or consultations conducted by Mas^{c}ūd end in his ordering letters written. The ritual of such letter-writing, and receiving, is almost always described in detail. Bayhaqī also uses correspondence as a form of narration. For example, he narrates the beginning of the brothers' war between Mas^{c}ūd and Muĥammad exclusively with letters they wrote to each other; what has survived of his account of the brothers' war between Maĥmūd and Ismā^{c}īl indicates that he had handled it in a similar manner.[47] This approach is unusual because other historians of the Ghaznavids, like the author of *Ta'rīkh-i Sīstān,* concentrate almost exclusively on Mas^{c}ūd's military side. It is also interesting because Mas^{c}ūd was not a diplomatically successful man, either in keeping peace abroad or in keeping peace at court.

Obviously one could argue that Bayhaqī concentrated on those things that he knew best and on which he had the best information—diplomatic contact with foreign thrones and the workings of the court and central administration. To some extent this is true, but the preference for these matters was based on more than availability of information or closeness to activity. First of all, Bayhaqī *had* done more with Maĥmūd's religious and military activities, from what can be seen in the material from *Ta'rīkh-i Yamīnī* that survives. Where Mas^{c}ūd was concerned, Bayhaqī had access to military information as well, as is evidenced in his rare accounts of battles; but his treatment of battles is not nearly so long as that of court intrigues. He shies away from the gore of battle, which interested other historians, giving casualty figures in summary fashions. This is a civilian's history written from one particular secretary's point of view. Because of this, Bayhaqī saw the chancery and the other bureaus as the heart of Ghaznavid history; but in many senses it was the heart, as much or more so than the army. It was constant communication and surveillance that held large empires like the Ghaznavid, with many of its units semiautonomous (see map 3, page 32), together. In such a structure the chancery was vital.

Second, the issues that interested and concerned Bayhaqī about Mas^{c}ūd's reign and that dominated that reign in his mind—issues of government and authority—were best examined at court and not in the army. The themes with which Bayhaqī dealt are those that struck him as important, though it is also true that his long exposure to court circles had commended these themes to his attention.

If Mas^{c}ūd's administrative and diplomatic behavior is stressed over his military and religious activities, there are numerous sections of the book in which Mas^{c}ūd loses the spotlight altogether, loses it to a number of ongoing subplots, most of which are connected with the careers of a large number of *buzurgān* ("eminent men") at court or with the affairs of various tributaries, like the Khvārazmshāh Altūntāsh or the Saljūqs. This ability and desire on Bayhaqī's part to follow a number of different characters, stories, and subplots contrasts with the tendency of Muslim dynastic historians, if not most dynastic historians, to focus almost exclusively on matters related to the monarch. Bayhaqī's vision of the important events of history thus extended beyond the ruler and his immediate affairs, but not far beyond. He does mention ordinary people (*umm, ummah*) but usually as crowds partaking in, or reacting to, court-centered events. Natural disasters take him temporarily away from the center, such as a flood in Mas^{c}ūd's reign or a drought in Maĥmūd's. But though some scholars have been impressed with his inclusion of social and economic information and his interest in natural phenomena, such information is very slight when weighed against information on administration and diplomacy.[48] But to explain his principles of selection simply by saying that he naturally wrote mostly about what was familiar to him, as one scholar has done, does not seem adequate.[49]

In the midst of the stories about Mas^cūd and other great men is a third element—frequent long digressions on chancery practice and personnel that sometimes have little to do with the narrative although they have been prompted by some event in it. Bayhaqī casually includes a number of technical terms as if his audience would understand. He includes the particulars of letter writing and copying almost routinely, for example, the states of the rough (*savād;* literally, "black") and clean (*bayāẓ;* literally, "white") copies or drafts.[50] Elsewhere much space is devoted to the choice of a new *dabīr*.[51] And again, after reporting negotiations between Masᶜūd and a tributary, Bayhaqī turns to a description of the rather gossipy interchange between Bū Naṣr-i Mushkān and his opposite number in the administration of the tributary, in which the two underlings discuss their respective situations, like chauffeurs waiting to drive their masters home. The technicalities of chancery practice are so evident that a reader knowing nothing of Bayhaqī's biography would guess his occupation within the first twenty-five pages.

In Bayhaqī's treatment of all these topics, there is one overwhelming feature: this is a historian intensely interested in human speech, emotion, activity, and interaction—in how people communicate and manage each other; there is only a rare mention of divine intervention. The bulk of the material on Masᶜūd's reign, as well as much of the interpolated material, is in the form of dialogue and correspondence, either directly overheard or seen by Bayhaqī, or reported to him at the time of the event in question or later; and he stresses the human rather than heroic qualities of the individuals treated, including Masᶜūd.

Clearly, the use of direct speech has a purely stylistic side. But the presence of so much direct quotation also raises an obvious methodological issue: no matter how good Bayhaqī's notes were, and no matter how strong his memory, it does not seem possible for him to have reproduced so many conversations verbatim. Bayhaqī did not content himself with communicating the substance of conversations, but put them in the form of lengthy direct speeches. Whether he thought them verbatim is not clear. One suggestion that comes to mind is that, lacking the documentary evidence he preferred, he turned human speech into a documentary form to make it seem more reliable.

As a result, it is clear that many apocryphal stories appear as direct documented speech. There are a number of repeated patterns in conversations supposedly far apart in time. In one interesting example the same exchange between the same two people, Masᶜūd and Bū Naṣr-i Mushkān, is reported to have occurred on two different occasions, the first of which would have made the second unlikely. To be precise, at the high point of an intrigue early in Mas^cūd's reign, Bū Naŝr is said to have been told that two men, ^cUbayd Allāh and Bū'l-Fatĥ Ĥātimī, had been spying on him for Mas^cūd during the reign of Mas^cūd's father.[52] Bū Naŝr is said to have replied:

> "What a great fraud that I have known of this situation [just] today."
> The *Amīr* said: "If you had been informed [or, had become aware] of it earlier, what would you have done?"
> He [Bū Naŝr] said: "I would have thrown them both out of the *dīvān,* because a treacherous *dabīr* is not useful" [*dabīr-i khā'in bikār nayāyad*].

Almost two hundred pages later, in a different year, Mas^cūd "again" tells this story to Bū Naŝr, but this time only about Bū'l-Fatĥ. Bū Naŝr is said to have replied:

> "Alas, that I today hear these words!"
> The *Amīr* said, "If you had heard them at that time, what would you have done?"
> "I [Bū Naŝr] would have said that . . . he be expelled from the *dīvān* because a treacherous *dabīr* is not useful" [*dabīr-i khā'in bikār nayāyad*].[53]

Because these conversations are clearly patterned, it is difficult to know whether any of their content is true. And the existence of patterning in this case makes one wonder how many other speeches and conversations are patterned and how many not, and how close any of them is to what was really said.

Dramatic dialogue is not uncommon in Islamicate historiography, even in the early historians; but Bayhaqī uses it much more than usual and with more claim to be able to reproduce conversations than many other historians who include them; and he is more able to make his readers take the conversations as real. It is clear for now that Bayhaqī was fascinated with communication of all sorts, which, after all, was his business. In his work his own narrating often serves simply to link up the lengthier conversations and documents.

Another particularly noticeable feature of the account of Mas^cūd's reign is a large volume of personal names. The index to the Fayyāẑ and Ghanī edition lists 635 names (in 691 pages), many of them used repeatedly. Bayhaqī not only uses names frequently but explicitly argues for the importance of using them, sometimes going into long explanations of honorific titles and epithets so as to be able to use them. In so doing he felt he was consciously breaking with existing historiographical practice; the exploration of names was much more the province of biographers.[54] Another technique relevant to naming is the prevalence of character sketches. This frequent analysis of character is part of Bayhaqī's larger notion that having the proper background information is necessary for a full understanding of any individual or event.[55]

This emphasis on name, both in the literal and figurative sense of reputation, runs through *Ta'rīkh-i Bayhaqī* and has been remarked by at least one other scholar.[56] Clearly, knowing names and being precise about them was vital to the work of a scribe. But there are elements of this emphasis on naming and being able to name, even down to the slaves of the *amīr*'s household, that have not been weighted heavily enough. First of all, if being able to give detail showed Bayhaqī close to the sources, being able to give names showed him especially so. Second, there is throughout the work an element of the pride of the not-so-great man in having been associated with the great. Just as serious reporting could descend to gossip, naming could and did become name-dropping, for example, when Bayhaqī mentions unnecessarily that he was a friend of a famous man he is describing.[57] Finally, one must acknowledge the element of personality, that Bayhaqī took an interest in people and their backgrounds and personalities and indulged himself in it by making it part of his history.

In attempting to summarize Bayhaqī's method in the narrative material, there are a number of ways available to conceptualize and explain the qualities of historical composition discussed thus far—inordinate length, predilection for detail, use of documents and eyewitness accounts, preference for direct speech, interest in names and biography. One scholar, K. A. Luther, has recently offered a new provocative vision of these qualities cast in terms of social psychology and in particular of communications theory.[58] According to this view, the qualities thus far discussed should be seen fundamentally as a style of communication. Luther argues that, for a complex series of cultural reasons, the Ghaznavid *dabīr* was given in his official work to the same style of communication used by Bayhaqī in his history, a style inherited in turn from the Sāmānid bureaucracy. The style of communication in question, according to this argument, is, though detailed, basically to the point and concise, just as the style of language, though elaborated, is relatively unadorned and unembellished. The function of this style is mainly to "expedite the business at hand. . . . " In the Ghaznavid chancery, according to Luther, "the premium was upon detailed yet concise reporting."[59] Luther goes on to assert, though not to prove, that "the possibility that a scribe would deviate sharply from his communications behavior in political correspondence when he turned to write political history is a very remote one."[60] Luther, then, believes that the "norms" of communication behavior become so deeply ingrained as to be second nature.

When Luther turns to Bayhaqī's historical style, he completes his argument by saying that

> Bayhaqī writes his own narrative in the same manner, as a Ghaznavid secretary, long schooled in observing and recording in a business-like fashion. . . .
> . . . Good *dabīrī* also involved detailed, accurate observation, discussion, and reporting. These are the skills Bū Naŝr Mushkān repeatedly displays in his work and the things which Bayhaqī clearly prizes in writing his history.[61]

The advantage to this type of argument is that it provides a reason for all the detail, which modern scholars have found alternately tedious and praiseworthy, other than mere self-indulgence. The latter explanation has been offered by Savory, who calls Bayhaqī an "oriental Pepys," saying that the length and detail which Bayhaqī has permitted himself in his book "has militated against the exercise of any self-discipline by the historian in the selection of his material, and has encouraged him to pad the work out with extraneous anecdotes and digressions of all kinds. . . ."[62]

But Luther's argument also poses two methodological problems. First, Luther has derived the norms of typical Ghaznavid communications behavior with which to evaluate Bayhaqī mainly from Bayhaqī's own chancery material.[63] Perhaps the norms inferred from the chancery material Bayhaqī has preserved in his history are not typical in fact, or perhaps other norms of accuracy and detail, from non-chancery sources, could have also affected Bayhaqī's historical style.

Second, this focus leads Luther to a skewed vision of *Ta'rīkh-i Bayhaqī* as a whole. He so concentrates on the material that interests him and fits his theory that he views the mass of interpolated material as merely "some embellishment" added to the narrative. His vision of the work as a whole is stated as "an extended intelligence report on Mas^{c}ūd."[64] But it is particularly when one looks at the interpolated material that one sees Bayhaqī's attempt to go beyond the norms of chancery communication, if such norms are assumed to have existed, to say other things in a less straightforward, less businesslike manner. This sort of explanation, if used monolithically, turns a work into a product of something outside itself. Often it becomes impossible to explain many aspects of the work, aspects that must then be explained away. For instance, though detail might be ascribed to chancery norms, can the presence of earthy imagery, to be discussed in chapter 5, be so explained? However, in making a possible explanation for why the interpolated material, a discussion of which completes this chapter, differs in many ways from the narrative material. Perhaps the narrative material, coming from chancery-related sources, tended to be communicated more strictly in scribal style than the interpolated material.

INTERPOLATION

Sources and Contents

The sources of the interpolated materials are by necessity different from most of the narrative sources. The sources of the poetic interpolations are easier to identify than those of the prose because Bayhaqī usually, though not always, names the sources or authors of the poetry. The poems are generally of tenth-eleventh century provenance, far more Persian than Arabic; Ghaznavid poets predominate over Sāmānid, but Sāmānid poets like Rūdakī (fl. end ninth/beginning tenth century) play a large role; more than thirty Ghaznavid poets are named, some famous, some not even poets by profession. One non-Sāmānid/Ghaznavid, non-Persian poet stands out—the Arab poet made famous by his stay at the Hamdānid court of Sayf al-Dawlah, al-Mutanabbī (303–44/915–55), who was a master of royal praise and satire.

The form of the poems is largely the long *qaŝīdah,* and several are included in their entirety; the epic *Shāhnāmah* of Firdawsī (completed about 401/1010) does not play a part, just as in the prose interpolations mentions of heroic pre-Islāmic Persian themes and characters are minimal. It is an interesting comment on the fate of bilingualism in Muslim civilization that though Bayhaqī included Mutanabbī's poems in Arabic, the modern Arabic translators of *Ta'rīkh-i Bayhaqī,* working in 1960, not only did not include all the Persian poetry intact but only summarized it briefly in Arabic.[65]

The sources of the prose interpolations are not so easy to identify. Bayhaqī names the sources of only four unambiguously: (1) Ibn al-Muqaffā''s (fl. ca. 133/750) translation of the old Persian book *Khudaynāmah,* referred to by Bayhaqī as *Ta'rīkh-i mulūk-i ᶜajam;* (2) al-Ŝūlī's (d. 335/946) *Awrāq al-Ŝūlī;* (3) al-Ŝābī's (fl. 361/971) *Kitāb al-Tājī;* and (4) al-Bīrūnī's (363–442/973–1050) *Musāmarah Khvārazm.*[66] Of these four named sources, three are from the tenth century, as are most of the books quoted in the narrative materials. Although earlier, Ibn al-Muqaffā' fits with al-Ŝūlī and al-Ŝābī in that he was a well-known figure in the *adab* tradition. Bīrūnī, who delved into almost every field, was a major figure attracted to the Ghaznavid court.

Bayhaqī either does not document the other interpolations at all or gives them vague references like "akhbār al-khulafā'" (stories of the caliphs). Whether he meant these designations in a general way or was referring to titles of works, like that of Ibn Abī Ŧāhir (third/ninth century), has not yet been determined. This author has begun a search for the sources of these undocumented anecdotes, but it is not yet complete. Among books checked unsuccessfully for such stories and anecdotes are Ŧabarī's *Ta'rīkh al-rusul wa'l-mulūk,* Ŝūlī's *Awrāq al-Ŝūlī* (mentioned above), Tanūkhī's *Nishwār al-muhādharah* (begun 361/971), and Ibrāhīm ibn Muĥammad al-Bayhaqī's (fl. ca. 300/912) *Al-Maĥāsin wa'l-Masāwī.*

Bayhaqī does definitely say that he read the interpolated stories while delving into many books of special *(khaŝŝah)* stories, some of which he collected or picked out *(iltiqāt kardah)* and later put into his history.[67] Some of the undocumented materials clearly do come from books because the *isnād*s for them are given, something Bayhaqī does not do with his own material; but the *isnād*s are always very short, indicating possibly that the stories to which they are attached may be from *adab* collections of historical anecdotes rather than from histories based on *ĥadīth*s. This theory would also fit with Bayhaqī's reference to books of special stories. One scholar has also suggested that, though Bayhaqī may have read all these stories in books at one time, he did not consult the book or written notes on it before including them.[68] This idea would accord with the implication in Bayhaqī's statement above that he collected stories some time before deciding which ones to include in his history.

A consideration of the contents of the interpolations may shed further light on the difficult problem of sources. The first feature, the same feature that struck another scholar studying the *adab* literature of the Ṭāhirid era, is that most of the themes of the interpolated material (see Appendix C) are post-Islāmic.[69] Even those figures from pre-Islāmic Persian times are figures that had been taken over into the Islāmic *adab* tradition and reworked, like Ardashīr and Alexander, and like Buzurgmihr, the prime minister of the Sāsānian emperor Nūshīrvān and the hero of a story of major importance in *Ta'rīkh-i Bayhaqī*. In the case of Buzurgmihr, it has even been argued that he was actually the creation of the Islāmic writers of *adab*.[70]

Among the Islāmic themes many are recent to Bayhaqī's time, like the Sāmānids and Būyids. Those from before the ninth century, like stories from the history of the caliphs, overwhelmingly emphasize figures like Harūn al-Rashīd and his Barmakid prime ministers and others who were also popular in *adab*-type historical collections. The table of contents of an early fourth/tenth-century *adab* collection of historical stories, by a fellow Bayhaqī, Ibrāhīm ibn Muḥammad, contains many of the figures found in the interpolated stories. However, that particular book does not appear to have been a source for Bayhaqī.[71] Although Bayhaqī's sources are not clear, many of the characters in his anecdotes are very similar to stories included in later works of *adab*, particularly in "Mirrors for Princes" literature like Ghazālī's (d. 1111) *Naṣīḥat al-Mulūk*. There are also a large number of aphorisms in the work that can be found in "Mirrors" literature, for example, definitions of justice and magnanimity. One particular story, about a miraculous occurrence between Moses and a lamb, could easily be a story from *adab*, where animal fables and omens were common.[72] It should also be noted that Bayhaqī seems to exempt prophets from his prejudice against miraculous stories, saying that God gives prophets the special powers to perform miracles.

It would be very interesting to know whether Bayhaqī actually had plodded through the many voluminous chronicles on the periods to which he refers or whether he availed himself of the "readers' digests of history" compiled by *adībs* for the more pleasurable reading of a wider audience. And even if he did make use of compendia of historical anecdotes, it is interesting to note that his anecdotes are generally much longer than those in the *adab* collections. If and when it is possible to find all the sources of these anecdotes, one might find other ways in which Bayhaqī altered the materials he used. Such discoveries would in turn cast more light on his method and values as a historian. At the moment his foremost principle of selection for any one of these materials seems to have been its appropriateness to the theme or incident being interrupted. As will be seen below, the subject of each interpolation responds directly to that event in the narrative which it is interrupting or following. It may also be assumed for the time being that the thematic patterns in the interpolations reflect either Bayhaqī's historical preferences or the preferences of the body of stories on which he drew or both.

Standards of Evidence

The high standards of accuracy that Bayhaqī attempted to apply to his material on Mas^{c}ūd's reign were not operative on the interpolated material. Minovi has already pointed to the general historical inaccuracy of these materials; and Bayhaqī was satisfied with vague references, often saying he got his interpolated material from *kutub-i muṣbat* ("established" or "reliable books").[73] These facts have led Minovi to argue that Bayhaqī probably did not sit down to consult a book before writing the stories up.[74] But there are four further possibilities that Minovi has overlooked: (1) that many of these stories did not come directly from books, despite what Bayhaqī says, but rather from an oral tradition; (2) that they did come directly from books but that they were purposely altered by Bayhaqī to fit his needs without concern for accuracy; (3) that they were inaccurate in the books used and Bayhaqī was unaware of it; and (4) that he did not have access to the books in question when he wrote his versions of stories that he had read in them.

Even if Minovi is right in that Bayhaqī was simply careless, one must remember two things. First, for Bayhaqī, history of the distant past could come only from reliable books; but there was no way he could make even reliable books live up to the standards of accuracy that he had derived from, and applied to, documentary and eyewitness accounts. All he could say was, and he says this repeatedly, that he had really read these things in books that he trusted and had not simply made them up. Despite the inaccuracies, which Bayhaqī may or may not have recognized, the interpolated material is told in a much more realistic and serious *manner* than is usually the case in *adab* writers.

Second, in material outside the narrative, historical reality was less important to him than the usefulness of *patterns,* not particulars, inasmuch as these patterns were to be related to, and compared with, the events of Mas^{c}ūd's reign. More than he does for narrative material, Bayhaqī stresses the moral values of the interpolated stories. For him it can be said that present or near-present history is both real *and* useful; past history is mostly useful for what it teaches, existing as it does *dar qadīm* (his phrase), in the old days, a Persian counterpart of the phrase, *in illo tempore*. He explicitly says that stories from the past are a fund of information to be culled as needed, not studied for themselves: "And to use [*fā'idah*] of books [*kutub*] and stories [*hikāyāt*] and biographies [*siyar*] from the past is that they can be read little by little [*bitadrīj*] and whatever is necessary or useful can be removed."[75] And yet, though there are inaccuracies in the interpolated material, Bayhaqī does not tell the stories in the purely moral-seeking way common to writers of *adab*. He tells them in detail, like the material in the narrative, in a serious manner, with an obvious interest in their content as well as in their usefulness. In this regard, as in his handling of the narrative material, Bayhaqī has begun to move beyond one of the problems of the *adīb*'s use of historical material to a more serious interest in the history for its own sake. The strongest statement of the usefulness of stories from the past has a curiously Qur'ānic ring: ". . . so that sleepers and those having become too enamored with the physical world will wake up."[76] The question, "To what should they awaken?", leads naturally into a discussion of the function of the interpolated material.

Function

The function of the poetic interpolations is a study in itself and will not be attempted here except for a few brief remarks. The poetic interpolations do not seem to function exactly as do the prose interpolations. Like the prose interpolations, which outnumber them, they are relevant to the material in the narrative they interrupt; in fact, one poem was composed especially for sections of the work.[77] Unlike the prose interpolations, the poetic interpolations seem to require no apologies for their inclusion, though Bayhaqī often stresses their moral benefits. This may indicate that the taste of the audience was established for poetry or simply that the audience was more accustomed to seeing poetry added to a narrative history. Surely, the inclusion of poetry as interpolation is more common in Islāmicate historiography as a whole than the inclusion of prose. Then, too, poetry was a very popular medium at the Ghaznavid court.

The consensus of historians on the purpose of including all interpolations, prose and poetry, has been that Bayhaqī put them there for adornment and amusement, as mere decoration.[78] There is some small amount of truth in this theory. Bayhaqī uses some words familiar to readers of *adab,* the same words used for the narrative material, to excite audience interest, words like *wonders, curiosities, rarities, embellishments.* He says himself that the inclusion of such stories makes his history special *(khaṣṣah)* and pleasant *(khūsh).* And some few interpolations do seem amusing and nothing else.

One is first led to be suspicious, however, by the fact that Bayhaqī is constantly explaining and apologizing for the inclusion of these stories that are supposed to be for audience amusement and diversion. Then one finds that stories specifically labeled *ārāstah* (adornment) are among the most serious and least amusing stories in the book.

There is a strong possibility that Bayhaqī wants to allow the ordinary person to look no further than he wishes or than is safe. For those who are more intelligent, Bayhaqī provides clues and encouragements to look and think much further, as far as they can in fact, using lines like "You may think this is irrelevant but look again," "Anything no matter how tedious it seems is worth reading once," Pause and think and you will agree with me," "Wise men will know there is more to say," "I want to explain everything fully and leave nothing hidden," "Wise men know what the profound moral of these stories is."[79] As in almost all Islāmic scholarship, the possibility of reading on different levels is built in. Throughout the work there are all sorts of signs of *taqiyyah:* radical statements in harmless mouths, explicit statements contradicted in practice, juxtaposition of contradictory ideas, and especially the raising of possibilities and ideas in interpolated material not raised in the narrative.

It is not clear whether Bayhaqī felt any immediate need to dissimulate his true feelings, or whether he is not hiding his true feelings but rather provocative ideas and suggestions. Most of the people about whom he was writing were dead, and he was himself not working for the *amīr*. But he definitely intended the work to be read in his lifetime and could not afford to say anything offensive about the royal family. He also seems to have been flirting with ideas that could have been offensive to a variety of readers unconnected with the court; and he often says that he desired the well-wishes of his readers. So the general self-protective tendency to esotericism seems to have prevailed.

It is in this context that Bayhaqī makes particular use of the interpolated material to raise all sorts of ideas that he does not choose to raise in the narrative. In *Ta'rīkh-i Bayhaqī* the interpolated stories seem to serve two related purposes: to reiterate or reinforce the morals of stories in the narrative, but also to expand, contradict, and comment on the narrative stories to which the interpolations are appended or to set up issues to watch for in narrative stories to come. This latter use may be similar to Ṭabarī's inclusion of various versions of the same story discussed in chapter 1.

The two functions are tied together in a circular process. Bayhaqī has come to the writing of the history of Mas^c^ūd's reign with a serious interest in accuracy and detail but also with certain issues and interests in mind. In the course of recording the history of Mas^c^ūd's reign, additional issues and patterns are suggested that, together with the original issues, lead Bayhaqī to look for, or to remember, similar situations from other histories. These other situations are then used to illuminate further the recent history that resembles them.

This process requires the reader to be able to reason analogically. Early in his work it seems that Bayhaqī is trying to instruct the audience to think in terms of analogy; later this faculty seems to be taken for granted. The first interpolated story is a very long one, and Bayhaqī interrupts it several times to tell his readers that he knows it is a *qiṣṣah-yi dirāz* ("long story") but that it is useful and really does come from the history of the caliphs.[80] The story itself is about the brothers' war between the two sons of Caliph Harūn al-Rashīd (r. 786–809). It has clear parallels to the brothers' war between Mas^{c}ūd and Muĥammad, an account of which it interrupts. The suggestion of its being intended analogically is heightened by the fact that the losers in both cases are named Muĥammad.

Fifty pages later a direct exhortation for wise men to think analogically occurs.[81] One of Bayhaqī's eyewitnesses has included in his account two lines of poetry on the inconstancy of lovers that used to be recited at the court of Amīr Muĥammad (r. 421/1030). Bayhaqī then argues that wise men should have understood these lines to have been analogous to the situation that existed between Amīr Muĥammad and his followers.

One hundred twenty-five pages later, Bayhaqī says he has brought up two stories so that readers can compare them with the pattern of relationships between man and his friend and the man and his mother that has emerged in a story about one of Mas^{c}ūd's officials, and seems to assume that the audience can make the necessary connections.[82]

In the process of making use of the interpolated material in so many different ways, Bayhaqī, perhaps without even realizing it, has begun to suggest that there are repeating patterns in human history—a theory that emerged explicitly in Islāmicate historiography only in Ibn Khaldūn's (1332–82) introduction to his history. The patterns in Bayhaqī's work are not nearly so broad as those in Ibn Khaldūn's, but they are clearly present. By telling his interpolated stories in the same amount of detail as the narrative stories, by treating them not as myth but as historical reality, and by fitting them so carefully to the issues and themes in the narrative, Bayhaqī gives the impression that the patterns and problems in Ghaznavid history are not at all new. One problem of particular significance in Ghaznavid history—contest over, and succession to, the throne—is explored especially often.

For example, in the midst of his account of the Ghaznavid *amīr* Maĥmūd's (r. 388–421/998–1030) changing of the succession from one son to the other and the ensuing brothers' war between them, Bayhaqī introduces a long story about the ^{c}Abbāsid caliph Harūn al-Rashīd's (r. 170–193/786–809) change of designation from one son to another and the ensuing brothers' war between *them.*[83] In the story about Harūn, Bayhaqī is able to suggest things about the Ghaznavid example that he was not able to suggest directly while narrating it. Specifically, in the story about Harūn, he suggests the basic foolishness of changing the designation from a more-popular to a less-popular son and the inevitable violent consequences, though before beginning the story about Harūn he has spent some energy justifying the very same decision by the Ghaznavid Maĥmūd. Thus what has begun as a narrow interest in Ghaznavid court life becomes, through the use of the interpolations, a much broader vision of human history.

The structure described in this chapter is obviously very complex: grounded in a scribe's interests and skills, it has been molded also by ideas from at least two other traditions—*adab* and philosophical history. The particular issues, themes, and problems that Bayhaqī explores in this complex structure, as well as their sources, are the subjects of chapter 4.

1. The only scholar who has attempted to look at Bayhaqī's historical method is Roger Savory, "Abo'l Fazl Bayhaqī as an Historiographer," in Mashhad University, Faculty of Letters and Humanities, *Yādnāmah-yi Abū'l-Fażl-i Bayhaqī* (Mashhad: Mashhad University Press, 1971), pp. 84–128. Savory has translated and commented on Bayhaqī's longest explicit declaration of method and has extracted a number of what he calls "distinctive" elements in the work itself, but has not attempted to put them into a pattern or to see the explicit declarations in the context of the work as a whole.

2. *TB*, pp. 156/192, 160/196, 241/311 (first phrase); 160/196 (second phrase); 154/189 (third phrase); 244/316.

3. Mas^cūdī, *El Masudi's Historical Encyclopedia, Entitled "Meadows of Gold and Mines of Gems": Translated from the Arabic by Aloys Sprenger, M.D. (Murūj al-dhahab),* trans. Aloys Sprenger, Oriental Translation Fund, London, Oriental Publications, vols. 54–56 (London: Oriental Translation Fund of Great Britain and Ireland, 1841), 1:27–28.

4. For Bayhaqī's quotation from *Kitāb al-Tājī*, see *TB*, p. 194/244. The information about Khalīfah ibn Khayyâṭ, author of a work known simply as *Ta'rīkh Khalifah ibn Khayyâṭ*, comes from an oral communication from Professor Michael Zwettler of the Ohio State University. For information on Abū Isḥaq al-Ṣābī, see Mohammed Arkoun, *Contribution à l'étude de l'humanisme arabe au IVᵉ/Xᵉ siècle: Miskawayh philosophe et historien,* Etudes musulmanes, vol. 12 (Paris: Librairie Philosophique J. Vrin, 1970), pp. 53 and 121.

5. For a case of the former, see *TB*, p. 109/130.

6. Ibid., p. 96/112. See also Appendix B, selection 2.

7. E.g., see *TB*, p. 255/333.

8. Ibid., p. 109/130.

9. Ibid., pp. 198 ff./249 ff.

10. Ibid., p. 354/452.

11. Ibid., pp. 260/340 ff. and 198/249 ff., respectively.

12. Persian city histories also tended to include documents. See Ann K. S. Lambton, "An Account of the Tarīkhi Qumm," *Bulletin of the School of Oriental and African Studies* 12 (1947–48): 586–96.

13. *TB*, p. 288/381.

14. Ibid., p. 294/389. Compare W. Barthold's translation of this passage in *Turkestan Down to the Mongol Invasion*, E. J. W. Gibb Memorial Series, n.s., vol. 5, 3d ed. (London: Luzac and Co., Ltd., 1968), p. 23. His rendering of the word *nādir* as "really valuable" does not communicate the significance Bayhaqī intended: that the inclusion of the lost papers would make his history unique, would distinguish it from others.

15. This extraction of the palatable from the technical is comparable to the way in which Mas^cūdī extracted from his more technical works material appropriate to a popular audience.

16. Barthold, *Turkestan,* p. 23, seconding Sachau's evaluation.

17. Ibn Funduq, *Ta'rīkh-i Bayhaq,* ed. Aḥmad Bahmanyār, 2d ed. (Tehran: Islāmiyyah Press, 1385/1965), p. 175.

18. *TB*, pp. 159/196 and 294/390, respectively.

19. Ibid., p. 286/379.

20. Ibid., p. 109/129. See also p. 199/250, where he refers to fifty years' coverage and several thousand pages written.

21. Ibid., pp. 378/483 ff.

22. Savory, "Abo'l-Fazl Bayhaqī as an Historiographer," has overlooked this fact in his evaluation of pace and detail.

23. On Bayhaqī's gossipiness, see ibid., pp. 104–7.

24. *TB*, pp. 331–32/422–23. He also gives two other accounts, as if unsure of which is true: pp. 320/407 and 323–24/411–12.

25. Ibid., pp. 666–67/903–6; for a not always literal translation, see Savory, "Abo'l-Fazl Bayhaqī as an Historiographer," pp. 85–88.

26. Savory, p. 85.

27. Ibid., pp. 85–86. See also Appendix B, selection 12.

28. *TB*, p. 666/904. See also Appendix B, selection 12.

29. H. A. R. Gibb, "Tarīkh," in H. A. R. Gibb, *Studies on the Civilization of Islam,* ed. Stanford J. Shaw and William P. Polk (Boston: Beacon Press, 1962), p. 117.

30. *TB*, pp. 666–67/903–6, adapted from Savory's translation, "Abo'l-Fazl Bayhaqī as an Historiographer," p. 87. See the interesting remarks on Bayhaqī's reference to this legend in S. H. Hodivala, *Studies in Indo-Muslim History: A Critical Commentary on Elliot and Dowson's History of India as Told by Its Own Historians* (Bombay: n.p., 1939), 2:151. See also Appendix B, selection 12.

31. *TB*, p. 99/117. See also Appendix B, selection 2.

32. Tanūkhī, *The Table-Talk of a Mesopotamian Judge (Nishwār al-muhādharah),* trans. D. S. Margoliouth, Oriental Translation Fund, n.s., vol. 28 (London: Royal Asiatic Society, 1922), p. 8.

33. Ibid., p. v.

34. Ibid., p. 10.

35. *TB*, p. 360/459.

36. Tanūkhī, *Table-Talk,* p. 8.

37. *TB*, p. 194/243, for example.

38. Muhsin Mahdi, *Ibn Khaldūn's Philosophy of History: A Study in the Philosophic Foundation of the Science of Culture* (Chicago: University of Chicago Press, 1957), pp. 63–65. For a collection of passages related to Bayhaqī's use of *ᶜibrah,* see Husayn Bahār al-ᶜUlūmī, "Ta'rīkh-i Bayhaqī ya A'inah-yi ᶜIbrah," in Mashhad University, *Yādnāmah*, pp. 54–67.

39. *TB*, pp. 109/130, 238/307 (*qāᶜidah*); 238/307 (*qānūn*); 254/333, 339/432, 404/519 (*rasm*), 12/12, 339/432, 397/509 (sharṭ). These are only a few of the available examples.

40. E.g., ibid., pp. 108/128, 196/246, 421/543.

41. E.g., ibid., pp. 108/128, 238/307.

42. E.g., ibid., pp. 52/51 and 247/320. It should also be noted that this tendency for the author to intervene to explain himself to his readers was a relatively new feature in Islāmic historiography, a feature that was to become even stronger. One of the most well-known examples is Ibn al-Athīr's (d. 631/1233) justification for writing about the Mongol devastation of the Dār al-Islām: "O would that my mother had not borne me, or that I had died and become a forgotten thing ere this befell! Yet withal a number of my friends urged me to set it down in writing, and I hesitated long; but at last came to the conclusion that to omit this matter [from my history] could serve no useful purpose." Translated in Edward G. Browne, *A Literary History of Persia* (Cambridge: Cambridge University Press, 1902), 2:427.

43. *TB*, p. 11/11.

44. E.g., ibid., p. 193/241, 196/245.

45. E.g., ibid., p. 11/11.

46. See Bayhaqī's account of Maḥmūd's qualities in Said Nafisi, *Dar Pīrāmūn-i Ta'rīkh-i Bayhaqī* (Tehran: n.p., 1342/1923), 1:64 ff. On the lack of religious information, see Kan Kagaya, "Religious Groups in Khorasan under the Ghaznavids," in Mashhad University, *Yādnāmah*, pp. 5–13.

47. Ibid., p. 36/39. Mas^cūd, the "hero" of *Ta'rīkh-i Bayhaqī*, came to the throne after a successful challenge to his brother Muḥammad's prior claim; their father, Maḥmūd, had similarly come to the throne after a successful challenge to his brother Ismā^cīl's prior claim.

48. E.g., Mujtaba Minovi, "The Persian Historian Bayhaqī," in *Historians of the Middle East*, ed. Bernard Lewis and Peter M. Holt, Historical Writings on the Peoples of Asia (London: Oxford University Press, 1962), p. 111.

49. Barthold, *Turkestan*, p. 23.

50. *TB*, p. 148/180.

51. Ibid., p. 245/319.

52. Ibid., p. 145/176.

53. Ibid., p. 322/410.

54. E.g., ibid., p. 110/131. ^cAbbās Zaryāb Khu^cī, "Ta'rīkh Nigarī-yi Bayhaqī," Revue de la Facultè des Lettres et Sciences Humaines de Machad, vol. 4, no. 7 (1972), p. 767, has, I think, arrived wrongly at the opposite meaning: that Bayhaqī tried to adhere to existing historiographical practice with regard to naming.

55. See Savory, "Abo'l-Fazl Bayhaqī as an Historiographer," pp. 96–102, for a discussion of these character sketches.

56. Ibid., pp. 96 ff.

57. *TB*, p. 242/314.

58. Kenneth A. Luther, "Bayhaqī and the Later Seljūq Historians: Some Comparative Remarks," in Mashhad University, *Yādnāmah*, pp. 14–33.

59. Ibid., pp. 24, 27.

60. Ibid., p. 23.

61. Ibid., pp. 24 and 28.

62. Savory, "Abo'l-Fazl Bayhaqī as an Historiographer," p. 92.

63. Luther, "Bayhaqī and the Later Seljūq Historians," p. 27.

64. Ibid., p. 24.

65. See Abū'l-Fazl Bayhaqī, *Ta'rīkh al-Bayhaqī (Ta'rīkh-i Bayhaqī)*, trans. Sādiq Nash'āt and Yahyā' al-Khashāb (Cairo: Dār al-Ṭibā^cah al-Ḥadīthah, 1380/1960), passim.

66. *TB*, pp. 105/125, 602/801, 194/244, 668/907.

67. Ibid., p. 194/243.

68. Minovi, "The Persian Historian Bayhaqī," p. 140.

69. See Clifford Edmund Bosworth, "The Ṭāhirids and Arabic Culture," *Journal of Semitic Studies* 14 (1969): 45–79. The poetry, whose contents were not subject to manipulation by Bayhaqī, does contain more pre-Islāmic themes.

70. Cf. F. R. C. Bagley, "Introduction," in Ghazālī, *Ghazālī's Book of Counsel for Kings (Naṣīḥat al-mulūk)*, trans. F. R. C. Bagley (London: Oxford University Press, 1964), p. xii.

71. Ibrāhīm ibn Muḥammad al-Bayhaqī, *Al-Mahāsin wa'l-masāwī*, ed. Muḥammad Abū'l-Faḍl Ibrāhīm (Cairo: Progressive Press of Egypt, n.d.), 2 vols. Thanks to Professor Michael Zwettler for pointing out this work.

72. *TB*, pp. 204–5/258–59. The story also appears in Midrash.

73. Ibid., p. 414/534. Also 29/36.

74. Minovi, "The Persian Historian Bayhaqī," p. 140.

75. *TB*, p. 36/39.

76. Ibid., p. 194/243.

77. Ibid, pp. 275/361 ff. (composed by the *faqīh* Abū Ĥanīfah Iskafī).

78. E.g., Minovi, "The Persian Historian Bayhaqī," p. 140; Luther, "Abū'l-Fażl Bayhaqī and the Later Seljūq Historians," p. 27.

79. *TB*, pp. 11/11, 108/28, 179/222, 28/30, 11/11, 35/38–39.

80. Ibid., pp. 29/31 ff.

81. Ibid., p. 76/87.

82. Ibid., p. 193/242. See also Appendix B, selection 5.

83. Ibid., pp. 29–36/31–39.

4

The Pattern in Bayhaqī's Carpet: An Analysis of the Themes of *Ta'rīkh-i Bayhaqī*

INTRODUCTION

Bayhaqī based his method as a historian on a blend of philosophical and secular views of history with the habits and attitudes of a *dabīr* and *adīb*. He pulled materials together from a number of sources. The interaction between his values as expressed in his work and his interpretation of history, both in general and in particular, also involved a blend: of ideas from several intellectual and religious traditions, often competing and conflicting, with the ever changing perceptions and values that the author had accumulated in the course of a long life.

Chapter 3 concentrated largely on structure and on structural elements of the contents of *Ta'rīkh-i Bayhaqī.* This chapter goes on to examine themes, patterns, motifs, problems, and issues raised by the materials selected, and the values of the author expressed through them. But structural considerations are still strong here because in these works it is often through elements of structure that themes, values, and attitudes are conveyed.

The pattern of the carpet into which Bayhaqī weaves his materials and ideas is Persian, like its maker.[1] Motifs and themes intertwine and ramify without hierarchical or geometric resolution. Bayhaqī was not a systematic thinker, and his ideas should not be forced into a rigid order. But just as structure was part of his method, there is a pattern to the motifs, themes, issues, and problems with which he deals, and to his own values that lie behind them.

The dominant themes raised by the materials in *Ta'rīkh-i Bayhaqī* can be broken down into two large interdependent categories: morality and responsibility, and government, each of which has a number of subdivisions. In each category the influence of several different traditions can be seen.

AN ANALYSIS OF THE FIRST KHUT̂BAH

There is one section in *Ta'rīkh-i Bayhaqī* where the major themes and values and the traditions behind them are contained in miniature. This is the first of the two *khut̂bah*s ("sermons") in the book.[2] The first step in analyzing this important passage is to determine how it fits into the book as a whole. Because of the brothers' war, which took up all of Muĥammad's reign (421/1030), Bayhaqī has already gone into Mas^{c}ūd's affairs extensively before actually getting to Mas^{c}ūd's reign. When in the narrative it becomes clear that Mas^{c}ūd has established himself as *amīr* over his brother Muĥammad, Bayhaqī pauses and says that instead of continuing the narrative about Mas^{c}ūd's takeover, a narrative that Bayhaqī has brought up to Mas^{c}ūd's arrival at Balkh, Monday, 7 Dhū'l-Hijjah 421/Monday, 6 December 1030, he will begin the entire section on Mas^{c}ūd with a *khut̂bah* and then several related but distinct sections *(faŝl).* Only then will he resume the narrative proper.

Having just said that he will not resume the narrative until after the *khut̂bah,* Bayhaqī begins his account of Mas^{c}ūd's reign officially anyway, under a large new heading followed by a brief paragraph reviewing the chain of events that led up to Mas^{c}ūd's reign. One can interpret the contents and placement of this section to support a hypothesis that Bayhaqī was a partisan of Mas^{c}ūd in his struggle with his brother Muĥammad. This would be interesting to know in light of the fact that Bayhaqī makes it seem throughout his account of the war between Muĥammad and Mas^{c}ūd that most of the officials of the court (and Bayhaqī was an official of the court at the time) supported Muĥammad and viewed Mas^{c}ūd as a usurper. But in reviewing the chain of events that led up to Mas^{c}ūd's reign, Bayhaqī passes over Muĥammad's reign entirely, attaching Mas^{c}ūd directly to Sabuktigīn, the founder of the Ghaznavid dynasty, through Mas^{c}ūd's father Maĥmūd.

There are other indications that Bayhaqī is legitimizing Mas^{c}ūd not simply because any dynastic historian needs to legitimize every member of a dynasty but because he favored Mas^{c}ūd over Muĥammad, or at least was neutral or pragmatic enough always to favor the winner. First, Bayhaqī writes his account of the very last part of Muĥammad's reign (which survives as the first ninety-five pages of *Ta'rīkh-i Bayhaqī*) largely from the perspective of the challenger, Mas^{c}ūd's camp, emphasizing how many people hoped Maf^{c}ūd would win and thought he should. Second, Bayhaqī explicitly says that his mentor, Bū Naŝr-i Mushkān, had known that Mas^{c}ūd would win and so purposely tried not to offend him or his supporters.[3] This would help explain why Bū Naŝr and his associates escaped the purge of the old guard that Mas^{c}ūd conducted after his accession. After the paragraph of introduction to

Mas^{c}ūd's reign, Bayhaqī explains that he has promised in the beginning of the entire history a *khut̂bah* at the start of each new reign; he then proceeds to the *khut̂bah* itself.

The placement of this *khut̂bah* at this point in the narrative has two felicitous stylistic effects as far as Bayhaqī is concerned. First, it allows Bayhaqī to avoid the subject of what happened to Muĥammad (who actually outlived Mas^{c}ūd) after Mas^{c}ūd's arrival at Balkh. Second, it solves the problem of how to make Mas^{c}ūd's reign separate and distinct, and by extension legitimate, instead of going right into it from the treatment of the brothers' war. The *khut̂bah* serves to break off the narrative and give a proper start to a new narrative, in which Bayhaqī will go back to Mas^{c}ūd's boyhood, having already treated some of his affairs in the accounts of Maĥmūd and Muĥammad. One of Bayhaqī's own remarks suggests this function. Before announcing that the *khut̂bah* will precede the narrative, he says that the narrative will necessarily take on a different tone now that he has shown Mas^{c}ūd established over his brother.

The *khut̂bah* itself runs five printed pages, and is mainly about good and bad kingship, in general and with regard to the Ghaznavids.[4] The first section of the *khut̂bah* contains a comparison of two figures popular in *adab* lore, Alexander the Great and Ardashīr (Sāsānian emperor of the third century C.E.), showing the superiority of Persian over other kings. He says that miracles *(mu^{c}jizāt)* similar to those performed by prophets have been attributed to these two.[5] Bayhaqī contrasts the meteoric rise and fall of Alexander, followed as it was by the reigns of the *mulūk-i t̂avā'if,* the lesser kings, that is, the Parthians, with the long line of just rulers who followed Ardashīr. For Bayhaqī lastingness is the mark of a great dynasty. For the first time he argues that the great dynasties of Persia, like the Ghaznavids, have followed directly on the greatness of the Sāsānians. Bayhaqī is here stating a view of the Ghaznavids that is much more exalted than the view held by certain contemporary authors. For example, the author of *Ta'rīkh-i Sīstān* and Gardīzī minimize the role of the Ghaznavids in Persia, viewing them as outsiders who control only the eastern Persian provinces, like Khurāsān.

The relevance of this discussion of kingship becomes clear when Bayhaqī inserts an answer to a hypothetical critic who would say that the greatness of the Ghaznavids came originally from smallness. Bayhaqī has already referred to Sabuktigīn as a general of the Sāmānids. Now he describes the political genealogy of the Ghaznavids to run from Adam to Muĥammad to the early caliphs to the Ghaznavids.[6] This is not to say that Bayhaqī confuses the line of prophets with that of secular rulers, but that he is arguing that the Ghaznavids as secular rulers are contributing to the expansion of Islām that Muĥammad as prophet began. Bayhaqī somewhat ambiguously refers to a group of people called *yārān,* or helpers of the Prophet—a category that seems to include the caliphs but may or may not include the Ghaznavids. Although Bayhaqī does not explicitly put the Ghaznavids on a par with the caliphs, he seems to view the role of the Ghaznavids to be some sort of extension of that of the caliphs.

To explain why the Ghaznavids superseded the Sāmānids, a more aristocratic dynasty of Persia that Bayhaqī admires, Bayhaqī uses the defense used throughout his book: ever since Adam, God has placed *mulk* ("kingship") where, when, and on whom He wants, taking into account the public welfare *(maṣlaḥah)* of his creatures. Wise men know that God can see the unseen and knows secrets ordinary mortals do not know. This pious remark signals, as usual, that Bayhaqī does not wish to carry the argument any further. This theme of transference of *mulk* according to God's will and the public welfare also occurs in the systematic political theory of the age as represented in Mawardī (d. 450/1058) and was taken up a generation after Bayhaqī with the work of Niẓām al-Mulk (d. 488/1095) writing under the Saljūqs.[7] After describing the transference of *mulk,* Bayhaqī connects the greatness of the Ghaznavids with the current ruler, Farrukhzād, in a perfunctory manner. Whether there is any implicit criticism of the Ghaznavid origins in Bayhaqī's decision to raise the issue in the first place is not known.

The second section of the *khuṭbah* is curiously announced by Bayhaqī as one that may be closer to people's hearts ("chunānkah bar dilhā nazdīktar bāshad"), fall on their ears more quickly, and not require a high degree of wisdom—a leading introduction. Then he immediately launches into a quotation that appears to be directly out of a work of orthodox theology, though the source has not yet been found.[8] One will notice in it a contradiction of his previous statement about the miracles attributed to Alexander and Ardashīr:[9]

> Know that God Most High has given to prophets (God's blessings on all of them!) [one] power and to kings another. And has made it incumbent on earthly beings that they must obey those two powers and acknowledge that true path to God. And anyone who acknowledges that to be from the stars and planets and signs of the zodiac, he disregards the Creator in their midst, and is a Mu^{c}tazilite, or *zindīq*, or *dahrī* [atheist?], and his place is in hell! We seek refuge in God from disappointment.[10]

Bosworth, quoting as far as "that true path of God" has argued that this passage shows that "as a typical representative of the Persian secretarial class, it is unlikely that Baihaqī's views on kingship and the divine order of events were much different from the accepted Perso-Islāmic tradition."[11] Nowhere does Bosworth define what he means by "typical representative of the Persian secretarial class" or "accepted Perso-Islāmic tradition." In the current state of knowledge, the accepted Perso-Islāmic tradition seems to have varied according to who was doing the accepting. Some Persian dynasties, like the Būyids, wanted to restore the sense of divinity that had been associated with the Sāsānian monarchs; others did not. Some writers exalted kings; some made fun of them. And surely with as little as is known of the individual personalities and values of the vast Persian bureaucracy, it is impossible to talk of typicality.

When the entire quotation is considered, it becomes clear that this is, rather, a theologically inspired passage in which Bayhaqī is setting out an alternative to the statement about the miraculous powers of the kings Ardashīr and Alexander that he had made a page earlier.[12] His own views, which cannot be assumed to be identical with this quotation, seem to vacillate when he comes to treat actual kings, like Mas^{c}ūd, as will be explored later in this chapter.

That this statement may be related to Islāmic theology and political theory becomes more likely when one analyzes the sentiments that follow it. Bayhaqī goes on to distinguish between kings *(pādshāhān)* and tyrants *(mutaghallibān)*. Kings are just, do good, behave well, leave good impressions, and must be obeyed. Tyrants are oppressive, do bad, and must be deserted so that holy war *(jihād)* may be waged against them. Rulers must, then, be judged according to their actions. As for the Ghaznavid emperors, they have been guided by God, have behaved well, and must be obeyed even though they are descended from slave Turkish soldiers. If any of them should be disappointing, wise men know that God's will is written and cannot be changed, again a signal from Bayhaqī that he has raised as many sides of this argument as he cares to. This rather ambiguous attitude toward authority and respect for it resembles the decisions of orthodox political theorists of the age: kings, unless thoroughly bad, must be obeyed for the sake of security. One must admit that they have been appointed by God; but since they do not have divine powers, one cannot expect them to exhibit perfection in all instances.

This argument ends the *khuṭbah* proper according to Bayhaqī. There is some confusion on this point, however, because he also says that another section ends the *khuṭbah* nine pages later.[13] Apparently Bayhaqī forgot that he had said originally that the two final sections appended to the *khuṭbah* were not supposed to be part of it. To summarize the contents of the *khuṭbah* to this point, Bayhaqī has said all the things he could be expected to say but has injected a number of doubts and qualifications. He has given the usual explanations of kingship both in terms of a Persian view that stresses the divinity of kings and of an Islāmic one that does not, and has fitted the Ghaznavids only into the latter. But he has also raised issues unnecessarily. For example, he has raised the question of the lowly origins of the Ghaznavids but has not explored it seriously, a characteristic form of *taqiyyah*. And again, he suggests the possibility that the real and ideal rulers are not one and the same but does not resolve it; it reappears in different guises throughout the history.

The section that follows the *khuṭbah* is longer and switches onto a different plane.[14] It is less theoretical and more practical, intended to be instructive and useful for those who are kings and those who are not. In it one can isolate two elements, one of which is found in *adab* works of counsel for kings and the other of which reflects a *ŝūfī* religious orientation. Some of the issues from the *khuṭbah* are also explored, but on a different level and in a different way. This material that follows the *khuṭbah* is not just the idle wisdom literature it seems, but further expresses a pattern of issues that concern Bayhaqī throughout his treatment of Ghaznavid history.

In the beginning Bayhaqī makes a direct reference to the possibility that what he is about to discuss can be understood on different levels: it is for each to take his position according to the amount of his understanding.[15] He then elaborates further on his distinction between wise, just men and oppressors. The oppressor is ignorant, a source of oppression not mentioned in the *khuṭbah,* where God's will is stressed; the source of good rule and a good reputation for a ruler is wisdom.

The question he then hopes to raise is, how is wisdom for ruling to be obtained, a central theme in his entire work. The first answer given to this question is a bit surprising—through self-knowledge. Although the context of this statement is not immediately clear, the quotations he adduces to support it are clearly *ŝūfī,* just as *ŝūfī* themes and images are noticeable throughout the work. Bayhaqī says that in the old days people used to say from ancient wisdom that God sent prophets to tell people "Know your own essence [*z̲āt*], for when you know your own essence, you will discover things."[16] Then comes a quote from Muḥammad: "Whosoever has known [*ᶜarafa*] himself [*nafsahū*] by virtue of that has known his God [*rabbahū*]."[17] The theme of self-knowledge was nowhere more important than among the mystics. And it should be remembered, in light of Bayhaqī's reference to old wisdom, that it was through ŝūfism that many folk ideas were taken into Islām. Bayhaqī then explains that what one must know about himself is his mortality, another theme of the work, and resurrection; then he will have achieved the right religion and truth, just as a body rests on four "things," no one of which can be taken away without severe damage to the entire being.

There follows an extended metaphor that expresses the necessity of kingship and the role of the king, all of whose images are familiar to both *adab* literature and philosophy. The metaphor is a body with three faculties: *khirad u sukhan* (also *nafs-i guyandah,* "intelligence and speech"), located in the head and heart; *nafs-i khashm* ("anger"), located in the heart; and *nafs-i ārizū* ("desire"), located in the liver. Since according to Bayhaqī there is so much to be said that it would become too long, he will treat the metaphor just enough to make his point. The first faculty can distinguish good and bad and is the king; the second is the army; the third, the subjects. The first must, moreover, dominate the other two. In this attempt at philosophical or pseudo-philosophical analogy, in which he merely gives new explanations for problems that he has already raised, Bayhaqī is clearly ill at ease. Although he alludes to knowing of the philosophers (*faylasūfān*),[18] he may have taken the analogy from a book of *adab*. Bayhaqī's confusion with it is revealed when shortly thereafter he says that each of the three faculties must be in perfect balance, so that none must dominate the others, for the health of the owner to be preserved. He further says that the king is the possessor of all the faculties, so the king becomes the whole as well as a part. Apparently Bayhaqī cannot consistently conceive of a "state" in the abstract as the whole body. Since the sovereign was himself the state in the Ghaznavid view, the pseudo-philosophical analogy becomes confused. If the body is healthy, Bayhaqī argues, the king will be able to distinguish between good and bad and act accordingly. But then he again says that rather than being in perfect balance, the three faculties must be dominated by the first to keep the king from falling into error.

One can resolve the confusion in all this only by realizing that Bayhaqī's seemingly abstract formulation, with which he is awkward, is actually a statement of practicality. Clearly, the king must not allow his army or subjects to dominate him, just as within his own person he must not allow the faculties that are lesser to take hold of his intelligence and reasoning faculty. At the same time it would be bad for the king to be the only strong element in the state, since he needs a strong army and productive subjects to survive. The analogy may be a failure by philosophical standards, but the practical points Bayhaqī makes through it are fairly clear. It should be added that this tripartite division between king, army, and everybody else was a common one in areas that Turkish-Islāmic dynasties ruled.

The final point made in these sections that follow the *khuṭbah*, and a theme of major importance in the work as a whole, is that the other way in which a good ruler can learn good from bad and keep himself in balance is through constant consultation with wise men. Bayhaqī says he has read in Ibn al-Muqaffā''s translation of the *Khudaynāmah,* the old Persian book of kings, that just kings take counsel night and day and that the function of a counselor is to help them, through experience and knowledge of history books, to avoid anger and find the right way (*shar^{c}*).[19] The word used for "right way," *shar^{c}*, is, incidentally, the one associated with Islāmic law as well.

To buttress this notion, Bayhaqī gives another very important historical example read by him in the histories of the Sāmānids, who had been superseded by the Ghaznavids. One of the Sāmānid rulers, Naṣr ibn Aḥmad (r. 864–92), was well-trained but became oppressive after coming to the throne (a pattern repeated many times in Bayhaqī's accounts of various individuals, including Mas^{c}ūd himself). Of course, Naṣr ibn Aḥmad knew that he should discuss the situation with his advisers, who, like all advisers, had been given by God qualities to help a king control his anger. Naṣr approves their advice and decides to have them not put any angry order of his into effect for three days after its issuance, so that the ''flame of anger'' would have a chance to die down and a decision could be made coolly about the rightness of the order. And again it is said that the advisers helped him rule according to the *sharī^{c}ah,* the holy law, another form of the word *shar^{c}* mentioned originally. (It should be noted that rule according to the *sharī^{c}ah* is not a quality that Bayhaqī ever associates with Mas^{c}ūd's advisers.) Naŝr then asks his advisers to summon to the Sāmānid court the seventy wisest men of the realm so that they may be tested. Out of the seventy Naŝr chooses three to stay with him and guide him.

The *khut̂bah* and the sections that follow it at first seem confused and rambling, but they were clearly not meant to be. A Persian secretary could have said many things about the issues they contain; Bayhaqī's choice of what to say must in some measure reflect his interests and background, and those interests then become the centers of his account of Mas^{c}ūd's reign. The themes of the *khut̂bah* reverberate in the account of Mas^{c}ūd. For example, at one point in the treatment of Mas^{c}ūd's affairs, Mas^{c}ūd, like Naŝr, is informed by his advisers of the need to control anger and tells them to delay angry orders for three days.

Bayhaqī also stresses the importance of these introductory sections explicitly. Near the end he says that he knows wise men will approve of what he has said, no matter how prolix he has been, because there is nothing written that is not worth reading once, one of the implications being that these sections might even be worth reading more than once.[20] He also expects that after his era men will come back to what he has written and will understand what he is trying to say.

To summarize, in the *khut̂bah* and related sections Bayhaqī explores a number of problems in several different vocabularies and at many different levels. The moral and political problems and issues he raises—good and evil, self-knowledge and mortality, the ideal versus the real ruler, authority and consultation, the transference of *mulk* (possession of a kingdom)—are the themes that dominate his treatment of Mas^{c}ūd's reign. The intellectual and religious traditions that lie behind his ideas are numerous and not always consistent with one another—*adab,* philosophy to a small extent, orthodox theology, and ŝūfism—and show an intellectual breadth that extends beyond the narrowest interests of a *dabīr,* just as is the case with his method. The dynamics of the interaction of these themes and traditions forms the subject of the rest of this chapter.

ISSUES OF PERSONAL MORALITY AND RESPONSIBILITY

There are two preconditions for undertaking a study of Bayhaqī's moral views: (1) that one realize that any *dabīr* at the Ghaznavid court in the eleventh century would probably have been exposed to a variety of not always compatible moral and religious outlooks; and (2) that in any work written from memory and notes twenty-five or more years after the event(s) described, and at a significantly different stage in life and employment, one can expect a mixture of different levels of moral awareness.

Because of these two factors, a number of seeming ambiguities or conflicts have arisen in Bayhaqī's thought. The tendency to want absolute answers or to feel that one must resolve conflicts in another's thoughts to understand them will not prevail here. Conflicts and ambiguities are part of the dynamics of a man's thought and can be explained without being reduced to agreement. It is even quite possible, as happens in Bayhaqī's case, for a man to hold two contradictory beliefs or to do in one area what is condemned in another.

Not only were there a number of competing formal legal and theological schools, with differing views on personal morality, in Nishāpūr when Bayhaqī was being educated; there were also a number of styles of Muslim personal piety, no two of them mutually exclusive. In addition to these Islām-centered religious factors, there were other popularized beliefs embedded in the substratum of Irānian folk religion. These beliefs were connected with the Zoroastrian and Manichean traditions that had existed in Irān for a long time before the Muslim conquest. In fact, one style of Islāmic piety, the mystical, had absorbed many such basically anti- or a-Islāmic ideas.

These heterodox views were not restricted to the folk consciousness. At least as late as the middle of the third/ninth century, Persian authors were composing defenses of Zoroastrian dualism in Pahlavi, for example, Mardānfarūkh's "Sikand-gumanik Vigar" [Doubt-dispelling explanation],

> to prove the correctness of the fundamental doctrine of the Mazda-worshipping religion, that good and evil do not proceed from the same source, and to show that other religions, while professing to believe in the unity of creation, can only account for the origin of evil, either by degrading the character of the sacred being, or by attributing evil to a corrupting influence which is really a sacred being.[21]

This explanation has been quoted at length because it will be relevant to Bayhaqī's ambivalent views on evil.[22] In addition, a vast pastiche of proverbs, anecdotes, and aphorisms of *adab* pervades Bayhaqī's moral expressions. The evidence for Bayhaqī's exposure to all these elements in the sphere of morality is not merely circumstantial; there are enough quotations and references in his work to show at least his awareness of all and the influence of many.

The effects of exposure to many moral outlooks on Bayhaqī's writing of history are further complicated by the age difference between Bayhaqī the observer of Mas^cūd's reign and Bayhaqī the historian of it. He reveals the moral reflections that age brought (he was thirty-six when Mas^cūd came to the throne and at least sixty-two when he began to write about him) in his nostalgic and sentimental musing at the end of most stories he tells. He is apparently able to report what happened and how he felt at the time and then reflect on what moral lessons he can derive now. In some ways the disillusionment that one expects in an older man can be found in Bayhaqī as he compares the real with the ideal; but more often the older man is more idealistic than the younger one, largely because another factor has entered into Bayhaqī's old man's morality—a rejection of the world's follies and treacheries—as he contemplates death.

BAYHAQĪ'S OWN PERSONAL PIETY, MORAL VALUES, AND RELIGIOUS AFFILIATION

The superficial signs of "orthodox" piety that characterize histories written by Muslim religious scholars are, not unexpectedly, absent in Bayhaqī's work. He keeps his use of pious phrases—for example, "Praise be to God!", "Mercy comes from God!"—to a minimum. Often when he does use them, they seem a kind of insurance, an apology for having transgressed some felt limit; for example, "Some say Mas^{c}ūd was having an affair with so-and-so's mother, and may have fathered him, but only God knows!"[23] At other times, they serve more the function of saying that Bayhaqī is not able or willing to go any further with an argument; for example, "They used to say that he [Qāẑī Abū Ṭāhir Tabbānī] was brought a roasted fowl that was poisoned; he ate from that and died. But only God the mighty and glorious knows the unseen."[24]

Bayhaqī's use of Persian rather than Arabic words for religious figures and institutions may also be relevant, though it is not known yet whether this can be taken as a measure of piety. Some examples are *payghambar* for *nabī* or *rasūl* ("prophet"), *ādīnah* rather than *jum^{c}ah* ("Friday"), *afarīdgār* for *khallāq* ("Creator"), *namāz* for *salāt* ("prayer"), and *īzād* for *allāh* ("God"). Bayhaqī also has a few pious expressions in Persian, though most of them are kept in Arabic.

Bayhaqī quotes only occasionally from the Qur'ān and rarely from *ĥadīth*. This feature is a more certain indicator that his type of piety was not steeped in the sources of his formal religious teachings. Aphorisms from *adab* are much more common as supporting fillips than quotations from religious sources.[25]

Most interesting is the scarcity of mentions of the relationship between Mas^{c}ūd and religion, religious people, or religious law. Although the Ghaznavids under Maĥmūd had made a special point of ruling according to religion and holy law, and although Bayhaqī describes the Sāmānids in this way, he treats Mas^{c}ūd's relationship to religion as a political matter. This feature may be argued to show more about Mas^{c}ūd's piety than about Bayhaqī's, but it is also the case that in general, in Bayhaqī's book, religion, religious figures, religious rituals, and religious celebrations are only minor topics.

All this does not mean that Bayhaqī was totally secular or impious or that the effects of his religious education and beliefs are nonexistent in his work, but that new standards must be developed to evaluate the personal piety of a historian who is not also a religious scholar. The need for new standards can be seen in the following example. One scholar has seen signs of the effects of Bayhaqī's religious education in his alleged opposition to the Ghaznavid internal spy system:

> . . . There are some indications that the education in the Muslim religious sciences undergone by all literate persons at this time had made Baihaqi and his fellow-officials conscious of the claims of justice and morality in official life and had disinclined them from wholly accepting the most ruthless aspects of the theory of the power state.[26]

This hypothesized relationship is worth examining at length, both in terms of methodology and in terms of substantive conclusions. Understanding Bayhaqī's personal moral values can come, after all, only through a careful reading of his treatment of history.

The quotation above has a number of unsubstantiated assumptions: (1) that the complex process of the effect of education on behavior can be taken for granted without carefully defining the "Muslim" sense of justice and analyzing its relevance in this context; and (2) that it was the Muslim education that made Bayhaqī conscious of the claims of justice and that without it he would have not had an ethical reaction to the system.

In the first instance it is also possible that a serious acceptance of certain "Muslim" values toward morality and government—and it is not known exactly what Bayhaqī's religious education contained anyway—would have disinclined a man from *all* elements of the power state. In the second instance it is possible that there were other sources of ethical dictates, in the tradition of *adīb* and *dabīr,* that could have been responsible for the same reaction. The systematic political theory of Bayhaqī's age makes clear how the demands of so-called Islāmic ideals, which are themselves not monolithic, could be openly compromised in an attempt to deal with the "power state." Furthermore, a self-consciously "Muslim" theorist, Niẓām al-Mulk, who was alive when Bayhaqī died but who wrote later, wholeheartedly encouraged the reestablishment of the spy system under the Saljūqs in the name of the security of the Muslims. Any sensitive reading of *Ta'rīkh-i Bayhaqī* must then show the need to reevaluate the current assumptions about the effect of the precepts of the Islāmic religious sciences on political theory.

Although Bayhaqī does indeed relate numerous instances of opposition by him and some of his colleagues in the chancery to certain aspects of governmental practice under Mas^{c}ūd, particularly the internal spy system, the opposition is never cast in terms of Islāmic precepts nor is there any tacit indication that Islāmic precepts are unconsciously involved. An analysis of one of Bayhaqī's most biting critiques of the spy system can provide many clues as to the reasons for his opposition and have the side benefit of illustrating the way in which he communicates moral values without committing himself to them.

As Bayhaqī describes it, the spy system was so convoluted as to be laughable. In fact, his most effective critique of the spy system is contained in a humorous story (and after all, humor is an effective form of satire) purportedly told by a source whose trustworthiness Bayhaqī has gone to some length to establish. The story is not even nominally about the spy system, but is presented as a story about Mas^{c}ūd's circumspection. This is a common form of *taqiyyah,* making it possible to talk about topics without talking about them as such. A scene of agents and counteragents worthy of a spy classic, this longish story is about a pleasure house that Mas^{c}ūd had constructed for him in the Adnānī Garden (at Harāt).[27] "This house had pictures from top to bottom, erotic pictures, of all sorts of copulation between men and women, all naked. . . ."[28] The story continues that Mas^{c}ūd's father, Maĥmūd, had spies on his own son, spies who found out about the house. Maĥmūd sent men to catch Mas^{c}ūd at his pleasures, but meanwhile Mas^{c}ūd's counterspies warned him in time to have the house whitewashed. Mas^{c}ūd forced his father's agents to check every building in town anyway, to be sure they had looked at the right one. The father ends up being led by this charade to regret his having suspected his son.

It is interesting first to note that Mas^{c}ūd's actions do not offend, or at least do not seem to offend, Bayhaqī. He even includes his reporter's statement "and it is a characteristic of young men to do things like this"; in other words, boys will be boys. Earthiness is a feature of Bayhaqī's writing, and any excuse for it is welcome. What Bayhaqī seems to oppose, in this story told by someone else and in others of his own, is the atmosphere of intrigue and mistrust that naturally results in inconsistent, vindictive government.

In this context the effects of such a relationship between father and son on the son's behavior when on the throne are also being explored. This is a theme that interested Bayhaqī and other Persian historians.[29] In Bayhaqī's work his explanation of the events in Mas^{c}ūd's reign in fact depends heavily just on this atmosphere of intrigue and treachery in which Mas^{c}ūd had been embroiled before coming to the throne.

In addition, Bayhaqī constantly exposes, in little remarks, the inhumanness and unfairness of the spy system. In a story about the imprisonment of the prime minister of a Sāsānian monarch, he remarks that spies were set over him who counted his every breath. When Mas^{c}ūd had his uncle Yūsuf spied on, Bayhaqī asks, "How could Yūsuf know that his 'heart and liver and beloved' (i.e., his closet servant) were spying on him." In the affair of Tughril, the slave who was persuaded to spy on Yūsuf (his master), the instigators of the plot are not criticized but rather Tughril—for being ungrateful of benefits his master had conferred on him and for being a stupid enough Turk (*Turk-i ābilah*) to believe the lying promises of the reward of a better position.[30]

In short, there is nothing in Bayhaqī's critique that could not have come from his general sense of ethics, civility, and propriety, which by and large must have been derived from the *adab* and *dabīrī* traditions. He did not oppose the use of spies altogether. What he protested was that things had gone too far, beyond the norms acceptable to a good *dabīr*. When his master Bū Naŝr opposed a scheme of Mas^{c}ūd's to reclaim the money his brother had given out on his accession, he did base his opposition on the fact that the scheme was unprecedented in the annals of the kings of Islām.[31] But it was precisely the existing Perso-Islāmic tradition of government, represented by the heads of the bureaus and their *dabīrs,* that was in conflict with tendencies in the new Turkish states; and this conflict was to be taken up and resolved later in the century by Niẑām al-Mulk. The Islāmic ideals upon which Bosworth calls would more likely not have made room for any spies, good or bad. Islāmic ideals, if they were influential here, were not influential directly as a result of Islāmic education but in the form in which they had already been compromised by, and taken into, the *adab* tradition.

Bayhaqī in general is not nearly so concerned about the definition of virtue and morality in the abstract as some philosophers and philosophical historians were. He uses the word *fāẑil* ("virtuous") for men of whom he approves, but does not define their virtue in the abstract but rather in terms of the activity it produces: they are loyal and do their jobs well, are careful and relatively honest, qualities apparently in short supply in the Ghaznavid regime. He accepts the fact that a degree of manipulation and deceit are necessary in government, like it or not, as is well illustrated in a work of animal fables popular among secretaries and whose figures appear in the poetry in *Ta'rīkh-i Bayhaqī—Kalīlah and Dimnah.* But gentlemen know the limits of such activity.

In obvious areas where a postulated "good Muslim" would react, for example, drinking, Bayhaqī is characteristically worldly and humane, and condemns a vice for its effects, namely, for leading a man beyond the limits of decency and gentility.[32] Furthermore, Bayhaqī is not against trickery when it comes out right, for example, when his master outfoxes someone else,[33] and also remarks positively that kings have many useful tricks. His is not a general sense of morality in the abstract but a pragmatic ethics, an evaluation of what ends the means are put to. He talks about knowing right from wrong, but usually judges these two qualities according to their effects. Like Machiavelli, he is not satisfied with the existing system, but he at least wants to make it as fair and effective as possible. As his master Bū Naŝr says when asked what he would have done had he known two of his *dabīrs* were spies against him, "I would have expelled them both from the bureaucracy, because a treacherous secretary is not useful.''[34] Finally, Bayhaqī opposed the system because it made trust between counselor and master impossible, though he is at the same time uncritical of his master Bū Naṣr's secret contacts with one of Mas^{c}ūd's tributaries because they served a good cause.[35] To summarize, Bayhaqī's personal piety is not of a *sharī^{c}ah*-minded sort. The ethics he exhibits in the area of governmental abuse are practical rather than abstract or religious. Other aspects of his personal piety and moral values will continue to be exposed in the discussion of moral issues that follows.

MORAL RESPONSIBILITY AND THE ORIGINS OF EVIL

Bayhaqī is concerned throughout his work to explain why the men he considers evil have become evil. ''Become'' is the appropriate word, since he seems to want to avoid saying they were born evil. At the same time he seems to be under the constraint of the more orthodox Muslim view of God's omnipotence and the unchangeability of his determination. This ambivalence between an independent source of evil and the one God as the creator of it makes Bayhaqī unclear on the degree to which men are morally responsible for their acts. These are all, of course, questions that have arisen in every monotheistic religion. Throughout *Ta'rīkh-i Bayhaqī,* Bayhaqī explores the distinctions between good and evil and gives assurance that they can be distinguished. In some parts of the narrative, the intrigues of the court become struggles between the forces of good and evil. In a complex moral statement, elements of which are repeated in two other places connected with other men, Bayhaqī says of Bilkātigīn, a *ḥājib,* or military commander, of Mas^{c}ūd, ''. . . He was a man than whom few are seen to be bolder or more generous or braver, but a powerful darkness [*tīrigī*] had hold in him and a levity which is abhorrent, but no man is without fault; perfection belongs [only] to God the Mighty and Glorious.''[36]

There is an echo of the first part of this statement elsewhere in a statement that makes it clear that the good qualities precede the bad. When Bayhaqī first comments on his *éminence grise*, Bū Sahl Zawzanī, he says, ''This Bū Sahl was a man born of an *imām* [religious leader] and eminent [*muhtasham*] and virtuous [*fāẓil*] and genteel, but wickedness [*sharārah*] had become [*shudah*] confirmed [*mu'akkad*] in his nature [*ṭab^{c}ah*],'' followed this time by another Muslim piety, ''God's creation cannot be altered.''[37]

The second part of the statement about Bilkātigīn appears again in the mouth of Buzurgmihr in an interpolated story, ''Do not blame men [*^{c}ayb nakunīd*], because no man is without blame. . . . '' This time Bayhaqī adds a further twist: ''. . . Whoever is unaware of his own fault [*^{c}ayb*] is the most ignorant of men,'' a variation of a theme from the *khuṭbah,* which also reminds one of the oriental adage, ''Whosoever desireth a faultless friend remains friendless.''[38]

In what he is saying here about good and evil Bayhaqī is indecisive. At least certain men have begun good and either had or acquired bad natures, which may or may not be seen to have been created by God. Further, whatever faults they have they should not be blamed for because no man is perfect or because God has created their faults. The question of responsibility cannot be decided, then, entirely from Bayhaqī's remarks on good and evil; one must also consider his views on life and death and on human motivation as a cause of historical events. One can only speculate whether the dualistic thinking prevalent in Persian religious thought was a source of any of this moral confusion.

THE MEANING OF LIFE AND DEATH

Although Bayhaqī includes a separate section on the meaning of the world that sums up his attitudes on life and death, his major comments on the subject come as editorial reflections on each of a series of falls of great men and in several interpolated stories about asceticism.[39] Undercutting Bayhaqī's treatment of the affairs of kings and great men (*pādshāhān* and *buzurgān*) is a melancholy sense of human frailty, foolishness, and mortality, mixed with a strong element of an old man's world-weariness. After almost every death or dismissal or fall from grace, or shaming of a great man (and such occurrences abound in the work as they do in the work of Tanūkhī), there is usually moralizing on the meaning of their lives and accomplishments and of life in general. This moralizing is sometimes aphoristic and cliché, sometimes not.

The most dramatic and cryptic such reflection comes after the gibbeting of Hasanak (prime minister of Maĥmūd fallen from power under Mas^{c}ūd): "Va Hasanak tanhā mānd chunānkah tanhā āmadah būd az shikam-i mādar." ("And Hasanak was left alone—as alone as he came out from the belly of his mother.")[40]

In all this moralizing, though Bayhaqī assumes the afterlife and takes the Day of Judgment for granted, he mentions them only rarely, perhaps as something God does to show rulers they are weak and mortal, too.[41] On the other hand, he constantly stresses the *finality* of death and the fleetingness of the material world in a number of ways throughout the book, usually leading to the conclusion that the world must not be trusted or emphasized too much in the conduct of one's life.

Having described Hasanak's execution in a passionate way, in one of the most beautiful passages in his book, Bayhaqī looks back and writes:

> He [Hasanak] is gone, and those people who plotted this trick are also gone (Peace be upon them!) and this story [*afsānah,* a word that has the connotation of fable] has in it many lessons for observers, and all these causes of quarreling and personal abuse for the sake of the vanities of the world they left behind [*bi-yak sūyi nahādand*]; the most foolish man is he who ties himself to this world which gives blessing but [also] takes it back in an ugly way.[42]

In another instance, after describing the death of Khvājah Aĥmad ibn Ĥasan Maymandī, Bayhaqī is more open (as he usually is in interpolated material) in his condemnation of materialism:

> I have always marvelled at [man's] avarice and mutual contention and at such sin and fault, reckoning and punishment, for a hungry dervish in misery and emaciation and a rich man with all his wealth, when death approaches, cannot be distinguished from each other; man is such that [only] his name goes on living after death.[43]

After the death of Aĥmad Ĥasan, who did die with a good name, Bayhaqī explicitly compares the lives of great men in terms of that "hungry dervish." Although it is the case that the exhortation to reject the trickery of the material world can be found originally in the Qur'ān, it was the *ŝūfīs*, the mystics, who emphasized it more than any other group. In another instance Bayhaqī adds a social aspect to all these themes:

> A wise man is such as not to be deluded by the boons and coquetries that time gives out, and is on guard against having them taken back, because it [time] takes back in a rough and merciless manner, and [he] must endeavor . . . that a good name be remembered of him and that it not be the case that he eat or dress entirely by himself (that is, he should not isolate himself), because no man has gotten a reputation this way.[44]

This emphasis on the maintenance of a good name and on a degree of asceticism, which anyone can have, brings up two other elements to be kept in mind. First of all, Bayhaqī is very much interested in the social context of morality—to have lived a good life others must go on remembering one's reputation. He stresses the maintenance of a good reputation where the after-life is not even mentioned. Worldly accomplishments cannot go to the grave, as Bayhaqī has one mother say to her warrior son, so why bother too much with them.[45] But this same chain of reasoning leads to an ascetic sense that seems at first incompatible with an emphasis on social behvaior. It is not incompatible, however, with reputation if the reputation is not one based on wealth alone.

The second factor to be kept in mind relates to Bayhaqī's age and position. For a not-so-great man, himself once fallen from office, there seems to be some satisfaction in having outlived all the men who gave him and others grief and took their affairs seriously, just as he himself had once done, and in being able to see through their foolishness. The view that all human activity ends up the same tends to vitiate the very significance of the great events described; to show that all men share universal problems brings great men down to the level of all. Bayhaqī's social snobbery has been argued by another scholar.[46] It seems more the case that his snobbery is of a spiritual or intellectual sort, as when he describes certain wealthy men of his day who have all the right outer accoutrements and horses and horse equipment but, when put near people who are civilized in the arts of conversation and intellect, are as awkward as "khar bar yakh" ("an ass on ice").[47] Then, too, the preoccupation with death and its meaning, after a life of seeking after the things he criticizes, must have to do partly with Bayhaqī's being old and out of office.

Any formal link, though, between Bayhaqī and ṣūfism must remain purely circumstantial for want of further biographical information. The image of the older experienced man turning to ṣūfism, and particularly to ascetic ṣūfism, in middle age was not unknown in eastern Irān, Ghazālī (d. 505/1111) being the most famous example. In addition there was in Nishāpūr a form of ascetic personal piety apart from organized ṣūfism known as *zuhd*. Finally, there was also a strain of asceticism in the *adab* tradition, especially in counsels for kings materials. Even if this latter was the source for Bayhaqī's ascetic expressions and stories, as it was the source for so much of his material, it is significant that he chose to use and emphasize them to a greater extent than did the *adab* tradition.

HUMAN MOTIVATION AND ITS ROLE IN CAUSATION

The sense of fatalism described above extends to questions of causation and then makes a full circle back to questions of individual human responsibility. Ultimately Bayhaqī feels that most events, if not all, could not be avoided completely, though he often shows in interpolated material how they could have been ameliorated, yet another form of *taqiyyah*. Human motivation and emotion are of great interest to him and are used by him to explain events on a superficial level. He explores rather complex emotions in the course of explaining events. For instance, when Mas^{c}ūd's defeated rival and brother Muḥammad is being led from one prison to another, he learns that the man who had led his own army over to Mas^{c}ūd has been executed by Mas^{c}ūd. Muḥammad then says that no matter what happens to him he will be happy knowing that the traitor has received his just reward.[48] In *Ta'rīkh-i Bayhaqī* Bayhaqī shows persons acting out every conceivable emotion—depression, anxiety, fear, love, greed, jealousy, and maternal feeling, to name a few.

Bayhaqī's sense of fatalism is not, however, usually one of divine judgment or of fate or chance. The figures who fall, for example, Muḥammad, Hasanak, Hasīrī, Aryāruq, Asaftigīn, Yūsuf, are not tragic in the Greek sense; they do not fall because of a flaw in character. They are, rather, pathetic, enmeshed in a situation with inevitable consequences, in patterns that are shown to have repeated themselves throughout history.[49] Mas^{c}ūd behaved suspiciously because he grew up in an atmosphere of suspicion. Two Turkish generals fell because they had bad advisers and were in a situation they could not be expected to handle.[50] The Sāmānids came to an end because their time had come, they had grown weak, they had a stronger adversary, and there was nothing they could do. This notion of situational causation that goes beyond individual personal emotion and motivation is present in rudimentary form in Bayhaqī but not well developed. On the one hand, people cannot help themselves and are not totally responsible; but on the other hand, they have the option to live right, an ambiguity that for the Muslim tradition began with the Qur'ān itself and persisted even in orthodox theology.[51] It is a question for Bayhaqī, but one that, like many, remains explored but unanswered.

IMPARTIALITY

Bayhaqī's ethical sense also shows up in his insistence on the need for impartiality and care, which in turn is based on his feeling, already discussed, that fullness of detail in reporting leads to accuracy. On close examination, it seems impossible that so many judgments of total impartiality and objectivity have been laid on Bayhaqī.[52] It is true as other scholars have argued that he believed in, and asserted, his impartiality. It is also true that he says some good things about his enemies and a few bad things about his friends. He shows his friends in a critical light, true, but never nearly so critical as his enemies. And it is certainly true that he insists on his impartiality every time he is about to condemn an enemy (though not, interestingly enough, when he is about to praise a friend). But in Islamicate historiography such vehement denials often precede admission of guilt and express a sense of stepping beyond some norm. In Bayhaqī's case it is precisely where he argues for his impartiality that he senses he is most open and liable to the charge of partisanship. It is odd for a man describing an atmosphere of partisanship in which he himself was deeply involved to plead complete lack of partisanship, but Bayhaqī believed hindsight could neutralize partisanship. Whenever he is about to say something bad about his enemy, and he often slips into gossipy slurs in their cases, he makes a disclaimer like "I am not saying this because he hurt me but because it is true." It may be true or it may be still partisan; but unfortunately we have no outside check, and most modern historians have uncritically accepted his slant on the intrigues of Mas^cūd's reign.

Bayhaqī also has a sense of those issues where he might be accused of partisanship that his view will involve for many readers a reevaluation of the past; it is never clear whether he saw things the way he tells them at the time they occurred or only through hindsight.[53] At first he begs off talking about his worst enemy, Bū Sahl Zawzanī. He piously says that Bū Sahl was not always bad and besides is dead and what is the use of stirring up the past? Better to let God decide. And in general, for characters he has chosen to describe, he leaves, like a good Muslim, the *judgment* to God, but not necessarily the criticism. When figures out of the distant past are concerned, he freely judges who has gone to hell or heaven, another form of *taqiyyah*.[54] Having left Bū Sahl's judgment to God, he later goes back on his commitment and goes deeply into Bū Sahl's behavior during Mas^cūd's reign.

In his oft-quoted views on the conflict between the old and new guards, the Maĥmūdīyān and the Mas^{c}ūdīyān, during Mas^{c}ūd's reign, and particularly in his view of the role of Bū Sahl in Hasanak's execution, he is very sure that he will be accused of partisanship if he does not defend himself ahead of time. He insists that he does not say anything that he says in his book out of partisanship *(ta^{c}assub)*:

> Readers may say, "This old man should be ashamed of himself," but I say that when readers pause with me in these matters, they will not find fault with me.[55]

About Bū Sahl's evil he says,

> I do not say this because I experienced many injuries from Bū Sahl, but I am explaining the truth. And I know it to be the case that wise men who have experienced those times and read this today will find no fault with me on account of what I write.[56]

Bayhaqī clearly knew he was susceptible to partisanship and tried to overcome it. He did to an extent, but his treatment of three figures in particular is not free from partiality and subjectivity: Bū Naŝr, Bū Sahl Zawzanī, and Mas^{c}ūd. Although it is true that good things are said about Bū Sahl, whom he disliked, he does not say any bad things about Bū Naŝr, or puts what could be interpreted as bad things in a good light. On Bū Sahl he stoops to the pettiness of quoting a servant on how wasteful Bū Sahl was of clothing, using twenty to thirty robes yearly. Of Bū Sahl he tells a hideous story of how he served Hasanak's head for dinner as a practical joke, but avoids stories of Mas^{c}ūd's cruelty.[57]

Although it is true that on the surface the schemes of Bū Sahl that Bayhaqī opposed, like reclaiming the money Muĥammad had given out and assassinating the Shāh of Khvārazm, seem objectively bad, Bū Sahl's motives are not evaluated impartially. In fact, they are not evaluated at all. In the milieu of Ghazna in the eleventh century, he could be said to have been playing the game of power politics his way. Bū Naŝr's group, as represented by Bayhaqī, were critical of Bū Sahl's political rules but never so critical of the equally vicious intrigues of their own friends at court, as in the plot to disgrace the two Turkish generals Aryāruq and Asaftigīn.

It is also true that Bayhaqī bases his accounts of crucial events, particularly intrigues, on the eyewitness accounts of his master in the Dīvān-i Risālat, Bū Naŝr, and tries to report them as fully as possible. But Bū Naŝr-i Mushkān was a deeply involved participant in the intrigues himself, often, according to Bayhaqī, fighting for his life and position. He had an automatic dislike for all Mas^{c}ūdīyān, as he called them, hangers-on of Mas^{c}ūd who did play the game of politics according to Bū Naŝr's rules. His lack of objectivity in Mas^{c}ūd's case is both negative and positive. He tries to protect Mas^{c}ūd, yet also criticizes him for acts that could be objectively justified. The failure of

Bayhaqī to maintain complete impartiality in these three cases, though he thought he had throughout, is connected with the fact that these three figures are for him expressions in their activities of the problems that most concern him in government—ideal rule, consultation, and succession—problems to which this chapter now turns.

ISSUES OF GOVERNMENT

By way of introduction, one must point out that the issues of government that Bayhaqī explores, partly through Ghaznavid materials and even more through examples from the past, had all been and were to be analyzed by writers of *adab* and in particular of "mirrors for princes." But Bayhaqī has concentrated only on those issues that were raised by the events of Mas^cūd's reign he has chosen to report. Whether the questions were in his mind before his observation and analysis of Ghaznavid history, the issues he chooses to treat are those suggested by, and rooted in, fairly recent events, and also illumined by examples from other history, largely the ^cAbbāsid caliphs since Harūn, the Būyids, and the Sāmānids. At the same time many of his examples, as has been discussed, are similar to later works of "counsel for kings" like Ghazālī's *Naṣīḥat al-mulūk*.

Bayhaqī's vision of the history and status of Muslim government are a product of the tenth century as are his method and sources already discussed. For him the questions of legitimate rule raised by the period of the first four caliphs—the Rāshidūn, or "Rightly-Guided"—questions so troubling to historians like Ṭabarī and Ibn Qutaybah, were dead issues. His piety as expressed in his historical vision was not of that sort. He is post-tenth century; he has accepted what some Muslims called a bad situation and tried to make it work, which after all was his job. His one story from the period of the Rāshidūn is ribald and already *in illo tempore (dar qadīm).* His attitude toward the caliphs of his stories is not exalted; it is clinical, like the attitude he sometimes turns on Mas^cūd. It also reflects his ideas about how the real lived up to the ideal: this is what went wrong, and this is what was good. For him the caliphs are still real people and have not been mythologized to the extent that they were in some other histories.

A scholar of Muslim political thought has drawn a distinction between the "mirrors" literature and systematic political theory like that of Ibn Khaldūn that is relevant to Bayhaqī's attitudes on government. The distinction has to do with the way in which information is arrived at from history in the two traditions.[58] The former is said to be deductive; the latter, inductive. In this regard, as has been seen, Bayhaqī veers away from the "mirrors" tradition, which has obviously been influential on his attitudes toward government, and in the direction of inductive reasoning, beginning to see patterns emerging from history.

In another case a difference has been alleged between Bayhaqī's views on government and those of the "mirrors" literature that is actually a similarity. Bosworth has argued that because Bayhaqī had actually served in government, "his philosophisings on the position and duties of his own class, that of the secretaries, have a rather more practical cast than much of the material in the 'Mirrors for Princes' literature." However, Bosworth is arguing from a quotation whose source is not known. In fact, most of Bayhaqī's suggestions in *Ta'rīkh-i Bayhaqī* are precisely that mixture of practical and ethical for which the "mirrors" literature has been criticized.[59] All in all, Bayhaqī was very much influenced by "mirrors" literature and *adab,* both in practical and ethical terms, but differed from them in his handling of history. What one is seeing in his book is a convergence of style, ideas, and aphorisms from "mirrors" and *adab* with more serious historical concerns whose sources are not always easy to pinpoint.

The three issues of government most frequently treated in Bayhaqī's historical accounts, and which appear in the *khuṭbah* discussed at the beginning of this chapter, will now be discussed in turn: the role of the king, ideal and real; the function of royal consultation and its relationship to authority; and the transference of kingship, from king to king and from dynasty to dynasty. All these issues were important in the Perso-Islāmic traditions of government that developed under the caliphs and became particularly important in the emerging military dynasties of the east, the first of which was that of the Ghaznavids.

The Role of the King, Ideal and Real

It is axiomatic for Bayhaqī that a strong absolute ruler is needed, not so much because God has ordained it (which he also says) but for security and stability. The support for this hypothesis comes from analogies and anecdotes from the "mirrors" literature, which are most pronounced during Bayhaqī's eulogy of the dead ruler Farrukhzād:

> The relationship between a *sulṭān* and men is like a firm tent supported on one pole, with ropes stretched down and affixed [to the ground] by strong pegs. The tent of the Muslims is *mulk* [the kingdom] and the pole is the *pādshāh* and the ropes and pegs are the *riᶜayah* [literally, "the herd," i.e., the common people, subjects]. Thus when you look well (you will see that) the main [part] is the pole and the tent stands because of that. Whenever it [the pole] is weak and falls, no tent remains nor any ropes nor any pegs.[60]

One should note that the hope for *imāmah,* for religiously justified rule as distinguished from *mulk,* has been abandoned by Bayhaqī's time by all but the *shīᶜah*.

In this justification, expressed through the tent analogy, and a quotation that follows, Bayhaqī concurs with the mainstream of Sunnī political theory.

On the next page after the tent analogy, Bayhaqī incorporates an old Persian figure, the Sāsānian monarch at the time of Muḥammad's birth, Nūshīrvān, who had been reworked into an ideal figure for Muslim *adab* tradition. It was a characteristic of Muslim *adab* and "mirrors" writers to assume a continuity between Sāsānian and Islāmic times:

> And Nūshīrvān said: "Don't settle in a city where there is no victorious and conquering king and no just judge [*ḥākim*] and no perennial rain and no wise doctor and no running water and [even] if there are all these things and there is no victorious king, all these things become insignificant."[61]

In other words, kings are a fact, nay, a necessity, of life; in addition there are certain ideal qualities that the good ruler *should* have; do the best you can to encourage these qualities and to conceal their faults while you help them overcome them.

Because the need for a strong king is axiomatic, as is the hope for ideal qualities, Bayhaqī feels free to present the real Masᶜūd but then usually qualifies his picture in terms of the ideal. This is the psychological mechanism that seems to control Bayhaqī's portrayal of Masᶜūd as a king, except that though he and his cronies apparently concealed Masᶜūd's faults when he was alive, by the time Bayhaqī is older and Masᶜūd dead, Bayhaqī tells all and then finds ways to excuse all. Even if he did not wish to tell all about Masᶜūd, he cannot help it because he cannot attack those others at court whom he wishes to attack without involving Masᶜūd too.

Kingship and Masᶜūd as Ruler

In his treatment of the first major theme, the attributes and role of the king, Bayhaqī gives lip service to the ideal qualities expressed in the "mirrors" literature, for example, magnanimity, compassion, control of anger; but Bayhaqī also allows a real Masᶜūd to emerge. Cliché praise such as, "His words dropped from his mouth as pearls," is rare.[62] In fact, Bayhaqī considers himself innovative in this regard, saying that he has read other histories whose authors treated their royal subjects with excessive flattery or detraction just to decorate their books. He says he will not have to do that because he has the proof for what he says that is good about Masᶜūd. But clever readers could also take his statement to mean he has the proof for bad things as well.[63]

In contrast to the "mirrors" literature, Bayhaqī's treatment of other kings and caliphs is not totally paradigmatic and idealized, but has a degree of historicity lacking in *adab* material. Alexander as ideal philosopher-king becomes Alexander a real king with real problems and faults.[64] Ardashīr does seem to be more idealized, but probably because Bayhaqī is using Ardashīr to take the house of the Ghaznavids back to an illustrious origin. Caliph ᶜUmar I, revered by many Muslim historians, is treated with the same earthy reality as Masᶜūd, just as he was treated by historians in the period before he became romanticized. Bayhaqī has taken a story about him from an early *dīwān* of Arabic poetry, the *dīwān* of Hutayah, rather than from a work of history or *adab*.[65]

Although Bayhaqī never discusses Mas^cūd as a divinely inspired ruler, the question of the relationship between prophecy and kingship was an important, and confusing, one for him. It has already been shown that there was a contradiction in the *khuṭbah* precisely on this point, and that Bayhaqī thought a distinction between kings and prophets would be more acceptable to his readers. However, there is one point at which his arrangement of two stories indicates again the possibility that kings and prophets are similar. These two stories come within a frame of stories that begins after Bayhaqī's gruesome account of Hasanak's execution and implicit condemnation of Mas^cūd's role in it. The placement of these two stories is significant because both the stories have to do with religion or piety of kings and contrast sharply with Mas^cūd's behavior during the affair of Hasanak.

Bayhaqī begins the frame of stories by showing what good relationships the Ghaznavid *amīrs* have had with the Tabbānī family of *gāzīs*, then interrupts his flashback to the history of that family to give a story about Sabuktigīn and his qualities and piety and a story about Moses.[66] The story about Moses is very similar to the last part of the story about Sabuktigīn. Sabuktigīn and Moses are both shown, in stories that may come from *adab* material, to have experienced omens of their greatness in incidents involving mother animals and their babies. These incidents were God's way of showing them how great they would be. The comparison between God's appointing of king and of prophet is thus made implicitly through the arrangement and placement of the stories without ever making the comparison explicit. After these two interruptions, Bayhaqī returns to finish the story of the Tabbānī family and thus the frame. Then he returns to the narrative.

In non-crucial areas of personality, Bayhaqī has few illusions about Mas^cūd, and his humanness comes through strongly, though Bayhaqī has stressed some qualities to excess: Mas^cūd jokes, plays, covets, rests, errs, fights (occasionally), hunts, laughs, swears, sleeps, eats, drinks (and gets drunk), mopes, shouts, commands, wenches (only once), but most of all schemes and *talks*. In fact, he is sometimes shown talking and scheming so much that one wonders how anything else got done. Mas^cūd, at least the young Mas^cūd, also has more exalted qualities, for example, refusing to rebel against his father even though his father has wronged him. Part of Bayhaqī's ability to convey the reality of Mas^cūd comes from the fact that he knows the reality and has a record of it; but the real Mas^cūd is not the only Mas^cūd in the book.

There is one critical area in which a confrontation with the implications of Mas^cūd's real nature is avoided. Contrary to Barthold, who claims Bayhaqī feels no compunctions about reporting Mas^cūd's weaknesses, it is the case that time after time Bayhaqī defends Masᶜūd's judgment in major events at court and absolves him of responsibility for carrying out his advisers' suggestions.[67] Other speakers are made to absolve him even more than Bayhaqī does. In a secret communication to Bū Naŝr, the Khvārazmshāh Altūntāsh is made to say, "There is no fault coming from His Majesty; the fault is from bad advisers. . . . "[68] At other times Bayhaqī falls back on the old line that a ruler's actions may seem odd, but rulers know and can see things ordinary mortals cannot know or see. Or he says that Masᶜūd actually knew better than, for example, to give the prime ministership to a certain man, rather than admit that Masᶜūd gave it to the man's rival because he feared his opposition.[69] The most serious critiques of Masᶜūd are put in the mouths of others, particularly women. One such case occurs in Bayhaqī's description of the aftermath of Hasanak's execution (Hasanak had been favored and protected by Maĥmūd but was abandoned by Masᶜūd), the dramatic high point of the book. Bayhaqī has already hinted that Masᶜūd was misled into executing the man and was not really responsible. Then after the execution Bayhaqī has the mother of the dead man say, "What a fortune my son had! That *sulṫān* [Maĥmūd] gave him this world; this one [Masᶜūd] gave him the next!" A more beautifully composed evocation of the "slings and arrows of outrageous fortune" would be hard to find. Bayhaqī compounds the sense of *taqiyyah* by adding that any wise man who hears the remark will approve of it and that no *man* would make such a remark. It is also important to know that Hasanak's mother's remark may very well have been stereotyped, since a similar remark appears in a contemporary history in the mouth of the mother of a fallen prime minister of the Saljūq Sulṫān Tughril.[70]

In another place Bū Naŝr-i Mushkān makes a revealing comparison between Maĥmūd and his son Masᶜūd in regard to their attitude toward consultation:

> This Lord [Masᶜūd] is the opposite of his father [Maĥmūd] as to spirit and emotion [*bi-himat u jigar*]. His father was a man stubborn yet far-sighted. If he said something not right [saying], "I will do thus," he said so out of rulership, and if someone explained the right and wrong of that, he would become angry and contest it and give [us] abuse. Then when he had thought it over he would return to the right path. But the nature of this Lord is otherwise. He acts despotically and thoughtlessly. I do not know what will be the outcome of this matter.[71]

Of course, this statement contrasts for the reader with all the ideal qualities Masᶜūd has been given earlier in the book, and it is on the other hand similar to the behavior of other kings with regard to consultation. Bayhaqī adds indirectly his approval to Bū Naŝr's evaluation by saying after it, "I said to myself [at the time he heard this statement] that this man [Bū Naŝr] is very farsighted." And on the next page Maĥmūd is again praised for some quality Mas^{c}ūd has clearly been shown not to possess.

It is interesting to note that just before this long quotation the most idealized and flowery treatment of kings had been occasioned by the death of Farrukhzād (451/1059). Bayhaqī says he stopped the narrative when he got the news. Then he launched into a very stylized elegy uncharacteristic of his work, in which the mystical feeling for kings emerges, particularly in the following quotation in Arabic: "All these [material] things [of life] revolve around the *amīr* like the revolution of the earth around the pole, and the pole, that is the king."[72] Thus when Bayhaqī describes Mas^{c}ūd's weaknesses shortly thereafter, the contrast is all the sharper.

Consultation

The question of the necessity of consultation has plagued all observers and commentators on absolute rule, from the author of the story of Joseph to Bossuet in seventeenth-century France. Bayhaqī lays out all the possible answers, drawn from the lessons of past and present history, and then retreats in utter confusion. He takes it for granted that a king must consult; but since he also takes it for granted that the king is the absolute final authority, the question arises, How can he consult and not erode his absolutism thereby? Or, putting it the other way around, How can the possible harshness of his absolutism be mitigated by consultation? Bayhaqī seems to want absolutism both mitigated and buttressed at the same time. Perhaps he had begun his career and even his writing of history with a feeling of the need to defend absolutism, and later with hindsight could see the insolubility of the dilemmas inherent in it. Persian political writers and thinkers had run the gamut from deifying the ruler to viewing him as a helpless child.

Over and over in the narrative and interpolations, Bayhaqī explores every possible relationship between ruler and adviser(s) and emphasizes the necessity of good advice. He shows Mas^{c}ūd encouraging advisers to disagree, using phrases like "the prime minister is our *khalīfah*," stubbornly refusing counsel, and being totally led and manipulated by bad advisers.

A curious twist to the critique, implicit and explicit, of Mas^{c}ūd's government comes in an interpolated story about Buzurgmihr, the prime minister of the Sāsānian emperor Nūshīrvān.[73] A story rather out of tone with most of the stories in the book, it occurs at an odd place, after a long series of descriptions of the ignominious deaths or falls of great men. Some of these deaths Bayhaqī has considered justified; most, however, have been problematic in his eyes. The story about Buzurgmihr is left intentionally vague as to how it is to be read; it is not directly analogous to any similar situation that has preceded it, though there are elements of many stories in it. It is, though, definitely about a case where the killing of a servant by a king was unjustified. The hero of the story is a religious reformer and ascetic, perhaps to make it even clearer that his killing was unjustified.

The story is simply that Buzurgmihr converted to Christianity and tried to convert Nūshīrvān, who in reply sent his entire body of Zoroastrian holy men, whom Bayhaqī describes anachronistically as *ᶜulamā',* the word for Muslim religious scholars. These men argued with Buzurgmihr, but he refused to repent, was imprisoned, and still refused to repent. Partly because he had a frightening degree of popular support (just as had some of the men Masᶜūd killed), he was executed. And Bayhaqī bluntly ends the story with the statement, "Nūshīrvān went to hell for this and Buzurgmihr went to heaven."

This story is full of evocative symbols that have echoes elsewhere in the work. Buzurgmihr during his imprisonment is dressed in *ŝūf,* wool, a word involved in the term ŝūfism. When asked to repent, Buzurgmihr says, "I have come out of the darkness into the light and will not return into the darkness where I would be ignorant, without wisdom."[74] These are images common to ŝūfism and to the Zoroastrian tradition. In fact, if his lecture to the Zoroastrian wise men is analyzed, there is nothing particularly *sharīᶜah*-minded in it, but much of a *ŝūfī* sort. Again, the themes of Buzurgmihr's reply to the crowd are universal and *ŝūfī* in tone.

This is a potentially explosive story, placed so as not to call attention to it, labeled mere decoration, so that it likely would have been passed over as such by readers not attuned to its implications. Those who were, however, might have been led to ask, Does this mean Masᶜūd will go to hell for rejecting sound advice or for participating in unjust executions? From another point of view one might ask, Why does God let Buzurgmihr die and Nūshīrvān live even though of course their scores will be settled in the afterlife?[75] Hasanak's mother has said the same thing about her son's death and Masᶜūd's role in it, making the suggestion of a possible identification between Nūshīrvān and Masᶜūd stronger.

The crux of the conflict between absolutism and consultation is expressed in a pithy statement said to have come from a *zann-i ᶜāqīlah*, a wise woman, the mother of Bū Naŝr-i Mushkān. She is said to have remarked prophetically to her son when Maĥmūd appointed Hasanak his prime minister, "Oh, son, when the Sulṫān gives someone the prime ministership who is a friend, in a week he will be an enemy, because kingship cannot be exercised in partnership."[76] Again, a case of situational causation is being explored and the dilemma of consultation and authority in absolute monarchy left unresolved.

The use of wise women to say important things is, by the way, another form of *taqiyyah*.[77] In many folk traditions old women are seen to possess the world's secrets; at the same time readers can be expected to dismiss old women's words as silly if they want to, since old women are absolved from having to make sense or to be taken seriously.[78]

Succession

Succession was a problem that troubled all Muslim dynasties, and the Ghaznavids were no exception. Both internal succession and passage of rule from one dynasty to another troubled Bayhaqī, and there are many explanations and examples of both in his work. In particular, he was interested in cases of the division of a kingdom between two sons, as had happened in the reigns of two Ghaznavid *amīrs,* Sabuktigīn and Maĥmūd. To explore the issue, he brings up other similar cases from Sāmānid and ᶜAbbāsid history. Any criticism of Maĥmūd's actions are found as usual in interpolated stories. In one such story, about Harūn al-Rashīd's decision to divide the ᶜAbbāsid caliphal empire between his two sons Amīn and Ma'mūn, Bayhaqī critically explores Harūn's motivations in a way that could be applied to Maĥmūd if one wished.

There are two particularly interesting things about Bayhaqī's handling of problems of succession. Especially where passage of rule from one dynasty to another is concerned, he sees the end result as all but inevitable. Where internal succession is concerned, he treats conflicts largely as personal issues. In his long description of the interaction between Muĥammad and Masᶜūd while they were at war, he dwells on questions not of legitimacy and right but of power and personality. The tragedy that befalls Muĥammad was built into his father's arrangements for succession and is treated as a personal tragedy for the losing brother, as Bayhaqī explores Muĥammad's descent into depression and withdrawal with some degree of psychological finesse.

PATTERNING IN "TA'RĪKH-I BAYHAQĪ"

In *Ta'rīkh-i Bayhaqī* it is clear (1) that there are a number of repeating patterns, particularly in the case of consultation between rulers and advisers; (2) that stories are told to make a point with much editorializing and with some accuracy sacrificed; and (3) that there are words used for some of the narrative and interpolated stories that suggest fictionalization—words like *afsānah, qiŝŝah, hikāyah*—as well as words like *khabar* and *ĥadith* that suggest straight reporting.

Has the selection and form of materials been made with exclusively didactic considerations in mind? Does Bayhaqī care more about accuracy and historicity or about the lessons that can be learned? Or is his history a case in which, in J. H. Plumb's words, "every fact [is] true, yet the picture totally false."[79] It is impossible to answer these questions definitively. Even were Bayhaqī's accounts to be compared as systematically as possible with every other contemporary history, there is a large amount of his material not contained in any other.

One *can* say, contrary to current scholarly opinion, that the book is not entirely a case of straight and accurate reporting. Bayhaqī seems to have thought that he could be attentive both to accuracy and to moral value, but it is clear that a certain amount of patterning has occurred.

Bayhaqī did not and could not have come to the writing of the history of the Ghaznavid dynasty with a *tabula rasa* as far as issues of morality and government were concerned. In dealing with these issues, he brought with him a wide variety of ideas from different sources—*adab,* "mirrors for princes," orthodox theology, folk traditions, philosophy, mysticism, and possibly some type of dualism. At the same time he had a serious interest in history, and his observation of, and reflection upon, Mas^{c}ūd's reign guided him to an extent in his selection of issues to be treated.

1. The metaphor is borrowed from the title of a book by Francis Ferguson, *Shakespeare: The Pattern in His Carpet* (New York: Dell Press, 1971).

2. An analysis of the second *khuṭbah* can be found on pp. 57 ff., above. See also Appendix B, selection 12.

3. *TB*, p. 179/222. See also Appendix B, selection 5.

4. Ibid., pp. 96–100/112–18. See also Appendix B, selection 2.

5. Ibid., p. 97/114.

6. Ibid., pp. 98–99/114–17.

7. Niẑām al-Mulk, *The Book of Government or Rules for Kings: The Siyāsāt-nāma or Siyar al-Mulūk of Niẓām al-Mulk,* trans. Hubert Darke (London: Routledge & Kegan Paul, 1960), p. 1.

8. Clifford Edmund Bosworth, *The Ghaznavids: Their Empire in Afghanistan and Eastern Iran,* 994:1040 (Edinburgh: Edinburgh University Press, 1963), p. 63, quotes only the first half of this passage and argues that it is a product of typical Perso-Islāmic views on kingship.

9. *TB*, p. 99/117; see p. 81, above.

10. Ibid. *Zindīq* means "free-thinker" in general; but in Bayhaqī's time it was associated with Zoroastrians and Manicheans in particular.

11. Bosworth, *The Ghaznavids,* p. 63.

12. See p. 81, above.

13. *TB*, p. 109/129.

14. Ibid., pp. 100–109/118–29.

15. Ibid., p. 100/118.

16. Ibid.

17. Ibid.

18. Ibid., p. 104/124.

19. Ibid., pp. 105–6/125–26.

20. Ibid., p. 108/128.

21. E. W. West, "Introduction," in Mardān-farūkh, "Sikand-gumanik Vigar," in *Pahlavi Texts,* part 3: *Dina-i Mainog-i Khirad; Sikand-gumanik Vigar; Sad Dar,* trans. E. W. West, vol. 24 of *The Sacred Books of the East,* ed. Max Mueller (Oxford: Clarendon Press, 1885), p. xxv. For a translation of "sikand-gumanik," see ibid., pp. 115–251.

22. It is possible that even though Bayhaqī condemns the *zindīqs* to hell (any outwardly good Muslim would have done the same), he might still consciously or unconsciously use their images and ideas. A similar phenomenon occurs in the work of Ghazālī, who in one context systemati-

cally destroys the arguments of the philosophers and in another quotes their sayings. See F. R. C. Bagley, "Introduction," in Ghazālī, *Ghazālī's Book of Counsel for Kings (Naṣīḥat al-mulūk)*, trans. F. R. C. Bagley (London: Oxford University Press, 1964), p. lxx.

23. *TB*, p. 401/515.

24. Ibid., p. 425/548. Cf. William H. McNeill, "Herodotus and Thucydides: A Consideration of the Structure of Their Histories" (M.A. thesis, University of Chicago, 1939), p. 16, on Herodotus's use of pieties.

25. E.g., *TB*, p. 180/223, on three things a king needs.

26. Bosworth, *The Ghaznavids*, p. 63.

27. *TB*, pp. 121–23/145–47. See also Appendix B, selection 4.

28. Ibid., p. 121/145.

29. In particular, this was a theme in some Safavid histories, for example, in the work of Iskandar Munshī, according to an oral communication from Ms. Guity Nash'at.

30. *TB*, pp. 252 ff./329 ff.

31. Ibid., pp. 257–60/334–40.

32. Ibid., pp. 161–62/197–99.

33. Ibid., p. 148/180.

34. Ibid., p. 145/176.

35. Ibid., pp. 421–23/543–46.

36. Ibid., p. 161/197.

37. Ibid., p. 179/222.

38. Edward G. Browne, *A Literary History of Persia* (Cambridge: Cambridge University Press, 1951), 1:x–xi. Of course, there are also a number of similar folk sayings, the most common being, "Those who live in glass houses should not throw stones." The Buzurgmihr story is in *TB*, p. 335/426–27. See also Appendix B, selection 10.

39. See TB, pp. 376 ff./480 ff., for section on the meaning of the world.

40. Ibid., p. 188/235.

41. Ibid., p. 249/325, in the story of the brides of Muḥammad and Mas^{c}ūd.

42. Ibid., p. 187/234.

43. Ibid., p. 366/466.

44. Ibid., p. 238/308.

45. Ibid., p. 190/237.

46. Roger Savory, "Abo'l-Fazl Bayhaqī as an Historiographer," in Mashhad University, Faculty of Letters and Humanities, *Yādnāmah-yi Abū'l Faẓl-i Bayhaqī* (Mashhad: Mashhad University Press, 1971), p. 103.

47. *TB*, p. 408/526.

48. Ibid., p. 76/86.

49. McNeill, "Herodotus and Thucydides," has observed different types of causation in stories composed by Herodotus and those borrowed intact from other sources; this pattern does not seem to exist in the case of Bayhaqī.

50. *TB*, p. 220–32/282–300. See also Appendix B, selection 8.

51. Gustave E. Von Grunebaum, *Classical Islam* (Chicago: Aldine Press, 1970), p. 33.

52. W. Barthold, *Turkestan Down to the Mongol Invasion*, E. J. W. Gibb Memorial Series, n.s. vol. 5, 3d ed. (London: Luzac and Co., Ltd., 1968), p. 23; Bosworth, *The Ghaznavids*, p. 10; Savory, "Abo'l-Fazl Bayhaqī as an Historiographer," p. 91 and passim.

53. *TB*, p. 31/33

54. Ibid., p. 336/428. On page 26/28 he leaves the judgment on Bū Sahl to God on the Day of Judgment, but in so doing suggests there may be more to say.

55. Ibid., p. 179/222.

56. Ibid., p. 154/189.

57. Ibid., p. 188/235.

58. E. I. J. Rosenthal, *Political Thought in Medieval Islam: An Introductory Outline* (Cambridge: Cambridge University Press, 1962), p. 69.

59. Bosworth, *The Ghaznavids*, p. 64; Bagley, "Introduction," p. xi.

60. *TB*, p. 379/485.

61. Ibid., p. 379–80/485.

62. Ibid., p. 20/21.

63. Ibid., p. 109/129.

64. Ibid., pp. 96–100/112–19.

65. Ibid., p. 238/308.

66. See ibid., pp. 198–210/249–67. See also Appendix B, selections 6–7.

67. E.g., ibid., pp. 231/298, 322/409–10; Barthold, *Turkestan*, p. 23.

68. *TB*, p. 93/107.

69. Ibid., p. 154/189.

70. S. H. Hodivala, *Studies in Indo-Muslim History: A Critical Commentary on Elliot and Dowson's History of India as Told by Its Own Historians* (Bombay: n.p., 1939), 2:151.

71. Ibid., pp. 399–400/513–15.

72. Ibid., p. 380/624.

73. Ibid., pp. 333–36/425–28. See also Appendix B, selection 10.

74. Ibid., p. 335/427.

75. Muhsin Mahdi has pointed out in an oral communication that similar stories from *The Thousand and One Nights* contain an implicit dualistic critique of the Muslim God.

76. *TB*, p. 340/434.

77. See also the story of the peacocks and an old woman's dream interpretation, ibid., p. 113/135.

78. The role of wise old women can be found in Western fairy tales like Aesop or Grimm, as well as in Eastern, like *The Thousand and One Nights*. Cultural anthropologists have noted this phenomen in some Iranian tribes—that women past child-bearing age become free to say the most outrageous things, things that younger women could not get away with.

79. J. H. Plumb, "An Englishman's Love Letter to New York," *New York Times Magazine*, 2 Sept. 1973, p. 14.

5

History and Language: The Style of *Ta'rīkh-i Bayhaqī*

INTRODUCTION

It is a rare compliment indeed to call any historical work, especially one from eleventh-century Persia, consistently interesting—intriguing (no pun intended), and even suspenseful at times—but *Ta'rīkh-i Bayhaqī* can be so complimented. The interest comes partly from the structural juxtaposition of story line with interpolation and the richness of universally meaningful themes. But the interest is generated as much by the literary style of the work as by structure and thematic content.

Now *style* is a word upon whose definition even students of literature have difficulty agreeing. In the broadest sense possible, everything discussed so far is a part of "style"; but this chapter will deal more with those elements of style that have to do with the use of language rather than with structure and themes, though these latter two factors will inevitably creep in. Language, structure, and thematic content, though they have been separated for purposes of analysis, are really, of course, interdependent and interrelated.

Just as the structural method and themes of *Ta'rīkh-i Bayhaqī* combine a number of elements, the style of language is also a blend. It is a blend of forms and modes of expression from two different linguistic and cultural traditions, Arabic and Persian, and from different levels of linguistic expression, from ornate to colloquial, all leavened by Bayhaqī's own sense of humor and imagery.

CRITICAL JUDGMENTS

Scholarly and critical judgments of Bayhaqī's style have varied widely, usually over issues of clarity and conciseness versus archaism and elaboration. The two poles are represented by Nafisi, for whom Bayhaqī's style is "archaic and sometimes complicated," and Minovi, for whom the expressions of *Ta'rīkh-i Bayhaqī*" set a model for composition in an accurate and sparing language"; and again by Bahār, a historian of Persian literature (and the author of the most thorough technical analysis of Bayhaqī's style), who is impressed with the length and elaboration of Bayhaqī's sentences, and Luther, who finds Bayhaqī concise and to the point.[1]

Each pole has its justification, depending on the standard of comparison employed and the aspects of style considered. *Ta'rīkh-i Bayhaqī* is obviously archaic when compared with modern Persian works. But at least its vocabulary is also archaic even when compared with a contemporary history like *Ta'rīkh-i Sīstān* or with slightly later histories. Although *Ta'rīkh-i Bayhaqī* shares many words and meanings special to the Ghaznavid era with a work like *Ta'rīkh-i Sīstān,* most it does not share.[2] Bayhaqī was a "professional" official; as a consequence his language is full of a number of words and expressions that were meaningful to his associates in government service but had already become obsolete shortly after his time, when the Ghaznavids were replaced in Irān by the Saljūqs. Nafisi's argument is supported to some extent by the difficulties that modern translators have encountered. It is a paradox that these features that make *Ta'rīkh-i Bayhaqī* eloquent, interesting, and unusual, features remarked upon as far back as Ibn Funduq,[3] are the things that make it difficult for a modern scholar to translate. Not only have early twentieth-century translations been faulted, but even very recent ones as well.[4]

To argue for the other pole, as represented by Minovi, it is ironic to note that these same "special words, terms, expressions, and turns of phrase" that make the language seem archaic and complicated to Nafisi mark it as accurate and concise for Minovi.[5] The problem lies in managing to understand all these items, for which most dictionaries are totally inadequate. Once they are understood, they become sources of clarity and precision in Bayhaqī's style. Again, what is sparing language for Minovi is obscure for those who have not managed to understand it, or have had a difficult time understanding it, precisely because it is sparing.

Bahār has emphasized the elaboration in Bayhaqī's sentences and descriptions because he is comparing them with the Persian prose that preceded Bayhaqī, which was underdeveloped in these areas. But Bayhaqī's sentence structure can also seem more complicated than a slightly later writer, like Ghazālī.[6] On the other hand, when one compares *Ta'rīkh-i Bayhaqī* with later Persian historians of the Saljūq and Mongol periods, like Rashīd al-Dīn and

Vaṣṣāf, his style seems inelaborate and inornate—refreshingly simple. And it is clearly this type of comparison that Luther has in mind when he calls Bayhaqī concise and when he explains that Bayhaqī's style failed to persist among the Saljūqs not because it was inherently unattractive or obsolete but because it was not appropriate to many aspects of culture and literacy at the Saljūq court.[7]

Another scholar, brushing all this controversy aside, has commented that Bayhaqī's style seems simply to have baffled everyone else. He himself, using audience interest as his measure, calls the style lively and enjoyable and leaves matters at that.[8] Thus it becomes clear that part of the problem in analyzing Bayhaqī's style is that the comparative study of Persian literature is not far enough advanced to provide adequate categories and measures. It is also the case that in the analysis of the style of *Ta'rīkh-i Bayhaqī* that follows, it will be necessary to keep in mind the natures of Persian style before and after Bayhaqī as standards of comparison.

BILINGUALISM

The issue of bilingualism, which is basic to any study of Bayhaqī's style, is unresolved at this time. Bahār, a leading historian of Persian literature, has argued that the development of a new, expanded Persian prose in the late tenth century was stimulated by contact with the Arabic prose tradition, which enriched its anemic Persian counterpart.[9] However, Bayhaqī's Arabic is relatively little compared with later authors. Bayhaqī's use of Persian words where Arabic words might be expected has already been noted in chapter 4. Bayhaqī also seems to use a technique common in Persian prose in a new way. This technique involves the use of two synonymous words, joined by "and," for emphasis. It has been suggested that this technique could also be used as a form of dictionary, developing new meanings for Persian words by linking them with their better-known Arabic equivalents.[10] This is often the case in *Ta'rīkh-i Bayhaqī*. Another form of writing Persian-style is Bayhaqī's preference for substituting the Persian connective "-i" for "ibn" in Arabic names, for example, ᶜUmar-i Khaṭṭāb for ᶜUmar ibn al-Khaṭṭāb.[11]

The question of the actual proportion of Arabic words in Bayhaqī's work has been impressionistically but never quantitatively measured. The usual impression is that the vocabulary is heavily or predominantly Arabic, but an unsystematic count of a few random pages indicates that this may not actually be so. As the study of the work of Bayhaqī and other Persian historians progresses, it will become necessary to make quantitative measurements of many aspects of style, something that has not yet become popular in the study of Persian literature.

Of course, even when quantitative measures are ready, there will still be the qualitative question of not only how many Arabic words are used but what kind. All one can say at this point is that Bayhaqī uses a large number of purely Arabic words, that is, words that do not appear to have been completely absorbed into Persian at his time and do not generally appear in classical Persian dictionaries (for example, *tarabbud, zā'irah*).[12]

It is also the case that where Bayhaqī uses wholly Arabic phrases or sentences, other than pieties and dates, he inserts them with no preparation.[13] Sometimes sentences entirely Arabic in vocabulary contain a Persian syntactical element.[14]

The social factors in bilingualism are important to bear in mind, too. Although one of Maĥmūd's prime ministers had attempted to make Arabic the exclusive language of the Ghaznavid administration, by Bayhaqī's time all *dabīr*s had to be able to read and write in Persian as well as in Arabic.[15] Bayhaqī seems to have been proud of his bilingual ability, which was particularly necessary for someone, like himself, who was engaged in diplomatic correspondence. He made copies in Arabic for letters to the west and in Persian for letters to the east. The best among the Ghaznavid officials, for example, Bū Naŝr-i Mushkān, could, on receipt of an Arabic or Persian letter, read it aloud and translate it orally into Persian or Arabic respectively without written preparation.[16] Thus the *dabīr*s had a stake in seeing that both language traditions were kept alive. But though bilingualism came naturally to Bayhaqī when he sat down to write his history, it would appear that in terms of vocabulary and syntax his style was predominately Persian. In this regard the Persian of the Ghaznavid chancery was unlike the Ottoman Turkish of the Ottoman chancery, which blended Arabic and Persian with Turkish much more thoroughly. The language of the Ghaznavid chancery kept Persian and Arabic much more distinct, and so they appear in *Ta'rīkh-i Bayhaqī.*

RELATIONSHIP OF FORM AND CONTENT

Among all the words that scholars have written about the style of *Ta'rīkh-i Bayhaqī,* no one has pointed out that the style of language is the opposite of many aspects of the content. Where the style of language is basically light and simple, the content is lengthy, detailed, and involved. The sense of prolixity that bothered the author himself is ameliorated by the language, which in turn enhances the fundamentally interesting topics that Bayhaqī chose for treatment. In short, the style makes the content more palatable.

From this point of view, most of the stylistic devices can be fitted into two types: hastening features and enlivening features. The major hastening feature is suspense. The enlivening features are more numerous: earthiness and humor; interesting colloquial, local, and folksy idioms; graphic imagery and figures of speech; emotional language and portrayal; variety of vocabulary, tenses, and constructions; a degree of rhyming; and a preference for active over passive verbs. *Ta'rīkh-i Bayhaqī* also contains a number of syntactical characteristics that do not fit either of these categories but that are useful for comparison with other works.[17]

Hastening Feature

There is one way in which Bayhaqī speeds up the lengthy, detailed accounts in *Ta'rīkh-i Bayhaqī;* by using them to build suspense. Bayhaqī often tells what the end of a long story will be—an execution, for example—so that the very lengthiness of treatment can make one read faster to get to a known end. When, for example, Bayhaqī is describing negotiations over the appointment of a prime minister and one knows who the winner will be, one becomes very anxious to find out how the end result is to occur by way of all the meanderings of the intrigues that have led to it.

Enlivening Features

The most striking "enlivening" feature to this reader is a certain earthy humor that can be found in at least one other work by an old, experienced man looking back—Usāmah's *Memoirs* (written ca. 581/1185).[18] One example is the use of vernacular words and expressions like "kashkhanak" ("little cuckold"; "pimp" in modern Persian) and like calling one's enemies "dogs."[19] These are definitely not usages one would expect from a self-consciously pious historian like Ṫabarī, even though "cuckold," it must be admitted, is used affectionately as well as negatively in Bayhaqī's writing.

Another example is Bayhaqī's choice of a scatological story about the caliph ᶜUmar (r. 644–56), the Prophet's companion Zibriqān, the Arab poet Hutayah, and the blind poet Ĥasan ibn Thābit.[20] It should be mentioned first that the relevance of this interpolated story is among the most questionable in the book, for its inclusion seems very contrived. The story goes that Zibriqān was given to eating and dressing in private, and was thus offended when Hutayah wrote a line of poetry that said: "Give up your noble deeds, neither go forth aspiring to them. Just sit down, for you are the well-garbed glutton."[21]

Zibriqān appealed to the caliph for redress against this satirist; but ᶜUmar, in the version Bayhaqī has chosen (there are many other versions), summons Hutayah, who says he sees no satire and that furthermore "literary criticism" is not the business of the Commander of the Faithful. So ᶜUmar sends for the blind poet Ĥasan ibn Thābit for an impartial opinion. Then comes Ĥasan's famous reply, "Ma haja' walakinna salaha ᶜala Zibriqān." ("He didn't satirize Zibriqān; he shat on him.")[22] Bayhaqī's detailed description of the pornographic pictures on Masᶜūd's pleasure gazebo, discussed in chapter 4, is obviously also relevant here. He also includes a story which hints that Maĥmud's commander in India was his illegitimate son.[23]

Bayhaqī also seems to enjoy describing the effects of drunkenness; at least he does so frequently. His descriptions include a man's getting into a street brawl because he had drunk too early in the morning (and, Bayhaqī adds, all wise men know that is a bad thing to do); a man's swearing and saying obscene things because he is drunk; and a man's (Aryāruq Ghāzī, a Turkish general) being tricked into being drunk when summoned by the Sulṭān so as to give the Sulṭān an excuse to demote and exile him.[24] This latter case goes to the extent of describing the man's attempt to sober up, including eating ice. The drunk man's plaintive reply on being summoned to court is particularly pathetic: "How can I come in this state? What kind of attendance can be performed by me?"

Again there is an element of earthiness in Bayhaqī's description of Mas^{c}ūd's brother Yūsuf's falling in love with one of Mas^{c}ūd's male slaves, Tughril. It is remarked that Yūsuf is not able to keep his eyes off Tughril after seeing him for the first time.[25]

Related to earthiness is a use of lively idioms, some of them folksy, colloquial, or local. Savory includes as examples of colloquialisms "kharī az kharān" (literally, "an ass among asses"; figuratively, "the most stupid ass imaginable") and "^{c}aṭsah-yī Maḥmūd" (literally, "the sneeze of Maḥmūd"; figuratively, "the spit and image of Maḥmūd").[26] One would want to add especially "as awkward as an ass on ice," which has a curious resemblance to the midwestern American farm expression, "as awkward as a hog on ice."[27]

Examples of other interesting idioms are: "If you want me to take the cotton out of his ear" (i.e., "give him the word"); "he chews the thistle," ("is idle," [zhāzh mīkhāyad]); namāyam hāl-i mu^{c}āmilat-i dānistān-u nādānistān" (literally, "I will show [you] what happens when the knowing and unknowing interact;" i.e., "I will separate the men from the boys"); and "hamigān zabān dar-dahān-i yakdīgar dārand" ("All had their tongues in each others' mouths;" i.e., "they were all parroting each other").[28] Another particularly informal pair of sentences is spoken by Sulṭān Mas^{c}ūd to an adviser who is informing him of the wrongful "entrapment" of one of Mas^{c}ūd's generals: "Būdanī būd. Aknūn tadbīr chīst?" ("What's done is done. Now what do we do?").[29] One of Bayhaqī's reporters, ^{c}Abd al-Ghaffār, speaks the following local expression: "As the old men [*zālān*] of Nishāpūr say, 'Mother dead and ten dirhams in debt!'"[30] ^{c}Abd al-Ghaffār uses this expression to describe someone in a down-and-out state.

Perhaps the most important enlivening features are images and other figures of speech, of which metaphors and analogies are the most common. It is important to note that these figures, which got out of hand in later Persian writers, like another Bu'l Faẓl (1550–1602), the author of the *Akbarnāmah*, this Bayhaqī controls well and uses sparingly. They do not overwhelm the meaning, nor do they detract from it. They are usually not cliché and usually enhance the meaning and interest. There *are* a few trite phrases, such as "pīrāhan-i mulk" ("the shirt [or more idiomatically, "mantle"] of kingship'') or the comparison of spoken words with scattered pearls, but in general the images and figures are fresh.

One of the first things one notices is the large number of images and figures that involve horses, tents, riders, elephant drivers, and caravans, elements one has come to expect in the visual arts of the Turkish and Mongol dynasties. Horse-rider images are the most frequent.[31] One caravan figure is particularly striking: ''This revolving earth is not permanent, and we are all lined up in a caravan and go after one another and no one will remain here. One must live so that after one's death good prayers are said [for one].''[32]

The next thing one notices is that images and detail are more often than not graphic and concrete, sensual in the literal sense, with the visual predominating over the other senses. Some of the graphic images are ''lashkar . . . chūn kūh-i ahan'' (''the army was like a mountain of iron''); ''khār dar mūzash uftād'' (''a thorn fell into his boot,'' similar to ''he had a thorn in his side''); ''ābī bar ātish āmad'' (''water fell on the fire,'' that is, ''things quieted down''); and ''murg khānah-yi zindigānī ast'' (''death is the house of life'').[33] The details given about people are graphic as well; for instance, ''Aĥmad dast bar dast zad'' (literally, ''Aĥmad touched one hand on the other,'' that is, ''Aĥmad wrung his hands'').[34] In addition, Bayhaqī is particularly fond of detailing *color* and other details of physique and dress, even for slaves, as in the following passage about a wine-drinking affair hosted by Amīr Mas^cūd:

> One day it happened that the Amīr [Mas^{c}ūd] was drinking wine at the Fīrūzī Garden, among the roses, and so many many-leaved roses [a popular variety in Persia] were scattered about that they could not be counted. And these handsome [lit. moon-faced] creatures, the cup-bearers, were coming [around] in turn two by two. This Tughril came in dressed in a ruby-colored tunic [*qabā*] and his partner had a turquoise *qabā,* and they were absorbed in taking the wine around, and both were handsome as the world. Tughril stood with colored wine [*sharābī rangīn*] in his hand, and the wine had [just] got to Amīr Yūsuf [Mas^{c}ūd's brother], when his [Yūsuf's] eye rested on [Tughril's face], and he [Yūsuf] fell in love.[35]

This discussion of figures and images leads into another feature of Bayhaqī's style, a fondness for conveying emotions of all sorts and pathos. One of his favorite emotional words is *tangdil* (''narrow of heart,'' that is, ''anxious''); but there are numerous others, like *ghamnāk* (''melancholic''), *khūsh* (''joyful''), and *khashmnāk* (''angry''). Bayhaqī frequently describes entire emotional states as reactions to some occurrence or other; he seems particularly interested in depression. One of the most interesting cases of depression he describes is that of Ṭāhir Dabīr, a secretary in the chancery whose work began to go poorly and who was criticized by Bū Naṣr-i Mushkān, causing Ṭāhir to take to drink.[36] Bayhaqī also gives much space to a rather detailed account of the emotional state of increasing withdrawal displayed by Amīr

Muḥammad during his confinement. He describes with a great degree of pathos the rough handling Muḥammad received on being transferred from one prison to another. And he includes a pathetic request by Muḥammad to a messenger departing from the prison: "Please don't forget me," a sad state indeed for a man who only seven months before had acceded to the Ghaznavid throne.[37]

Clearly, the situation that evokes the most pathos, as described by Bayhaqī, is the execution of Ḥasanak. Bayhaqī describes the event in his usual graphic detail, including the color of Ḥasanak's clothes and the fact that Ḥasanak's body was left hanging for so long that the feet and legs withered away. Bayhaqī even includes an emotional description of the reaction of Ḥasanak's followers in the crowd, who refused to stone the body as ordered by the executioners. He concludes with a sympathetic account of the fact that Ḥasanak's supporters were kept from rebellion only because Masᶜūd's officers threatened them with extermination.[38] In these cases graphic imagery and emotionalism work together, as also in a description of the clothing and armor stripped from a man being arrested.

For any hopeful Arabist-Persianist/historian who has been assured by his peers that historical writings in Arabic or Persian are easy to read because the authors establish their working vocabularies in the first twenty-five pages, Bayhaqī's vocabulary comes as a shock. Halfway through *Ta'rīkh-i Bayhaqī* new words are still appearing frequently. Bayhaqī was never satisfied with using the same verb in two subsequent sentences. If *pūshīdah* ("hidden") is used in one sentence, and "hidden" also appears in the next sentence, *panhān kardan* will be used. Or if *āghāz kardan* ("to begin") is used on one page, its Arabic equivalent, *ibtidā' kardan,* will be used on the next. And this is one place where bilingualism really helped, because it is always possible to "create" an Arabic equivalent of a Persian verb by using one of a number of nominal Arabic forms with a Persian verb like *kardan*. There are even words from a number of other languages: Turkish, Mongol, and Pashtu.[39]

Another type of vocabulary variety and interest is the use of the same word in two different connotations. For example, on the same page Bayhaqī uses *shāgirdān* to mean legitimate apprentices and apprentices in the ironic sense of partners in crime.[40] Yet another type of vocabulary expansion is the use of a larger number of verbs to form the passive and impersonal constructions than is common in modern Persian. For example, *guzashtan, uftadan, raftan,* and *āmandan* are all frequently used for impersonal constructions. The use of *āmadan* in addition to *khvāstan* for passive constructions also lends variety. There is also a wide variety of verb tenses and verb constructions. One very common usage is to employ both possessive constructions like *khānih-yi man* and *marā khānih ast.* Another is to alternate between adjectives, for example, *khashmnāk,* and adjectival verbal constructions, like *khashm dasht.* There is also some degree of rhyming, for example, *vāfī-u kāfī*.[41]

Finally, Bayhaqī enlivens his style by his preference for active over passive verbs.[42] He is also given to using verbal forms as adjectives.

Other Syntactical Features

There are also a number of noticeable syntactical features that do not fit in either the hastening or the enlivening categories, but that have been described as common classical forms by grammars.[43] Most usual are the particle *bi* before past tenses of verbs for finality, particularly *biraft,* which is very frequent; the use of *āmadan* for constructing the passive, for example, *ẕikr kardah āmad,* "mention has been made"; *ra* for dative and possessive, for example, *marā būd,* "I had"; the impersonal use of *giriftan*; and *i* attached to the end of a verb for habitual or conditional past, for example, *bā khvud guftamī* ("I used to say to myself"), and *kardamī,* "had I done." *Hamī* is also affixed as a prefix to form habitual past. The pleonastic use of *rā* is rare.

Finally, there is also a small degree of understatement, including a number of frequently used *nā*-prefix words like *nādān* ("not-knowing," "ignorant"), and understated figures like "shedding blood is not a game."[44] There is a limited amount of periphrasis, both in the form of euphemism and in the form of circumlocution. A favorite euphemism, and one that has given translators much trouble, is "firmān yāft," "he received the summons [from God]," that is, "he died." According to Hodivala, this phrase is common in Vaŝŝāf and Gardīzī as well.[45] A frequent kind of circumlocution takes the form of "so numerous they could not be counted," or "so wonderful nobody present [or nobody old] could remember the like of it." Over-all, however, periphrasis is uncommon in the work, inappropriate as it is to Bayhaqī's basically simple style.

Apocope of a number of sorts appears in *Ta'rīkh-i Bayhaqī.* The most common is cutting off the last part of perfect tenses, for example, *shudah* for *shudah būd.* A technique related to apocope is the internal shortening of words, the most common being *āram* for *āvaram.*

Bayhaqī also uses a device that in music is called anticipation. An example, which occurs frequently, involves putting the particle *kih* before the referent of the relative clause it introduces: perhaps writing *kih īn mard* instead of *īn mard kih,* or *man kih* instead of *kih man.* Another example is something that has been noticed in Ghazālī's writing: putting the object before the cardinal number that defines it. Another case is putting the direct object after the verb, or, put the other way around, moving the verb up from the end of the sentence.[46]

"House that Jack built" sentences are also frequent, that is, more than one *kih* relative clause per sentence, giving a sense of speed to the pace. A sense of speed also comes from the long strings of sentences connected by *va* that tend to lead the reader on faster than if the sentences were chopped up. The verb is not always at the end of the sentence; it is often followed particularly by the adverb that qualifies it. Another way verbiage is cut is by the extensive, and sometimes confusing, use of the indefinites *īn* and *ān,* and by personal pronouns whose referents are some way back, making it necessary to pay attention and follow a story closely all the way through.

Many critics have tried to label the total effect of Bayhaqī's style, using adjectives like ''lively'' and nouns like ''memoirist.'' Although this is the last place where another word needs to be added, there is one that comes to mind—''journalistic.'' For in the current idiom Bayhaqī's style is journalistic rather than scholarly. He reports fully but is not erudite; he is given to popularization and colloquialism; he emphasizes graphic imagery and human interest. His style is not popular nor is it elitist; it appeals to an intelligent, refined, but not scholarly audience.

Two questions, however, remain: if Bayhaqī's style is so interesting, was he then a great writer; and why does he seem to have had no literary heirs? To answer the first question without being a linguistic specialist is difficult, but Bayhaqī seems, at least to the non-linguist, to have been a stylistic master. His style is compelling, being straightforward and eloquent at the same time. His is an eloquence or simplicity with elaborate rhetoric unnecessary to its success. It is for precisely these qualities of style that Bayhaqī appears to have had no linguistic heirs. The style that Bayhaqī carried over from his work in the chancery and expanded was not maintained by the literati at the court of the Saljūqs, who even during Bayhaqī's lifetime had already encroached on Ghaznavid domains in Irān.

The fact that language and style were Bayhaqī's business throughout most of his life has made this chapter particularly important. Although his historical style is basically similar to the examples of chancery writing that he includes, it is not nearly so formal; it is much more relaxed and seems to ạim more at dramatic effect and striking qualities. Thus just as Bayhaqī went beyond the narrowest secretarial vision in terms of structure and thematic content, so in terms of style of language he has expanded the chancery style with which he was familiar to enhance the interest of his work.

1. Said Nafisi, ''Bayhakī,'' *Encyclopedia of Islam,* 2d ed., 1:1130; Mujtaba Minovi, ''The Persian Historian Bayhaqī,'' in *Historians of the Middle East,* ed. Bernard Lewis and Peter M. Holt, Historical Writings on the Peoples of Asia (London: Oxford University Press, 1962), p. 140; Mālik al-Shu^{c}arā' Bahār, *Sabk Shināsī* (Tehran: Maḥfūẓ Press, n.d.), 2:67; and Kenneth A. Luther, ''Bayhaqī and the Later Seljūq Historians: Some Comparative Remarks,'' in Mashhad University, Faculty of Letters and Humanities, *Yādnāmah-yi Abū'l-Fazl-i Bayhaqī* (Mashhad: Mashhad University Press, 1971), pp. 14–33.

2. See the list of idiomatic terms and phrases in *Ta'rīkh-i Sīstān,* ed. Mālik al-Shu^carā' Bahār (Tehrān: Zavvār Publishing House, 1312/1894), pp. xvi–xx.

3. Ibn Funduq, *Ta'rīkh-i Bayhaq,* ed. Aĥmad Bahmānyār, 2d ed. (Tehran: Islāmiyyah Press, 1385/1968), p. 175, refers to its great eloquence and rhetoric.

4. First, see the extensive corrections of an early English translation of *Ta'rīkh-i Bayhaqī* in S. H. Hodivala, *Studies in Indo-Muslim History: A Critical Commentary on Elliot and Dawson's History of India As Told by Its Own Historians* (Bombay: n.p., 1939), 2:150–70. Then see Roger Savory, "Abo'l-Fazl Bayhaqī as an Historiographer," in Mashhad University, *Yādnāmah,* pp. 115–16, for a critique of a translation in Clifford Edmund Bosworth, *The Ghaznavids: Their Empire in Eastern Iran and Afghanistan, 994:1040* (Edinburgh: Edinburgh University Press, 1962). Finally, see my critique of a translation by Barthold, note 14, p. 75, above. There are also places where the Arabic translation of *Ta'rīkh-i Bayhaqī,* trans. Sādiq Nash'āt and Yahyā' al-Khashāb (Cairo: Dār al-Ţibā^cah al-Ĥadīthah, 1380/1960), could be questioned, as in the rendering of "rasm-i ta'rīkh" as "uŝūl al-ta'rīkh."

5. Minovi, "The Persian Historian Bayhaqī," p. 140.

6. See the comments on Ghazālī's style in F. R. C. Bagley, "Introduction," in Ghazālī, *Ghazālī's Book of Counsel for Kings (Naŝīĥāt al-mulūk),* trans. F. R. C. Bagley (London: Oxford University Press, 1964), p. xi; Bahār, *Sabk Shināsī,* 2:67.

7. Luther, "Bayhaqī and the Later Seljūq Historians," pp. 25 ff.

8. Savory, "Abo'l-Fazl Bayhaqī as an Historiographer," p. 108.

9. Bahār, *Sabk Shināsī,* 2:63–66.

10. Thanks to Professor Frederic Cadora, Ohio State University, for suggesting this possibility.

11. *TB*, p. 238/308.

12. See also Bahār, *Sabk Shinasī*, 2:85–87. See also G. Lazard, "Les emprunts arabes dans la prose persane du Xe au XIIe siècle: aperçu statistique," *Revue de l' Ecole Nationale des Langues Orientales,* 2 (1965): 53–67.

13. E.g., *TB*, top of p. 380/485.

14. E.g., ibid., p. 239: "Inqadtu hādhihi'l qiŝŝah wa in kāna fihā ba^cdū'l, kih'al-bādi^cah ghayru mamlūl."

15. Muĥammad Nāẑim, *The Life and Times of Sulţān Maĥmud of Ghazna* (Cambridge: Cambridge University Press, 1931), p. 136: "Shortly after taking office he [Maymandī] ordered Persian to be replaced by Arabic in all official correspondence." Nāẑim has taken this information from ^cUtbī.

16. *TB*, pp. 289/383, 372/474.

17. The best and most thorough analysis of Bayhaqī's style, and one that goes far beyond the scope of this work, is Bahār, *Sabk Shināsī,* 2:62 ff.

18. Usāmah ibn Munqidh, *Memoirs of an Arab-Syrian Gentleman,* trans. Philip K. Hitti (New York: Columbia University Press, 1929). See also Savory, "Abo'l-Fazl Bayhaqī as an Historiographer," p. 109.

19. *TB*, pp. 153/187 and 318/404, 324/412, respectively.

20. Ibid., p. 238.

21. Professor Michael Zwettler, of Ohio State University, has provided this wording of the translation of this line.

22. *TB*, p. 238/308.

23. Ibid., p. 401/515.

24. Ibid., p. 228/293.

25. Ibid., p. 252/330.

26. Savory, "Abo'l-Fazl Bayhaqī as an Historiographer," p. 108, referring to *TB*, pp. 223/286 and 401/515, respectively.

27. *TB*, p. 408/525. Thanks to Mr. Robert Demorest, of the Ohio State University Press, for pointing out that "hog on ice" can also mean the opposite, that is, coordinated and independent.

28. Ibid., pp. 362-63/463, 338/430, 148/180, and 87/100, respectively.

29. Ibid., p. 322/409.

30. Ibid., p. 76/86.

31. E.G., see ibid., pp. 101/119, 104/122, 108/129, 109/129, 247/322.

32. Ibid., p. 365/466.

33. Ibid., pp. 347/442, 242/314, 229/295, and 334/426, respectively.

34. Ibid., p. 324/412.

35. Ibid., p. 252/330. See also Appendix B, selection 9.

36. Ibid., p. 146/178.

37. Ibid., p. 11/10.

38. Ibid., pp. 178 ff./221 ff. See also Appendix B, selection 5.

39. See Qiyām al-Dīn Piā^cī, "Turkish, Mughal, and Chinese Language in *Ta'rīkh-i Bayhaqī*," in Mashhad University, *Yādnāmah*, pp. 182–98; and ^cAbd al-Shākūr Rashād, "Several Pashto Expressions in *Ta'rīkh-i Bayhaqī*," ibid., pp. 199–200.

40. *TB*, p. 337/429.

41. Ibid., p. 146/177.

42. See Muḥammad Javād Sharī^cat, "Active Verbs and the Method of Their Use in *Ta'rīkh-i Bayhaqī* and Their Direct Objects," in Mashhad University, *Yādnāmah*, pp. 364–73.

43. For example, A. K. S. Lambton, *Persian Grammar* (Student's Edition; Cambridge: Cambridge University Press, 1963), pp. 161–65.

44. *TB*, p. 182/226.

45. Hodivala, *Studies in Indo-Muslim History*, 2:157.

46. *TB*, p. 357/456: "Tabībī az Samānīyānrā silat-i nīkū dād panj hizār dīnār."

6

Bayhaqī's Place in Persian and Islamicate Cultural History

INTRODUCTION

A full determination of the place of any thinker or work in Persian or Islamicate cultural history is impossible because no complete scholarly history of either Persian or Islamicate culture exists. But there are a number of possible ways to begin to place Bayhaqī and his work. This chapter will first compare Bayhaqī and his history with three other contemporary or near contemporary historians and their works. Then it will relate ideas and work to Gibb's analysis of the secularization of Islamicate historiography and to Arkoun's view of the development of Arab and Islamicate humanism. Finally, it will explore the relationship between Bayhaqī's ideas on government and the development of Islamicate political theory.

COMPARISON WITH CONTEMPORARY HISTORIANS

Problems

It is possible to compare Bayhaqī's account of the reign of Mas^{c}ūd with the accounts of other contemporary and near contemporary historians. There are, however, three major problems with the results of any such comparison. First, the length of the other accounts is not comparable to the length of Bayhaqī's. What remains of Bayhaqī's account—all of Mas^{c}ūd's reign except the last year—is about 600 printed pages. The lengths of three other contemporary or near contemporary accounts are 15 pages of approximately 300 in Gardīzī, *Zayn al-akhbār* (ca. 441–44/1050–53); 4 pages of 415 in *Ta'rīkh-i Sīstān* (ca. 448/1056); and 5 pages of 1,250 in Juzjanī, *Ṭabaqāt-i Nāṣirī* (ca. 658/1259).[1]

The author of one of these works—Gardīzī—explicitly commits himself to brevity in all matters, in marked contrast to Bayhaqī; the other two have written fairly long works but devoted only brief portions to Mas^{c}ūd.[2] Although Gardīzī's entire scope is smaller than that of the other two authors, the proportion of space he devotes to Mas^{c}ūd is larger.

The second problem is related to the first: the works of all these authors had a much broader scope than *Ta'rīkh-i Bayhaqī,* so that the Ghaznavids naturally loom less large in them. Gardīzī's *Zayn al-akhbār* is a history of Persia from legendary times to the Ghaznavid ruler ^{c}Abd al-Rashīd (r. 441–44/1050–53), to whom the work was dedicated. *Ta'rīkh-i Sīstān* is, as its name implies, a history of Sīstān and its surrounding province from pre-Islāmic times to the reign of the Saljūq *sulṭān* Tughril (r. 429–65/1038–63). Jūzjānī's *Ṭabaqāt-i Nāṣirī* is a history of Islām with an emphasis on the rulers of Irāq, Irān, and India, from Adam down through the early years of the Mongol invasions. It contains only a brief "universal" pre-Islāmic summary. For none are the Ghaznavids as a dynasty at all central.

The third problem is that the authors of two of these three works did not live and write where Bayhaqī did, so that their geopolitical focus is different. Gardīzī may have lived in Ghazna and worked for the Ghaznavids; but the author of *Ta'rīkh-i Sīstān* was a native and partisan of that province, and Jūzjānī lived in India during the latter part of his life and wrote from that perspective. These latter two have a vision of the political role and significance of the Ghaznavids that necessarily differs from Bayhaqī's. The occupations of the author of *Ta'rīkh-i Sīstān* and Gardīzī are not known; Jūzjānī was a *qāżī* for the Slave Kings of Delhi.[3]

Comparisons

When one makes comparisons, one must be cautious not to overemphasize any similarities or differences between Bayhaqī and other authors that might be the natural result of these circumstantial and situational factors—length, scope, and geopolitical perspective. With these cautions in mind, one can go on to make a number of comparative points about Bayhaqī's method, substance and interpretation, and style.

There are five striking features of methodological comparison: Bayhaqī is (1) more explicit about his method; (2) much more introspective; (3) much less tied to a strictly annalistic or regnal framework and all that it implies; (4) less dependent on other books, particularly history books; and (5) much more detailed and reflective than all three of the other authors. Gardīzī, as has been mentioned above, explicitly commits himself to brevity, whereas Bayhaqī emphatically commits himself to fullness of detail.

In terms of substance and interpretation, Bayhaqī, Gardīzī, and the author of *Ta'rīkh-i Sīstān* contrast with Jūzjānī's great degree of stylized royal adulation. Among the three former authors, Bayhaqī has the most cliché royal praise and mention of the "exploits" of rulers; but even in Bayhaqī this is slight. Gardīzī, with his commitment to brevity, omits even some of the more famous exploits of Maĥmūd and Mas^{c}ūd. The author of *Ta'rīkh-i Sīstān* is very matter-of-fact and adulatory about the Ghaznavids.

Some of these differences can be explained by differences in locale and occupation. The author of *Ta'rīkh-i Sīstān* viewed the Ghaznavids as temporary outside rulers and stressed popular support there for other less orthodox dynasties like the Saffārids (253–91/867–903). In fact, the Ghaznavids exercised control in Sīstān only for a short time. Even Gardīzī, in *Zayn al-akhbār,* grouped the Ghaznavids together with other rulers *(umarā',* pl. of *amīr)* of Khurāsān, from the governors of the caliphs through the Sāmānids and Ghaznavids down to Mawdūd.[4]

Bayhaqī, on the other hand, seems to take the Ghaznavid role in Irān, at least during Mas^{c}ūd's reign, more seriously. For the early part of Mas^{c}ūd's reign, the Ghaznavids' control was effective at least in the east of Khurāsān, which is Bayhaqī's focus, but not in south and central Irānian provinces like Sīstān. However, even in the capital of Khurāsān, Nishāpūr, there were local partisan groups that did not support the Ghaznavids. Bayhaqī himself mentions the leaders of these groups, but, of course, not their hostility or indifference to the Ghaznavids. He comes closest to doing so in a description of the partisans of various men executed by Mas^{c}ūd—Hasīrī, Hasanak, and Asaftigīn Ghāzī. But even in these cases he describes their hostility in terms of narrowly personal feelings rather than in terms of more generalized social grievances against the regime or dynasty as a whole.

Bayhaqī's attitude toward, and information on, Mas^{c}ūd is far more complex than that of the other authors, who all treat Mas^{c}ūd in a distant, impersonal fashion, stressing his military side to a greater extent than does Bayhaqī. Understandably, all the information on intrigues and great men that is contained in *Ta'rīkh-i Bayhaqī* is absent in the others. The author of *Ta'rīkh-i Sīstān* does not mention members of Mas^{c}ūd's bureaucracy at all, and does not even mention Mas^{c}ūd himself as often as he mentions the governors Mas^{c}ūd sent to Sīstān. Gardīzī mentions some of the same government officials and messengers as does Bayhaqī and some that Bayhaqī does not mention, like the caliphal messenger Abū Sahl b. Manŝūr b. Aflākh Gardīzī.[5] Gardīzī's treatment of Mas^{c}ūd's reign is almost like an epitome of *Ta'rīkh-i Bayhaqī,* though Gardīzī's book was published six to ten years before Bayhaqī's. The difference between the two is that Gardīzī treats the diplomatic and internal in the same depth as the military. But Bayhaqī's view of court intrigues, of the conflict between the Mas^{c}ūdīyān and Maĥmūdīyān, of Mas^{c}ūd at the mercy of his advisers, is completely absent in the other accounts. To give an example, Gardīzī devotes a few sentences to the choice of Maymandī as prime minister; Bayhaqī devotes many pages; and the author of *Ta'rīkh-i Sīstān* does not mention the event at all. For Juzjanī, writing somewhat later, Mas^{c}ūd has become known as the "martyr" because he died ignominiously after a humiliating defeat by the Saljūqs; but Jūzjānī's sympathetic perception is lacking in the other accounts.

The style of Gardīzī and of the author of *Ta'rīkh-i Sīstān* is similar to that of Bayhaqī, but Bayhaqī's style is syntactically more complex, more detailed and richer in vocabulary, just as his material is more complex. Of Gardīzī and the author of *Ta'rīkh-i Sīstān,* Gardīzī is closer to Bayhaqī.[6] It is interesting that Gardīzī includes emotional detail similar to that included by Bayhaqī (for example, "^{c}Alī Hājib bāng bar vay zad," "Hājib ^{c}Alī shouted at him"), and also similar sentence construction (for example, "har rūz [lashkar] fawj fawj hamī āmadand," "each day the army would come troop by troop"), but in general Bayhaqī is much more detailed.[7] For example, where Gardīzī mentions that Mas^{c}ūd bestowed a fine *khil^{c}ah* on Maymandī, Bayhaqī describes it in detail.[8] Or where Gardīzī unemotionally relates the causes and nature of Hasanak's execution, in eleven lines, Bayhaqī takes as many pages for an intricate, complex, and dramatic account.[9] And finally, where Gardīzī calmly mentions the act of *muṣādarah* (extortion under torture from men fallen from office), Bayhaqī gives its pros and cons, as well as the feelings of all participants.[10]

Bayhaqī's Place in Persian Historiography

Some of these points that have emerged from the comparison of Bayhaqī with other authors can be and have been explained. Many others are difficult to explain. One author has suggested that Bayhaqī was simply a very special person, calling him a "talented *dabīr.*"[11] And personality factors and natural gifts doubtless constitute a partial explanation. Age and experience were also clearly factors in Bayhaqī's style as a historian. Other interesting works were written by older men who had experienced a series of ups and downs, men like Ibn Khaldūn, Usāmah, and Ghazālī.

But the strikingly unusual features of Bayhaqī's work—complex structure, variety of materials, emphasis on accuracy and reality, the pattern of ethico-political themes, the undercurrent of asceticism, the lively and appealing style—cannot be explained simply in terms of personality, age, or practical experience. The fact that Bayhaqī's work appears at this time to be unique in Persian history, that his work was popular and respected but not directly imitated, is relevant here. Bayhaqī was exposed to, and wrote in response to, a number of developments, not all of which outlasted him to influence others. The simple yet interesting style that Bayhaqī developed from his chancery experience was related to the literary developments of the Sāmānid and Ghaznavid periods, developments that were replaced by a more ornate style of historical writing in the Saljūq era. The degree to which his method moved beyond either the views of secretary or annalist was a response of some sort to the influence of the new ways in history of the Būyid period. His reflective, introspective, sometimes ascetic *ṣūfī*-like response to much of what he reported was somehow connected to the growing importance of ṣūfism in the time and place of his education. His themes were enriched by his immersion in the *adab* tradition. All these things came together in his work in a way that they did not in any other work of Persian historiography known today.

The fourth to the sixth (tenth to twelfth) centuries—which includes the time during which Bayhaqī arrived at his unique blend of materials—has been called an "Islāmic renaissance."[12] Gibb has noted that during this period of general intellectual innovation and experimentation in Dār al-Islām, cultural achievements were largely personal and individual.[13] Bayhaqī's very uniqueness was a characteristic of the period in which he wrote. He was not, then, the only thinker during this so-called Islāmic renaissance to have developed a lively, imaginative, idiosyncratic style that did not become part of any school. Unique cultural productions were a feature, as yet unexplained, of the fourth to the sixth centuries.

This connection of Bayhaqī, who spent most of his life far to the east of the central Islamicate lands, with cultural developments originating there raises an important issue: Bayhaqī seems to have been, to a larger extent than other eleventh-century Persian historians, influenced by historiographical and intellectual trends in the central lands and in the Islamicate mainstream. A possible explanation might be that the Sāmānid and Ghaznavid rulers before and during Bayhaqī's lifetime were committed to bringing the best creators of Islamicate culture to their courts. These figures included some of the most creative, experimental geniuses of the Islamicate renaissance, in philosophy, science, and other branches of learning. But why this atmosphere influenced Bayhaqī more than other historians of the age is still hard to explain. Three particular developments in the Islamicate mainstream can be related to Bayhaqī: the secularization of Islamicate historiography, the development of Arab humanism, and the emergence of a new Islamicate political theory.

THE SIGNIFICANCE OF THE SECULARIZATION OF ISLAMICATE HISTORIOGRAPHY: A REEVALUATION OF GIBB'S ARGUMENT

Using as his standard the type of history written by religious scholars from the second to the fourth (eighth to tenth) centuries, Gibb sees the development of the type of history represented by Bayhaqī as essentially negative and deleterious for two reasons:

> 1) It was inevitable that their [the clerks' and secretaries'] presentation of events would reflect the bias and narrow outlook—social, political and religious—of their class. The old theological conception which had given breadth and dignity

> to history was discarded, and annalistic [*sic*] tended to concentrate more and more upon the activities of the ruler and the court.[14]
>
> 2) The secularization of history had another serious consequence. In place of its earlier theological justification, the historians now pleaded the moral value of its study: history perpetuates the record of virtuous and evil actions and offers them as examples for the edification of future generations. Such a plea was highly acceptable to the host of moralists and dilettantes; if history were merely a branch of ethics, not a science, they need not scruple to adapt their so-called historical examples to their own ends. The *adab*-books and *Mirrors for Princes,* full of such perversions, went far towards vitiating public taste and judgment, and even historians and chroniclers themselves were not always immune from such perversions.[15]

The problem with these arguments is twofold: they assume that historical writing in its ideal form is broad in focus and free from didacticism, and they assume that Islāmic history written by religious scholars possessed these qualities and that "secular" history did not. This latter assumption in turn rests on an overly simplistic view of "theologically inspired" as opposed to "secularized" history.

With regard to "theologically inspired" history, the idea of justifying or elucidating theology through historical study did not always give breadth to history, even before the fourth/tenth century. Nor was history written by religious scholars always "theologically inspired," as in the case of the *qāżī* Jūzjānī mentioned above, who wrote a history similar to those written by secretaries and clerks. Theologically inspired history was not always the objective science that its authors claimed it to be; it, too, was basically didactic. The didactic nature of all pre-modern Islāmic historical writing is clear. But didacticism can be of all kinds—from Ṭabarī, who saw history as an illustration of the *ḥadīth*-minded pious view of the world, to the consciously philosophical lesson-seeking of Ibn Khaldūn. Bayhaqī's didacticism is not of Ṭabarī's piety-minded type, though he was pious in his own way, nor is it truly philosophical like Ibn Khaldūn's. His didacticism falls somewhere in between the two extremes.[16]

With regard to "secularized" history, such as that written by Bayhaqī, it is clear from *Ta'rīkh-i Bayhaqī* that, though the immediate outlook of a secretary writing history might seem narrow, this historical vision could be broad and that the search for moral values in history could be combined with as strong a concern for accuracy and as strong a sense of piety as in the theologian-historians. And if after the fourth/tenth centuries the secretary-historians began to concentrate more on court affairs, it was also the case that in their day the court had a pervasive influence. Vision, concern for accuracy, and piety were present in a secretary-historian like Bayhaqī; but they were a vision, accuracy, and piety different from, not better or worse than, the vision, accuracy, and piety of a religious scholar-historian like Ṭabarī.

Theologically inspired history and secularized history were sometimes different from one another, sometimes not; but they share, along with all other Muslim historical writings, most basic features.

BAYHAQĪ'S RELATION TO THE DEVELOPMENT OF "ARAB HUMANISM"

There is another development of the fourth to the sixth (tenth to twelfth) centuries to which Bayhaqī can be related. This movement is what Arkoun has labeled the development of Arab-Islāmic humanism.[17] Arkoun argues that it was the genius of the fourth/tenth century to try to reconcile three existing humanistic tendencies: religious, literary (associated with *adab*), and philosophical. He isolates six features of the new humanism:

> 1) An overture to sciences considered foreign;
> 2) A rationalization of religious and parareligious phenomena . . . an elimination of miracle, of the marvelous, of superstitions, in order to replace them with scientific explanation;
> 3) Priority attention to ethico-political problems;
> 4) Development of scientific curiosity and of a critical sense which entailed a new organization of knowledge;
> 5) Esthetic values (architecture, decoration, furniture, painting, music), . . . still very poorly known;
> 6) An inadequate mastery of the world of the imagination. Arkoun goes on to describe the intense hostility of many groups to the new intellectual developments, pointing out that they died down because they were inappropriate particularly to many of the nomadic groups who came to prominence in the Dār al-Islām after the fourth/tenth century. According to Arkoun, the gradual decline of the humanities and the humanistic attitude explains why Ibn Khaldūn, who, according to Arkoun, perfectly assimilated all these humanistic tendencies, was poorly received and never emulated.

If one measures Bayhaqī against Arkoun's six characteristics of Arab-Islāmic humanism, one finds that he possesses most of them in one degree or another. The only attribute that does not relate to his work directly is the first, though since he was familiar with the work of Bīrūnī, who stayed at the Ghaznavid court, it can be assumed that he was exposed to an open attitude toward "foreign" sciences. The second characteristic is made explicit in his work, except that instead of replacing miracles and superstitions with a scientific explanation, he rules them out of his history entirely. The third feature, a preoccupation with ethico-political problems, is also an obvious feature of his work. If in the fourth attribute the word *scientific* is taken broadly, as Arkoun meant it to be, Bayhaqī's attention to accuracy and care and rejection of questionable information is relevant.

The fifth characteristic deserves discussion. Although Arkoun is thinking of nonverbal arts, one could argue that Bayhaqī was working on a new aesthetic sense in prose similar to that being developed in the visual arts. His prose has a graphic, visual quality, almost as if he were describing in words scenes that also could be captured in miniature painting. Certain passages in their totality call up a visual image that is quite complete and effective, operating on the senses in a way unusual for pre-modern Persian prose.

As for the sixth and last attribute, Bayhaqī's imagery is concrete rather than abstract and intellectual. His handling of dream material in the book—three occasions—is stilted and straightforward. In general, Bayhaqī is disdainful of what has not been observed or what is part of the world of the imagination.

Although Bayhaqī clearly was not deeply immersed in the intellectual developments of the century of his birth, he did respond to them in his own way. To the explanations of his singularity given above should be added the fact that Ghazna was far from the centers of these developments; there it would not be expected that many, engaged full-time in an occupation such as his, would have the time or interest to become involved in them. The failure of his efforts to catch on with later historians is to be explained by the fact that the developments to which he was responding and in which he was partaking did not outlast him with any strength.

ISLAMICATE POLITICAL THEORY AND "TA'RĪKH-I BAYHAQĪ"

There is one final perspective from which Bayhaqī's work should be viewed, that of the development of Islamicate political theory. In terms of time Bayhaqī is located between the theologically based theory of Mawardī, who was responding to the very beginning of new forms of government in the Muslim world, and Niẑām al-Mulk, who was responding to the fact that these new power arrangements were to be permanent. In terms of substance Bayhaqī is located somewhat between these two as well. His ideas about government resemble those of Mawardī. He was also involved with the "Mirrors for Princes" tradition, which had less to say on the problems of the breakdown of caliphal power, in which Mawardī was interested. Bayhaqī also, however, shows signs of beginning to be aware of the problems that Niẑām al-Mulk took up less than twenty years after Bayhaqī's death. These problems involved the confrontation between the Perso-Islamicate political theory and practice of the "Mirrors" literature with the power-oriented, military politics of nomadic groups like the Saljūqs, under whom Niẑām al-Mulk worked. Bayhaqī's negative reaction to many of the abuses of government and absolutism that developed under the Ghaznavids was later systematized and rationalized by Niẑām al-Mulk. Bayhaqī himself was able to explain away his reaction in vocabularies familiar to him; Niẑām al-Mulk attempted to reconcile the two tendencies and make them workable. In the short run, Bayhaqī's feeling of hopelessness was more correct; not until the Ottoman Empire were the various tendencies in politics and political theory reconciled in any lasting way.

1. Abū Sa^{c}īd ^{c}Abdū'l-Ĥayy b. al-D̂ahhāk b. Maĥmūd Gardīzī, *Kitāb Zaynū' l-Akhbār,* ed. Muĥammad Nazim, E. G. Browne Memorial Series, vol. 1 (London: Luzac & Co., 1928), pp. 95–110; *Ta'rīkh-i Sīstān,* ed. Mālik al-Shu^{c}arā' Bahār (Tehran: Zavvār Publishing House, 1314/1896); Jūzjānī, *The T̂abak̂at-i Nāŝirī*, trans. Major H. G. Raverty (rpt.; New Delhi: Oriental Books Reprint Corp., 1970), 1:91–97.

2. Gardīzī, *Kitāb Zaynū' l-Akhbār,* pp. 61–62.

3. The dynasty popularly known as the Slave Kings of Delhi, more properly called the Mu^{c}izzīs, ruled from 602 to 689 (1206–90). Jūzjānī served Iltutmish (r. 607–33/1211–36) and his three successors, Rukn al-Dīn, Jalālat al-Dīn, and Mu^{c}izz al-Dīn (all three r. 633–39/1236–42) and then Maĥmūd Shāh (r. 644–64/1246–66), to whom his work is dedicated.

4. See "Table of Contents" in al-D̂ahhāk b. Maĥmūd Gardīzī, *Zayn al-akhbār,* ed. ^{c}Abd al-Ĥayy Habībī, Irānian Culture Foundation, Publications on the History and Geography of Irān, vol. 11 (Tehran: Offset Press of Muĥammad ^{c}Alī ^{c}Ilmī, 1347/1928), pp. viii–ix.

5. Gardīzī, *Kitāb Zaynū' l-Akhbār,* p. 95.

6. I have not yet read Jūzjānī in Persian.

7. Gardīzī, *Kitāb Zaynū' l-Akhbār,* p. 98.

8. Ibid., p. 96.

9. Ibid., pp. 96–97.

10. Ibid., p. 97.

11. Kan Kagaya, "Religious Groups in Khorāsān under the Ghaznavids," in Mashhad University, Faculty of Letters and Humanities, *Yādnāmah-yi Abū' l-Faẑl-i Bayhaqī* (Mashhad: Mashhad University Press, 1971), p. 5.

12. H. A. R. Gibb, "An Interpretation of Islamic History," in H. A. R. Gibb, *Studies on the Civilization of Islam,* ed. Stanford Shaw and William R. Polk (Boston: Beacon Press, 1962), pp. 17–21.

13. Ibid., p. 18.

14. H. A. R. Gibb, "Tarīkh," in *Studies on the Civilization of Islam,* p. 120.

15. Ibid., p. 121.

16. There are fascinating comparisons to be made between these features in Bayhaqī's work and the mixture of sophism and tragedy that has been observed in Thucydides. See John H. Finley, *Thucydides* (Ann Arbor: University of Michigan Press, 1963).

17. Mohammed Arkoun, *Contribution à l'étude de l'humanisme arabe au IVe/Xe siècle: Miskawayh philosophe et historien,* Etudes Musulmanes, vol. 11 (Paris: Librairie Philosophique J. Vrin, 1970), pp. 356–63.

7

Ta'rīkh-i Bayhaqī in the Light of Speech Act Theory

''Perhaps I have trained myself to see what others overlook.'' – Sherlock Holmes to Dr. Watson, ''A Case of Identity''

Without yet applying any systematic critical theory, we have managed, by asking an eclectic assortment of contextual and textual questions, to move far beyond existing criticism of *Ta'rīkh-i Bayhaqī* and to raise problems and issues that would merit further research. First of all, the structure of *Ta'rīkh-i Bayhaqī* is not simply a chronological-political narrative casually ''embellished'' or ''adorned'' with interpolations, but rather a self-consciously innovative statement about how history should be done. The historiographical significance of the interpolated material as commentator on, and expander of, the narrative is now clear. The degree to which Bayhaqī saw repeating patterns in history deserves further study, as does the relationship between the roles of *dabīr* (''secretary''), *adīb* (''bellelettrist''), and *mu'arrikh* (''historian/chronicler'') that he combined so well. For Bayhaqī was not only secretary—patiently keeping records as clearly as possible—but also raconteur—elaborating and expanding his message with well-chosen, well-written, amusing anecdotes—and chronicler—following political, military, and diplomatic events from year to year to record the greatness of a dynasty.

Second, the analyses of the structure and thematic content of *Ta'rīkh-i Bayhaqī* have raised doubts about Bayhaqī's accuracy, objectivity, and impartiality, qualities that have impressed other observers. That certain themes, such as the relationship between absolutism and consultation or between ruler and ruled, dominate his book and recur within it so often forces one to question whether illustrating the themes became for him as important as, or even more important than, reporting observations. There is clear evidence of patterning and stylizing—particularly of speeches and conversations. It appears that his concern for accuracy was greater in the narrative than in the interpolated material, but even in the former there are small inaccuracies that raise doubts. And certain important figures he does not treat with impartiality.

Third, the image of Bayhaqī as a talented secretary dabbling, albeit successfully, in history must yield to a picture of a man whose basic interests, perspectives, and skills were those of a *dabīr* but who was also responding to numerous other intellectual traditions and influences, including *adab,* ṣūfism, Persian dualism, Islāmic *sharīᶜah*-mindedness, philosophical history, and political theory. Scholars also have not taken enough into account the impact of hindsight and of aging, which may be particularly relevant to Bayhaqī's gossipiness, prolixity, and interest in emotional situations.

Finally, Bayhaqī in his unique accomplishment is very much a part of developments in the Islamicate mainstream. His innovativeness in structure and style can be compared with similar accomplishments during the "Islāmic renaissance" of the tenth to twelfth centuries. His work may also be a Persian counterpart of the development of "Arab humanism." And he is concerned with the same problems that troubled political theorists—both systematic and popular—in his day. In some ways his dabbling in philosophical history and in criticism of his sources foreshadows the more systematic contributions of Ibn Khaldūn. Above all, his work stands as a study of human interaction that does not scorn the intricate and complex for the general, but carefully analyzes the former to understand the latter and vice versa.[1]

Just as the preceding analysis suggests new directions, it has also borne out all five of the assumptions about Islamicate historiography made in chapter one.

1. The book reflects the values, concerns, experiences, and occupation of the author and, in turn, those aspects of his time that influenced him.
2. The book is didactic, stressing that there are lessons to be learned from history; but it is also concerned with accuracy and historical "realities." However, it is not always clear what lessons the author himself wants to teach. To some extent he has molded the behavior of the individuals he describes into patterns and typologies, but it is hard to determine the extent of the patterning.
3. There is a pervasive element of *taqiyyah* ("dissimulation"), both in terms of esotericism and encouragement to read on different levels, and in terms of hiding the author's feelings.

4. Structural features communicate the author's values; but in this case structure seems to communicate his questions and doubts even more than it does his confirmed values. Structural features both conflict with explicit declarations of values and serve where such declarations are absent.
5. Although Bayhaqī's work adheres to certain literary conventions of form and style, it is less a genre piece than most histories written by Muslims up to his time. It is rather a combination of genres, particularly of *adab* and *ta'rīkh,* blended with a personal and professional style of language. It is difficult to determine how conventional the author's style is because complete information is lacking on the style of language and expression in which he was trained. It appears, however, that his style is innovative, even though the standard chancery style has clearly influenced the form and content of his work.

Despite its accomplishments, however, the preceding analysis lacked a holistic framework or system to tie its findings together and help organize future research—a perspective that will keep scholars from again reducing texts to one or another monolithic explanation. I believe that, as hypothesized in chapter one, Pratt's nascent theory of display texts can provide that framework. This chapter will explain how the preceding analysis has substantiated this hypothesis, how Pratt's ideas help explain what has been observed, and how implications are to be drawn for the future study and use of historical narratives.

TA'RĪKH-I BAYHAQĪ AS DISPLAY TEXT

Bayhaqī makes it easy for the reader to tell whether he is, in Pratt's words, "not only reporting but also verbally displaying a state of affairs, inviting his addressee(s) to join him in contemplating it, evaluating it, and responding to it."[2] Indeed, Bayhaqī tells his reader he is so doing at the end of almost every set of narratives and interpolations. His use of words that encourage interpretation abounds. His *khuṭbah* on history explicitly argues for telling "tellable" history. He constantly calls upon the reader to reflect, marvel, condemn. Implicitly as well, by his use of interpolation to comment on, and expand the meaning of, events, by his inclusion of human detail unnecessary to sheer informing, Bayhaqī displays a preoccupation with the relevance of tellability.

If, then, Bayhaqī's narrative can be considered a display text, it should also, according to Pratt, be structured according to Labov's divisions for natural narratives, which are:

1. abstract (a short, one- or two-sentence summary, encapsulating the point or topic of the story, perhaps even in the form of a title);

2. orientation (the identification of time, place, persons, and their activity and possibly the speaker's relationship to it, placed usually before the first narrative clause);
3. complicating action;
4. evaluation (a separate section here but also embedded as a secondary structure in the complicating action);
5. results or resolution (a passage that ends with the last narrative clause);
6. coda (something that "closes off the sequence of complicating actions and indicates that none of the events that followed were important to the narrative," and "leaves the listener with a feeling of satisfaction and completeness that matters have been rounded off and accounted for," often bringing the reader back to the point where the larger narrative left off).[3]

That Bayhaqī's narrative organization corresponds to Labov's divisions could be illustrated with any of the translated portions in the Appendix; but let us take, for ease of handling, a shorter one, "Buzurgmihr's Imprisonment."[4] A very brief abstract is contained in the sentence that precedes the subheading "A Story" and in the subheading itself: this will be a story about a prisoner (and by implication, about the relationship of one imprisonment story to another that has been interrupted). The orientation consists of the entire first paragraph, which gives time, persons, and situation. The orientation ends before the first narrative clause, "This story was carried to Khusraw Nūshīrvān," which in turn begins the complicating action. The result or resolution ends with the last narrative clause, "In the end he ordered that he be killed and mutilated in order to set an example," and seems to include the whole paragraph of which it is a part. In this case the evaluation may actually follow the resolution if it is taken to be "Buzurgmihr went to heaven and the Khusraw went to hell"; but if one wished to see that as part of the resolution (where it should be in Labov's scheme), one could easily see the paragraph that includes Buzurgmihr's last words as an evaluation. Wherever one places the formal evaluation, it is clear that evaluative devices are, as Labov suggests, also scattered throughout the narrative as well, particularly in Buzurgmihr's lengthy replies to questioners (one of Bayhaqī's favorite techniques) and in his interchange with Nūshīrvān, in which the Khusraw is portrayed as indecisive, short-sighted, willful, and vindictive (characteristics assigned to other rulers described by Bayhaqī, too). When the resolution comes, it is no surprise.[5] In the coda, the sentence following the last narrative clause, the reader is made to feel that the story was worth reading before continuing the main narrative. Unfortunately, any future analysis of Bayhaqī's narrative style will have also to proceed on relatively small units, since neither the whole multivolume narrative nor the whole volume of which the extant work is a part remain.

If Bayhaqī's narrative can be shown to be a display text that conforms to the narrative divisions Pratt has adopted from Labov, one should proceed to test the existing use maxims for such narrative (adopted by Pratt from Grice's conversational maxims) before developing new ones. For just as Pratt has assumed that any theory of literary narrative should be able to account for "natural narrative," so I assume that any theory that can account for literary narrative and natural narrative should be able to account for historical narrative, too. In my view (a view implicit in speech act theory itself), the composition of a historical narrative, and the ways in which it is read, are not necessarily affected in any fundamental way by the fact that it claims to be responding to a series of "real" past events—either experienced or read about, just as a novel that represents historical events need not be distinguished for all purposes from one that represents imaginary events as long as the *representations* and *readings* are comparable. Furthermore, the chronological structure of historical narrative is not a distinguishing feature; in fact, the basic structures of historical narrative may actually be closer to those of natural narrative—chronology undergirded by evaluation—than those of what Pratt views as literary narrative. Therefore I hold that developing a theory of historical narrative will entail concentration on types of representation and reading, not on the historical validity of its contents.

When we begin to try to look at a historical narrative like *Ta'rīkh-i Bayhaqī* in the light of a possible speech act theory of literary narrative, any inconsistencies should at first reflect on the theory, not on the appropriateness of placing historical narratives within its purview. We may find that the appropriateness conditions or maxims for the historical narrative speech situation are in fact different; but our first step should be to test existing use maxims, as Pratt has done for nonhistorical literary narrative.

Pratt has found Grice's use maxims for conversation to be the best starting point; to replicate her experiment, so will I. Grice bases his maxims on a phenomenon that he calls the Cooperative Principle, which seems particularly appropriate to historical narrative: "Make your conversational contribution such as is required, at the stage at which it occurs, by the accepted purpose or direction of the talk-exchange in which you are engaged."[6] This principle can be adapted to written narrative, in which actual exchange or interruption by receiver is suspended for the duration, in the following way: the author must make his whole narrative, and the order and relationship of its component parts, appropriate to the speech situation (genre) in which he and the audience are involved. The maxims to be observed if such a principle is to be maintained are, according to Grice,

I. Quantity
   1. as informative as required
   2. no more informative than required

II. Quality
  1. true
  2. not believed by speaker to be false or inadequately evidenced
III. Relation
  1. relevant
IV. Manner
  1. perspicuous
  2. free from obscurity, ambiguity, prolixity, disorderliness[7]

According to Pratt, and of course Grice, when these maxims are not followed, the speaker must make it possible for the audience to reconcile the speaker's non-following with the Cooperative Principle; that is, the speaker must manage to "implicate" the reason for his non-following in such a way that the audience can make enough sense of his behavior to maintain the Cooperative Principle. There are four intentional ways in which any speaker can break the rules:

1. Violation (just quietly not observing a maxim, often with misleading effect);
2. Opting-out (refusing to do enough to fulfill a maxim);
3. Clashes (experiencing inability to fulfill one maxim without violating another);
4. Flouting (blatantly failing to fulfill a maxim in a way that cannot be confused with any of the first three).

In conversation all four cases of rule-breaking can be resolved so as to maintain the Cooperative Principle. In a "literary" situation, according to Pratt, in which the necessary audience participation is impossible, the audience may lose faith or interest in an author who uses the first three. Implicature in itself may not work in those cases. Only in the fourth case is implicature always demanded, says Pratt, and the Cooperative Principle never jeopardized.[8] It is, then, through understanding the rules, rule-breaking, and deviance appropriate in a given speech situation, that we come to understand the meaning of the composition and reading of a work, that we "decoded the speaker's utterance, detected deviance, and calculated implicature."[9]

When *Ta'rīkh-i Bayhaqī* is looked at in this light, a certain feature of the work that was problematic for more conventional analysis takes on new, and possibly crucial, meaning—Bayhaqī's continuously expressed fear of losing his audience and his constant effort to keep them on his side. Bayhaqī, in Grice and Pratt's terms, must have been knowingly violating whatever maxims were in force in such a way that he felt the audience might not be able to resolve his behavior through ordinary means and thus keep faith in him.

Let us look first at his behavior in terms of Grice's maxims and forms of rule-breaking. Bayhaqī does not seem guilty of Violation, of unostentatiously breaking maxims; but at this stage in our understanding, such violation might be hard to detect. He does, however, frequently opt-out, often concerning issues on which he could have been accused of Violation had he not opted out. For example, in the following passage Bayhaqī is clearly in danger of violating the maxims of Quantity and Quality by saying more than is informative and by saying it on questionable evidence, when he opts out: "He [Aĥmad Yinaltigīn] was called the sneeze [i.e., spit and image] of Maĥmūd. They used to gossip about the story of the mother and the birth of Yinaltigīn and Amīr Maĥmūd. And there *had* existed between the *Padshāh* and his mother a state of friendship, but [only] God (May He be exalted and glorified!) knows the truth."[10] Just as Bayhaqī frequently opts-out in this situation, he also opts-out when there is no danger of Violation, as do many Muslim historians. In fact, Opting-out seems for Muslim historians to be a form of rule-breaking that also does not endanger the Cooperative Principle, since it too seems always to demand implicature that the audience always expects to have to make. With regard to Opting-out, Pratt's understanding of the rule-breaking tolerable in literary discourse will have to be examined.

Bayhaqī also seems to experience, and try to resolve, Clashes constantly—between maxims of Manner and Relation and Quantity, if not Quality as well. He frequently acknowledges that his prolixity will conflict with what the reader assumes to be informative enough, or that being informative enough demands that they abandon their notion of what is relevant, or that being informative enough involves apparent disorderliness. Here, though, Pratt's understanding is probably not in jeopardy because although Bayhaqī experiences Clashes, he also realizes that such Clashes ordinarily would endanger the Cooperative Principle unless he instructs the audience in their resolution.

Finally, Bayhaqī also blatantly fails to fulfill maxims (but not to the degree to which he suffers from Opting-Out and Clashes). For example, the story whose narrative was analyzed earlier is inserted into the larger narrative in such a way as to violate maxim III, Relation, especially when its insertion is compared with other similar insertions. Bayhaqī offers a justification that is flimsy at best, whereas in other cases he goes to great lengths to justify relevance; so the reader is naturally immediately alerted to the need to find a reason for the story's presence. Whatever revisions will be needed to account for a historical narrative like *Ta'rīkh-i Bayhaqī,* the fact that its author explicitly acknowledges a Cooperative Principle seemingly similar to Grice's and frequently pinpoints the circumstances that endanger it for the reader could be the starting point of our future understanding of the maxims that governed such compositions before, during, and after Bayhaqī's time.

One theory might argue that Bayhaqī was demanding new kinds of implicature, or at least forms of implicature new to the audience for that speech situation. Earlier historical texts could still have been "world-creating," but in noticeably different ways. As discussed in the last chapter, a change in the nature of Islamicate historical writing seems to have been initiated in the few generations before Bayhaqī, from juxtaposition of different *ḥadīth* narratives on the same topic to continuous narrative perhaps closer to oral story-telling techniques.[11] Our findings here would lend support to the idea of such a change and provide ways to measure and study it.

What, then, would we have to know to be able to carry this type of analysis further? Obviously we would have to know the rules that governed the speech situation of which a given work is a case, which in turn would require defining a spectrum of speech situations for a particular time and place. If a work was called, for example, "Ta'rīkh," and written on a certain subject, what did readers expect when they picked it up? To answer this question, one would need to know how authors were legitimized and how books were edited and deemed worthy of selection for copying (in this case, manuscript copying) and distribution.

However, according to Pratt, answering these questions is not, as many literary-minded historiographers like myself have tended to assume, enough. Within the larger speech situation of the genre are enclosed a series of other speech situations with whose maxims readers can be assumed to be familiar and whose rule-breaking those same readers can assess and resolve. Although the bulk of *Ta'rīkh-i Bayhaqī,* for example, is in the form of a large narrative enclosing smaller and smaller narratives, composed either by the author or other speakers or even other speakers within other speakers, much of it involves distinctly different speech acts—formal and informal correspondence, formal and informal dialogue or conversation, addresses, and poetry—some of each type author-generated, some not. The reader of *Ta'rīkh-i Bayhaqī* would have had to use implicature to resolve any rule-breaking in these other speech situations as well; and according to Pratt the range of deviance acceptable from speakers other than the main author is even greater than that acceptable from him. Therefore,

> in order to account for the full range of implicatures for which the reader of a literary work is responsible, a description of the literary speech act will, at least in some cases, have to take into account both the CP [Cooperative Principle] and maxims as defined for the work's genre and the CP and maxims as defined for the fictional speaker's utterance. While only the latter are required to decode what the fictional speaker is saying and implicating as well as what the author is saying, both sets of appropriateness conditions are required to decode what the author is implicating.[12]

If we really want to analyze a historical narrative like *Ta'rīkh-i Bayhaqī* in terms of speech act theory, we will have to come to understand the Cooperative Principle and rules for each type of speech situation within the larger whole. In particular, we will need to study the relationship of Bayhaqī's various narratives to the other narrative styles of his day, perhaps even narrative poetry.

The question remains, has *Ta'rīkh-i Bayhaqī* done more for a speech act theory of literary discourse than that theory has done for it? What have we really added to our understanding of the work itself? Have we merely restated conclusions arrived at through conventional analysis or have we truly brought the dismembered elephant to life again? In any empirical method, the case study *should* do as much for the theory as the theory does for it. But that justification aside, the fact that conventional analysis of *Ta'rīkh-i Bayhaqī* seemed to lead so naturally into speech act theory promises that we will be able to use it to tell us in a systematic way what we need to know in order to understand historical narratives. If we can establish suitable maxims and types of rule-breaking and implicature, we can eventually specify the nature of the interaction between author composition and reader reception, that is, the sociological situation in which this special kind of communication took place and the mutual concerns reflected by it. Once all of this has been established, the possibility of systematic comparisons of texts will be enormously expanded; and the need to arrive at a single authentic reading, obviated.

But any approach such as the one just described raises further questions about the uses of historical narratives, questions with which this book will end and others, hopefully, begin. If historical narrative can and must be understood as a use of information for purposes other than sheer informing, for what purposes can it best be used? The germ of an answer is planted in Marc Bloch's contributions to the handling of historical evidence. As H. Stuart Hughes has expressed it,

> Bloch shifted the emphasis [from history as an internal process of thought] to what was external and tangible. He did not deny the subjective character of historical judgment. He simply drew attention once again—and far more systematically than had been true of his nineteenth-century forebears—to the realities that the historian can actually see or hear or touch: archaeological remains, languages, folklore, and the like. These, he argued, provided the fixed points on which the thought of the historian could come to rest, and from which it could also take a new start—much as the surveyor makes his first reading from a metal plaque on the ground of whose accuracy of elevation he can be fairly certain.
>
> It is no surprise, then, to find that Bloch wrote of his chosen endeavor as a metier. He viewed himself as a craftsman, not merely "re-enacting" the past in his mind, as the classics of the idealist tradition taught, but tracing with a technician's precision the basic processes of past eras, whether in patterns of settlement or in the tilling of the soil. And these, he found, since they were tangibly present—since they could *actually be confronted* [emphasis added] by the historian rather than just "rethought" from the dubious evidence of documents—were by their very nature less subject to debate.[13]

But how can we use Bloch's promising notion of viewing as history's hard evidence what can "actually be confronted rather than just 'rethought,'" when Bloch himself views historical narrative reports—that is, "intentional" history—as "tracks" or realities, not as any kind of realities in themselves?[14] We can if we expand Bloch's definition of "confrontable" hard data, which already includes "a linguistic characteristic, a point of law embodied in a text, a rite, as defined by a book of ceremonial or a stele,"[15] to include historical narratives as hard data for what they allow us to confront directly, that is, verbal narratives. This use ironically would coincide with Bloch's insistence on not relying on intentional historical narrative to write narrative history. In a society like the Islamicate, in which the past came to be a unique vehicle for expressing the needs and concerns of the present, historical narrative provides an invaluable source.

I would like us to come to see and use historical narratives like *Ta'rīkh-i Bayhaqī* according to a spectrum that ranges from what they allow us to confront directly to what they allow us to confront only indirectly. In my view, a work like Bayhaqī's provides, in order, from hard to soft:

1. A direct confrontation (hard) with a particular case of a larger category of speech acts (still to be determined) and a particular form of language use.
2. A less direct confrontation (medium hard) with a world-creating representation and explanation of events the author thought important, or believed the audience would or should think important; less direct by virtue of being composed according to certain rules and filtered through the author's cognitive and emotive faculties; by extension a confrontation with related genre pieces.
3. A somewhat indirect confrontation (medium), by virtue of genre limitations, with the values of one relatively low-level administrator and subject whose expectations the ruler would have to fulfill to some extent (by extension, a confrontation with other similarly placed individuals). In fact, if we follow the ideas of sociologists like Eisenstadt about leadership roles, such confrontations with the expectations of men like Bayhaqī can tell us more about how leaders would have had to behave than would Bayhaqī's descriptions of a particular leader's behavior.[16]
4. A more indirect (medium soft) confrontation with what the audience would have valued.
5. An indirect (soft) confrontation with the reign of Sulṭān Mas^{c}ūd of Ghazna, subject to all the problems of any witness's accounts.[17]

The foregoing description of a possible spectrum is entirely tentative, but its overall shape argues for the use of historical narratives principally in writing the history of that for which they are events in and of themselves—the history of images and representations of the past, and a corresponding deemphasis of extracting or mining presumed historical realities from them. After all, each piece of such a narrative is embedded in, and serves, an entire composition. What I am calling for is a reversal of the traditional ways in which historical narratives have been used—not to demote them, as authors like Bloch and Cantor have done, to the role of confirming what hard evidence suggests, but rather to elevate them to the role of providing crucial evidence for a unique dimension of the history of language, culture, ideas, and communication.

I do not know what shape Islamicate historiography will take or how we will come to know, without circularity, all we need to know; but in the future, along with Hayden White, " . . . I will consider the historical work as what it most manifestly is—that is to say, a verbal structure in the form of a narrative prose discourse that purports to be a model, or icon, of past structures and processes in the interest of *explaining what they were by representing* them."[18]

And in the end, may the reaction to this exercise in analysis be quite different from the response of a client to Mr. Sherlock Holmes's explanation of his conclusions, which he had drawn from logical reasoning and close observation:

> Mr. Jabez Wilson laughed heavily. "Well, I never!" said he. "I thought at first that you had done something clever, but I see that there was nothing in it, after all."
>
> "I begin to think, Watson," said Holmes, "that I make a mistake in explaining. *'Omne ignotum pro magnifico,'* you know. . . . "[19]

1. See Finley, *Thucydides,* passim, for a discussion of this same circular process in Thucydides' work.

2. Pratt, *Toward a Speech Act Theory,* p. 136. Throughout the analysis that follows, the reader is encouraged to make full use of the extensive translations provided in the Appendix.

3. Ibid., pp. 45–46.

4. The closeness of many of Bayhaqī's narratives to Labov's natural narratives might be explained by the possibility that they could have been oral or natural themselves, despite the fact that Bayhaqī says, as in this case, that he read them. See Appendix B, selection 10.

5. Labov considers the most effective evaluation to be the most embedded. By *embedded* Labov means that which is furthest away from the speaker and his own time, for example, placed in the mouth of a neutral observer. Using Labov's measurements, Bayhaqī's evaluations are often deeply embedded. According to Luther, "The Literary Analysis of *Inshā'* Texts," the possibility exists that in narratives such as Bayhaqī's, the most important evaluation is centered, not at the end. In the case of this narrative, then, Buzurgmihr's speech before he is imprisoned might contain the evaluation. Although I have chosen to explore the narrative structure here, the symbols (entombment and resurrection, light and dark), values, and other features that enhance the effect would be part of any complete analysis.

6. Pratt, *Toward a Speech Act Theory,* p. 129.

7. Ibid., p. 130.

8. Ibid., pp. 159–60.

9. Ibid., p. 202.

10. *TB*, p. 401/515.

11. See Hodgson, "Two Pre-Modern Muslim Historians," on the nature of Ṭabarī's "representation" of the past.

12. Pratt, *Toward a Speech Act Theory,* p. 203. One might eventually want to consider Pratt's belief that excessive deviance from the unmarked or normative case for a genre constitutes social deviance and rebellion (pp. 210 ff.).

13. H. Stuart Hughes, *History as Art and as Science* (New York: Harper and Row, 1964), p. 16.

14. Marc Bloch, *The Historian's Craft* (New York: Vintage Books, 1953), pp. 61 ff.

15. Ibid., p. 54.

16. S. N. Eisenstadt, "Social Institutions," *International Encyclopedia of the Social Sciences*.

17. For example, see ibid., pp. 56–57. In this regard, studies of perception like Ernst H. Gombrich, *Art and Illusion* (Princeton: Princeton University Press, 1961), are particularly important.

18. White, *Metahistory,* p. 2; in this effort at reconceptualization, semiotics will undoubtedly play an important role (e.g., Umberto Eco, *A Theory of Semiotics* [Bloomington: Indiana University Press, 1976]).

19. Arthur Conan Doyle, "The Red-Headed League," in *The Complete Sherlock Holmes,* p. 177.

Appendix A

Genealogy of the Ghaznavid Dynasty

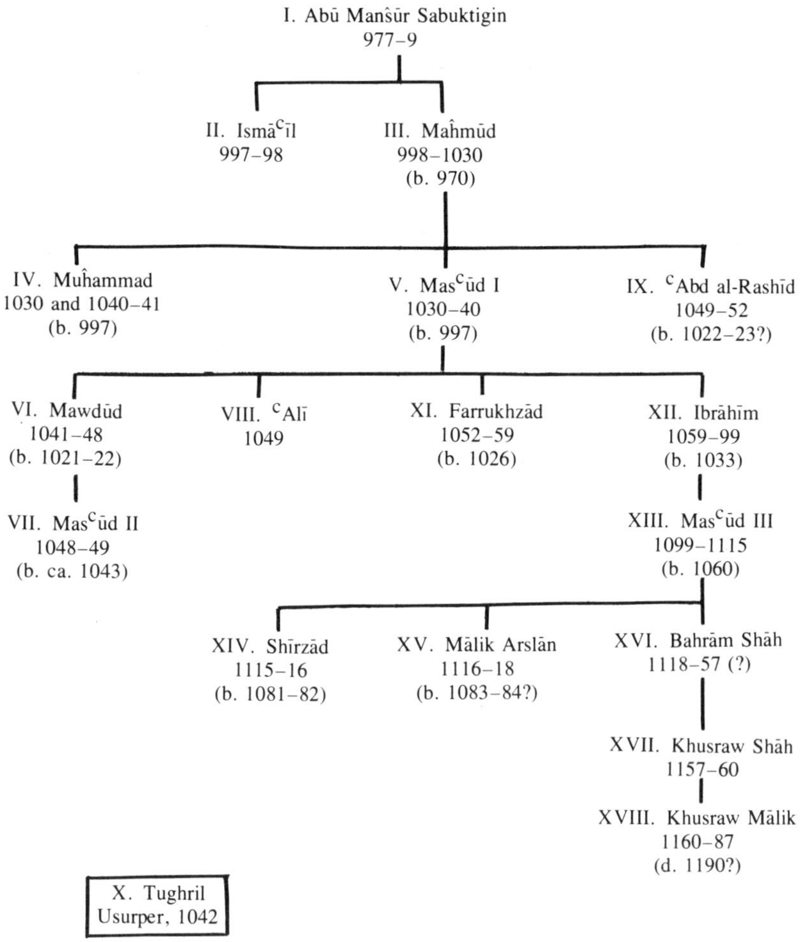

Source: Adapted from Bertold Spuler, "Ghaznawids," *Encyclopedia of Islam*, 2d ed., 3:1051.

Appendix B
Translated Selections from "Ta'rīkh-i Bayhaqī"

1. Amīr Muĥammad's Imprisonment
2. *Khut̂bah* on Kingship
3. Early Signs of Mas^{c}ūd's Greatness
4. Mas^{c}ūd's Pleasure House
5. Ĥasanak's Execution
6. Sabuktigīn's Dreams of Greatness
7. Moses and the Lamb
8. Aryāruq's Fall
9. The Amīr Yūsuf and the Slave Tughril
10. Buzurgmihr's Execution
11. An Occasion for a Royal Drinking Bout
12. *Khut̂bah* on Historical Method

GENERAL INTRODUCTION

If texts like *Ta'rīkh-i Bayhaqī* are to be studied from a number of theoretical perspectives, they will need to be made available to persons other than those who can read them easily in the original. What follows is the first extended English translation of parts of *Ta'rīkh-i Bayhaqī* since Morley's unreliable nineteenth-century effort.

I have tried to be as faithful to the original as possible—in syntax, vocabulary, and even word order—without rendering it either clumsy or elegant, neither of which it is. Wherever a literal translation of phrases and words in the Persian text cannot be made idiomatic in English, I have provided a free translation (enclosed in brackets) to clarify meaning. I have tried to translate the same Persian word with the same English word each time, but have had to take liberties with such fluid words as *ḥāl* and *kār*. Certain technical terms—particularly military, bureaucratic, and religious ones—have been left untranslated; where explanations are not provided in brackets, the reader is referred to the glossary at the end of this appendix. Poetry that I have chosen not to translate is indicated by ellipses. Both the Fayyāż and Ghanī 1324/1946 edition and the Fayyāż 1350/1971 have been used; where their readings differ, the one yielding more sense has been chosen or the ambiguity noted. Paragraphing from the latter has been preferred; pagination from both is provided.

The passages whose translations follow have been chosen because they have been used illustratively in the foregoing analysis and because taken as a whole they represent most of the different types of material in *Ta'rīkh-i Bayhaqī*. To paraphrase Bayhaqī himself, the stories may be long but there is nothing not worth reading once; the "plurality" of these texts, and the pleasure they afford any reader, may even inspire multiple readings and extensive further study.

Finally, my thanks go out to a number of colleagues and students who have made important suggestions about the wording of various sentences in the translation: Pouneh Alcott, Azam Attar, Joseph Roberts, Kasem Suleiman, and Michael Zwettler. Whatever errors remain are of course mine alone.

1. AMĪR MUḤAMMAD'S IMPRISONMENT (*TB*, pp. 8–11/8–11; 70–77/79–87)

Translator's Note

One of the first problems Bayhaqī encountered in presenting Sulṭān Masʿūd's accession was to explain his successful usurpation of the claims of his brother in such a way as to invalidate neither man. In these passages he focuses on a relatively sympathetic portrayal of the brother Muḥammad; in selections 2 and 3, on a complex validation of Masʿūd. To place the story that follows, it is important for the reader to know that when the first great sulṭān of the Ghaznavid house, Maḥmūd, died in 421/1030, Muḥammad succeeded in Ghazna as his father had decreed. But since he refused to divide power with his brother Masʿūd, as had also been decreed, Masʿūd, who was then in the far west of the empire, marched east and was proclaimed sulṭān by the troops of Khurāsān province, whereupon the troops of Ghazna (the imperial capital to the southeast) deposed Muḥammad at a place near Ghazna, Takīnābād. What follow are descriptions of the order for the imprisoning of Muḥammad at the fortress in Takīnābād, where he had taken refuge, and of the transfer of Muḥammad from the fortress at Takīnābād to a fortress in the region of Ghūr to the northwest. There it was decided that he be exiled to India, where later, in 432/1041, he was briefly raised to the throne again by the very rebels who had just killed his brother.

The first passage contains an example of the correspondence from Amīr Masʿūd that served to notify his new followers of his wishes. In the second passage Bayhaqī concentrates on the pathos and psychology of the situation, allowing character to emerge from speech and action, as did many Hellenistic historians in much earlier times. In a later passage he finds an instructive parallel in the third/ninth-century conflict between the sons of the famous caliph, Harūn al-Rashīd, reflecting the similar Hellenistic interest in history's repetitive patterns. In fact, in each of the twelve selections that follow, similarities to Greek and Roman historiography can be pointed out.

ʿAli [Ḥājib-i Buzurg of Muḥammad] gave Bū Ṣaʿīd-i Dabīr a letter to read, in the handwriting of Amīr Masʿūd, that they had not seen before; it had been written in his own hand:

> It is certain for us, and was certain at that time when our father the late Amīr passed away and the honorable Amīr [my] brother Abū Aḥmad [i.e., Muḥammad] was summoned to sit on the throne, that there was no fitting option for the realm other than that. And we had opened up a very significant far-away province and were heading for Hamadān and Bāghdād because those Daylamites [in the conquered province] did not present any danger. And we wrote a letter with that royal messenger to [our] brother in condolence and congratulations and sincere advice, [that] if he would listen and be our assistant and send right away whatever we had wanted, in no circumstances would we make it difficult for him; and we would summon [only] those individuals from the notables and Muqaddams of the army whom it was reasonable to summon; and we would head for Bāghdād so that the realm of the Muslims would be under the *firmān* of us two brothers. But [our] brother shut off his way to the right course, and imagined that perhaps he was on a level with the policy of us servants of the decree of God. Now since the affair has reached this point and he is staying at the Kūhtīz Fortress openly with his people in such a way that under no circumstances can he be sent to Gūzgānān, and it would be ugly bringing him by himself as if he had become a prisoner (for when he reaches Harāt we cannot see him in that condition), the right way is that he remain with honor and respect at that fortress together with all his people and such people who are at work there with him; for the *firmān* is not that anyone from his people be imprisoned. And Buktigīn-i Ḥājib is, with that degree of wisdom which he has, staying with his own people at the foot of the fortress; and we entrusted the province of Takīnābād and the police of Bust to him, so that he send an assistant to Bust; and he has an excess of kindness, which he will use in serving [Muḥammad]. For we are heading from Harāt to Balkh so that [our] residence this summer will be made there; and when Nawrūz [Persian New Year; falls at beginning of spring] passes, we will go to Ghazna and make the arrangements for our brother such as must be made, since no one is dearer to us than he. Let all this be recognized, if God the Mighty and Glorious wills!

And when they heard this letter, all of them said, "The Amīr had shown complete fairness at that time when he sent the messenger and now showed [even] more complete [*sic*]; what has the Ḥājib judged in this matter?" He said, "If you say [so], this letter must be sent to Amīr Muḥammad so that he know that he is remaining here by *firmān* of the Master, that his [Mas^{c}ūd's] guardianship and protectiveness are apparent and that we were all dismissed from his affairs.They said, "It must necessarily be sent so that he become aware what the situation is and then speak himself with Buktigīn-i Ḥājib." He told Dānishmand-i Nabīh and Muẓaffar-i Ḥākim, "Go to Amīr Muḥammad and present this letter to him and give him a bit of counsel and say nice things and explain that the opinion of [our] Master the Sulṭān in his case is very good, and when we servants arrive at the royal palace, we will make it better; and that in these two or three days these people will go entirely from here and your supervision is now with Buktigīn-i Ḥājib, and he is a prudent and wise man and will preserve your great rights—until you say to him what must be said."

And these two individuals went and told Buktigīn what task they had come for, for without his order no one could be at the fortress. Buktigīn assigned his Kadkhudā [to go] with them, and they went to the fortress and came before Amīr Muḥammad and performed the ceremonies of attendance. The Amīr said, "What is the news from my brother and when will the army go to him?" They said, "The news of our Master the Sulṭān is entirely favorable and in these two or three days all the army will go and the Ḥājib-i Buzurg after it, and the servants [i.e., we] have come for this," and they gave the letter to the Amīr. He read it, and a slight somberness appeared in him. Nabīh said,

"Long live the Amīr! The Sulṭān who is [his] brother protects the rights of the Amīr and shows benevolence; he [Muḥammad] must not be disheartened and must be content with the will of God and return to joyousness, for as they have said, 'The foreordained exists and worry is superfluous'" [in Arabic]. And the Amīr praised them and said, "Do not forget me." They went back and told Ḥājib-i Buzurg ᶜAlī what had gone on.

And the people entirely disbanded and took to preparing to go to Harāt because the Ḥājib [ᶜAlī] gave a *dastūr* for their going. And he also gave an order that they calculate the salaries and pensions of Amīr Muḥammad. And he ordered the ᶜĀmil of Takīnābād to take good care so that there be no error. And he summoned Buktigīn-i Ḥājib and turned over to him a *manshūr* with the royal signet for [him to supervise] the police of Bust and the province of Takīnābād. The Ḥājib got to his feet and turned to his Excellency and kissed the ground. Ḥājib-i ᶜAlī gave him a *dastūr* and praised [him] and said, "Keep your horsemen and send back the other army that is at the foot of the fortress with you to the campground so that they go with me. And be prudent and alert so that no error occur." He said, "I will obey." And he went back and sent the army that was with him to the campground and summoned the Kūtvāl of the fortress and said, "Caution of every kind must be taken now that the army is going, and without my order no one must be given way to the fortress." And all matters were settled, and the people began to go to Harāt to attend [Amīr Masᶜūd].

Mention of the Rest of the Affairs of Amīr Muḥammad (God Be Pleased with Him!) after He Was Imprisoned until He Was Transferred from Kūhtīz Fortress to Mandīsh Fortress

I have already explained before this that [when] Ḥājib-i Buzurg ᶜAlī went from Takīnābād to Harāt, how careful he was in the case of Amīr Muḥammad on account of the royal *firmān* of Sulṭān Maṣᶜūd that had arrived concerning assigning Buktigīn-i Ḥājib and putting the good and the bad [i.e., all responsibility for] this prisoner on his shoulders [lit., neck]. And now that I have finished [the account of] the going of the armies to Harāt and the seizing of Ḥājib-i ᶜAlī Qarīb and of the gaining of control over other affairs, so I have reached that [point] when Sulṭān Maḥmūd moved from Harāt to Balkh; that story I have halted to take up the rest of the circumstances of that prisoner so that what went on in that period when the army went from Takīnābād to Harāt and transported him from this Kūhtīz Fortress to the Mandīsh [in the region of Ghūr] be completely explained and the story completed. And when I have finished this, then I will return to when Amīr Masᶜūd moved from Harāt to Balkh, if God wills.

From Ustād ᶜAbd al-Raḥmān Quvvāl, I heard:

> When the army went from Takīnābād to Harāt, I and those like me who were the attendants of Amīr Muḥammad were like a fish cast out of the water and left on dry land, both plundered and helpless, and we were not heartened by the fact that we would be staying some distance from the base of Kūhtīz Fortress. And we were hoping that perhaps Sulṭān Masᶜūd would summon him to Harāt and a light [would] appear. And every day as was my custom I would go to attend [Amīr Muḥammad]—I and my friends the musicians and storytellers and old Nadīms, and we would eat something and go back at the time of Namāz-i Shām. And Ḥājib-i Buktigīn became increasingly cautious, but he did not keep any one of us from him [i.e., Amīr Muḥammad]. And each day there were more fine gifts such that if for instance he had wanted bird's milk [i.e., anything extraordinary], he would produce it right away. And Amīr Muḥammad (God be pleased with him!) even became somewhat more contented and began drinking wine, drinking continually.

One day we were drinking wine on that Khażrā', seated in front of him, the musicians playing; a host appeared from afar. The Amīr (God be pleased with him!) said, ''What could that be?'' They said, ''We cannot tell.'' He spoke to a confidant, ''Go down and hurry and see what that host is.'' That confidant left hurriedly and after a long while came back and said something in the Amīr's ear. And the Amīr said, ''Praise be to God,'' and became very refreshed and joyful, so that we all supposed that it was very good news, but we did not have the nerve [lit., face] to ask. When Namāz-i Shām was about to arrive, we went back. Me alone he called up and had himself very near to me, so much so that in all [my] life he had never had me so near, and said, ''Bū Bakr-i Dabīr went safely to Garmsīr so that now he is going on the Kirmān road to Irāq and Mecca. And my mind [lit., heart] has been set at ease for him, because he did not fall into the hands of these dishonorable [ones], especially Bū Sahl Zawzanī, who is thirsty for his blood; and that was his host and he was going by camel with complete assurance.'' I said, ''The kindness of God the Mighty and Glorious is such that the heart of a prince can be sure of Him [play on words—*khudā* and *khudāvand*].'' He said, ''There is [yet] another wish. If that [too] comes to pass, whatever happens to me, my heart will be happy.'' He turned away, keeping this [other] story to himself, so I went back.

And several days after that a camel-mounted express messenger arrived from Harāt at Ḥājib-i Buktigīn's [post], near Namāz-i Shām. And the Amīr (God be pleased with him!) was told, and Bū Naṣr-i Ṭabīb, who was one of [the group of his] Nadīms [and probably his physician] he sent to Buktigīn, giving the following message: ''I heard that an express messenger has arrived from Harāt; what is the news?'' Buktigīn answered, ''It is favorable. The Sulṭān has given an order concerning something else.'' When it was day, we were intending to go to the fortress to attend [Amīr Muḥammad]; some of Ḥājib-i Buktigīn's people said, ''Turn back today, because there is some obligatory task for the Amīr [to do]. A *firmān* has arrived with favor and kindness that that [task] be completed. Then you will [again] be going according to [your] custom.'' We became very anxious and turned back extremely uneasy and sorrowful.

Amīr Muḥammad (God be pleased with him!), when the second day arrived, grew frantic. He had said to the Kūtvāl, ''The Ḥājib must be asked what is the reason that none [of my people] are coming to me.'' The Kūtvāl sent someone to ask. The Ḥājib sent his own Kadkhudā to him and he delivered this message: ''An express rider has arrived from Harāt with a royal letter. A *firmān* has been given with complete favor and kindness in the case of the Amīr, and a confidant is coming from Harāt to the Amīr with several messages [containing] obligations [i.e., for Muḥammad to comply with]. He may arrive today. This is the reason, so he has said for you not to become anxious because there is nothing but good will.'' The Amīr said (God be pleased with him!), ''It seems very fine''; and he took a little comfort [from this], but not so much as was needed.

And at Namāz-i Pīshīn that confidant arrived. And he was called Aḥmad-i Tasht Dar, from the closest and most special ones of Sulṭān Mas^c^ūd. And Ḥājib-i Buktigīn sent him to the fortress right away, to stay until Namāz-i Shām and then come back down. And then it was verified that the messages from Sulṭān Mas^c^ūd were good: ''We have been informed of what has gone on, and the planning of any action now will be ordered out of necessity. My brother the Amīr must be of stout heart and not give way to any suspicion, because this winter we will be in Balkh and in springtime when we come to Ghazna, the plan of bringing [our] brother will be made. It is necessary that a list of whatever has been sent from the treasury with his Kadkhudā to Gūzgānān be given to this confidant, and also that whatever has been taken from the treasury by his order, of gold coins and clothing and jewels, either placed anywhere or which he has with him or in the Sarāy of the ladies of the Ḥaram, he give over entirely to Ḥājib-i Buktigīn for it to be returned to the treasury, and that a list of whatever is given to the Ḥājib be handed over to this confidant so that he will be informed of that." And Amīr Muḥammad (God be pleased with him!) gave the lists and gave over to the Ḥājib whatever there was from the treasury with him or the secluded ones of the Haram. And two days were spent until they finished this. And in those two days no one was allowed to go near the Amīr.

And the third day the Ḥājib mounted and went nearer the fortress and elephants with howdahs were brought there, and he gave a message that the *firmān* was such that the Amīr would be taken to Mandīsh Fortress because there he would be better taken care of, but that the Ḥājib would come with the army that was stationed at the base of the fortress, because it was necessary for the Ḥājib to go with those people who were with him for something important. Amīr Jalāl al-Dīn Muḥammad wept when he heard this, knowing what was going on. Whether he wished it or not, he would be brought out alone from the fortress, and lamenting rose up from the members of his household. The Amīr (God be pleased with him!), when he came down called out to the Ḥājib to say whether the *firmān* was such that he be transported alone. The Ḥājib said, "No, all [his] people will go with him; but [his] children are prepared for the journey as a group, because transporting them with him would be ugly. And I will stay here until all are brought safely and well after him, so that they may arrive near him safely at Namāz-i Dīgar."

The Amīr was transported and with him 300 horsemen and the Kūtvāl of the Kūhtīz Fortress with 300 foot soldiers; the Ḥaram ladies were seated in howdahs and [their] attendants on mules and asses. And many indignities occurred in the name of keeping scrutiny over them, and [people] were calling [it] indecent, and that was in order; after all, he was the son of Maḥmūd. And Sulṭān Mas^cūd when he heard even reproached Buktigīn severely, but there was still no escape [from it]. And that master of speech, Laythī the poet has spoken very well about this situation, and here are some verses:

. . . .

And at Namāz-i Dīgar this group caught up with Amīr Muḥammad; and when he saw them together with him, he returned thanks to God the Mighty and Glorious and chalked his experiences up to profit and loss. And the Ḥājib, also arrived, alighted farther [away] and ordered that Aḥmad-i Arslān [one of Amīr Muḥammad's most notable servants] be bound there and [then] transported to Ghazna for Sarhang-i Kūtvāl Bū ^cAlī to send him to Mūltān so that the city of [his] confinement would be there. And his [Muḥammad's] other servants, like Nadīms and musicians, were told, "Everyone go about your own business, because it is not the *firmān* for anyone of you to go near him [Muḥammad]." ^cAbd al-Raḥman-i Quvvāl said, "The next day they dispersed; but I and my friend, and also Nāṣirī and Baghavī, secretly went with him; for the heart of a friend would not allow taking our eyes off him, and I promised that we would go to the fortress and would go back when he was brought there. When they took him out of the Iyāz Forest and got him to Kūr and Alasht, the Mandīsh Fortress appeared from afar on the left. They turned off the road and went to the left, and I and this free man went with them to the base of the fortress. We saw the fortress, very high, with endless staircases and of such an extent that it would be much toil for someone to be able [to climb them]. Amīr Muḥammad came down from the howdah (and he had fetters) and stood still, in simple shoes and hat, and a ruby-colored brocade *qabā*. And we saw him but it was impossible to attend or signal. We fell to weeping such a flow of tears as the Tigris and Euphrates, just like a river. Nāṣirī and Baghavī, who were with us were driven away. And one [of them] was of the Nadīms of this Pādshāh and used to speak sweet melody and poetry; he wept and then spoke a fine impromptu poem:

"Oh Shāh, what was this that happened to you
Your enemy even came from a kinsman's shirt
[i.e., womb, amniotic sac]
Your trial surpassed [all] other trials
Your share of your father's realm turned into Mandīsh."

Then two very strong [men] grabbed his upper arms and he began walking with great effort; and every few steps he would go, he would sit for a good while and rest. When he had gone far but was still in eyeshot, he sat; a camel-mounted express messenger appeared from afar; Amīr Muḥammad saw him from the road; he did not go again until he asked why the express messenger had come. And he sent someone from his own to Ḥājib-i Buktigīn. The express messenger arrived with a letter; it was a letter in the handwriting of Sulṭān Mas^cūd, his brother. Buktigīn-i Ḥājib sent that up right away. The Amīr (God be pleased with him!) had sat at that point in the road, and we were watching; when he read the letter, he prostrated himself, then got up and went to the castle and disappeared from sight. And they delivered [his] family in there together, and several of his men servants whom the *firmān* [also] included. And Ḥājib-i Buktigīn and that group [of his] departed. I, ^cAbd al-Rahman Fuẓūlī, as the old men of Nishāpūr say, "orphaned and ten *dirhams* in debt," overtook those two persons who had grabbed the Amīr's arms and asked why the Amīr had prostrated himself? They said, "What business of yours is this story? Why don't you read what the poet says, and that is this:

Does our time return, oh tents,
Or is there no way to it after its passing?" [in Arabic]

I said, "Verily it is the day for the sound of this verse, but I will stick with that [question of mine] until I hear this one other point [i.e., the answer to my question] and [then] I will go." They said, "It was a letter in the handwriting of Sulṭān Mas^cūd to him that, 'We [have] ordered ^cAlī Ḥājib-i Buzurg, who has imprisoned the Amīr at [Takīnābād], to be imprisoned [himself] and his punishment be given over to his hand [Muḥammad's], because no servant shows this insolence with his own master. And I want this joy to be delivered to the heart of my brother, because I know that he will be very joyful.' And Amīr Muḥammad prostrated himself to God the Exalted saying, 'Today whatever happened to me made me happy, since that faithless ingrate was brought low and his wish in the world came to an end.'" And I went [away] along with my friend.

And I also heard from Ustād ^cAbd al-Raḥmān Quvvāl, seven years after I had begun this Ta'rīkh, Saturday the 11th of Rajab, 455 [Monday, 10 July 1063], and I was speaking about the story of the reign of Muḥammad, he said with several uncommon verses: "I remember Amīr Muḥammad requested this verse from me many times, so much so that there used to be few sessions in which I did not read [them], and the verses are:

> Your faithlessness is not a novelty nor a wonder
> But your faithfulness is the most novel of novelties
> There is no substance in your faithfulness
> The substance is in my desire and with my trust in the words
> of untruth and deception.

And although these two verses are the speech of a lover to a beloved, the wise man must look upon this with an eye to [its] lesson, because this has been an omen that was passing over the tongue of this Pādshāh (God's mercy upon him!). And there have been in his time all kinds of dark deeds of which he was unaware, along with such good things that he did with the army and the Ri^{c}āyah during his own Amīrate, just as is the subject of these two verses. The foreordained exists, and whatever God the Mighty and Glorious decides will come to pass. (God wakes us from the sleep of the incautious by his favor.) And after this I will relate in its own place whatever went on in the case of this prisoner. And Ĥājib-i Buktigīn, when he finished with this job, went to Ghazna as ordered so as to go from there to Balkh with the mother of Sult̂ān Mas^{c}ūd and other ladies of the Ĥaram and Ĥurrah-yi Khuttalī [Mas^{c}ūd's aunt], so as to get them there with caution.

2. KHUT̂BAH ON KINGSHIP (*TB*, pp. 95–109/111–30)

Translator's Note

This passage is one of the most difficult to translate, because Bayhaqī's usually fairly straightforward style is often contorted when he tries to express abstraction, metaphor, and analogy. The wide-ranging erudition, the intellectual virtuosity, that he seems to display is hard to evaluate, especially since it is absent in his narrative presentation. And any references to "ancient" teachers are overwhelmed by ideas and reworkings of clearly Islāmic origin. After all, Bayhaqī need not have seen the original sources but could easily have taken them from other compendia in which similar selections from a variety of works had already been made into a kind of reader's digest. Still the passage reflects a degree of integration and thematic coherence that makes it relevant to the narrative rather than extraneous as it might well have been.

The word *khut̂bah* usually refers to the sermon given in a mosque during the weekly communal prayer on Friday, a sense derived from its basic meaning of a somewhat formal address. Here both the formality and preaching are present, and the word is used to distinguish this from *ta'rīkh* or annalistic narrative. Clearly, too, Bayhaqī is concerned that his readers might react negatively to these sections, and, as in other cases where he digresses, he promises to return to the real thing, i.e., the narrative, as soon as possible.

Beginning of the History of
Amīr Shiĥāb al-Dawlah [Mas^{c}ūd] ibn Maĥmūd

Says Abū'l-Fažl-i Muĥammad ibn al-Ĥusayn al-Bayhaqī (God's mercy upon him!), although this section of the *Ta'rīkh* is preceded by whatever was mentioned previously, nevertheless in rank it takes precedence. To begin with, one must know that the deceased

Amīr (God's mercy upon him!) was the blossom of a young tree, from which tree *mulk* appeared; and it matured when Amīr Shahīd-i Mas^{c}ūd occupied the throne and the place of his father. And those learned ones who told the history of Amīr ^{c}Adīl Sabuktigīn (God be pleased with him!) from the beginning of his childhood to that point when he fell to the *sarāy* of Alptigīn (Ĥājib-i Buzurg and Sipāhsālār of the Sāmānids), and [who told] the harsh circumstances that passed over him to that point when he acquired the rank of the Amīrate of Ghazna and in [the course of] that became mighty and the business reached Amīr Maĥmud such as has been written and explained (and I also wrote to the end of his lifetime), [those learned ones] had done whatever there was on them [i.e., Sabuktigīn and Maĥmūd], and I also did whatever assisted me in the amount of my own learning until I reached this great Pādshāh [i.e., Mas^{c}ūd]. And I, who do not have learning and am not in their rank, have been like a passenger until I reached this point. And my desire is not that I explain to the people of this era definitively the situation of Sult̂ān Mas^{c}ūd (May God illuminate his proof!), because they have seen him and been assured of his greatness and courage and his singularity in all the tools of government and administration. Rather, my desire is this: that I write a history-foundation [or fundamental history] and erect a great structure [on it], such that the memory of them will last till the end of time. And complete success in that [endeavor] I wish from the Lord Everlasting, and God is the friend of success. And since in the *Ta'rīkh* I made the condition that in the beginning of the reign of each Pādshāh I write a *khut̂bah,* then occupy myself with telling the *ta'rīkh* [itself]. I now observe that condition, with the will of God and His help.

Section: Such I say, that the most excellent past kings are a group who were the greatest [kings]. And from that group two individuals are well known: one, Alexander the Greek; and the other, Ardashīr the Persian. Since our Masters and Pādshāhs have surpassed these two in all things, one must of necessity know that our kings have been the greatest on earth, because Alexander was a man whose princely flame took hold forcefully and flared up for only a very little while and then was reduced to ashes. And those great kingdoms that he took, and in the cultivation of the world that he opened up, his aim was [simply] this—that anyone could pass through [his] regions for any amusement. And when he asked of those Pādshāhs whom he conquered that they submit to him and call themselves his lessers, truly it resembles when one has administered a serious oath but has fixed it up so that it not be false. The revolution of the world's turning, what benefit [is it]? A Pādshāh must be commanding, for when he takes *mulk* and land and cannot command them, and soon his hand falls on another kingdom and it passes in the same way and he neglects that, he has given all voices [lit., tongues] every opportunity to say that he is weak. The greatest traces they have of Alexander, which have been written in books, [are] that he killed Dārā, who was King of ^{c}Ajam [i.e., Persia] and Fūr, who was King of Hindūstān. And with each one of these individuals he is known to have made a big, ugly error. His error with Dārā was that he took himself to Nishāpūr in the guise of a messenger to Dārā's army; they recognized him and wanted to seize him, but he fled. And his [Alexander's] companions [actually] killed Dārā himself, but the matter got turned around [i.e., in people's memory]. As far as his error with Fūr, it was that when the battle between them became protracted and drew long, Fūr invited Alexander to a duel so both would engage with each other. And it is not proper for a Pādshāh to choose this danger, but Alexander was a crafty and artful man. Before he came near Fūr, he prepared a trick for killing Fūr: from beside Fūr's army came a mighty cry and Fūr became anxious and looked to that side and Alexander took the opportunity and struck and killed him. So Alexander was a man with power and ambition and noise and lightning and thunder, as if he were a cloud in spring and summer that has passed over the Pādshāhs on the face of the earth, rained, and dissipated. "And verily the clouds of summer soon disperse'' [line of poetry in Arabic]. And for 500 years after him, the *mulk* of the Greeks that he held and spread over the face of the earth was true to a policy that Aristotle the teacher of Alexander made; and he said, ''The realm must be divided among kings so that they may be occupied with each other and not be engaged with Rūm [Arabic term for the Hellenic Mediterranean and Europe]. And they are called the 'party kings''' [i.e., the Parthians].

And as for Ardashīr-i Bābakān: the greatest thing that is related about him is that he revived a Dawlah-become-foreign and established a custom [*sunnah*] of justice among kings, and after his death a group went on with that [custom]. And upon my life this was [a] great [thing], but God the Mighty and Glorious had brought the period of the ''party kings'' to an end so that the job would go to Ardashīr with such ease. And the miracles that they tell of these two have been such as the Messengers [of God] have; and the family of this great Dawlah [i.e., the Ghaznavid] has had those effects and qualities that no one [else] has had, such as came [already] in this *Ta'rīkh* and others that will also come [later]. So if a slanderer or envier says that the lineage of greats of this great family has come from a slave-boy of obscure note, the answer to him is that since God (Mighty be His remembrance!) has created Adam, he has decreed such that *mulk* be transferred from this people to that people and from this group to that group. The greatest testimony to that which I am saying is the word of the Creator (Glorious be His Gloriousness, Sanctified be His names!), who has said, ''Say: O God, You are King of *mulk;* You give *mulk* to whom You will and remove *mulk* from whom You will; and You strengthen whom You will and humble whom You will; in Your hand is the Good because You are the Master of all things'' [Qur'ān 3:26] Further, one must know that the drawing off by the decree of God (Mighty be His remembrance!) of the shirt of kingship from one group and putting it on another—in that is Divine wisdom and the general welfare of the creatures on the face of the earth, since the grasp of men of the understanding of that has remained feeble, and no one has managed to reflect why this is so, let alone talk about it. And although this rule is correct and true, and there is no escape from being satisfied with the will of God the Mighty and Glorious, wise men if they commit this matter to consideration and keep drawing conclusions and deducing until they find light of this proof, they will be assured of the fact that the Creator (Glorious is his Gloriousness!) is the Knower of Secrets, who knows events not yet existent and has gone [forward] in knowledge of the unseen—that in the world in a certain land will be found a man with whom His servants will be content and secure, and that land will have blessedness and florescence. And he sets up reliable rules such that when it [*mulk*] arrives from that seed to that man, such has passed that the men of his time submit [to] his status and nobility and be obedient and submissive, and in that obedience they not give way to any shame. And just as He makes manifest this Pādshāh, He will make a crowd of people arrive with him, his helpers and servants who are fitting to him, one more great and sufficient and worthy and courageous and knowing than the other, so that the land and people of that [place] become more adorned by that Pādshāh and by those helpers for that period which God the Mighty and Glorious has decreed (May God bless the most virtuous of mortals!).

And from those Messengers (God's blessing upon them all!) such it has occurred from the time of Adam (Peace be upon him!) up to the Seal of the Prophets, Muŝtafā [i.e., Muĥammad] (Peace be upon him!). And one must observe that since Muŝtafā (Peace be upon him!) was unique on earth, [God] gave him helpers of such a sort that after his passing, how they acted and made Islām reach such a station as is apparent in *Ta'rīkh*s and *Sīrah*s [biographies of the Prophet]; and until the Day [of Judgment], this will be the Way [*Sharī*ᶜ*ah*], each day stronger and more visible and more eminent, even if the Associators [i.e., the idolatrous opponents of Islām] detest it [last phrase in Arabic].

And the work of the victorious, right hand [of God], pious, [Divinely] assisted *dawlah* that is today apparent, and [that] Sult̂ān Mu^{c}aẑẑam Abū Shujā^{c} Farrukhzād bin Nāŝir al-Dīn Allāh (May God lengthen his life!) has inherited (a lawful inheritance), even *it* has occurred in this manner. God (Mighty be His remembrance!), since He wants a dynasty with this greatness to become visible on the face of the earth, made Amīr ^{c}Ādil Sabuktigīn arrive from the ranks of infidelity to the ranks of faithfulness, conferred him on the Muslims as a blessing, and then raised [him] up until from the root of that blessed tree many branches appeared at many levels [and] stronger than the root. On those branches he arranged Islām and tied the strength of the successors of the Messenger (Peace be upon Him!) in them; so when it is looked at, Maĥmūd and Mas^{c}ūd (God be pleased with both of them!) were two bright stars concealed by a morning and an evening so that when morning and evening have passed by, the light of those suns is revealed. And behold, from those suns so many countless illustrious stars and glowing planets have been produced. May this great *dawlah* last forever, every day stronger against the force of the enemies and enviers!

And when I finished this section, I began another section such as may be closer to the heart, and the ears will grasp that more quickly and no great trouble be produced for the intellect. Know that God the Exalted has given a [i.e., one] power to Messengers (God's blessing on them all!) and another power to Pādshāhs, and has made it incumbent on creatures on the face of the earth to adhere to those two powers and to acknowledge that God-given straight path. And anyone who recognizes that [as coming] from the heavens and planets and zodiac signs removes the Creator from [their] midst, and be he a Mu^{c}tazilite or *zindīq* or atheist, his place is in Hell! ("We seek refuge in God from abandonment" [in Arabic].) After [i.e., From] the power of the Messengers (Peace be upon them!), miracles came, that is, things whose like mortals seem incompetent to bring. And the power of the Pādshāhs is clear thought and a long reach [lit., arm] and conquest and victory over enemies and the justice that they give, in accordance with the decrees of God the Exalted; for the distinction between [divinely] assisted victorious Pādshāhs and the tyrannical Khārijī is that since Pādshāhs have justice-giving and good conduct and good character and good effects, one must be obedient to them and must acknowledge their rightful appointment over them. And the tyrants, who have oppressiveness and bad conduct, one must call Khārijī and must wage *jihād* against them. And this is a balance on which good behavior and bad behavior are weighed and made manifest, and by necessity one can know which one of those two persons he must obey. And our Pādshāhs (those who have passed [on] may their God forgive [them], and those who are still living may He continue them!), one must observe what sort of their conditions have occurred and are occurring in [the way of] justice and goodness of character and virtue and piety and purity of life and making people and lands submit and shortening the reach [lit., arm, hand] of the tyrants and oppressors, until he become assured that they have been among the chosen of the Creator (Glorious is His Gloriousness, and Holy His names!) and that obedience to them has been and is a duty. If in the midst of this a defect appears in the place of these Pādshāhs of ours such that they experience a disappointment, and rarely does it happen that in this world they have seen many, one must observe wise men with the eye of wisdom and must not give errors a way to himself, because the decree of the Creator (Glorious is His Gloriousness!), which is preserved in pen as it has been uttered, is never changed; and there is no refutation of His judgment (Mighty be His remembrance!) [last phrase in Arabic]. And truth must always be recognized as truth, and falseness as falseness, as has been said, "Verily the truth is the truth even if mortals are ignorant of it, and the reprehensible is the reprehensible even if ordinary people do not think so." And I ask God the Exalted to guard us and all the Muslims from error and mistake with His power and beneficence and the abundance of His mercy [last two sentences in Arabic].

And when I finished the Khuṭbah, I saw it necessary to compose another section that is also useful to Pādshāhs and others as well, in order that each rank benefit from it according to the amount of its knowledge. So I begin with that wherein I explain what the quality of a wise man is such that it allows him to be called learned and what the quality of an unjust man is such that there is no escape from calling him ignorant; and one can be certain that anyone whose intellect is stronger, tongues [i.e., voices] are more outspoken in praise of him; and one whose intellect is smaller, in the eyes of men he is of less weight.

Section: The greatest sages that there have been in olden times have said such, that among the olden revelations that God the Mighty and Glorious sent to the Messengers of that time was that they tell men: "Know yourself, for when you know yourself, you will understand [other] things." And our Messenger (Peace be upon him!) has said: "He who knows himself therefore knows his Lord"; and this is an expression short but with many meanings; for anyone who cannot know himself, how can he know other things? He is like the beasts but cut off from the beasts, because they have no discernment and he has. Then when it has been well reflected on, beneath this very light saying and short statement is much benefit, for everyone who knows himself—that he is living and in the end cannot escape death and will rise again from the grave by the will of the Creator (Glorious be his Gloriousness!)—he knows his Creator and is sure that the Creator is not like one created, [that] He turns him to right faith and correct belief. And therefore he knows that there is a mixture of four things [humors, elements?] on which a body rests, and whenever one of those falls into error in the correctly set balance, deficiency becomes apparent.

And in this body are three faculties, one intellect and speech, and its locus is the head in partnership with the heart; and another, anger, and its locus is the heart; and the third, desire, and its locus is the liver; and they recognize each faculty [to be] the location of a spirit [*nafs*], although the source of those [spirits] is a single one. And speaking about this matter is long, for if one becomes concerned with explaining that, [his] motivation [soon] becomes lost. Therefore, I have concerned myself with a [few] points in order that [some] profit will become apparent. As for the power of intellect and speech, it has three loci in the head. One is called imagination, the first level [of which] can see and hear things; the other level is that which can discriminate and retain; so from this one can know truth from falsehood and beautiful from ugly and possible from impossible. And the third level is that which can understand and retain whatever may be seen. After this one must know that the greatest approximate analogy to this is that it is like a sage with whom they consult on matters, and the judgment and rules are with him; and that first [level] is like the just and truthful witness who tells whatever he hears and sees to the sage so that he give it to a third [party], and when he questions, gets [an answer]. This is the condition of the Nafs-i Gūyandah (spirit of speaking). And as for the Nafs-i Khashm-i Gīrandah (spirit of anger), with it is reputation and shame-avoidance and not experiencing injustice, and being concerned with vengeance when injustice is done to it. And as for the Nafs-i Arizū (spirit of desire), with it is love of food and drink and other pleasures.

Then one must know very well that the Nafs-i Gūyandah is the Pādshāh, predominant, victorious, prevailing; he must have a quite complete and strong administration and rule, [but] not so [strong] as to be destructive; and kindness [but] not such as resembles weakness. And then [Nafs-i] Khashm is the army of this Pādshāh, through which he finds out weaknesses and makes borders fast and stymies enemies and watches over the *riᶜāyah*. The army must be prepared and with preparedness carry out his *firmāns*. And the Nafs-i Arizū is the *riᶜāyah* of this Pādshāh; it is necessary that they fear the Pādshāh and army, fearing completely, and give [them] obedience. And every man whose condition is of this sort that I recalled, and who manages these three powers completely such that they fall into correct balance with each other, calling that man learned and full of complete intellect is permissible. Therefore, if in man one of these powers gains ascendancy over another, there inescapably will come about a deficiency in the amount of [i.e., corresponding to] the dominance. And when the makeup of man is well scrutinized, in that regard the beasts are one with him. But man, on whom God (Mighty be His remembrance!) has conferred these two blessings that are knowledge and action, of necessity is separate from the beast, and receives reward and punishment. Therefore, one can now necessarily know that anyone who attains this rank, on him it becomes incumbent to have his own self under his own management so as to go on whatever path is more praiseworthy and to know at what point the distinction is between good and bad, so as to incline toward whatever is most praiseworthy and be far from whatever is most blameworthy and abstain [from it].

And since this situation has been related, two ways are now going to be made clear: one path good and the other path bad. And that [situation] has signs through which one can know good and bad. The observer must reflect on the conditions of men; whatever of them seems good to him, he should know that it is good and then compare his own condition with that; for if he does not find [it] of that sort, then he will know that it is wrong. For men cannot know their own fault. And a wise man has confirmed that enigmatically—"'No one has the fault-seeing eye."

I see that every man sees the fault of another
He is blind to the fault which is in him
Every human being, from him are hidden his faults
And the fault which his brother has is obvious to him.

[Arabic poetry]

And when a man happens [to have] complete intellect, and the power of anger and the power of desire prevail in him, the faculty of intellect is put to flight and there is no escape from this person's falling into error. And it should be that he knows that he has fallen between two great enemies and that both are stronger than his intellect and that he must play many tricks on his intellect in order that he can overcome these two enemies, as has been said: "Woe to the strong among the weak" [in Arabic]. So when a weak [thing] falls between two strong [ones] one can know what the situation will be like, and therein faults and defects become conspicuous and virtues and merits remain hidden. And sages have likened the body of man to a house in which are a man and a pig and a lion, and to the man they assign intellect; and to the pig, desire; and to the lion, anger. And they have said whichever is strongest of all these three, it is his house. And this situation they see with clarity and know analogically that every man who can keep his own body under control and can break the back [lit., neck] of greed and desire, it is permissible to call him a wise and self-possessed man; and that man whose desire can become completely superior such that all inclines toward desire and the eye of his intellect remains unseeing, he is in the place of the pig, just as that person whom anger gains a hold over and in that anger nothing inclines to sparing and mercy, is in the place of the lion.

And one must necessarily make this problem clearer: "If a taunter says that if desire and anger should not have to exist, God the Mighty and Glorious would not have created them in the body of men, the answer to that is that in whatever the Creator (Glorious be His glory!) has created there is a benefit, general and perceptible. If he did not create desire, no one would incline toward food, which is the mainstay of the body, and toward copulation, in which is the perpetuation of reproduction, and man would not continue and the world would become depopulated. And if He did not create anger, no one would turn toward revenge-taking and guarding himself from shame and injustice and being concerned with retribution and keeping his wealth and household far from usurpers, and the public welfare would become wholly cut off. Notwithstanding that such must be, the praiseworthy thing is that the faculty of desire and the faculty of anger be in obedience to the faculty of intellect, that he recognize both [to be] in the place of a horse on which he is seated and rides around as he wishes. And if it is not docile, he makes it afraid with the whip right away and, whenever the need arises, beats [it]; and when desire comes, he shackles it and ties up its stall so it cannot be opened, for a man knows that these two enemies who are with him are enemies than whom he cannot be rougher and more powerful, so he must always beware of them lest one time they cheat him and make it appear to him that they are his friends, as is intellect, so that he do something ugly and think that it is beautiful, and cause someone injustice and think that he has done justice. And whatever he is about to do, he makes known to intellect, which is truly his friend, so that he may be secure from the deceitfulness of these two enemies.

And every servant upon whom God the Mighty and Glorious bestowed clear intellect and [who], with that intellect which is truly his friend, examines matters and with that intellect becomes a friend of knowledge, and reads the stories of those past and considers [them] and also looks to the deeds of his own time, [that servant] can know what a good deed is and what bad conduct is, and whether the consequence of both is good or not; and what men speak [about] and what they admire and what it is that remains memorable of man [is what is] the most excellent.

And there are many sages who have men go on that right path but as for themselves do not go on the path they have pointed out. How many men I see who do the "bidding unto good and the rejecting of the reprehensible" [according to Islāmic law, the duty of every Muslim] and say to men that such-and-such a deed must not be done and such must, but view themselves far from that, just as there are many physicians who say one must not eat such-and-such a thing because some illness results from it, and then eat a lot of that thing. And there are also Faylaŝūfs, and they are known as physicians of moral qualities, who prohibit very ugly deeds and when a place is empty, do them. And the community of ignorant ones who do not know deep thinking and what is the outcome of such acts, they are excused because they are ignorant; but the knowing ones, because they know, are not excused. And a wise man with resolve and sound judgment is he who, on account of his own clear reason, was of one heart with the community, and subdued [his] enthusiasm for vain desire. So if a man does not find complete assistance from his own power of resolution, he chooses a few persons (whichever ones are purer and more virtuous) to point out his faults to him; for when he strives with strong enemies who hold a place in the midst of his heart and soul, if from them he will come out weak, he consults with these sincere advisers in order that they show him the right direction, as Muŝtafā [i.e., Muĥammad] (Peace be upon him!) has said, "The faithful one is the mirror of the faithful one" [in Arabic]. And Galen, and he was the greatest sages of his era such that there is no equal who has come forth in the science of medicine and anatomy [lit., flesh and blood] and the dispositions of the body of men, and there is none who was more equal [*sic*] than he was in treatments of moral qualities, and he has in those Risālahs very fine [parts] about everyone's self-knowledge from which readers may have many benefits. And the main part of this work is the following; it says: "Everyone with intelligence who cannot recognize his own fault and is in error, it is necessary that he do such that he choose a friend from the group of friends [who] is wisest, most sincere, and most accomplished, and entrust to him the inquiry into his own conditions and habits and qualities so that he show him his good and evil unsparingly. And Pādshāhs are more needful than their fellow men of all this which I am saying because their *firmān*s are sharp like a sword, and no one has the gall to disagree with them; and an error that issues from them, that can be difficult to understand. And I read in the *Akhbār-i Mulūk-i*

^{c}*Ajam*, translated by Ibn al-Muqaffā^{c} [723–59], that the greatest and most learned of their Pādshāhs had the custom that continually by day and night until they would go to sleep wise men used to be seated with them from the wisest of those days, like guides and spies over them, who would explain to them something that went well and something that went badly from the affairs and customs and *firmāns* of those proud ones who were Pādshāhs. Then when a desire stirred him [one of the Pādshāhs] that is bad and he wanted to drive away that anger and aggressiveness wherein are [the causes of] instances of bloodshed and the eradicating of families, they would perceive that and show him the virtues and offenses [i.e., pros and cons] of that, and speak with him of stories and reports of past kings, and inform and instruct him in the way of *Shar*^{c}, in order that he deduce that with his own intellect and reason, and that anger and aggressiveness quiet down and he go along with that which appears to be necessary by virtue of justice and rectitude; because every time he gets angry and aggressiveness appears in him, in that hour a great bane has gained mastery over his intelligence and he becomes needy of a doctor to cure that bane so that that affliction subside.

And men, whether Pādshāh or other than Pādshāh, each one [of them] has a soul, and they call that Rūĥ, very large and substantial, and has a body, and they call that Jism, very small and insubstantial. And since physicians and healers choose the body, in order to treat quickly any sickness that appears, and make medicine and foods for that to make it return to well-being, [it would be] worthier for physicians and healers also to select the Rūĥ in order to also treat afflictions of that, for any wise man who does not do this, it is a bad choice that he has made, for he has passed over the most important and handled the most unimportant. And just as those physicians have medicines and herbs brought from Hindūstān and every [other] place, there are also medicines for these physicians, and those are intellect and selected experiences, whether seen or read from books.

And such I read in the reports of the Sāmānids, that Naŝr-i Aĥmad-i Sāmānī [r. 913–42] was eight-years-old when he survived his father; for Aĥmad was killed on the hunting ground, and this little one was seated on the throne in place of [his] father. That kingly-born whelp came out very well, mastered [lit., rode] all the manners of kings, and seemed without equal. But in him were wickedness and malevolence and aggressiveness and pride in excess. And he gave important *firmāns* out of anger, so that people became afraid of him. And with all this he would return to intelligence and would know that those qualities are very unacceptable.

One day he retired alone with Bal^{c}amī, who was his greatest Vazīr, and Bū Ŧayyib-i Mas^{c}abī, Sāĥib-i Dīvān-i Risālat, and both were unique [*sic*] in [their] day in all tools of learning. And he described his condition to them completely and said, "I know that this which comes from me is a great sin, but I do not overcome my own anger; and when the flame of anger subsides, I repent; but what use does it have, because heads have been cut off and households uprooted and the rod applied without limit. What is the [appropriate] course of action in this matter?" They said, "Perhaps the right way is that the Master station the wisest Nadīms before him in whom, with the complete wisdom that they have, may be mercy and compassion and forebearance, and give them a *dastūr*, that unsparingly when the Master becomes angry in excess, they intercede and subdue that anger with kindness; and when he commands [something] good, that thing praise in his sight so that he order more [like it]. Such we know, that if it be [handled] in this manner, this affair will return to [a state of] well-being."

This suggestion pleased Naŝr-i Aĥmad very much, and he approved their speech and praised this which they said, saying, "I [will] attach something else to this so that the matter be complete, and by [my] oath, I swear whenever I give a *firmān* in anger that for three days it not be signed into order so that during that period the flame of my anger may have become cool and conversations with intercessors have taken place; and then I will consider that and ask questions, so that if I have thus become angry justifiably, they will beat them with the rod somewhat, so that it be less than 100 [strokes; i.e., mitigated punishment]. And if I have taken to anger unjustifiably, I will nullify that punishment and will remove [it from] those persons concerning whom I have ordered that course of action, if they merit the removal. And if the punishment be according to the requirement of the Sharīᶜah, just as the Qāẑīs judge, it will be carried out." Balᶜamī said, and Bū Ṭayyib, that nothing remained [to be planned] for this affair to return to [a state of] well-being.

Then he [Naŝr] ordered, saying: "Go around and seek in my realm the wisest men, and whatever number is found, let them be brought to the place in order that I command whatever there is to command. These two eminent men went back very joyful because the greatest evil was theirs [to correct]; and they made a careful search of the whole body of wise men of the realm, and from the whole, seventy or so people were sent to Bukhārā. And Naŝr-i Aĥmad was informed; he ordered that the seventy-or-so individuals who had been chosen must be tested for one year until there have been chosen the few wisest persons. And they did just this until from among that group three old men emerged, wiser and more learned and more experienced. And they were brought before Naŝr-i Aĥmad and Naŝr tested them one week. When he found [them] unique [*sic*], he told them his secret and copied a very solemn oath in his own hand and recited it, and gave them a *dastūr* on interceding in any case and speaking freely. And one year went on like this; Naŝr had become another Aĥnaf-i Qays [a figure known among Arabs for forebearance] so much so that in forebearance he was compared to him, and unworthy qualities had become far from him once and for all.

This section has also come to an end and I know such that wise men, however long I have dragged out my remarks, will agree that nothing has been written that does not merit reading one time. And after this era men of other eras will return to that and understand [it]. And it is certain for me that today as I am composing, under this great majesty (May it always be!), there are great men who if they occupied themselves in telling the history of this Pādshāh [i.e., Masᶜūd] would shoot the arrow on the target [i.e., hit the mark] and demonstrate to men that they are the cavalry and I am the foot soldier, and that I do foot service for them with gouty lameness, and such would be necessary that they would write and I would learn, and when they would speak I would listen; but since the *dawlah* has employed them so that they care for larger tasks and do enough and be girded so that in no circumstance does weakness occur that an enemy or envier or rebel would rejoice and obtain his purpose, [so] how can they accomplish history-telling and observing such situations and reports and writing them, and how can they be devoted to that? So for [the purpose of] assistance to them I undertook this work, for if I hesitated, awaiting that time when they would complete this task, it might be that they would not, and when a long time would go by, these stories would rest far from the eye and heart of men and someone else would want [to do] this work who would not have that horsemanship on the horse [i.e., expertise] which I have and [thus] the great effects of this illustrious family would be effaced.

And when I finished these sections from the *khuṭbah*, I returned to the telling of the *ta'rīkh*, and I wish success from God (Mighty be His remembrance!) in completing that according to the rule[s] of Ta'rīkh.

3. EARLY SIGNS OF MASᶜŪD'S GREATNESS (*TB*, pp. 109–13/129–35)

Translator's Note

This passage follows on the heels of selection 2 and seems to apply Bayhaqī's general points about succession to Sulṭān Mas^c^ūd's in particular. The passage is particularly interesting because it contains examples of how Bayhaqī decided what to include, validated his witnesses, extolled the virtues of old pious women, described dream interpretation, and characterized the style of life of the upper classes.

And when I finished these sections of the *khuṭbah,* I returned to the telling of the *ta'rīkh*, and I wish success from God (Mighty by His remembrance!) in completing that according to the rule[s] of Ta'rīkh.

And before this in the previous narrative I have brought two cases among those concerning the career of this great Pādshāh (May God illuminate his proof!), one, of whatever significant deeds were done of his own accord after Amīr Maḥmūd (God be pleased with him!) returned from Rayy and entrusted that province to him; and the other of whatever went to him of good fortune by virtue of God (Glorious be His remembrance!) after the passing of his father, in the province of his brother in Ghazna up to when he arrived at Harāt and his affairs coalesced and his aims became completely fulfilled, so that readers be informed of those. And there were rarities and wonders that befell him in the days of his father; several were events that I brought entirely into this *Ta'rīkh* in their own places in the history of the years of Amīr Maḥmūd; and there were several other fine points quite worth knowing that had taken place in the days of [his] youth when he increased [his] stature and his father made him heir. And I had heard a little of those at that time when I was at Nishāpūr, not having obtained the good fortune of serving this *dawlah* (May God strengthen it!); and I was always wanting to hear them from a reliable man who would have seen them with his own eyes; but this opportunity did not occur. Until in those days when I took up this history-telling, my desire for accomplishing that increased, because it is long years since I am occupied in this task, and I am thinking that when I reach the blessed times of this Pādshāh [i.e., Mas^c^ūd], if those fine points have not come to hand, it might be negligence to omit them. Just such a good opportunity occurred in the beginning of the year 450 [1058] when Khvājah-yi Bū Sa^c^īd ^c^Abd al-Ghaffār Fākhir bin Sharīf Ḥamīd Amīr al-Mu'minīn (God prolong his strength!) did me the favor and sought me out in this corner of [my] retirement and took pains [to be] near me. And whatever I was in search of he gave me and then wrote in his own hand. And he is so trustworthy that anything his intellect and learning registers does not need any witness. For this Khvājah (May God continue his blessing!) was connected with the service of this Pādshāh since [he, Mas^c^ūd, was] fourteen years old; and in his service he experienced many ups and downs [lit., hot and cold] and experienced troubles and did great dangerous things with the like of Maḥmūd (God be pleased with him!). So necessarily when [his] master reached the throne, he considered him such that he held him in quite complete esteem and trust. My friendship with this Khvājah came about in the remaining days of the year '21 [1030], when the banner of Amīr-i Shahīd [i.e., Maḥmūd] (God be pleased with him!) reached Balkh. I found him quite completely learned, and he would sit in the Dīvān-i Risālat with my teacher, and most of his days he would be before this Pādshāh in special private sessions. And he made it necessary, rather it was [my] duty, that I observe the correct form of his address; but in the narrative that I wrote before this, that is not the custom. And any wise man who has discernment can know that "Ḥamīd Amīr al-Mu'minīn" is in the form of an epithet of the majesty of the caliphate, and may any address be greater than this? And he acquired this honor in the blessed days of Amīr Mawdūd, who sent him to Bāghdād as a messenger with a very significant task; and he went and did that task as wise men and experienced ones [would] do. He came back [having served his] purpose, as I will detail after this when I reach the days of Amīr Mawdūd. And in the days of Amīr ^c^Abd al-Rashīd, from among the whole lot of reliable men and servants, the trust fell to him for a journey to the region of Khurāsān, on a quite significant task of [arranging] a covenant with a group of eminent men who today hold the province of Khurāsān; and at that time I was taking up [my] job with the Dīvān-i Risālat, and those circumstances I [will] also detail in their place. After that circumstances both smooth and rough passed over this Khvājah, and in these auspicious days of Sulṭān Mu^{c}aẓẓam Abū Shujā^{c} Farrukhzād bin Mas^{c}ūd (May God lengthen his life and aid his standard!) the Ra'īs-ship of Bust was turned over to him, and he was in that region for a long time and showed good effects. And today he is residing in Ghazna honored and respected, at his own house. And I wrote these few fine points of his career; and I will reveal the particulars of his situation very clearly in this *Ta'rīkh* in their own places if God wills. And these few fine points from the *Maqāmāt* of Amīr Mas^{c}ūd (God be pleased with him!) that I heard from him [^{c}Abd al-Ghaffār] I wrote here in order that they be known. And when I finish this, then I will take up the seating of this Pādshāh on the throne at Balkh and narrate the history of his auspicious days.

A Maqāmah about the Designation of Amīr Shihāb al-Dawlah Mas^{c}ūd
and What Went on of His Circumstances
[from ^{c}Abd al-Ghaffār]

During the months of the year 401 [1010] Amīr Maḥmūd (God be pleased with him!) went on the conquest of Ghūr, from Bust on the Zamīndāvar Road [region in the southeast of present-day Afghānistān], and ordered that two of his children, the Amīrs Mas^{c}ūd and Muḥammad, and his brother Yūsuf (God's mercy on them all!) stay in Zamīndāvar, and that the heaviest baggage also be kept there. And these two princes were fourteen years old and Yūsuf was seventeen. And he had them remain there for the reason that he was honoring Zamīndāvar because that region was the first province that the Amīr ^{c}Ādil Sabuktigīn his father (God be pleased with him!) gave him. And he [Maḥmūd] ordered my grandfather (I who am ^{c}Abd al-Ghaffār)—at the time when that Pādshāh went to Ghūr and those Amīrs were brought down there at the house of Bayātigīn-i Zamīndāvarī who was Vālī of that region [i.e., Zamīndāvar] from the hand of Amīr Maḥmūd—to remain in attendance on them and keep in order whatever must be [kept] of their stipends and allowances. And my grandmother was a devout, self-possessed, Qur'ān-reciting woman, and she knew writing and Qur'ān commentary and dream interpretation, and she also [had] memorized many *ḥadīs* and reports of the Prophet (God bless him and grant him peace!). And along with [all] this, she used to make wholesome [lit., clean] things to eat and extremely fine sherbets, and in this was a past mistress [lit., a miracle; i.e., a marvel, a wonder]. So my grandfather and grandmother both occupied themselves in attending to those royal princes who had been brought down there, and from that old woman they would request sweets and foods and [other] wishes, and she would be very fastidious in that so that it would seem very agreeable. And they would summon her continuously so she would tell them *ḥadīs* and recite stories, and they would take pleasure in that. And I was very big, going to Qur'ān-recitation school, and I would attend them such as children do and [then] return. Until it happened that Amīr Mas^{c}ūd said to my Adīb, whom they used to call Bisālimī [*sic*]: "^{c}Abd al-Ghaffār must be taught something of *adab*." He taught me two or three *qaṣīdah*s from the *Dīvān* of Mutanabbī [Arabic poet, 915–65] and "Qifā' Nabki" [lit., 'Stay; let us weep," the opening words of the *Mu^{c}allaqah* of Imrū'l-Qays, pre-Islāmic Arabic poet], and for this reason I became more arrogant.

And in those days I saw them seated in that manner which Rayḥān-i Khādim was set over them by Amīr Maĥmūd [to oversee]; and he would bring Amīr Mas^{c}ūd and seat him in the *ŝadr* [seat of honor, probably raised, carpeted, or cushioned at head of a room] first; then Amīr Muĥammad would be brought and seated on his right, such that one of his knees would be outside the *ŝadr* and one knee on the mat [of the *ŝadr*]; and Amīr Yūsuf would be brought and seated outside the *ŝadr* on the left. And when they would mount for polo and [other] sport, Muĥammad and Yūsuf would be in attendance in front of Amīr Mas^{c}ūd with a *ĥājib* who was appointed [i.e., for that purpose]. And at Namāz-i Dīgar when the tutor would return, first those two individuals would retire and leave, then Amīr Mas^{c}ūd one hour after that. And Rayhān-i Khādim watched over all the arrangements, and if he would see anything improper, he would shout out.

And two times a week they would mount and pass out into the villages. And Amīr Mas^{c}ūd had the custom that each time he would mount he would offer them [i.e., the villages] his hospitality and many foods would be brought with great pains from my grandfather and grandmother, for many times he would request things secretly so that no one in the kitchen would have news [of it]. And there was a *ghulām,* Khurd Qarātigīn by name, who was in [on] this activity and would bring messages to my grandfather and grandmother (and they used to say that this Qarātigīn was the Amīr's foremost *ghulām;* at Harāt he found Naqīb-ship and after Naqīb-ship became Amīr Mas^{c}ūd's Ĥājib); and foods would be brought out to the Mughāsafah Plain, and he would also show great hospitalities [there] and invite Ĥasan, son of Amīr Farīghūn, the Amīr of Gūzgānān, and others who were his peers and bestow something on them after eating.

And Bayātigīn Zamīndāvarī, the governor of the region, was also a foremost *ghulām* of Amīr Maĥmūd; and Amīr Maĥmūd held him in high esteem. And he had a very useful and pious wife. And in those days when Amīr Mas^{c}ūd succeeded his father to the throne, he held this woman in great esteem out of respect for [her] past services, just as though she were on a par with the Queen Mother. And several times here at Ghazna in the Majlis of Amīr Mas^{c}ūd—and I was present—this woman would speak of those affairs of the times and explain those kingly qualities of the Amīr, and the Amīr would be very pleased by that and would question [her] much about those places and [their] villages and crops. And this Bayātigīn Zamīndāvarī, at that time when Amīr Maĥmūd acquired Sīstān and overthrew Khalaf [b. Aĥmad; Saffārid ruler deposed 393/1002], had brought with him 130 peacocks, male and female. They used to say they were indigenous to Zamīndāvar; and in our houses were some of them, and they used to hatch many babies in the domes. And Amīr Mas^{c}ūd used to like them and would go in search of them on the roofs. And at our house in a dome [they] laid eggs in two or three places and hatched babies.

One day from the roof he called out to my grandmother and summoned [her]. When she neared him, he said, "In [my] sleep I saw that I was in the land of Ghūr, and just the same as these places are, there was the light of a fortress, and there were many peacocks and roosters. I was taming them and putting them under my *qabā,* and they were fluttering under my *qabā* and clucking. And you [who] know everything, what is the interpretation of this?" The old woman said, "If God wills the Prince of Princes to seize Ghūr, then the Ghūrids will come to obedience." He said, "I have not taken over the authority of my father; how will I take them?" The old woman answered, "When you become great, if God the Mighty and Glorious wishes, this will be; for I remember the Sult̂ān your father when he was here in the days of [his] boyhood and he held this province. Now he has taken most of the world and is [still] taking; you will also be just like your father." The

Amīr replied, "If God wills." And in the end it came to be just as he had dreamed, and the region of Ghūr came to obedience of him. He has [had] a good effect in Ghūr such as has been recalled in this Maqāmah. And in the months of 421 when it happened that I, who am ^{c}Abd al-Ghaffār, became joined to the service of this Pādshāh (God be pleased with him!), he ordered me to bring with me several males and females from those peacocks; and six pairs were brought; and he ordered that those be placed in the garden, and they laid eggs and hatched babies. And at Harāt there is a lineage related to them. And the Amīrs of Ghūr came into the service of the Amīr willy-nilly, because he made such a strong impression [on them] that they were afraid of him and settled down. And for no time is it indicated nor read in books that the Ghūrids were so obedient and submissive to a Pādshāh as they were to him.

4. MAS^{C}ŪD'S PLEASURE HOUSE (*TB*, pp. 121–25/145–49)

Translator's Note

This passage, in its earthiness, humor, and irony, has a natural human appeal. Like Hellenistic historians, Bayhaqī took every opportunity to involve the varied emotions of his readers. Relations between royal father and royal son, on which the passage also focuses, seemed to fascinate Persian historians. But most of all, this story gives an insight into the complex and ubiquitous spy and communications network, or *barīd*, that was such an important source of imperial unity and control in ancient, as well as Islamicate, Irānian empires.

Now one [example] of the alertness and vigilance and circumspection of this magnificent Pādshāh [i.e., Mas^{c}ūd] (God be pleased with him!) is the following. In the days of his young manhood when he was [residing] in Harāt and, hidden from his father, used to drink wine, concealed by Rayhān-i Khādim he used to seek seclusion below the Sarāy and have male and female musicians brought to him by secret routes. In the palace complex of the Adnānī Garden he ordered them to renovate a house for midday naps, and make for it *muzammil*s [copper and brass pipes or taps that controlled the flow of water when turned from one side to the other] and hang pieces of linen in such a way that water from the pool would run, appear magically on the roof of the house, pass into the *muzammil*s, and moisten the [pieces of] linen. And they made pictures on this house from floor to ceiling, erotic pictures of [different] sorts of intercourse of men with women, all naked, such that the whole of that they painted [into] a "book" of pictures and stories and words. And outside these were drawn pictures befitting these. And the Amīr would go there at midday nap time and sleep there; and it is the mark of young men that they do such [things] and [things] like this.

And although Amīr Maĥmūd had a *mushrif* who was an associate of this Amīr his son, to be out with the Nadīms and "count his [i.e., Mas^{c}ūd's] breaths" and convey [them], it was agreed that that *mushrif* would not penetrate his private places. So he [Maĥmūd] had spies concealed from him among his own [Mas^{c}ūd's] people, like a slave or valet or old women or musicians or others than them who would report whatever they became aware of, so that of the affairs of this son nothing whatsoever remained hidden from him. But the associate would furnish him [Mas^{c}ūd] with names and give him bits of advice, because he was the heir-apparent and he [the associate] knew that someday the throne would be his. And just as his father had concealed spies on him, he also had [them] on his father, even to this extent, that whatever went on would be reported. And one of them was Nūshtigīn-i Khāssah Khādim, than whom no servant was closer to Amīr Maĥmūd. And his [Mas^{c}ūd's] aunt Ĥurrah-yi Khuttalī herself was his "seeker of knowledge."

So they wrote to Amīr Maĥmūd in total secrecy the report of this house with erotic pictures, and they indicated that "when one has passed from the Adnānī Sarāy there is a big garden; on the right side of this garden is a large pool and beside the pool on the left is this house. And night and day there are two locks on it, above and below. And they are opened at that time when Amīr Mas^{c}ūd goes there for a midday nap. And the keys are in the hands of a servant whom they call Bishārat."

And when Amīr Maĥmūd was informed of this situation, he came at midday nap time to the tent pavilion and spoke with Nūshtigīn-i Khāssah Khādim about this, and gave this order: "Tell Khayltāsh so-and-so, who is a fast rider who has no equal among fast riders, to prepare for himself to be sent someplace on account of something important, so that he go swiftly and verify the condition of this house. And no one must be aware of this matter." Nūshtigīn said, "I will carry out your *firmān*." And the Amīr slept, and he [Nūshtigīn] came to his own camp and entrusted a horseman from among his own crack horsemen with three of his own choice horses and instructed him to go to Harāt in total secrecy to Amīr Mas^{c}ūd in six days and six-and-a-half nights. In his own hand he wrote a *mulat̂t̂ifah* to Amīr Mas^{c}ūd informing [him] of these circumstances, saying, "After this horseman of mine, a royal Khayltāsh will arrive to see that house of yours, one-and-a-half days after the arrival of this horseman, someone who fears no one, who will go alone to that house and break the locks. The Amīr [will] take up this matter quickly as he sees [fit]." And that crack horseman went right away. And then someone summoned that Khayltāsh whose *firmān* it was [to be]; he came prepared. Amīr Maĥmūd arose from sleep in between two prayers, performed Namāz-i Pīshīn, finished, summoned Nūshtigīn, and said, "Did the Khayltāsh come?" He replied, "He came and is waiting at [my] camp." He said, "Bring paper and pencase." Nūshtigīn brought [them] and the Amīr wrote a safe conduct letter of this substance:

"In the name of God, the Merciful, the Compassionate. Maĥmūd ibn Sabuktigīn's order to this Khayltāsh is that he go to Harāt in eight days. When he arrives there he should [go] at once to the Sarāy of my son Mas^{c}ūd, fearing no one, drawing his sword and beheading anyone who prevents his going; and as soon as he enters the Sarāy, not looking to my son, enter the Adnānī Garden from the Sarāy; on the right side of the Garden is a pool and beside that on the left a house; he should go into that house and take a good look at what sort of walls it has and see what [is in] that house and return immediately, so as to converse with no one, and return to Ghazna. And the way of Qutlughtigīn-i Ĥājib-i Bihishtī [Mas^{c}ūd's Ĥājib] is that he will act according to this *firmān*, if he values his life (and if he shows respect, his life will go on) and to give the Khayltāsh any help that needs to be given until such time as he becomes satisfied, by the will and aid of God, and [so] Peace!"

When this [safe conduct] letter had been written, the Khayltāsh was summoned; and he [Maĥmūd] sealed that safe conduct letter and gave it to him, saying, "It must be such that you go to Harāt in eight days and do such-and-such and verify the circumstances [that] have been explained, and keep this story secret." The Khayltāsh kissed the ground and said, "I will carry out your *firmān*," and went back. The Amīr told Nūshtigīn-i Khāssah, "The Khayltāsh must be given a good-paced horse from the stable and 5,000 *dirhams*." Nūshtigīn came outside and spent time in giving the horse and silver, and in making the best selection of a horse. And he killed time [lit., burned the day] until Namāz-i Shām had been made, and [then] the Khayltāsh was given [his things] and left fast.

[Meanwhile] that crack horseman of Nūshtigīn, as he had been instructed, arrived at

Harāt, and Amīr Mas^c^ūd became aware of [the contents of] the *mulaṭṭifah*; and he ordered that the horseman be caused to alight someplace and at the same time ordered the plasterers to be summoned and to make that house white, and smooth it out as if there had never been paintings on those walls, and to furnish it and straighten it up and put the locks back on, and no one to know what the situation was.

And on the heels of this crack horseman the Khayltāsh arrived, at high noon on the eighth day. And Amīr Mas^c^ūd was seated on a sofa in the Adnānī Sarāy with his Nadīms. And Ḥājib-i Qutlughtigīn-i Bihishtī was seated at the threshhold with the other Ḥājibs and retainers and functionaries. And the Khayltāsh arrived, alighted from his horse, drew his sword, took his iron-headed mace under his arm, and left his horse behind. Immediately Qutlughtigīn got to his feet and said, "What is it?" The Khayltāsh did not answer and gave him the safe conduct letter and went down into the Sarāy. Qutlugh[tigīn] read the safe conduct letter and gave it to Amīr Mas^c^ūd and said, "What must be done?" The Amīr said, "Any *firmān* that there is must be carried out." And a commotion occurred in the *sarāy*, but the Khayltāsh kept on going up to the door of the house and went in. He saw a pure white house plastered and furnished. He came out and kissed the ground before Amīr Mas^c^ūd, saying, "There is no escape for servants from carrying out a *firmān*. And this unmannerly servant carried out the *firmān* of Sulṭān Maḥmūd. And the *firmān* is such that as soon as I have seen this house, I return. Now I [will] go." Amīr Mas^c^ūd said, "You came suddenly and carried out the *firmān* of the master my father the Sulṭān. Now by our *firmān* stay one day—for it may be that they have indicated [this] house by mistake—until they show [you] all the *sarāys* and houses." He [the Khayltāsh] said, "I will carry out your *firmān*, even though [this] servant has not been given this order [i.e., by Maḥmūd]." And the Amīr mounted, and two parasangs away is a garden that they call Bīlāb, a fortified place because he and his people used to have a place there, and he ordered that all the people of the *sarāys* gather there and evacuate [the *sarāys*], and the Ḥaram and the *ghulāms* left. And then Qutlughtigīn-i Bihishtī and the Mushrif and the Ṣāḥib-i Barīd brought the Khayltāsh around all the *sarāys* and showed each place to him one by one until he saw all of them and became assured that there was no house of that sort of which he had been informed. Then they wrote letters about the state of the case, and gave the Khayltāsh 10,000 *dirhams* and sent him back. And Amīr Mas^c^ūd (God be pleased with him!) came back to the city. And when the Khayltāsh arrived at Ghazna and retold completely whatever had gone on, and the letters had also been read, Amīr Maḥmūd said, "God's mercy upon him, about this child of mine many lies have been told." And he cut off any more of those searches and inquiries.

5. Ḥasanak's execution (*TB*, pp. 178–96/221–46)

Translator's Note

This detailed description of the arrest and execution of Ḥasanak is only one of several such descriptions. In the historiography of the ancient world, such descriptions were very popular, so much so that they often took the form of set pieces. There is no way yet to tell whether Bayhaqī's descriptions of the deaths of famous men are similarly stylized, but he clearly used them to play upon the emotions of his readers.

The Ḥasanak in question was a member of the prominent Mīkā'īlī family of Nishāpūr, who had served as Vazīr for Sulṭān Maḥmūd until his death. Because Ḥasanak took the side of Muḥammad in his dispute with Mas^c^ūd, when Mas^c^ūd won, Ḥasanak was arrested. His enemies at court, especially Bū Sahl-i Zawzanī, who was a confidant of Mas^c^ūd, reinforced the Sulṭān's desire to get rid of all his father's and brother's supporters and allies. He made it possible to justify in the case of Ĥasanak by reviving old rumors that he had been sympathetic to the Qarmatians, a Shī^{c}ī sect connected with the Fât̂imids of Egypt and enemies of the ^{c}Abbāsid caliph in Bāghdād and by extension of the Ghaznavids as well. As will be seen, the religious sympathies attributed to Ĥasanak had to be inferred from the fact that he had traveled through Fāt̂imid Syria and Palestine on his return from a pilgrimage to Mecca (414/1023) and while there had accepted a robe of honor from the Fāt̂imid caliph in Egypt. The parallel between Ĥasanak's and an earlier case, the execution of the general al-Afshīn by the ^{c}Abbāsid caliph al-Mu^{c}tasim (r. 833–42) on charges of Zoroastrian sympathies, did not escape Bayhaqī, who used it to preface the following description of Ĥasanak's arrest and execution. Bayhaqī's extended admiration for the valor of Ĥasanak's mother, and of a much earlier Muslim mother, is also to be noted, and resembles Hellenistic descriptions of female valor. Finally, the ways in which men at court are seen to influence the Sult̂ān's will is also significant.

Mention of the Execution of Ĥasanak-i Vazīr
(God's mercy upon him!)

I will write a section about the beginning of this affair of the execution of this man, and then the story [itself] will be explained in detail. Today when I am beginning this story, in Dhū'l-Ĥijjah in the year 450 [1058], in the auspicious days of Sult̂ān Mu^{c}aẑẑam Abū Shujā^{c} Farrukhzād ibn Nāŝir-i Dīn [r. 1052–59] (God preserve and keep him!), of these people about whom I will speak, one or two persons are living in forced retirement; and it is several years since Bu Sahl-ī Zawzanī [Mas^{c}ūd's ^{c}Ārīẑ] passed away. And I have no business replying to what came from him by way of trouble—even though bad came to me from him—since in any case, my lifetime has reached 65 and [I] must be about to follow him. And in the *Ta'rīkh* that I am doing, I make no statement that comes from prejudice or anger and [that will cause] the readers of this composition [to say], "Shame on this old man!" Rather I say that which readers can approve and not reproach.

This Bū Sahl was a pious, dignified, virtuous, cultivated man; but wickedness and maliciousness took hold in his nature—and there is no changing God's creation—and along with that wickedness he had no compassion and was always keeping an eye out for a great and powerful Pādshāh to become angry with a servant and punish that servant and dispose of him; this man [i.e., Bū Sahl] would jump out from a corner and look for an opportunity to stir things up and cause this servant a great pain, and then would boast, "*I* disposed of so-and-so!"—and if he did, he only saw and experienced it [i.e., he did so only indirectly]—and wise men would know that it was not so and would shake their heads and secretly laugh, "He is an exaggerator"; except for my teacher [i.e., Bū Naŝr-i Mushkān], whom he could not dispose of even with all that treachery he did concerning him, in whose case he could not attain his wishes since the judgment of God did not favor and assist his instigations. And besides that, Bū Naŝr was a farsighted man: in the days of Amīr Maĥmūd (God be pleased with him!), without betraying his own master, he observed the wishes of this Sult̂ān Mas^{c}ūd in all things, for he knew that the throne would be his [i.e., Mas^{c}ūd's] after [his] father. And Ĥasanak's situation was otherwise, for on account of a preference for Amīr Muĥammad and his supporting of the wishes and *firmān* of Maĥmūd, he offended this prince [i.e., Mas^{c}ūd] and did and said things that equals will not endure, much less a Pādshāh, just as when Ja^{c}far the Barmakid and these cohorts [of his] did the Vazīrship in the days of Harūn al-Rashīd [r. 786–809] and the outcome of their work was the same as issued from this Vazīr [i.e., Ĥasanak]. And for servants and slaves, watching the tongue with lords is necessary, since for foxes, quarreling with lions is impossible. And in his rank and riches and people, Bū Sahl was one drop of water from the river next to Amīr-i Ĥasanak—[his] learning occupies another place [i.e., higher]—but since transgressions issued from him [i.e., Ĥasanak] that I have brought up before this in the *Ta'rīkh* (one of which was that he said to ᶜAbdūs [Masᶜūd's servant], "Tell your Amīr, 'That which I do, I do by *firmān* of my master. If the throne ever comes to you, Ĥasanak will have to be executed.'"), [so] necessarily when the Sulṭān [Masᶜūd] became Pādshāh, this man sat on the wooden horse [i.e., the gallows]. And Bū Sahl and others than Bū Sahl, who are they in this? For Ĥasanak paid the consequences of his temerity and transgression. And the Pādshāh under no circumstances ignores three things: disorder in the realm, the disclosing of secrets, and insolence (and we seek refuge in God from abandonment!) [what follows colon is in Arabic].

When Ĥasanak was brought from Bust to Harāt, Bū Sahl-i Zawzanī handed him over to ᶜAlī Rā'iẑ, his servant; and there happened to him what happened to him of all sorts of contempt. For since there was no way out for him, his situation was subject to revenge and chastisements, and for that reason men censured Bū Sahl for being able to beat an [already] beaten and fallen man. The [real] man is that man whom they have said can accomplish "forgiveness along with his power" [phrase in Arabic]. God (Mighty be His remembrance!) said—and His speech is true—". . . the suppressers of anger and the forgivers of fellowmen, and God loves the virtuous ones" [Qur'ān 3:133].

When Amīr Masᶜūd (God be pleased with him!) headed for Balkh from Harāt and ᶜAlī Rā'iẑ transported Ĥasanak in chains and showed contempt for him, and there was revenge and intolerance and vengeance, I hear however from ᶜAlī (he told me once secretly) that from whatever Bū Sahl ordered of ugly actions in the case of this man, [only] one out of ten was done, and numerous kindnesses were [also] going on. And at Balkh he [Bū Sahl] persisted and kept nurturing [the idea] in the Amīr that Ĥasanak must necessarily be executed. And the Amīr was very forebearing and merciful, and did not reply. And a confidant of ᶜAbdūs said, "A day after the death of Ĥasanak I heard from my mentor [i.e., ᶜAbdūs] that the Amīr [had] said to Bū Sahl, 'There must be a justification and excuse for killing this man.' Bū Sahl said, 'The greatest justification is that this man is a Qarmatian and accepted the Egyptians' robe of honor so that the Amīr al-Mu'minīn al-Qādir Billāh [r. 991–1031] was annoyed and sent back a letter from Amīr Maĥmūd and now speaks of this continuously. And the Lord remembers that a messenger of the Khalīfah came to Nishāpūr and brought a banner and robe of honor, and what sort of letter and oral message there were on this matter. On this matter the *firmān* of the Khalīfah must be observed.' The Amīr said, 'Let me reflect on this matter.'"

After this my teacher [Bū Naṣr-i Mushkān] also told a story from ᶜAbdūs (who was on very bad terms with Bū Sahl): "Since Bū Sahl spoke so much about this case, one day the Amīr told Khvājah-yi Aĥmad Ĥasan, when he was returning from the levée, that the Khvājah [i.e., Aĥmad] should sit alone in the Ṭāram because there was a message for him to be carried by ᶜAbdūs. The Khvājah went to the Ṭāram and the Amīr (God be pleased with him!) summoned me [ᶜAbdūs] and said, "Tell the Khvājah-yi Aĥmad that the situation of Ĥasanak is not concealed from you, that in the days of my father he brought several pains to our heart and when my father passed away, what great designs he had in the time of my brother, but it did not go his way; and when God the Mighty and Glorious gave the throne and realm to us with such ease, [our] choice is that we accept the apology of sinners and not be preoccupied with the past. But concerning the belief of this man they are making statements to the effect that he accepted the Egyptians' robe of honor to the sorrow of the Khalīfah, and the Amīr al-Mu'minīn was offended and broke off correspondence with my father. And they are saying that he had given the messenger who had come to Nishāpūr and brought the covenant and banner and robe of honor a message that Ĥasanak, being a Qarmatian, must be executed. And we had heard this at Nishāpūr and do not quite remember it. What does the Khvājah say concerning this?" When I delivered the message, the Khvājah thought for a long time, then said to me, "What has happened to Bū Sahl-i Zawzanī that he has taken such an exaggerated interest in seeing his [Ĥasanak's] blood flow?" I said, "I am really not able to know. This much I have heard, that one day he was at Ĥasanak's Sarāy in the days of his [Ĥasanak's] Vazīrate, on foot and clothed in a *durā^{c}ah* [a coarse woolen upper garment worn by foot soldiers]. A Pardahdār had shown disdain for him and pushed him down." He said, "Oh Praise be to God! How much arrogance he must have in his heart!" Then he said, "Tell [your] master that at that time when I was a prisoner in the Kālinjar Fortress and they were intending to take my life and God the Mighty and Glorious protected [me], I made all sorts of vows to God that I would not make a statement about [shedding] someone's blood, true or not true. At that time when Ĥasanak came from the Ĥajj to Balkh and we headed for Mā Warā' al-Nahr [i.e., Transoxiana] and visited with the Qadr Khān, after returning to Ghazna they indicated to us that it was not known what had gone on in Ĥasanak's case and the late Amīr spoke in some way with the Khalīfah. (Bū Naŝr-i Mushkān has some true stories; it is necessary to solicit them from him.) And the Amīr is the Lord Pādshāh; what is to be commanded, he will command; for if he [Ĥasanak] is proved to be a Qarmatian, I will not make a statement about shedding his blood because I am pained by the shedding of all creatures' blood. And I spoke openly to that effect so that he [Ĥasanak] will not say that 'He [Aĥmad] has had a wish for this misery which I am in today.' And although it is so, I would not withhold my advice from the Sulṭān (for I would thereby be a traitor) in order that his blood and anyone else's blood not flow at all; for verily, blood-shedding is not a game." When I brought back this reply, he [the Amīr] reflected for a very long time, then said, "Tell the Khvājah that whatever is necessary will be ordered." The Khvājah got up and went to the Dīvān; on the way he told me, "^{c}Abdūs, as much as you can, keep the Lord on that [course; i.e., of not shedding Ĥasanak's blood], lest an ugly reputation be born [for him]." I [^{c}Abdūs] said, "I will carry out your *firmān*;" and I returned and spoke with the Sulṭān. Fate was lying in wait doing its work. . . . ' "

After this he [the Amīr] conferred with my teacher [Bū Naŝr]. He told me the story of what went on in that private session, saying, "The Amīr questioned me about the story of Ĥasanak, after that about the story of the Khalīfah, and said, 'What do you say about the faith and belief of this man and about [his] accepting the robe of honor from the Egyptians?' I exerted myself and elaborated entirely the situation of Ĥasanak and his going on the Ĥajj up to that point when he returned from Madīnah to Wādī al-Qura on the Syrian road and accepted the Egyptian robe of honor, and the necessity of [his] accepting [it], and turning back from Mawsil [Mosul] and not returning to Bāghdād, and deceiving the Khalīfah that the Amīr had ordered it. The Amīr said, 'Then in this case what sin has there been from Ĥasanak, for if he had come by the desert road, would not all his creatures have perished there?' I said, 'So it was, but they painted the Khalīfah some sort of picture such that he took great offense and lost his temper and called Ĥasanak a Qarmatian, and there has been correspondence and coming and going on this subject.' And the late Amīr such was his obstinacy and annoyance that one day he said, 'To this feebleminded Khalīfah it must be written that I for the sake of my estimation of the ^{c}Abbāsids have raised my finger in the whole world and am seeking a Qarmatian, and the one who is found and proved really to be one, [his] execution will be carried out. And if it is proved that Ĥasanak is a Qarmatian, a report will reach the Amīr al-Mu'minīn of what has gone on in his case. I have fostered him [i.e., Ĥasanak] and he is on a par with my children and brothers; and if he is a Qarmatian, I am a Qarmatian, too.' Although that statement was appropriate for a Pādshāh, I went to the Dīvān and wrote [instead] such writing as servants write to masters. And at last after [much] coming and going it was settled that the robe of honor Ĥasanak had accepted and those rare gifts which those Egyptians had sent to Amīr Maĥmūd he send with a messenger to Bāghdād to be burned. And when the messenger came back, the Amīr asked [him], 'At what spot were the robe and rare gifts burned?' for it had pained the Amīr greatly that the Khalīfah had called Ĥasanak a Qarmatian. And [even] with all that, the alienation and intolerance of the Khalīfah kept increasing, in secret, not openly, until Amīr Maĥmūd answered the Call [i.e., died]. The servant [i.e., Bū Naŝr] has explained what went on completely.' He [Amīr Mas^{c}ūd] said, 'I *knew* [it].'''

After this session, Bū Sahl still did not desist from his work at all. On Tuesday, the 27th of Ŝafar, when the levée broke up, the Amīr said to the Khvājah [Aĥmad] that ''he must sit in the Ţāram so that Ĥasanak be brought there with the Qāżīs and Muzakkīs in order that what has been acquired [by Hasanak] all be written in a title-deed in our name and witnessed for us.'' The Khvājah said. ''Such will I do,'' and went to the Ţāram. And a group of some of the Khvājahs and the A^{c}yān and the Sāhib-i Dīvān-i Risālat and Khvājah-yi Bū'l-Qāsim Kasīr (even though he was discharged from office) and Bū Sahl-i Zawzanī and Bū Sahl-i Hamdavī [also] came there. And he sent Amīr-i Dānishmand-i Nabīh and the Ĥākim of the army, Naŝr-i Khalaf, there. And the Qāżīs of Balkh and the Sharīfs and ^{c}Ālims and Faqīhs and Mu^{c}addils and Muzakkīs (persons who were of good reputation and well-known) were also present and seated there. When this entourage was ready, I who am Bū'l-Fażl and a group of people were seated outside the Ţāram by the shops awaiting Ĥasanak. In one hour Ĥasanak appeared, without bonds. He had an ink-colored *jubbah* [long open outer cloak] tinged with black, sort of shabby, a very clean *durā^{c}ah* and *ridā'* and a turban rolled Nishāpūr style [or made of Nishāpūr cloth] and new Mīkā'īlī boots on his feet and his hair smoothed down concealed under [his] turban with a little amount showing. And the Valī of the prison was with him, and ^{c}Alī Rā'iż and many foot soldiers on all sides. They brought [him] to the Ţāram, and he stayed until near Namāz-i Pīshīn; then they brought him back to the prison. And the Qāżīs and Faqīhs came out after him. I heard this much, when two people were talking with each other, ''What brought Bū Sahl to this, that he dishonored himself?''

After the Khvājah, he [Bū Sahl] came out with the A^{c}yān and went back to his own house. And Naŝr-i Khalaf was a friend of mine; I asked of him, ''What went on?'' He said, ''When Ĥasanak came, the Khvājah got to his feet; when he did this act of generosity, all got to their feet whether they wanted to or not. Bū Sahl-i Zawzanī did not have control over his anger. He got up, but not all the way, and muttered to himself in a rage. Khvājah-yi Aĥmad said to him, 'In all [your] deeds, not all the way.' [Then] he really was sorely troubled. And although the Khvājah wanted Amīr-i Ĥasanak to sit near him, he did not accept and sat on my right instead. And the Khvājah indicated his right side to Khvājah-yi Abū'l-Qāsim and Bū Naŝr-i Mushkān (even though Bū'l-Qāsim was long discharged, nevertheless respect for him was [still] very strong) and Bū Sahl was on the left side of the Khvājah. On account of this, he was even more out of sorts.

''And the Khvājah-yi Buzurg [Aĥmad] turned toward Ĥasanak and said, 'How are things going and how have your days been passed?' He said, 'There is cause for gratitude.' The Khvājah said, 'One must not be disheartened, because such circumstances come up for men; one must show obedience to the *firmān* in whatever the Master orders; because as long as there is life in the body, there is hope for 100,000 consolations, and there is a way.' Bū Sahl's self-control ran out. He said, 'Why does the Master talk so with some Qarmatian dog who is going to be executed according to the *firmān* of the Amīr al-Mu'minīn?' The Khvājah looked at Bū Sahl in anger. Ĥasanak said, 'I don't know who has been a dog; [all] mortals know my family and whatever I have had of means and servants and riches. I experienced [lit., tasted] the world and pursued my affairs, and the end of man's work is death. If fate has arrived today, no one can deny whether they take him to the gallows or other than the gallows, because I am no greater than Ĥusayn-i ^{c}Alī [martyred cousin and son-in-law of the Prophet Muĥammad]. This Khvājah [i.e., Bū Sahl] who is saying this to me has recited poetry to me and has stood at the door of my house. But the story of a Qarmatian must be better than this for them to arrest him for this accusation, but not [when they arrested] me. This much is well-known: I do not know of such things.' Bū Sahl's bile rose and he shouted out and was about to swear; the Khvājah shouted at him and said, 'Is there no respect for this assembly of the Sult̂ān that we are holding here? We are seeking to do a job here. When we have finished, this man will be in your hands for five or six months; then do what you want.' Bū Sahl grew silent and did not speak to the end of the session.

"And two title-deeds had been written for all the goods and properties of Ĥasanak [turning them] entirely over to the Sult̂ān; and one by one the properties were read to him, and he confessed to selling that willingly and gladly, and he received that silver [i.e., money] which had been specified, and those [reliable] persons wrote their witness and the Ĥākim registered [it] in the Majlis and the other Qāżīs also, according to the custom concerning things like that. When they finished with this, they said that Ĥasanak must go back, and he turned to the Khvājah and said, 'Long live the Khvājah-yi Buzurg! In the time of Sult̂ān Maĥmūd by his command I used to speak idly about the case of the Khvājah, which was altogether a mistake; but what escape is there from carrying out a *firmān*? They forced the Vazīrate on me, and that was not my idea. I had no bad intention whatsoever in the case of the Khvājah and I favored the Khvājah's people.' Then he said 'I have erred, and I am deserving of whatever punishment the Master orders, but our benificent Lord [i.e., God] will not abandon me. And I have renounced life, [but] my wife and children must be considered, and the Khvājah will pardon me.' And he wept. Compassion came to the faces of those present, and tears came to the eyes of the Khvājah and he said, 'From me [there is] a pardon, and he must not be so hopeless, for improvement is possible; and I considered and accepted from God the Mighty and Glorious that if the judgment goes against him, I will look after his people.'

"Then Ĥasanak rose and the Khvājah and his people rose. And when they all turned and went, the Khvājah reproached Bū Sahl much and he wished the Khvājah much apology and said, 'I could not overcome my own anger [lit., bile].' And the Ĥākim of the army and the Faqīh Nabīh reported on this session to the Amīr; and the Amīr summoned Bū Sahl and abraded him well, [saying], 'I have gathered that you are thirsty for this man's blood. Our Vazīr should have dignity and honor.' Bū Sahl said, 'I recalled that presumptuousness with which he treated the Master in Harāt in the days of Amīr Maĥmūd; I could not control myself, and no more such oversights will occur.'" And from Khvājah-yi Āmīd-i ^{c}Abd al-Razzāq [son of Aĥmad] I heard. "That the evening before the day they executed Hasanak, Bū Sahl came to my father at Namāz-i Khuftan; my father said, 'Why have you come?' He said, 'I will not go until the master goes to sleep, for he must not write a note to the Sult̂ān for intercession in the case of Ĥasanak.' My father said, 'I was going to write, but you have spoiled it, and that is very evil.' And he went to his sleeping place."

And that day and that night they took up the plan of Ĥasanak's execution, and they fixed up two messengers in the clothes of messengers who [supposedly] had come from Bāghdād and brought a letter from the Khalīfah [saying] that Ĥasanak the Qarmatian must be executed and must be stoned to death so that no one another time in defiance of the Khalīfahs would wear an Egyptian robe of honor, nor transport pilgrims through those regions. When the[se] matters were done, the next day (Wednesday, with two days remaining from Ŝafar) Amīr Mas^{c}ūd mounted and headed for hunting and a three-day revel, with [his] Nadīms and special attendants and musicians, and in the city ordered the city's deputy to have a gallows erected on the edge of the Musalla of Balkh, below the town [itself], and people were heading there. Bū Sahl mounted and came near the gallows and stopped above it; and horsemen had gone with foot soldiers to bring Ḥasanak. When they brought him out from beside the Bāzār-i^{c}Āshiqān and he arrived in the middle of the city, Mīkā'īl had halted his horse there. He came up to him and called him a traitor and gave him all sorts of ugly invectives. Ḥasanak did not look at him or make any reply. The common people cursed him [i.e., Mīkā'īl] for this bitter conduct he showed and for those ugly words he uttered; and the people of distinction themselves could not say what to do with this Mīkā'īl. (And moreover after Ḥasanak [died], this Mīkā'īl, who had married the sister of Ayāz [a favorite slave of Maḥmūd], saw many afflictions and suffered misfortunes, and today is alive and occupied in prayer and Qur'ān reciting. When a friend behaves in an ugly way, what escape is there from [his] being paid back?) And they brought Ḥasanak to the foot of the gallows (We seek refuge in God from a like fate!), and they had stationed the messengers who had [supposedly] come from Bāghdād, and Qur'ān-reciters were reciting the Qur'ān. They ordered Ḥasanak, "Take off your clothes." He put his hand underneath inside and tightened the string of his *izār* [loose breeches gathered at waist and ankle] and tied the ankle strings of his *izār* and drew [off] his *jubbah* and shirt and threw them [away] with his turban and stood naked except for his *izār,* his hands together, his body like white silver, and his face [beautiful] like 100,000 images, and all the people cried in pain. A helmet sheathed in iron had been brought, intentionally narrow such that his face and head were not covered, but they [i.e., others] called out, "Cover his head and face so that they not be marred by stones, since we are going to send his head to Bāghdād for the Khalīfah." And they kept Ḥasanak just like this, and he was moving his lips and reciting something until they would bring him a larger helmet; and meanwhile Aḥmad-i Jāmahdār came mounted and faced Hasanak and gave him a message, "The Lord Sultān says, 'This is your wish, that you had requested of us: "If you become Pādshāh, execute me." We would have forgiven you, but the Amīr al-Mu'minīn has written that you have become a Qarmatian, and you are being executed according to his *firmān*.'" Ḥasanak made no reply whatsoever.

After that they covered his head and face with the larger helmet they had brought. Then they called out to him, "Run!" He did not speak or pay any attention to them. Everyone said, "Have you no shame? [At least] *take* the man you are about to kill to the gallows!" [or "To take a man you are about to kill to the gallows by running him there."] And a big commotion was about to start; the horsemen rushed to the people and suppressed that commotion. And they took Ḥasanak toward the gallows and delivered him to the place [of execution], [seating him] on a mount he had never sat on [i.e., the gallows]. And his executioner bound him firmly and brought down the noose, and they called out for people to stone him; no one laid a hand on the stones and everyone wept bitterly, especially the Nishāpūrīs. Then they gave out silver [i.e., money] to a handful of rogues so that they would throw stones; but the man himself had died because the executioner had thrown the noose around his throat and strangled him. This is Ḥasanak and his fortune. And his saying which he used to say (God's mercy upon him!) was this: "The prayer of the Nishāpūrīs will save me." But it did not. And if the Muslims plunder the land and water, neither land remaining nor water, no amount of *ghulāms* and properties and goods and gold and silver and riches will avail. He went, and this group of people that had made this plot also went (God's mercy on them!); and this is a tale with many lessons. And all these causes of contention and strife for the sake of the vanities of the world, they left behind. How foolish the man who ties his heart to this world, which gives blessings but [also] takes them back in an ugly way.

When they finished this, Bū Sahl and his people returned from the foot of the gallows and Ĥasanak remained alone, just as alone he had come from the belly of his mother. And after that I heard from Bū'l Ĥasan Kharbalī, who was my friend and one of Bū Sahl's intimates: "One day he [Bū Sahl] was drinking wine and I was with him; the assembly was well-arranged, with many *ghulām*s standing around; and the musicians were singing so pleasantly. Meanwhile he had ordered that the head of Ĥasanak be brought secretly to our presence and kept in a large dish with a domed lid; then he said for them to bring the first fruits for us to eat from. All said, 'Let's eat'; so he said, 'Bring it'; so they brought that dish and from far away they removed the lid. When we saw the head of Ĥasanak, we were all shocked and I fainted; and Bū Sahl laughed [and] with a cup of wine he had in his hand poured [some wine] into the garden; and they took the head back. And the next day in private I reproached him much and he said, 'You are a chicken-hearted man. The head[s] of enemies must be [treated] like this.' And this story became public, and everyone censured him greatly on account of it and cursed him." And that day that they had executed Ĥasanak, my teacher [i.e., Bū Naŝr-i Mushkān] fasted and was very sorrowful and pensive such as I had never seen him, saying, "What hope remains?" And Khvājah-yi Aĥmad-i Ĥasan [Maymandī] was also in this condition and did not sit in the Dīvān.

And Ĥasanak was left hanging for nearly seven years; his feet were worn down and withered so that no trace was left of them when they took him down, as instructed; and they buried him such that no one knows where his head is and where his body. And the mother of Ĥasanak was a very brave woman; I heard that for two or three months this story was hidden from her. When she heard, she did not complain as women are wont to do. Rather she cried in pain such that those present wept blood from her pain. Then she said, "What a great man this son of mine was—that a Pādshāh like Maĥmūd gave him this world and a Pādshāh like Mas^{c}ūd gave him the next!" And she held for her son a very fine mourning. And any wise man who hears this will admire it, and so he should. And one of the poets of Nishāpūr spoke this elegy about his death:

> They cut off his head, which was the head of heads,
> Which was the ornament of the time and the crown of the realm.
> Whether he was Qarmatian or Jew or Pagan,
> Lowering him from throne to gallows was reprehensible.

And there has been a similar case to this in the world, which [has to do with the time] when ^{c}Abdallāh-i Zubayr (God be pleased with both of them! [i.e., Abdallāh and Zubayr, his father]) ascended to the Caliphate at Mecca, and the Hijāz and Irāq became committed to him. And his brother Mus^{c}ab, as his deputy, took Baŝra and Kūfah and the Savād [Lower Irāq]. And ^{c}Abd al-Mālik-i Marwān [Umayyad Khalīfah] headed for Mus^{c}ab with a very large army that contained his men and equipment and provisions. And a great battle broke out between them, and Mus^{c}ab was killed. ^{c}Abd al-Mālik returned to Syria and sent Ĥajjāj-i Yūsuf to Mecca with an ample and well-prepared army—such stories as are recorded in detail in the history books. Ĥajjāj arrived with the army and joined with ^{c}Abdallāh in battle. And Mecca was besieged and ^{c}Abdallāh took refuge in the Mosque of Mecca, and the battle grew fierce, and the catapults were prepared against the House [i.e., the Ka'bah], and stones were thrown until one pillar was brought down. And ^{c}Abdallāh, since his situation had become so restricted, stopped fighting. And Ĥajjāj sent a messenger to him [saying], "One or two days remain from your being taken, and I know that you will not come out on the safe conduct that I will give you; come out [then] by order of ^{c}Abd al-Mālik so that I can send you to Syria without bonds, honorably and respectably. Thus will he know [i.e., you], what must be done so that no more ruin occur in the Ĥaram [Sacred Precinct of Mecca] and no more blood be shed.'' ^{c}Abdallāh said, ''Let me think about this.'' That night he took counsel with his own people who had stayed with him. There were many indications that he must go out so that civil strife not take place and no grief come to him. He came to his mother Asmā', who was the daughter of Bū Bakr-i Ŝiddīq [father-in-law of Muĥammad and first Khalīfah] (God be pleased with him!), and discussed the whole situation with her. Asmā' thought for a time, then said, ''Oh my child, this secession which you made against the Umayyads [family of Arabs in whose hands was the Caliphate], was it for the faith or the world?'' He said, ''By God, it was on account of the faith, and the proof of that is that I have not taken one *dirham* from the world, and this is well-known to you.'' She said, ''Then resign yourself to death and killing and mutilation as your brother Mus^{c}ab did, for your father has been Zubayr-i ^{c}Awwām, and your grandfather on my side was Bū Bakr-i Ŝiddīq (God be pleased with him!). And look what Ĥusayn-i ^{c}Alī (God be pleased with him!) [cousin and son-in-law of Muĥammad, who had also opposed the Umayyads] did. He was forebearing and did not yield by the order of the son of Ziyād-i Ubaydallāh [Umayyad governor before Ĥajjāj].'' He said, ''Oh Mother, I had also inclined toward what you are saying, but I asked for your opinion and wishes [lit., heart] to know them in this matter. Now I know and martyrdom has turned pleasant to me, but I am [still] thinking [about the fact] that when I am killed, they will mutilate me.'' His mother said, ''When a sheep is killed, no pain comes to it from being mutilated and skinned.''

^{c}Abdallāh prayed and recited Qur'ān all night; at the time just before dawn, he made his ablutions and performed the morning prayer with the community and recited Sūrah ''Nūn and Qalam'' [Qur'ān 68] and ''Hal a'tī^{c}ala'l-insān'' [Qur'ān 76] [both of which encourage resisting the unrighteous and promise rewards to the righteous] in the two *rak^{c}ah*s [sections of prayer ritual]. And he put on his mail and fastened on his weapons; and among the Arabs no one had done war on foot like him. And right away he took his mother aside and bade her farewell. And his mother straightened his mail on him and stitched the armhole and said, ''Chew these sinners up!'', such that you would say she was sending him to eat *palūdah*; and certainly she gave him no complaint as women [usually] do. And ^{c}Abdullāh came out. He found his army disbanded and disordered and disaffected from him, except for a group of people who were from his very own who wanted to be loyal to him, laden down with cuirass and mail and helmet and weapons. He shouted, ''Show your faces to me.'' All showed their faces to him. ^{c}Abdullāh recited these verses:

> Verily when I recognize my day, I am patient.
> When they recognize it, then they deny [it].

When they arrived at the battle, they stopped. (The day was Tuesday, the seventeenth of Jumādah I, the seventy-third year from the Hijrah [Sunday, 6 October 692].) And Ĥajjāj-i Yūsuf came out from that side with a great army and arranged them. He placed the Hims contingent opposite the Ka'bah and the Damascus men opposite the Banū Shaybah, and the Jordan men opposite Safā and Marwah [spots in sacred precinct associated with Hagar and Ishmael], the Palestinian men opposite the Banū Jamah, and the Qinasrīn men opposite the Banū Sahm. And Ĥajjāj and Ţāriq b. ^{c}Amr stood with a mighty army at Marwah and a large banner was placed there. ^{c}Abdallāh-i Zubayr, when he saw a limitless army placed toward him from every side, turned to his own people and said [in Arabic], ''Oh family of Zubayr, if you gave yourselves over willingly to me, we would be one family among the Arabs, cut off entirely from others than us and not associated with any disgrace. Now then, oh family of Zubayr, pay no heed to the clash of swords, for I have not been present in any place except that I was brought out wounded from amongst those who were killed. And I have not found any medicine for wounds worse than what I found in the pain of their occurrences. Take care of your swords as you would take care of your faces. I have not known a person yet who broke his sword and kept his life. And if a man loses his weapons, he is like a barren woman. Cast your eyes away from the gleam of swords, and let every man busy himself with his opponents. And do not be distracted by asking about me and do not anyone say 'Where is ᶜAbdallāh b. Zubayr?' Should anyone ask about me, I will be in the first ranks."

Then he said, "In the name of God, oh freeborn men, charge!" And he came out like a lion, attacking on every side, and there was no side into which he sallied forth with less than ten men, nine of whom fled in terror in front of him, such as foxes flee before lions. Lives were lost; the battle grew fierce, and the enemies were many. ᶜAbdallāh waxed powerful until he was contending with the group of men across from the gates in front of Ĥajjāj. And they were so near to being defeated that Ĥajjāj ordered the banner taken forward more. And fresh men and distinguished fighters came out from the heart of the army and [all] contended with each other. In this contending a stone hit ᶜAbdallāh-i Zubayr hard on the face and blood ran down his face. He cried out, saying,

Our wounds do not bleed on our heels,
But rather the blood drips down on our knees.

And another stone hit him harder on the chest, such that his arms trembled from that. One of Abdallāh's *mawla*s, seeing the blood, shouted, "They've killed the Amīr al-Mu'minīn." And the enemies were not recognizing him because he had his face concealed; [but] when they heard from the *mawla*, and realized that he was ᶜAbdallāh, many men rushed to him and killed him (God be pleased with him!); they removed his head and carried it to Ĥajjāj. He prostrated himself and shouted out that ᶜAbdallāh-i Zubayr had been killed. The Zubayrids forebore until all were killed, and the *fitnah* quieted down. And Ĥajjāj came into Mecca and ordered that that pillar that had been ruined by a catapult's stone be repaired and other structures built. And the head of ᶜAbdallāh-i Zubayr (God be pleased with both of them!) he sent to ᶜAbd al-Mālik-i Marwān, and ordered that his body be put on the gallows. The report of his killing was brought to his mother, who complained not at all, saying, "We belong to God and to God we return. If my son had not done such as he did, he would not have been the son of Zubayr and the grandson of Bū Bakr-i Ŝiddīq (God be pleased with both of them!). And after a while she came out. Ĥajjāj asked, "What is this old woman doing?" They informed him of what she had said and of her forebearance. He said, "Praise be to God the Mighty! If ᶜA'ishah, Mother of the Faithful [Muĥammad's favorite wife], and this sister [of hers, Asmā'] had been men, this Caliphate would never have reached the Umayyads. This is [true] courage and forebearance. A trick must be played so that perhaps she can be caused to pass by her son so [we can see] what she herself will say." Then a group of women were delegated to this task, and they conspired and made a trick so that Asmā' was led to that side. When she saw the gallows, she realized it was her son; she turned to a woman from among the noblest women and said, "Will not the time come that the rider will be caused to alight from this horse?" And she did not add to this and went away. And this story was taken to Ĥajjāj, who remained astonished and ordered that ᶜAbdallāh be taken down and buried.

And this story, however long it is, has many benefits; and I will bring up another two situations so as to establish that Ĥasanak had comrades in the world greater than him; if something happened to him which had happened to them, do not be astonished; and also if his mother did not complain and spoke such words [as I have reported], do not reproach me that this could not be, for between men and women there is much difference, and your Lord creates what He will and what He chooses.

Harūn al-Rashīd, when he had ordered that Jaᶜfar, son of Yaĥya-yi Barmak, be killed, decreed that he be made into four pieces and hanged from four gallows. (And that story is well-known, and I am not bringing it up so that [my] words get drawn out to great length and [my] readers grow weary and forget that *ta'rīkh* [i.e., of Mas^{c}ūd's reign]: and also Bū'l-Fažl believes that [certain] things ought not be spoken.) And Harūn had secretly appointed some people so that when anyone would pass under the gallows of Ja^{c}far and show signs of grief and compassion, he would be seized [by them] and brought to him and punished. And when the time came that Harūn came to regret his overthrow of the Barmakids, one day a man from Baŝra passed by. His eye fell on one of Ja^{c}far's gallows. He said to himself,

If it were not that our fear of the informers and spies of the Khalīfah never sleeps,
We would go around your trunk and touch it as when people touch the Black Stone [sacred object in Ka'bah at Mecca].

In an hour this story and these verses reached the ear of Harūn and the captured man was brought before him. Harūn said, "You have heard our decree. Why did you commit this blunder?" He said, "I had heard, but the Barmakids have given me assistance [lit., hand] of a sort that is unheard of. I wanted to reciprocate, secretly, and I did. And a blunder occurred in that I did not observe the *firmān* of my Lord; and if they [the Barmakids] should be in that state [that they are in], whatever happens to me I will deem rightful." Harūn requested the story; the man told it. Harūn wept and pardoned the man. And these long stories are not empty of rarities and fine points and lessons. [As promised, Bayhaqī follows this with another story, also about the Barmakids.]

6. SABUKTIGĪN'S DREAMS OF GREATNESS (*TB*, pp. 201–4/253–55)

Translator's Note

Bayhaqī's *khuṭbah* on kingship, selection 2, established the idea that rulership and messengership are both God-given. The origins and behavior of rulers could make that hard to believe. The founder of the Ghaznavid dynasty, Sabuktigīn, was even a slave, as were many Islamicate rulers. This story echoes the theme of God-given rulership, again through dream interpretation.

The placement of this story is also of interest. It bisects a flashback description of the background and careers of the Tabbānids, a prominent Nishāpūrī family of legal scholars whose good will had always been cultivated by the Ghaznavid sulṭāns. That flashback in turn interrupts the narrative that follows the account of Ĥasanak's execution (selection 5), a narrative of the negotiation of a marriage contract with the Qadr Khān, another important ally of Mas^{c}ūd. The Tabbānid account comes in because one of the messengers to the Qadr Khāns is a Tabbānid. The Sabuktigīn story comes in because the Tabbānids' relations with him are mentioned. Within that story is the story of Moses and the lamb (selection 7). Thus a four-level frame, or box, story is created, frame stories being, of course, an important technique of ancient Near Eastern narrative style, the most famous example being the *1,001 Nights*. It also reminds us how complex are the problems of organization of materials within an annalistic framework.

The Story That Had Gone on between Amīr ^{c}Ādīl Sabuktigīn
(God Be Pleased with Him!) and His Khvājah,
Whom He Had Brought from Turkestan, and
Amīr Sabuktigīn's Dreaming

Sharīf ᶜAbdū'l-Mużaffar bin Aḥmad bin Abū'l-Qāsim al-Hāshimī, nicknamed al-ᶜAlavī, told me a story in Shavvāl of the year 450[1058]—and this is a great free man with nobility and lineage, and learning and excellent poetry, and he has nearly 100,000 verses about this *dawlah* and past Pādshāhs (God be pleased with them and preserve Sulṭan Muᶜaẓẓam Abū'l-Shujāᶜ Farrukhzād bin Nāṣir-i Dīn Allāh!). He said:

At that time when Amīr ᶜĀdīl [i.e., Sabuktigīn] went to Bukhārā to meet with Amīr Rażī [i.e., Nūḥ b. Manṣūr, Sāmānid ruler 976–97], he sent my grandfather Aḥmad bin Abū'l-Qāsim bin Jaᶜfar al-Hāshimī to the Amīr of Bukhārā [i.e., Rażī], and he sent the Amīr of Gūzgānān [territory in eastern Khurāsān] with him by virtue of the fact that he was Sipāhsālār, for them to fix things up [for the meeting]. And the Amīr [Rażī] complimented him [my grandfather] and gave a *manshūr* about his taking part of the *kharāj-i hāyeṭi* [a kind of tax] that he [Rażī] held. And when my grandfather died, Amīr Maḥmūd assigned my father this rebate and ordered a *manshūr*, because he had become the Amīr of Khurāsān and the Sāmānids were overthrown and he had become Pādshāh. And my grandfather said, "When we finished the war of Harāt and were proceeding to Nishāpūr, every day the routine was such that the Amīr of Gūzgānān and all his magnificent Sālārs, from those of Sāmān and Khurāsān, would come to the entrance of the tent of Amīr ᶜĀdil Sabuktigīn after Namāz [-i Subh] and stop the horses [there]. When he would come out to mount, all these grandees would alight until he mounted, and [then] proceed to the next *manzil* [*manzil*s are way-stations at fixed intervals from each other]. When he arrived at a *manzil* that they call Khākistar [which may be on the road from Mashhad to Marv], one day he held a levée there and ordered much charity to the dervishes; and after the Namāz-i Dīgar he mounted and rode out into those plains, and all the notables with him; and from place to place in those plains were elevations and mountain bases; we saw part of a mountain. Amīr Sabuktigīn said, 'I found [it].' And he halted his horse and made five or six *ghulām*s get down and said, 'Dig in such-and-such a place.' They began digging and went down a little way; a thick iron pin was found such as might belong to a stable, its ring separated from it; they pulled it out. Amīr Sabuktigīn saw that, got down to the ground from his horse and thanked God the Mighty and Glorious and prostrated himself and wept much, and requested a prayer mat and made two *rakᶜah*s of prayer and ordered that [they] bring this pin away and mounted and stood still. And these grandees said, 'What is this situation that has just happened?' He said, 'It is a rare story; listen.'

'Before I fell into the *sarāy* of Alptigīn, the Khvājah from whose [*sarāy*] I was transferred me and thirteen friends of mine from the Jayhūn [Oxus River] and brought [us] to Shubruqān [place near Balkh] and from there to Gūzgānān. And the father of this Amīr was then Pādshāh of Gūzgānān. We were brought to him. Seven people other than me he purchased. Me and five he did not choose. And the Khvājah passed on from there to Nishāpūr. And at Marv al-Rūd and Sarakhs [northwest of Marv] he sold four more *ghulām*s. I remained, and two friends. And they used to call me "Tall Sabuktigīn," and by chance three of my master's horses had become [saddle-] sore under me. When we arrived at this Khākistar, another horse became [saddle-] sore under me and my master had beaten me much and had put a saddle on my neck. I was very sad on account of my situation and life, and my misfortune that no one was buying me. And my master had sworn that he would bring me on foot to Nishāpūr, and he made to bring me just that way. That night I went to sleep with very great sorrow. In [my] sleep I saw Khiżr [a well-known pre-Islāmic servant of God associated with Moses in a story in Sūrah 18 of the Qur'ān] come near me and question me, saying, "Why are you suffering [*lit.*, eating] such sorrow?'' I said, ''From my bad luck.'' He said, ''Have no sorrow. I give you good tidings that you will be a great and famous man such that sometime you will pass this plain with many important men and you the greatest of them. Have a joyful heart and when you reach this rank, do good with God's creation and give justice so that your life be prolonged and the *dawlah* remain for your offspring.''I said, ''I give thanks.'' He said, ''Give me your hand and make [me] a pledge.'' I gave him [my] hand and promised; he squeezed my hand tight and I woke up. And it showed such that the trace of that squeezing is [still] on my hand. I got up in the middle of the night, performed my ablutions and stood in prayer until the fiftieth *rak^{c}ah* had been done, and I supplicated much and wept, and I perceived more strength in myself. Then I removed this pin and came out into the plain and buried the sign. When day came, my master loaded up and searched for the pin but did not find it; he beat me much with a whip and swore mightily, ''I will sell [you] at any price they want to buy you!'' And I walked the two *manzil*s to Nishāpūr, and Alptigīn was at Nishāpūr as a Sipāhsālār of the Sāmānids with a great retinue; and he [my master] sold me and my two friends to him. And the story after that is long, until I reached this stage that you see, and God knows best what is right.'''

Story of Amīr ^{c}Adīl-i Sabuktigīn with the Gazelle and Her Baby and His Taking Pity on Them and His Dreaming

From ^{c}Abd al-Mālik Mustawfī at Bust I heard, also in 450 [1058]—this free man is a *dabīr* and pleasing in speech and useful and an accomplished master [lit., a miracle, i.e., a marvel, a wonder] in accounts:

At the time when Amīr Sabuktigīn (God be pleased with him!) took Bust and the Baytūzids were overthrown, there was a chieftain in the region of T̂āliqān whom they called Aĥmad Bū ^{c}Amr, a man old and just and wealthy; Amīr Sabuktigīn admired him among all the men of that region and favored him and brought him near to him, and his trust in him was to the degree that each night he would summon him and he would be near the Amīr till late, and he would also give him private audience [where] he would tell [him] of his joy and sorrow and secrets. And this old man was a friend of my father, Aĥmad Bū Nâsir Mustawfī; one day he was telling my father—and I was present—''One evening Amīr Sabuktigīn was telling me stories and explaining the circumstances and secrets of his goings-on, and then said: 'Much before I acquired Ghazna, one day I mounted near [the time of] Namāz-i Dīgar and went out into the plain at Balkh, and I had only that one horse and [it was] very fleet and had run in such a way that every prey that would come before me would not escape.

I saw a gazelle and a baby with her; I urged my horse on and made a very powerful [effort] and the baby was separated from the mother and grew sad and I captured it and placed it on [my] saddle and went back, and the day had reached Namāz-i Shām. When I had ridden for a while, a voice came to my ear; I looked back again, [and] it was the mother of the baby who was coming after me and crying and begging. I turned [my] horse around in hope that she might be captured too, and I gave chase. Since the wind was blowing from in front of me, I turned back; and two or three times the same thing happened, and this little helpless one was coming [with me] and moaning until I arrived near the city; that mother of it kept coming and moaning in the same way. My heart went out [lit., burned] and I said to myself, "What will become of this gazelle baby? Pity must be taken on this loving mother," [and] I threw the baby back onto the plain. It ran toward the mother, and they both cried and went into the plain; and I arrived home; the night had grown dark and my horse had remained without feed. I became very despondent and went to sleep like a sorrowful [one] in chains. In [my] sleep I saw an old man very wise who came near me and said to me, "Oh Sabuktigīn, on account of that mercy which you showed to this gazelle and your giving this little baby back to her and leaving your own horse without feed, we will confer the city they call Ghazna, and Zavūlistān, on you and your offspring; and I am a messenger of the Creator (Glorious be His Gloriousness! and Hallowed His names, and there is no god other than Him!)." I woke up and felt strong of heart. And I always kept reflecting on this dream, and lo, I have arrived at this station. And I know for sure that *mulk* will remain in my family and offspring until that period when God (Mighty be His remembrance!) has decreed.'"

7. MOSES AND THE LAMB (*TB*, pp. 204–5/258–59)

Translator's Note

Stories like this about biblical figures appear less frequently in *Ta'rīkh-i Bayhaqī* than they do in examples of other Islamicate genres like Mirrors for Princess and *akhlāq* (collections of incidents of exemplary behavior or speech). It is not clear how Bayhaqī came to use this particular story. It is interesting that a similar story appears in collections of the Midrash as well. Here it is used to give further time depth, and thus validity, to the exemplary behavior attributed to Sabuktigīn in selection 6. It also reflects an interest in omens that occur in the youths of famous leaders, an interest that Islamicate historians shared with the historians of the ancient world.

The Story of Moses the Messenger (Peace Be upon Him!) with the Lamb, and His Taking Pity on It

When Pīr-i Ṭāliqānī had told this story [about Sabuktigīn and the baby gazelle], my father said, "Extremely rare and fine dream it has been; this showing forgiveness and pity is fine indeed, especially on these speechless [creatures] like a cat and its like from whom there is no pain [i.e., who cannot force humans to pity them]; for such have I read in the stories of Moses (Peace be upon him!) that, at that time when he was shepherding, one evening he was running the sheep toward an enclosure. It was the time of prayer and a dark night and raining hard. And when he arrived near the enclosure, a lamb escaped. Moses (Peace be upon him!) became anxious and ran after it with the intention that when he found it, he would beat it with [his] staff. When he had caught it, his heart went out [lit., burned] to it and he led it aside and brought his hands down on its horns and said, 'Oh helpless *darvīsh,* you are neither fearful for what is behind nor hopeful for what is ahead; why did you run away and abandon [your] mother?' And although it had happened in eternity that he would be a Messenger, for this compassion which he showed, prophethood became more confirmed on him."

These two rare dreams and this story I have explained so that it will be known and confirmed that this *dawlah* will remain in this great family for a long time. Now then I go back to the story which I had begun in order that it be completed.

8. THE DOWNFALL OF ARYĀRUQ (*TB*, pp. 220–30/282–96)

Translator's Note

Again here, as in selection 6, the role of good advisers is emphasized. Although Aryāruq is singled out as an unsophisticated Turk in need of professional assistance, it should be remembered that the Ghaznavid Sul̂tāns themselves were also Turks who relied on "Persian" professional administrators. Court intrigue is particularly well described here, in the persons of the so-called Pidarīyān and Maĥmūdīyān—the old guard loyal to the deceased Amīr and his appointee Muĥammad. The Aryāruq in question had been one of Maĥmūd's generals who served him as commander-in-chief of the Indian army. During Mas^{c}ūd's reign his enemies at court are said to have managed to make his brashness and cockiness seem like a real threat to the throne.

Mention of the Seizure of Aryāruq, Ĥājib-i Ŝāĥib of the Indian Army, and How That Went on up to When He Was Killed in Ghūr (God Be Pleased with Him!)
[Title in Arabic]

I have brought up before this the situation of Aryāruq Sālār of Hindūstān in the days of Amīr Mahmud (God be pleased with him!), how the swelling in his head became of such a sort that they took him as almost [lit., half] a rebel; and in the reign of Muĥammad, how he did not give himself up to them; and how, in that time when Khvājah-yi Buzurg-i Aĥmad-i Ĥasan drew him back from Hindūstān by some ruse and when he saw the Amīr, he said, "If Hindūstān is [to be] of use [to us], Aryāruq must not be there again." And [I told about] the coming of Aryāruq each day to the palace with several functionaries and shield-bearers, together with Ghāzī Sipāhsālār; and [about] the vexatiousness of the advancement and arrogance of these two individuals to the Maĥmūdīyān and Pidarīyān. And the situation was of this sort because these two powerful [ones], Aryāruq and Ghāzī, did not have anyone from whom a [wise] policy could come. And these two Sipāhsālārs did not have two Kadkhudās able in Dabīrī, or experienced in ups and down [lit., who had tasted hot and cold], for it is obvious what can come from Ŝa^{c}īd the Moneylender and lackeys like him, of obscure note and little worth; and the Turks hang around such men entirely, and do not look to the [possible] outcome so that inevitably damage will occur; since they have no experience, however energetic and generous they are with their own persons, whatever possessions and resources they have, nevertheless in Dabīrī they do not know their way around and do not know today from tomorrow [i.e., night from day]—what escape is there from the occurence of error? The Maĥmūdīyān, when they became aware of this situation and found an opening through which they could trip up these two men, stood together in plotting how they could "drown" these two Sipāhsālārs.

And chance befriended these circumstances. One [instance] was that the Amīr induced ^{c}Abdūs to deceive their Kadkhudās; and he brought [them] in secret to the Majlis of the Amīr. And the Amīr flattered them and gave [them]hope and arranged with them that they "count the breaths" of their own masters [i.e., spy on them] and tell ^{c}Abdūs whatever went on so that he explain it [i.e., to the Amīr]. And those two of obscure stature and little worth were deceived by those blandishments that they received; and they never dreamed, and they did not know that when their masters fell, they would be "humbler than sandals and lower than the dust" [expression in Arabic]; and how could they know, for they were neither schooled nor well read. And these two men were useful, and whatever went on, true or false, they would turn and tell ᶜAbdūs. And the Amīr became more displeased with Aryāruq from what he heard. And Ghāzī also fell a little in his sight. And the Maḥmūdīyān became more outspoken, and when they would say something of these matters in the Amir's presence, he would take notice and listen. They persisted in the plot and arranged that first a trick must be played so that Aryāruq would be overthrown, and when he fell and Ghazi remained alone, it would become possible for them to be able to overthrow him. And the Maḥmūdīyān obtained a little bit of a story about the affairs of these two Kadkhudās, that while drinking they had boasted that they were the servants of the Sulṭān, and [thus] they demonstrated that they had been deceived [i.e., by the Amīr]. And they [the Maḥmūdīyān] began to flatter them and give them something and imply that if it were not for their masters, the Sulṭān would order for them important tasks.

And another misfortune came [out of the fact] that Sipāhsālār Ghāzī was a sly one whom Iblīs (God curse him!) used not to be able to ensnare. He had never drunk wine. [But] when he found his aims coalesced and his measure [of success] became full, he turned to wine and took up drinking. The Amīr, when he heard, gave wine to both Sipāhsālārs. And wine is a great calamity when it is out of bounds, and anything can be done with excessive winedrinkers. And he [Ghāzī] began, by virtue of the fact that he was a Sipāhsālār, flattering the army and every day bringing a troop back home and providing an opportunity for wine; and Aryāruq would be nearby as well, and he would also be his guest; and in both parties when the wine took effect, the notables would praise these two Sālārs in Turkish and call Ḥājib-i Buzurg-i Bilkātigīn a faggot and ᶜAlī Dāyah female and the Sālār of the Ghulāms of the Sarāy—Buktaghdī—blind and lame, and others likewise; everyone they would fault and revile.

From ᶜAballāh, who was the Kadkhudā of Buktaghdī, I heard it said, after these two Sipāhsālārs fell:

> One day when the Amīr had not held a levée and was drinking wine, Ghāzī came back, together with Aryāruq, and brought many men with them and drank wine. Sālār Buktaghdī sent me secretly to Bilkātigīn and ᶜAlī and gave the message that these two unself-controlled [ones] had gone too far; if he [read "they"] saw fit, they would mount on the pretense of hunting, with twenty *ghulāms*, until he come near them with Bū ᶜAbdallāh and some *ghulāms*, and they would make a plan of action for this business. He [read "they"] said, "It seems quite fitting; we will go in the direction of Mīkhvārān until the Sālār [i.e., Buktaghdī] arrives." And they mounted and went. And Buktaghdī also mounted and brought me with him, and they brought a falcon and a hunting panther and all sorts of birds of prey. When they had come two parasangs, these three persons stopped above with three Kadkhudās: I and Bū Aḥmad Taklī, (the Kadkhudā of the Ḥājib-i Buzurg) and Amīrak (the confidant of ᶜAlī); and they appointed the *ghulāms* as bird-handlers for the hunt, and we remained six persons [i.e., Buktaghdī and ᶜAbdallāh, Ḥājib-i Buzurg Bilkātigīn and Bū Aḥmad Taklī, and ᶜAlī Dāyah and Amīrak].
>
> [Our] masters entered into conversation and for a time despaired of the Amīr and of gaining ascendancy over these two Sipāhsālārs. Buktaghdī said, "The surprise is that in the *sarāy* of Maḥmūd there is no one of meaner stature than these two persons, and they have kissed the ground in front of me a thousand times; but both are brave and manly. Ghāzī is a crafty one among the crafty—and Aryāruq is a jackass among jackasses; so Amīr Maḥmūd pulled them up and placed them in a high rank so that they became respectable. And Ghāzī attended the Sulṭān very agreeably at Nishāpūr until he reached this great rank. And although the heart of

the Sulṭān is not inclined toward Aryāruq, but [is] inclined toward Ghāzī; since they turned to wine and are doing wanton things [pun on a kind of grape], the heart of the Sulṭān could also be turned away from Ghāzī. But as long as Aryāruq does not fall, a plan cannot be made for Ghāzī; but when the strands of the plot [lit., rope] entwine, then both will fall so that we will be delivered from this humiliating situation." Ḥājib-i Buzurg and ᶜAlī said to make a plan [connected with] wine or to induce someone openly to ruin Aryāruq. Sālār Buktaghdī said, "These two [suggestions] are nothing and will not turn out, and we will be dishonored and the affairs of both of them will become strong[er]. The [better] course of action is that we conceal this business and show friendship and assign some people to make instigations and whatever the Turks and these two Sālārs are saying, exaggerate it and inform [us] where the affair gets to." They settled on this and the *ghulām*-bird-handlers came back. And the day had grown late and the hunting chests were opened so that they could eat and the servants and *ghulām*s and attendants all ate. And they returned and took up that which had been prepared for these two individuals.

And several days passed in this manner, and the heart of the Sulṭān became hardened to Aryāruq; and he held a private session concerning seizing him and expressed his dissatisfaction with Aryāruq to the Vazīr, saying, "The situation has reached that point where Ghāzī has been tainted from this, and certain things a king cannot endure. And it is not proper for Sālārs of the army to act independently, for protégés may not have such boldness. And it is obligatory to seize him; for when he has been seized, Ghāzī will come [back] to well-being. What does the Khvājah say about this?" The Khvājah-yi Buzurg thought for a time, then said, "Long live [our] wise Master! I swear that in nothing whatsoever do I betray the well-being of the realm. And the matter of the Sālār and army is a very delicate thing and entrusted to the Pādshāh. If the royal judgment sees [fit], he will excuse the servant [i.e., the Khvājah] in this one matter. And whatever he himself sees as right, he will do and command. If a servant says something in such matters, it may be that it does not happen to agree with the opinion of the Master and he will be displeased with me." The Amīr said, "The Khvājah is our deputy and the most trustworthy of all [our] servants, and one must necessarily discuss such matters with him, so that he will repeat whatever he knows and we will listen to it. Then we will turn it over in our mind and command whatever seems necessary from reason." The Khvājah said, "Now the servant can make a statement. Long live the Master! That which has been said concerning Aryāruq, [i.e., previously by me] that day when he came back, was some advice that was made in the case of Hindūstān, that there from this man issued transgressions and rashness, and also that there fell to him a great fame there and that he corrupted it to such an extent that the late Amīr summoned him, and he showed sloth and negligence in going and gave [all sorts of] explanations for that; and that Amīr Muḥammad summoned him [and] he also did not go and [rather] answered that Masᶜud is the heir of [his] father. If he assents to the accession of [his] brother and does not head from Irāq to Ghazna, then he will come to attend him.' And when he heard the name of the Master and the servant [i.e., I] said what there was to say, he came with the servant [i.e., me]. And up to this point I have not heard that rashness and disobedience has come from him such that you must be concerned about. And this unceremonious behavior and manifestation of excessive means and drinking of wine without [your] *firmān* with Ghāzī and the Turks is very easy [to take care of]; and I can make this right in one session [with him] in such a way that nothing will have to be said about these matters [i.e., publicly]. And the Master's jurisdiction has increased and there must be men of action [to help], and [ones] like Aryāruq are slow to come to hand. The servant has now explained that which has occurred to him." The Amīr said, "I know, and it is entirely as you were saying. And this matter must be kept hidden until I consider it further." The Khvājah said, "I will carry out your *firmān*," and went back.

And the Mahmūdīyān did not refrain from stirring things up to that point where it was thrown into the ear of the Amīr, "Aryaruq has become disloyal and has arranged with Ghāzī to inititate some evil; and if they do not find the occasion, they will go [away]; and beyond this, the army is in allegiance to him." One day the Amīr held a levée and all the men were together; and when the levée broke up, the Amīr ordered, "Do not go; let us drink wine," And the Khvājah-yi Buzurg and the ᶜĀriż and the Ṣâḥib-i Dīvān-i Risālat also sat with him; they began bringing trays, one before the Amīr on his throne, and one in front of Ghāzī and one [in front of] Aryāruq; and one before the ᶜĀriż-i Bū Sahl Zawzanī and Bū Naṣr-i Mushkān and one in front of every two Nadīms (and Bū'l-Qāsim Kaṣīr was seated according to the custom of the Nadīms). And *lāgūshtah* and *rishtah* had been ordered and very much was brought. Then these grandees, when they had eaten, got up and came back to the Târam of the Dīvān and sat and washed their hands. And the Khvājah-yi Buzurg flattered these two Sālārs and said nice things. And they said, "From the Master all is warmheartedness and flattery, and we serve him our souls a ransom for him [i.e., we would sacrifice ourselves for him]; but we are anxious and do not know what must be done." The Khvājah said, "This is madness and wrong imagination; it will lift from your hearts right now; wait until I finish and you two will be summoned." And he went up alone and requested a private audience and repeated [their] point to the Amīr and petitioned [him] to reassure them; after that, "The judgement of the Master will be right in what he sees and orders." The Amīr said, "Let me consider it." And all the people were called back and the musicians came and took up their work, and the revelry grew and every type of activity was going on. When the day reached Namāz-i Pīshīn, the Amīr signaled the musicians to stay silent; then he turned to the Vazīr and said, "The rights of these Sālārs are to such an extent that we had to order them recognized, if it is Ghāzī [who] made that service at Nishāpūr that no [other] servant made (and we were with the armies), and came from Ghazna; and [if] when he heard that we reached Balkh, Aryāruq hastened with the Khvājah and came to attend [us]. And we keep hearing that some individuals are showing envy concerning them and speaking idly, and they [Ghāzī and Aryāruq] are anxious. One must not consider that; [rather] one must trust this view that we have spoken, for we will not listen to the statements of anyone concerning them." The Khvājah said, "There is nothing left to say, and what greater praise may there be than [what] issues from the royal utterance." And both Sipāhsālārs kissed the ground and also kissed the throne and returned to their places and sat down quite exultant. The Amīr ordered that two special *qabā*s with gold be brought, and two sword-belts set with jewels, such as the value of both was said to be 50,000 *dīnār*s. And he summoned both again and ordered that the *qabā*s of both be placed on their backs and tied with their own hands. And the Amīr with his own hand threw the [shoulder] sword-belts over their necks. And they kissed [his] hand and throne and ground and went back, mounted, and left, all the functionaries of the palace with them, until they were back at their own residences. And I who am Bū'l-Fażl was keeping watch this day—I saw all this [and] recorded it in the diary for that year.

After their departure, the Amīr ordered two parties [for them]: gold goblets with long necks full of wine and fruit and sweetmeat plates and pots of narcissus were prepared for the two Sālārs; and he told Bū'l'Ḥasan Karkhī-yi Nadīm, "Go to Sipāhsālār Ghāzī and these will be brought after you, and three special musicians will come with you; and say, 'From our party you returned incomplete; [now] drink wine with the Nadīms, along with the sounds of the musicians.'" And three musicians went with him and footmen delivered these favors. And the Khvājah made several remarks concerning this matter such as he knew to say, and went back near Namāz-i Dīgar. And the others also began to go back [i.e., from the Amīr's party]. And the Amīr, since it was near evening, got up and went eagerly into the *sarāy*. And the Maḥmūdīyān grew very despondent on account of this situation, which had taken a new turn. Neither they nor anyone knows what is in the Unseen. . . .

And these two Nadīms came to these two Sālārs with these favors and musicians. And they performed the ceremonies of attendance and, when they heard the oral message of the Sulṭān, cheerfully drank wine and rejoiced much; and when they became drunk, they gave the Nadīms horses and gold and horse ornaments and clothes and silver and Turkish *ghulām*s, and fortunately they were returned; and they even bestowed clothes and silver on some of the musicians; and Ghāzī fell asleep. And Aryāruq had such a habit that when he sat in wine-drinking, he would drink three or four days, day and night; and this night he drank until day from that joy and flattery which he had received.

And the Amīr held a levée the next day; Sipāhsālār Ghāzī, more swollen with pride, came to the palace with much excessive ceremony. When he was seated, the Amīr asked, "Why has not Aryāruq come?" Ghāzī said, "He has the habit of drinking wine three or four days and nights in a row, especially on account of today's joy and flattery." The Amīr laughed and said, "Today we too must drink wine, and we will send Aryāruq a tray." Ghāzī kissed the ground as he went back. He [the Amīr] said, "Do not go"; and they began to drink. And the Amīr ordered that Amīrak-i Sipāhdār-i Khamarchī be summoned (and he relished wine-drinking; and Aryāruq had complete trust in him; Amīr Maḥmūd had also sent him to Aryāruq, in India, [to tell him] to come to the palace; and he returned in that month he passed away, such as I have mentioned before this), and Amīrak came forward. The Amīr said, "Fifty flasks of wine will be brought with you to the Ḥājib of Aryāruq; go and stay with him for he has complete trust in you, until after he gets drunk and sleeps. And say, 'We give you a *dastūr* not to perform attendance [on us], but to drink wine according to your habit.' Amīrak left; he found Aryāruq as he had been told, and he was strolling around the garden and drinking, and the musicians were playing. He gave the message. He [Aryāruq] kissed the ground and wept profusely. And he bestowed money on Amīrak and the footmen, and they [the footmen] went away. And Amīrak stayed [with Aryāruq]; and Sipāhsālār Ghāzī stayed there with the Amīr until lunchtime, then returned and took several Sarhangs and Ḥājibs with him and sat [down] to drink; and that day he bestowed a wealth of *dīnār*s and *dirham*s and horses and *ghulām*s and clothing; and Aryāruq also according to his habit fell asleep and got up and drank *rishtah* and went back to drinking wine until he did not have the slightest idea of what he was doing; that day and that night and the next day he rested not at all.

And the Amīr held no levée the next day; he had prepared for Aryāruq to be seized. And he came and sat on the Khaẓrā' opposite the Ṭāram of the Dīvān-i Risālat, and someone was coming secretly and reports of Aryāruq were being brought. In the midst of this, the time of Namāz-i Pīshīn having arrived, ᶜAbdūs came and said something in the ear of Bū Naṣr-i Mushkān. He got up, saying to the Dabīrs to go away so that the garden would be vacated. Except for me [Bū 'l-Fażl] all got up and went. He secretly said to me, "Send the horses back to the house and sit in the Dihlīz of the Dīvān, for it is of first importance that that be done; and be careful to be sure of whatever happens, and then come to me." I said, "Such will I do." And he went, and the Vazīr and the ᶜĀriż and the other people also went away together.

And Buktigīn-i Ḥājib, the son-in-law of ᶜAlī Dāyah, came to the Dihlīz and went up to Amīr and stayed one hour and came back to the Dihlīz; and he summoned Muhtāj Amīr-i Ḥaras and spoke secretly with him and he left. He brought 500 foot soldiers with full arms from every side and sent [them] back to the garden so that they stay concealed. The Indian Naqībs came and brought 300 Indians, and they were also stationed in the garden.

And a Pardahdār and a Sipāhdār came to Aryāruq and said, "The Sulṭān is having a wine revel and summons you; some people [also] went to Sipāhsālār Ghāzī so that he come." And he was in such a state that from drunkenness neither his hands nor feet were working. He said, "In this condition how can I come? What attendance can come from me?" Amīrak-i Sipāhdār, whom the Sulṭān had planted with him, said, "Long live the Sipāhsālār! The *firmān* of the Master must be observed and [you] must be at the palace; for when he looks upon this situation, he will forgive and send [you] back. And not being there is very ugly, and the [wrong] interpretations will be placed [on it]." And Amīrak helped his [Aryāruq's] Ḥājib, Altūntigīn, to say with him that there was no escape from going. He called for clothes and boots and headgear and put [them] on, along with a mob of *ghulāms* and 200 foot soldiers. Amīrak told his Ḥājib, "This is ugly—he is in his cups—ten shield-bearing *ghulāms* and 100 footsoldiers would be sufficient." He [the Ḥājib] sent back that milling crowd of soldiers, and Aryāruq himself did not have an idea in the world of it. When he arrived at the palace, Buktigīn-i Ḥājib was again before him, and Amīr-i Ḥaras. They brought him in and preceded him to the Ṭāram and seated [him] there. Aryāruq was [there] one moment, got up and said, "I am drunk and cannot; I am going back." Buktigīn said, "It would be ugly to go away without an order; [stay] until we inform the Amīr." And he sat in the Dihlīz—and I who am Bū'l-Fażl was weeping for him; he summoned the water-carrier and he came and held a water pitcher before him; he reached down and brought up some ice and ate it. Buktigīn said. "Oh brother, this is ugly, and you a Sipālsālār are eating ice in the Dihlīz of the Ṭāram?! Go to the Ṭāram and do whatever you want." He went away and came into the Ṭāram (if he were not drunk and they wanted to take him, it would have been a long task). When he was seated in the Ṭāram, fifty Sarāy Sarhangs of the fighters of the vanguard arrived suddenly and Buktigīn came in, took Aryāruq aside, and the Sarhangs came in from left and right and seized him so that he could not move at all. He shouted at Buktigīn, "Oh unmanly brother, you have brought this act upon me?" Other *ghulāms* came in, took their boots off and in each boot had two short swords, and Muhtāj came in. Chains were brought, very strong, and put on his feet. And his *qabā* was removed; poison and amulets were found in the front of his *qabā*; all were taken away from him and he was taken out. And some fifty foot soldiers surrounded him and other foot soldiers ran and seized his horses and arms and *ghulāms*. And his Ḥājib escaped with three *ghulāms* openly; and his *ghulāms* took up arms and came onto the roof of the house; and a mighty commotion began. And the Amīr was with Buktigīn [while they were] seizing Aryāruq; and some [other] individuals had rushed to Buktaghdī and Ḥājib-i Bilkātigīn and the notables of the army, who had beforehand [been assigned] the task of mounting up; all who had thus been prepared were mounted. When they bound Aryāruq, and his *ghulāms* and attendants rebelled, this prepared group rode toward his Sarāy. And many other horsemen of every type were joined with them, and a great battle began. The Amīr sent ᶜAbdūs to Aryāruq's people with a message: "Aryāruq was a man not knowing himself [i.e., misguided], and you were with him in [his] affliction. Today the public welfare lay in his being suppressed. And we are your masters; do not behave like children and [with]draw your hands from battle, for it is apparent that your numbers are such that you will be killed in one hour, and that will be of no use whatsoever to Aryāruq. If you keep to yourselves, we will look favorably on you and reward you." And he [ᶜAbdūs] took a message and very fine warmheartedness to his Ḥājib. When ᶜAbdūs delivered this message, water fell on the fire [of revolt] and the Ḥājib and his *ghulāms* kissed the ground; this *fitnah* settled [down] right away and the Sarāy was seized and the doors sealed. And the sun set [on it] such that you would say it had never been the dwelling of humans. And I went away and told my teacher [i.e., Bū Naṣr-i Mushkān] whatever I had seen. And the Namāz-i Khuftan having been performed, Aryāruq was transported from the Târam to Kūhandīz [Fortress]; and then ten days after that he was dispatched to Ghazna and consigned to Sarhang-i Bū ᶜAlī Kūtvāl; and Bū ᶜAlī, by virtue of a *firmān,* had him at the fortress a little while in such a way that no one realized that he stopped there. Then he was sent to Ghūr to Bū'l-Ĥasan-i Khalaf to be imprisoned there, and his story came to an end; and I will bring it in its own place how his end and killing were.

This seizure of him in Balkh was on Sunday, the nineteenth of Rabī'l-Avvāl, 422 [Tuesday, 17 March 1031]. And the day after his capture, the Amīr sent to Aryāruq's Sarāy, Pīrūz-i Vazīri-yi Khādim and Bū Saᶜīd-i Mushrif (who is still alive today and staying at Ribât-i Kundī; and they had still not given [him] [the title of] Mushrif because the Ishrāf of the palace was in the name of Qāżī Khusraw) and Bū'l-Ĥasan-i ᶜAbd al-Jalīl and Bū Naŝr-i Mustawfī. And a Mustawfī and a Kadkhudā of his [Aryāruq] who had been seized were brought there and the doors were opened and much riches removed; and they gave a list that there was very great wealth [also] in Hindūstān. And it took three days until whatever Aryāruq had was completely copied down and sent to the palace. And those *ghulām*s of his who were choice were put in chains [and sent to the Amīr]; those who were mediocre he bestowed on Sipāhsālār Ghāzī and the Ĥâjibs. And Bū'Ĥasan-i ᶜAbd al-Jalīl and Bū Saᶜid-i Mushrif he [the Amīr] appointed to go to Hindūstān to bring Aryāruq's wealth back. Both individuals left quickly. And before his being seized, swift Khayltashes had gone with letters so that the people of Aryāruq [i.e., in Hindūstān] be observed carefully.

9. THE AMĪR YŪSUF AND THE SLAVE TUGHRIL (*TB*, pp. 247–55/322–33)

Translator's Note

There emerge in this selection two themes common to many Islamicate dynasties—competition within and among lineages and the rise to power of parvenus. Since in these dynasties competition for the throne occurred frequently and often along kin-related lines, all male relatives, especially uncles, could be threats to a new ruler. The most well known decimation of a corps of uncles took place under the ᶜAbbāsid caliph Harūn al-Rashīd (r. 786–803). Here the conflict is between Masᶜūd and his uncle Yūsuf. The parvenu is Tughril. Again the level of detail is high (note the brief but especially effective scene-setting for the Tughril story) and the organization complex, involving both flashback and "flashforward" and a digression to tell a parallel story from the relatively recent past.

Mention of the Seizure of Amīr Abū Yaᶜqūb Yūsuf bin Nāŝir al-Dīn and Abū Manŝūr Sabuktigīn al-ᶜÂdil (God's mercy on both of them!)

And the seizure of this Amīr was at this Balq [a section of Zavūlistān near Ghazna]. And the story and details of this affair must necessarily be written for the matter to be fully understood. Amīr Yūsuf was a man quite without malice and would not chase after [lit., grab the tail of] any sedition or dissension. And in the days of his brother Sulŝān Masᶜūd (God's mercy upon him!), he so occupied himself in rendering attendance two times a day that he would not accomplish any work, and in between, when he would finish attendance, he would be occupied in his play and revelry and wine. And in such circumstances, youth and good things and trouble-free desire, it is apparent he would acquire [only] a little experience. And when Amīr Maĥmūd passed on and the elephant driver was far from the head of the elephant [i.e., Yūsuf no longer had supervision] and Amīr Muhammad came to Ghazna and sat on the throne, he gave his uncle Amīr Yūsuf a Sipāhsālārate, and there occurred those events such as occurred and [such as] I have brought in before this. The straightening out of [the question of] that Pādshāhship, and his term as Sipāhsālār, took only a little amount of time, in which there could be for him [only] a little enlightenment. And then such an event occurred in the confining of Amīr Muhammad in the Kūhtīz Fortress at Takīnābād; and howsoever much they do out of desire for the great Pādshāhship and howsoever much getting close to them they allow, Pādshāhs at such a time accept such attempts to get close but do not rely on such people, as in the stories of Ya^cqūb-i Layth [founder of the Saffārid dynasty of eastern Irān, which overthrew the Tāhirids 259/872]. I read such that he was heading to Nishāpūr to seize Muhammad bin Tāhir bin ^cAbdallāh bin Tāhir, Amīr of Khurāsān, and the notables of the time of his [i.e., Muhammad's] *dawlah* had tried to get close to Ya^cqūb and sent fast couriers with letters that he must hurry faster "for from this master of ours [i.e., Muhammad] no activity issues except playing" so that the frontier of Khurāsān, which is a large frontier, not dissipate. Three individuals from the most aged, most learned elders did not look toward Ya^cqūb and did not try to get close to him. And they were at the door of the *sarāy* of Muhammad-i Tāhir until Ya^cqūb-i Layth arrived. And Muhammad-i Tāhir was taken and these three individuals were seized and brought before Ya^cqūb. Ya^cqūb said, "Why did you not try to get close to me as your friends did?" They said, "You are a great *pādshāh* and will become [even] greater than this. If we give a true answer, and you will not get angry, we will speak." He said, "I will not; speak." They said, "The Amīr has never seen us except for today?" He said, "I have not seen [you]." They said, "At no time has there been any correspondence or communication between us with him or him with us?" He said, "There has not been." They said, "Then we are men old and aged who have served the Tāhirids for many years and in their *dawlah* have experienced favors and found ranks. Would it be proper for us to take the way of ingrates and try to get close to their opponents even if they cut off our heads?" They said, "So this is our situation and we today are in the hand[s] of the Amīr and our master has been overthrown. Let him do with us what God (Glorious be His name!) approves and what befits his magnanimity and greatness." Ya^cqūb said, "Go back to your houses and rest assured that free men like you must be preserved and are useful to us; it must be that you be associated with our palace." They went back secure and grateful, and Ya^cqūb ordered that group of people who had tried to get close to him seized and whatever they had confiscated and [them] expelled. And he raised up these three individuals and confided in them on matters of the realm. And I bring in such stories on this account—so the slanderers do not speak hastily about this great Pādshāh Mas^cūd but [rather] say what is owing to him, for the nature of Pādshāhs, and their circumstances and habits, are not like others, and what they see no one can see.

And it was in this connection that Amīr Yūsuf had a preference for Amīr Muhammad—on account of [his] support of the inclination of heart [that] drew Sultān Mahmūd to that side [i.e., Muhammad] so as to annoy this side [i.e., Mas^cūd]. And Amīr Yūsuf had two daughters, one grown up and come of age, the other small and not come of age. And Amīr Mahmūd gave the former, come of age, to Amīr Muhammad and the [marriage] contract was concluded; and the latter, not come of age, he betrothed to Amīr Mas^cūd so as not to offend him, but the [marriage] contract was not concluded. And Amīr Mahmūd ordered a marriage ceremony, the likes of which no one remembered, in the *sarāy* of Amīr Muhammad, which is opposite the Maydān-i Khurd. And when the *sarāy* was decorated and things made ready, Amīr Mahmūd mounted and came there and complimented Amīr Muhammad much and gave [him] a royal robe of honor and gave out many gifts; and they went back and left the *sarāy* for the bridegroom and the women.

And by the arrival of fate, fever took the bride, and at Namāz-i Khuftan they brought a litter and the River of Ghazna became full of noble women and many lighted candles and torches in order that the bride be transported to the Kūshk-i Shāh; the inexperienced helpless one answered the Call adorned and laid out among gold and ornaments and jewels; and that affair was spoiled, and in one hour the news found its way to Amīr Maĥmūd; he grew quite sad, but with the arrival of fate what could he do, for God (Mighty be His remembrance!) shows such things as that to [His] servants so that they know their own weakness. The next day he ordered that the contract be concluded for the other daughter who was betrothed to Amīr Mas^{c}ūd to be betrothed to Amīr Muĥammad. Amīr Mas^{c}ūd became very distressed, but did not have the nerve [lit., face] to say [so]. And the young[er] girl was very small; they delayed bringing her home and time passed and circumstances changed and Amīr Maĥmūd answered the Call, and that affair came out in the end that this daughter reached the Sarāy-Pardah of Amīr Muĥammad at that time when he came to Ghazna and sat on the throne, and she was said to be fourteen years old. That evening when she was carried from our section, Sar Asyā, from the *sarāy* of her father to Kūshk-i Imārah, I saw much ceremony, beyond [normal] bounds. And then after the accession of Amīr Muĥammad. this daughter was sent on to him at the fortress and was there a time and went back because she became despondent; and today she is here at Ghazna. And Amīr Mas^{c}ūd was annoyed by this—for he saw such misfortunes [as coming] from his uncle—and overpowering fate helped with this until Yūsuf fell from palace to pit, and we seek refuge in God from adversity [in Arabic].

And when things came together for Sult̂ān Mas^{c}ūd at Harāt and got straightened out, such as I have brought up before, he sent Ĥājib-i Yāruq Tugmish Jāmahdār to Makrān with a large army to clean [it] out, and he stationed Bū'l-^{c}Askar there, [and] sent Amīr Yūsuf with ten Sarhangs and a troop of the army to Qusdār [in order] for him to back up the Jāmahdār, and the affairs of Makrān soon settled down. And this was a pretense insomuch as he wanted Yūsuf to remain for a little while far from his and the army's eye and be at Qusdār [as] a city of confinement and those Sarhangs as guardians over him. And secretly, according to the *firmān* of the Sult̂ān, they deceived his Ĥājib Tughril, whom he held dearer than [his own] children, and made arrangements for him to be a *mushrif* over him [i.e., Yūsuf], and report whatever went on so as to obtain the fruit of this service in the [form of the] great rank that he would acquire. And this stupid Turk swallowed this lie and did not know that ingratitude is [or may be] unlucky. And he assigned messengers from Qusdār to the task and would send [them] to Balkh, and they would explain the good and bad [lit., lean and fat] to ^{c}Abdūs secretly and they would be transmitted to the Sult̂ān; and Yūsuf, how could he know that "his heart and liver and beloved" [i.e., Tughril] were spying on him; and all the time, and even more in wine, he would grumble and speak looser statements that "What was this that we all did to ourselves, that we will all succeed one another, and necessarily such must be that it may be that we act in bad faith and disloyalty until the affair reaches [who knows] where?" And they wrote all this and exaggerated it until the Sult̂ān became more heavy-hearted.

And [this went on] up to that point where Tughril reported, saying, "Yūsuf is making to cast himself into Turkestan and has taken up correspondence with the Khāns." And the Sult̂ān secretly ordered letters to the notables who were his guardians [saying], "Great care must be taken in watching over Yūsuf until he comes to Ghazna. When we head from Balkh to Ghazna, we will summon him. If he wants to go in another direction, he must not be allowed and must be bound and brought bound before me. And if he comes straight to Bust and Ghazna, certainly he must not be informed of anything of whatever we ordered." And those notables carried out the *firmān*, and whatever care he made necessary they accomplished. And we were at Balkh and at several times—3 or 4 or 5—swift camel messengers arrived from Qusdār and brought Yūsuf's letters—and fine citrons and pomegranates and sugar cane—showing signs of subservience and detailing the condition of Makrān and Qusdār. And the Amīr again ordered favorable replies, and the form of address was this: "The Honorable Amīr [my] Uncle Abū Ya^{c}qūb Yūsuf bin Nāŝir al-Dīn." And he wrote, "On such-and-such a day we will move [out of] Balkh; and the affairs of Makrān having settled down, it must be that you go quickly, right upon [receiving] this order, so as to arrive opposite Ghazna with us, so that [your] rights will be properly acknowledged."

And Amīr Yūsuf went from Qusdār and arrived at Ghazna before Sultān Mas^{c}ūd. Since he heard that the army of the Sultān was planning to go from Parvān to Ghazna, they came for the ceremony of greeting, [he Yūsuf] with his son Sulaymān and this ingrate Tughril and fifty *ghulām*s, very lightly equipped.

And one watch remaining from evening, the Amīr had removed himself from Sitaj, and facing Balkh had given [the order] that they set up the Sarāy Pardah there. And he was in a woman's canopied elephant litter, torches lit and couriers running to and fro. Near the city a torch appeared from afar in that plain beside Ghazna. The Amīr said, "It may be my uncle whom I have summoned who wishes permission to come" and ordered two Naqībs to go with his permission. They rushed toward the torch and reached [it] and hurried back and said, "Long live [our] Master, it is Amīr Yūsuf." After one hour he arrived. The Amīr halted [his] elephant and Amīr Yūsuf got down and kissed the ground; and Ĥājib-i Buzurg-i Bilkātigīn and all the notables and grandees who were with the Amīr were on foot. And they called for his horse and helped him mount with as complete generosity as possible. And the Amīr questioned him very warmly, warm beyond what was normal. And they rode along and he conversed with him the whole [time] until it became day and they alighted for Namāz[-i Ŝubh]. And the Amīr got on a horse instead of an elephant and they rode along, Yūsuf on his left side, and they were conversing until they reached the campground. The Amīr turned to ^{c}Abdūs and said, "My uncle has come lightly equipped; right here in front of the Sarāy-Pardah tell [them] to set up a canopy and sofas [i.e., cushioned or carpeted platforms for sitting] and tents and [my] uncle will settle down here so he may be near us. He [^{c}Abdūs] said, "So will I do."

And the Amīr went into the tent [area] and alighted at [his] pavilion; and Amīr Yūsuf was seated in a little tent while they set up canopy and sofas; then he went there and they set up other tents and his *ghulām*s camped and low tray-tables were brought and set down—I myself was looking on from the Dīvān—he did not touch anything and had become [turned] into himself quite beyond bounds because he had formed a slight [notion] of the abomination that was occurring. When the tray-tables were removed and the notables dispersed [to] the palace, the Amīr retired and summoned ^{c}Abdūs and had him [there] a long [time]; then he came out and went to Amīr Yūsuf, and they were alone and conversed for a long [time] and ^{c}Abdūs was coming and going and conversing and his [Yūsuf's] treacheries enumerated. And his end was that when the day reached Namāz-i Pīshīn, three Muqaddims from the Indians were stationed there with 500 Indian horsemen with complete arms and three Indian Naqībs and 300 select foot soldiers; and horses with saddles were brought and halted. And I saw Amīr Yūsuf, who got onto his feet, and he was still in headgear and boots and [sword?] belt, and he took his son in an embrace and wept and took off [his] belt and threw it down and told ^{c}Abdūs, "I entrust this little one to God the Mighty and Glorious and after that to you." And he told Tughril, "May you be happy, oh ingrate. Was it for this that I fostered you and cherished you more than my [own] children, so that you did such [a thing] to me for the petty favors which you bought? May there happen to you whatever you are worthy of!" And he mounted his horse and they took him to the Sigāvand Fortress. And after that I did not see him at all; and the next year, 423, when we went back from Balkh, on the road a letter arrived that he passed away at the Darvanah Fortress (God's mercy upon him!).

And the career of this Tughril, it is a short kind of story but it is rare; I cannot resist telling [it], and then I will return to the narrative.

Mention of the Story of this Ghulām Tughril al-ᶜAżdī

This was a *ghulām* whose like would not emerge from among a thousand *ghulām*s, in visage, physique, complexion, grace, and skill. And Khātūn-i Arslān had sent him from Turkestan for Amīr Maĥmūd. And this Khātūn was accustomed each year to send Amīr Maĥmūd a rare *ghulām* and a virginal slave-girl by way of a gift; and the Amīr would send him Egyptian linen and fine muslin and pearls and Byzantine brocade. The Amīr admired this Tughril and had him after Ayāz [famed favorite of Maĥmūd, who was his chief cup-bearer] in a group of seven or eight *ghulām*s who were his cup-bearers. And two years having passed, one day it happened that the Amīr was drinking in the Bāgh-i Fīrūzī, among the roses, and so many 100-petaled roses were scattered around that they were uncountable. And these cup-bearers, handsome [as the] world [lit., moon-faced], were coming [around] in turn two by two. This Tughril came in dressed in a ruby *qabā*, and his partner had a turquoise *qabā*, and they were occupied in cup-bearing, both handsome. Tughril was standing still, colorful wine in hand, and had [just] poured wine for Amīr Yūsuf; his [Yūsuf's] eye rested on him and he fell in love; and however he tried to ignore him, he could not take his eyes off him. And Amīr Maĥmūd watched furtively and was seeing the loss of sense and stupefaction of his brother; but he took no notice until an hour passed, then said, "Oh [my] brother, you are still father's little one, and father said to ᶜAbdallāh-i Dabīr at the time of his death, 'It is decided that Maĥmūd will oversee the kingdom of Ghazna because Ismāᶜīl is not the man for that. Speak to Maĥmūd of my message, that "My heart is troubled for Yūsuf. I entrust him to you; it must be that you bring him up according to his nature and cherish him like your own offspring."' "And you know that to this end we have ordered toward you many favors. And we supposed that you had grown up replete with *adab*; and you are not such as we have supposed. In a drinking party why are you looking at our *ghulām*s? Does it [not] please you for no one to look at your *ghulām*s at a drinking party? And yet your eye has stayed on this Tughril for a long time, and if it were not for respect of the soul of [our] father, a most complete chastisement would come to you. I will forgive you this one time and present this *ghulām* to you, since for us there are many like him. Take care that such a blunder not occur another time, because with Maĥmūd such games do not go on." Yūsuf was dumbfounded and rose to his feet and kissed the ground and said, "I repent and another blunder like this will not happen." The Amīr said, "Sit down." He sat. And that affair was cut off and the joy of wine rose; and the wine overcame Yūsuf [so] he went away. And Amīr Maĥmūd called a special servant whom they used to call Ŝāfī, and there were several *ghulām*s under him [i.e., in his charge], and said, "Send Tughril to my brother." He was sent, and Yūsuf made much rejoicing and bestowed many things on his servants and gave much charity. And he raised this *ghulām* up and he became his Ĥājib and he held him dearer than his own children; and as when black night brings an end to its white day and eclipses the sun, he wanted a woman [for Tughril] from a distinguished family and took unusual personal pains in the marriage contract and his wedding such that the community of wise men did not approve. And [his] reward and recompense for that came out greater than that, as I explained. After the passing of his master, there occurred [for Tughril] a sort of rank from SulṭānMasᶜūd, but he became detestable both with him and with most men, and disloyalty twisted around in him, and he passed away in the youth of his days in disappointment, and the consequence of ingratitude is [always] the same. And may God (Mighty be His remembrance!) keep us and all Muslims in His protection and may He grant the best guidance so that it will lead to gratitude for His blessings and of His servants who are the beneficiaries, through His benevolence and the abundance of His mercy [last sentence in Arabic].

And after the passing of Amīr Yūsuf (God's mercy upon him!), his servants were dispersed. Struggles for survival befell Bū Sahl Lakshān, his Kadkhudā, and he returned his monies under forcible extortion. And he was a man very learned, wise, and self-possessed, and his end came out that the governorship of Bust was given to him, since he was a man from Bust, and in [the course of] that employment he answered the Call. And Khvājah-yi Ismā^c^īl experienced many hardships and experienced plenty of ups and downs [lit., hot and cold] and looked after the rights of this House [i.e., Yūsuf's] and took upon [himself] the affairs of the children of this Amīr [i.e., Yūsuf], and held himself responsible in their cases, and fell and rose; and in the days of Amīr Mawdūd (God's mercy upon him!) he became better known and began [to do] the most special tasks for this Pādshāh and showed such competence and trustworthiness that inevitably he became prominent, so that today in the auspicious time of Sulṭān Mu^c^aẑẑam Abu Shujā^c^ Farrukhzād bin Nāŝir al-Dīn Allāh there are entrusted to him the job of deputyship and special estates and many [other] tasks. And he has pursued these tasks for a long time in such a way that no fault has come back to him. And another was Âmavī. And Âmavī, when[ever] he looked work in the face, he successfully completed it [lit., grabbed the tail of its conclusion]; but after Yūsuf, he removed his hand from earthly service and chose the Mihrab and prayer and Qur'ān and devotion and has stayed like this; and several times Pādshāhs of this *dawlah* (God's mercy on all of them!) wanted him to work, and he did do the Sālārate of the Ghāzīs of Ghazna a little [while] (God grant them peace!) and was very fine in that; but finally he caused intercessors [to help] him escape that; and on several occasions they wanted him to go with messages, [but] he made tricks so that he got out [of it]. And in the 449 they pressured him to take the Ishrāf of the Avqāf of Ghazna, and from that they wanted [him] to receive all the glory; [but] he made tricks to terminate this affair. And it is a complete man who can do such and be able to break the back [lit., neck] of desire and greed. And any servant who keeps to the side of God (Mighty be His remembrance!), He (Glorious be His magnificance!) will not leave that servant lost. And Bū'l-Qāsim Hakīk, who was a Nadīm of Amīr Yūsuf and a pleasant and useful man, also served no one, and he was generous and loyal. And today these two individuals are alive, here in Ghazna, and are friends. What remedy do I have if I have not acquired the friendship of all, for this [kind of information] is not far from the convention[s] of Ta'rīkh. And since I have completed this story, now I return to the narrative of Sulṭān Mas^c^ūd, after the seizure of Amīr Yūsuf and the sending of him to Sigāvand Fortress.

10. BUZURGMIHR'S EXECUTION (*TB*, pp. 333–37/425–28)

Translator's Note

One could argue that this story, coming as it does in the middle of *Ta'rīkh-i Bayhaqī*, constitutes a kind of center for it. It is placed at the end of a series of descriptions of imprisonments and executions—Amīr Muĥammad, Ĥasanak, Aryāruq, Asāftigīn Ghāzī, Bū Sahl Zawzanī. An analogy seems to be indicated in the unusually brief, one-sentence introduction; and the shared question is obvious: How does an absolute ruler deal with other powerful individuals around him so as to maintain his absolutism without denying himself their usefulness? Over and over again the answer has been the same—imprisonment, exile, execution.

The Buzurgmihr in question was alleged by Muslim writers to have been the chief minister or Vazīr of Nūshīrvān, the Sāsānian monarch at the time of the birth of the

Prophet Muĥammad. Oddly enough, in Muslim lore Nūshīrvān was usually a symbol of perfect justice, but here the assessment of him is demonstrably other. It is now even thought by scholars that Buzurgmihr was actually a creation of early Muslim writers who then attributed to him all sorts of positive values.

In the story that follows, Buzurgmihr's long speech made upon arrest is an encapsulated version of many of Bayhaqī's values, be they Qur'ānic, Zoroastrian, Ŝūfī, or other. The "miracle" of Buzurgmihr's "entombment" and "resurrection" follows a familiar pattern, too.

When the report about this prisoner Bū Sahl Zawzanī [financial officer of Mas^cūd who fell out of favor in 1031] came to an end, I felt an obligation to tell the tale of [another] prisoner.

A Tale

I have read such that when Buzurgmihr the Sage left the religion of the Zoroastrians, which had been a harmful religion, and took the religion of Jesus the Messenger (God's blessing upon him!), he bequeathed to his brethren the following: "I have read in books that at the end of time a messenger will come whose name is Muĥammad Muŝtafā (God bless him and grant him peace!). If I live long enough, I will be the first person to pledge [myself] to him; and if I do not, I am hopeful that our resurrection will be with his *ummah*. You bequeath the same message to your offspring so that you will obtain paradise." This news was carried to Khusraw Nūshīrvān. The Khusraw wrote a letter to his ᶜĀmil: "As soon as you read this letter, send Buzurgmihr to the palace in heavy ropes and chains." The ᶜĀmil made to send him according to the *firmān*, and the report circulated in Fars [south central province of Irān, in which the Sāsānian capital was located] that the prisoner would be transported the next day. The *ĥukamā'* and *ᶜulamā'* kept coming to him [i.e., Buzurgmihr] and saying: "Give us the benefit of your knowledge and do not withhold anything in order that we become wise. You used to be our bright star because you showed us the right way; you used to be our fresh water because we bloomed from you; you even used to be our fruitful abundance, because from you we acquired all different kinds [of things]. The Pādshāh has become enraged on your account and they are transporting you, and you are no longer one of those sages because you have left the right path. Give us a remembrance of your knowledge."

He said, "I charge you to recognize God the Mighty and Glorious, the Unique, and to obey Him; know that He sees your good and evil act[s], that He knows whatever you have in your heart, that your life is according to His decree, that when you come to your end you will return to Him, that there will be a Resurrection and Judgment, with question and answer, reward and punishment. Speak goodness and do good act[s] because God the Mighty and Glorious created you for good; so take care not to do evil and to stay far away from it, for an evildoer has a short life. So be pure and keep [your] eye and ear and hand and private parts far from what is prohibited and from the property of [other] men. And know that death is the house of life; no matter how long you live, you must [still] go there. And wear the cloak of modesty that is the cloak of the pious; make truth-telling your practice, because it keeps the face bright, and men love truth-tellers, and truth-tellers will not be ruined; stay far away from lie-telling, because the liar will not be accepted even if he give true testimony. Envy diminishes a person, and the envier will never have any peace because he is perpetually at war with the decree of God, Mighty His name! So envy people's future, not their past. The greedy one has no ease because he is [always] desiring something that perhaps will not be given him. And stay far from [other] women, because they consume riches and destroy homes. Whoever desires that his wife stay pure does not go around among the wives of others. And do not find faults with people, because no one is without fault. Whoever is unaware of his own faults is the most ignorant of men. A good nature is the greatest gift of God, the Mighty and Glorious; so stay far from a bad nature because that is a heavy bond on heart and foot. A bad nature will always be in great pain, and people will be in pain from it; to a good nature belongs this world as well as the next, and it is worthy in both worlds. Whoever is greater in age than you, honor him more and take care to respect him and do not disobey him; and do not rely on hope [alone], such that you draw your hand away from your work. People who built cities and villages and buildings and canals and experienced [lit., ate] the sorrow of this world, they have all passed away and gone and all those things have been effaced. This which I have said should be sufficient, and this much I know, that we will see each other on the Day of Resurrection."

When they got Buzurgmihr to the square of the Khusraw, he ordered, "Bring him before me just as he is, in ropes and chains." When they brought him forward, the Khusraw said, "Oh Buzurgmihr, what dignities and ranks are left that you have not obtained on account of our excellent opinion [of you]? And you have reached the station of the Vazīrate, and the management of our realm rests on you. Why have you forsaken the religion of your own fathers? Why have you, a worldly sage, made it appear to people that this Pādshāh along with [his] army and *ri^{c}āyah* are not on the right path? Was this your desire—to excite the realm against me, and bring them, the élite and common [alike], out against me? I consider you fit to be killed, for no sinner has not been killed, and you have a great sin; nevertheless, repent and return to the religion of your grandfathers and fathers so as to gain forgiveness; for it would be a pity to kill a sage like you, and there is no other like you." He [Buzurgmihr] said, "Long live the king! People call me the sage and knower and wise man of the time; but now that I have come out of the darkness into the light, I will not return to the darkness, lest I become unknowing, without wisdom." The Khusraw said, "I will order them to cut off your head." Buzurgmihr said, "The Judge before whom I will go is just and does not require testimony and gives retribution and will take His mercy away from you." The Khusraw became angrier than he had ever been at any time before. He said, "Take him back until I order what must be done." They took him back. When the Khusraw's anger subsided, he said, "It would be a pity to destroy this [one]." He ordered that they put him in a house, very dark, like a tomb, and that they bind him with iron chains and clothe him with very thick wool [*ṣūf*] and each day allot him two barley loaves and one heap of salt and a small jar of water. He [Khusraw] appointed *mushrif*s who counted his breaths and conveyed [them] to him.

Two years he remained in this arrangement. One day they did not hear any words from him and told the Khusraw. The Khusraw became despondent and ordered them to open Buzurgmihr's prison. They brought his people to him so they could speak with him and perhaps he would answer. They brought him out into the light, finding him strong of body and in good color. They said, "Oh sage, we see you in thick wool and heavy chains, in a narrow dark place. How is it that your color is healthy and your body strong; what is the reason?" Buzurgmihr replied, "I have made for myself an aid to digestion out of six things; each day I eat a little of that so that I have stayed like this." They said "Oh sage, if you see [fit], teach us that medicine so that if something happens to one of our friends, and such a situation comes up, he will have it to take." He said, "First, I have sure trust that whatever God, Mighty His remembrance, has decreed will be; second, I am content with God's will; third, I have put on the shirt of patience because there is nothing like patience for misery; fourth, if I am not patient, I do not let the weight of desire and extreme impatience affect me; fifth, whenever I think that a created thing like me has situations worse than this, I am grateful; sixth, thus I do not despair of God (Glory be to Him Most High!), who gives [me] comfort hour by hour.'' Whatever went on and whatever he said was conveyed to the Khusraw, who talked to himself like this, ''How can such a sage be killed?'' But in the end he ordered that he be killed and mutilated in order to set an example; and Buzurgmihr went to heaven and the Khusraw went to hell.

Anyone who [has] read [this], I know he will not find fault with [my] bringing in this story because it is not without a moral and the narrative has been embellished by such stories, and now I return to the narrative [itself]. . . .

11. AN OCCASION FOR A ROYAL DRINKING BOUT (*TB*, pp. 656–58/888–92)

Translator's Note

Theoretically, Islāmic law prevented Muslims from drinking. Selections like this make it clear how much that prohibition was observed at court. Here the rapid transition from heavy drinking to prayer is particularly noteworthy. This story concerns a celebration of an event characteristic of many Islamicate courts—the assigning of a prince to a trusted adjutant, in this case Khvājah-yi Mas^{c}ūd, for training in the administration of a province. In this story and others, we are reminded of the importance of protocol. Here Bayhaqī introduces the man chosen by comparing him with another famous minister of Persian origin, Ja^{c}far the Barmakid, who served (and was executed by) the Caliph Harūn al-Rashīd (r. 786–803).

The Story of Ja^{c}far bin Yaĥyā bin Khālid Barmakī

In the stories of the caliphs such have I read that Ja^{c}far bin Yaĥyā bin Khālid Barmakī was singular in his time in all the skills of administration and learning and etiquette and wisdom and self-possession, and sufficient to the degree that he in the days of the Vazīrate of his father used to be called ''the second Vazīr'' and carry out many of his tasks. One day he was seated in the Maẑālim and was reading petitions and writing answers, such as was the custom. There were nearly 1,000 petitions, all of which he signed with the royal signet that in such-and-such a matter such-and-such must be done; and in so-and-so, such; and the last petition was a whole book, more than one hundred lines crowded with cramped narrow writing, and it had come from a special servant to be released from doing additional work. Ja^{c}far on the back of that petition wrote, ''Look into it and let it be done in its case whatever is done in similar cases.'' And when Ja^{c}far got up, those petitions were taken to the Majlises of Qaẑā and Vizārah and Aĥkām and Avqāf and Naẑr and Kharāj and scrutinized; and people remained astonished and congratulated Yaĥyā his father. He replied, ''Abū Aĥmad—that is, Ja^{c}far—is singular in his time in every aspect of bureaucratic procedure [*adab*] except that he is in need of hardship to refine him [last sentence in Arabic].''

And the situation of the Khvājah-yi Mas^{c}ūd (Peace be upon him!) was just the same [in] that he came from home and school [directly] before the throne. Undoubtedly he saw in his time whatever he saw and experienced whatever he experienced such as I will explain in this work in its [proper] place. And today in the year 451 [1059] by *firmān* of the exalted lord, Mu^{c}aẑẑam Abū'l-Muẑaffar Ibrāhīm (God lengthen the rest of his life and help his friends!), he is sitting in his house until there will be a *firmān* to come before the throne again. And it has been said that a *dawlah* must fall and rise to be stable, and that a *dawlah* that goes along level, according to intention and without any adversity, will fall at the same time as its lord.

The Amīr (God be pleased with him!) held a levée, and the Vazīr and notables attended. When they were settled, Khvājah-yi Mas^{c}ūd was brought forward and performed the ceremony of attendance and stood still. The Amīr said, "We chose you as Kadkhudā of [our] child Mawdūd. Be prudent and work according to the orders that the Khvājah [i.e., Badr, the Khvājah-yi Buzurg] gives." Mas^{c}ūd said, "[Your] servant is the prisoner of [your] *firmān*." And he kissed the ground and went back, and they performed what was owing to him very well; and he returned home, was there one hour, then came to Amīr Mawdūd; and whatever of his had been brought, was brought there. And Amīr Mawdūd treated him very kindly, and from there he came to the house of the Vazīr, his father-in-law; and the Vazīr showed him much favor, and he returned.

And Sunday the tenth of Muḥarram, Amīr Mawdūd gave robes of honor to the Vazīr and Badr Ḥājib-i Buzurg and Artigīn-i Sālār and others, so extremely fine that no one remembered their like in any time nor had such as these [ever] been given. And [their] people came forward and performed the ceremony of attendance and went back. And Amīr Mawdūd was given two elephants, male and female, and two kinds of drums, and many additional gifts comparable to these, and others [i.e., people] likewise, and matters were completely prepared.

And Tuesday the twelfth of this month, the Amīr (God be pleased with him!) mounted and came to the Bāgh-i Fīruzī and sat on the *khażrā'* of the Maydān-i Zarrīn. (And that building and square today have been altered, [but] at that time they were by themselves on their own.) And he had ordered a feast to be prepared with great formality and *harīsah* [thick grain dish with meat] to be set up. And Amīr Mawdūd and the Vazīr also came and sat [with him]. And the army began to pass in review, and first was the entourage of Amīr Mawdūd—umbrellas and broad banners and 200 men from among the *ghulām*s of the *sarāy*, all with coats of mail and short hunting-spears and many led camels and riding camels, and foot soldiers and broad banners and 170 *ghulām*s with full arms, and his horsemen decorated with complete splendor; on its heels, [the retinue of] Artigīn-i Ḥājib and 80 or so *ghulām*s of Artigīn; and on their heels a troop of 50 *sarāy ghulām*s and 20 Sarhangs, their leader much adorned, with many led camels and riding camels; and on their heels, much-adorned Sarhangs, until all passed by. And near the arrival of Namāz-i Pīshīn, the Amīr ordered his son and the Vazīr and the Ḥājib-i Buzurg and Artigīn and the Muqaddims to be seated at table and he himself sat and they ate, and this group performed the ceremony of farewell and left. And the concluding of the covenant happened at the assembly of this king (God's mercy upon him!) [last sentence in Arabic].

And the Amīr, after their going, said to ^{c}Abd al-Razzāq, "What [do you] say? Let us drink a few cups [of the large sort passed around after dinner] of wine." He said, "Such a day, [my] lord rejoicing; my Lord's son having gone, according to plan, with the Vazīr and notables; and [along] with all this, [our] having eaten *harīsah*, when [will] we again have such a day for wine?" The Amīr said, "It must be without formality, so we are going to the plain and drink wine in the Bāgh-i Fīrūzī." And much wine was brought; [and] right away he went from square to garden. And about 50 bumper glasses and up to 50 two-handled glass pouring vessels were set up in the middle of a tent and the bumper glasses made ready to pass [around]. The Amīr said, "Pay attention to justice and keep the bumpers even so that no injustice occur." Then they were passed around, each bumper half a *man* [a weight measure of about three kilograms], and the revelry grew and the minstrels took up their song. Bū'l-Ḥasan drank five, with the sixth he weakened, with the seventh he became insensate, and [with] the eighth he threw up and his footmen took him away. Bū'l-Alā'-yi Ṭabīb at the fifth dozed off and was carried out. Khalīl-i Da^{c}ūd drank ten, and Siyābīrūz nine, and both were carried to Kūy Daylamān. Bū

Na^{c}īm drank twelve and fled. Da^{c}ūd Maymandī got drunk, and the musicians and jesters all became intoxicated and fled. There remained the Sult̂ān and Khvājah-yi ^{c}Abd al-Razzāq. And the Khvājah drank eighteen, sought leave to go, saying to the Amīr, "Truly, if I am given any more of this, manners and judgement will leave this servant [of yours]." The Amīr laughed and gave him leave. And he rose and left with great politeness. And the Amīr continued to drink happily and finished twenty-seven half-*man* bumpers, got up, requested water and a basin and his prayer mat, rinsed his mouth and made his Namāz-i Pīshīn and Namāz-i Dīgar. And he appeared such that you would say, "He has not drunk wine." And all this was within my sight and vision, I who am Bū'l-Fažl. And the Amīr mounted his elephant and went to the palace complex.

12. KHUT̂BAH ON HISTORICAL METHOD (*TB* pp. 666–67/903–6)

Translator's Note

This last selection contains the second of Bayhaqī's two *khut̂bah*s. Here he concentrates on the nature of historical evidence in a way that reminds one slightly of Ibn Khaldūn's (1332–1406) much later denunciation of historians who include "nonsense" in their writings. The *khut̂bah* serves to introduce a section that Bayhaqī has taken from the famous author, Abū Rayhān al-Bīrūnī (362/973-ca. 442/1050), and apparently also to justify its potentially controversial contents about a very serious matter. The section taken from Bīrūnī concerns the province of Khvārazm, which came under Ghaznavid rule in 408/1017, when the Ghaznavids overthrew a local dynasty. Bayhaqī is at pains to demonstrate that in so doing the Ghaznavids were not guilty of stealing the province from the ^{c}Abbāsid caliphs at Bāghdād, and goes to great length to do so.

Since the situation of this province [Khvārazm] is of this sort [i.e., confused and controversial], I saw it necessary to place a *khut̂bah* at the head of this section and to speak a little of the uncommon stories and reports of that [province] in such a way that wise men will accept and not reject.

Khut̂bah

Know such, that men are called men by [the nature of their] heart, and [their] heart becomes weak or strong from hearing and seeing; for as long as they do not see bad and good, they do not know joy or sorrow in this world. So one must know that the eye and the ear are the lookouts and spies of the heart, for they transmit to the heart whatever they see and hear, and that which they transmit to it is useful for it; and the heart offers whatever it obtains from them to the intellect, which is the arbiter of justice, for it to separate the true from the false; and whatever is useful it takes in, and whatever is not it throws out. And for this reason it is the desire of man to know whatever is hidden from him and unknown and unheard, and to hear of the circumstances and reports of [other] times, whether passed or not [yet] come. And the past one can find with difficulty by traveling around the world and placing suffering on oneself and seeking out circumstances and stories, or [by] studying reliable books and rendering oneself knowledgeable of accurate stories from them. And as for what has not come, the way remains closed, for it is unalloyed unseen; for if man would know [that], he would find [it] all good and no bad would reach him. And no one knows the unseen save God the Mighty and Glorious.

And although it is so, wise men are tangled up in this and are searching [for it], and turn round and round that and speak about it seriously . . . [texts problematic to end of sentence].

And reports of the past are said [to be of] two sorts, and a third other than those is not recognized: either one must hear [them] from someone or one must read [them] from a book. And the requirement of the former is that the speaker must be trustworthy and truthful and also the intellect [must] give testimony that that story is true; and the word of God supports that, as has been said, "Do not deem as true from reports anything that does not have reason in it." And a book is just the same, that whatever stories have been read which the intellect does not reject, those the hearer believes, and wise men hear those and accept them. And most common people are such that they like absurd impossibility better, such as stories of the demons and fairies and ghouls of the deserts, mountains, and seas, as when a fool gives a public entertainment and a crowd just as [foolish] as he comes round, and he says "In such-and-such a sea I saw an island and we 500 souls landed on that island, and we baked bread, and set up pots, and when the fire got intense and the heat reached the ground, it moved; we looked [and] it was a fish." And, "On a certain mountain we saw such-and-such things, and an old woman conjurer made a man into a jackass," and again, "Another old woman conjurer smeared his ear with an oil so that he turned human," and whatever [else] resembles these from the fables that bring sleep to ignorant men when they are read to them at night. And those persons who want correct statements to believe are counted among the knowledgeable, and their number is very small, and they accept the good and throw out improper statements. And Bū'l Fatḥ Bustī has said (God's mercy upon him!), and has said very well, the verses "Intellects have scales with which they assess the rightness of matters,/And they are experience."

And I, who have taken up this *Ta'rīkh,* have made it a necessity that whatever I write either is of my own witnessing or of [my] correct listening [to] a trustworthy man. And a long time before this I saw a book in the handwriting of Ustād Abū Rayhān, and he was a man who had no peer in his time in *adab* and learning and arithmetic and *falsafah*; he would not write anything foolish; and I have this long [passage] about that [i.e., about excluding foolishness] so that it be established what care I have taken in this *Ta'rīkh*; and although these people of whom I speak, most have gone on and a very small number remain, and the truth is such as Bū Tammām has said, "Then there passed these years and their peoples,/And the former and the latter are [but] dreams," [still] I have no escape from completing this book [so] that the name of these grandees remain alive and also that a remembrance of me remain; for after me this *Ta'rīkh* will be read, and the condition of greatness of this family (May it last forever!) be firmly established. And in these stories of Khvārazm I have seen fit to begin with the history of Ma'mūniyān [i.e., from 385/955 on, before Ghaznavid control] just as I copied [it] from Ustād Abū Rayhān, who has explained what has been the reason for the length of their dynasty, and what is the connection with that province in the Maḥmūdī dynasty [i.e., the Ghaznavids]; and when the dead Amīr [i.e., Maḥmūd] (God be pleased with him!) went there, how it was that he brought that kingdom under his authority and established Altūntāsh there [408/1017] and himself went back, and after that what sort of circumstances occurred up to that point when the son of Altūntāsh, Harūn, rebelled at Khvārazm and took the way of traitors and the House at Khvārazm was overthrown; for in these stories are many morals and wonders such that readers and listeners can acquire much enlightenment and many benefits. And I wish success from God (Mighty be His remembrance!) in completing this composition, for verily Glory be to Him, the Good, who prospers and assists!

Glossary

Adab. The manners, tastes, skills, habits, literature, and culture of the urbane gentleman

Adīb. One well-versed in *adab* and practicing it

ᶜĀmil. Local tax collector

Amīr. Literally, commander; used in early days of Ghaznavid regime for central Ghaznavid ruler; later supplemented but not supplanted by *sulṭān*

Amīr al-mu'minīn. "Commander of the faithful," title reserved for the *khalīfah* and adopted in early days of Islāmic empire

ᶜĀriẓ. Head of the Dīvān-i ᶜArẓ, which handled organization and pay arrangements for the army; title also used for his subordinates

Ashrāf. Plural of *sharīf,* noble, but in this sense a nobleman descended from ᶜAlī, cousin and son-in-law of the Prophet Muḥammad

Avqāf. See *majlis-i avkāf*

Dabīr. Employee of one of the *Dīvān*s, synonymous with Arabic *kātib*, who gained his position by serving out a successful apprenticeship with a master of the skill(s) in question

Dabīrī. The skills and normative rules, practices, and knowledge of a *dabīr*

Dastūr. A type of order, generally in writing, authorizing, assigning, or giving permission for a specific act or task

Dawlah. Literally, a change in fortune, applied herein to the passing of *mulk* from one group to another and the period of time they held it; thus, by extension, a dynasty

Dihlīz. Literally, vestibule, hall, corridor, or passage; here probably an anteroom for the *ṭāram*

Dīnār. A gold coin in use in much of the premodern Islamicate world

Dirham. A silver coin in use in much of the premodern Islamicate world

Dīvān (dīwān). Literally, a recording or collecting of something; by extension, a government bureau (see also *majlis*)

Dīvān-i risālat. Bureau of correspondence

Falsafah. Philosophy in the Greek sense, including mathematics, music, medicine, astronomy, and so forth

Faylasūf. One who does *falsafah*

Firmān. An order or command, of an oral or written, general or specific, nature, generally used in connection with high-level authority, even in connection with God Himself

Fitnah. A trial or temptation, applied by many Muslim historians to four internal conflicts in the Muslim community between 656 and 813: upon the murder of the third *khalīfah* ᶜUthmān (656); upon the accession of the second Umayyad *khalīfah* Yazīd (684; the one in which ᶜAbdallāh-i Zubayr was involved); upon the assault on Umayyad rule that led to the founding of the ᶜAbbāsid dynasty (747); and upon the death of Harūn al-Rashīd and the accession of his son al-Amīn (809); these Muslim historians viewed internal conflict as a mark of God's testing the loyalty and wisdom of His community

Ghulām. Slave, used for domestic and military tasks, often given as tribute from one high-ranking individual to another

Ĥadīṣ (ĥadīth). A story or report about the Prophet Muĥammad, or sometimes about the early *Khalīfahs* or other Companions; many were incorporated into the four so-called sound collections of *ĥadīth* by the tenth century

Ĥājib. A title basically meaning chamberlain, doorkeeper, but could be applied to a variety of individuals at the Ghaznavid court at different and sometimes more exalted levels

Ĥājib-i buzurg. The great *ĥājib,* chief officer of the Ghaznavid court, used almost synonymously with *vazīr,* but more often than the latter in this text

Ĥājib-i ŝāĥib. Commander of a large provincial army (cf. *sipāhsālār*)

Ĥaram. An off-limits or sacred area, such as around the holy city of Mecca or around the women's quarters of a large household; also used, therefore, for the women's quarters and its occupants

Harīsah. According to Steingass, *Persian-English Dictionary,* "a kind of thick pottage made of bruised [i.e., cracked] wheat boiled to a consistency to which meat, butter, cinnamon, and aromatic herbs are added"; according to others, a delicacy that also includes sour milk

Ĥukamā'. Plural of *ĥakīm,* wise man, sometimes applied to philosophers and physicians, sometimes generically

Ishrāf. (dīvān-i shughl-i ishrāf). Inspection; i.e., the bureau in charge of overseeing and spying on various matters for the ruler, composed of persons with the title *mushrif*

Jihād. Self-exertion for the good of the faith, striving in the way of the Lord; came to mean legitimate militant acquisition of territory for Islām, either from non-Muslim or from Muslims of the wrong persuasion

Kadkhudā. Quartermaster appointed by the central ruler for provincial armies and armies of other great men, like the son of the ruler; under supervision of the *ᶜĀriż;* also a less official kind of adjutant or valet

Khalīfah (caliph). The title taken by the central leaders of the Muslim community after Muĥammad's death and occasionally by strong regional rulers (e.g., Umayyads of

Spain, Fâtimids of Egypt, Almohades of North Africa); in this text the word refers to the ᶜAbbāsid *khalīfah* in Bāghdād

Khazrā'. Judging from the usages in this text, any of a number of raised parts in a structure—a terrace, a balcony overlooking a rotunda, or second-story pillared observation portico similar to the one in the ᶜAlī Kapu palace in Isfahān; perhaps related to Arabic meaning of sky

Khayltāsh. Apparently a *ghulām* trained to serve in the cavalry of the central army

Khuṭbah. Literally, any public address; the sermon given in a mosque during the communal prayer on Friday; in this text a formal excursus of a quasi-philosophical nature

Khvājah. An honorific applied in general to a variety of men of distinction, from teachers to rich employers to court dignitaries

Kūtvāl. A man appointed directly by a ruler to supervise a fort and its supplies of provisions, fodder, and war material for the army

Majlis. Literally, an assembly of any kind, used in many senses, including synonymously with *dīvān* in the sense of government bureau

Majlis-i qażā. Bureau of matters pertaining to *Sharīᶜah* law

Majlis-i vizārah. Bureau run by *Vazīr* (chief minister), controlling civilian and sometimes military matters and probably the chancery as well

Majlis-i aḥkām. Bureau of government decrees (?)

Majlis-i avqāf. Bureau of *vaqfs* i.e., pious foundations, as to endow mosques and schools

Majlis-i Naẓr. Bureau of matters pertaining to court of administrative complaints (*maẓālim*)

Majlis-i kharāj. Bureau of taxation

Manshūr. A royal mandate or diploma assigning or protecting specific tasks for an individual, sometimes not sealed with royal signet

Maqāmah (pl., maqāmāt). A genre of *adab* mixing poetry and prose, in which episodes of adventures in the life of a heroic figure are portrayed with stylistic virtuosity in a series of separate compositions

Mawla. in Bedouin society, a nonmember of a tribe attached to it for a period of time (sometimes prior to adoption) in a form of clientage; in early Islāmic society, by extension, a non-Arab convert to Islām, who had to attach himself to an Arab tribe as a client to participate in conquests and receive concomitant benefits

Muqaddim. High military rank, usually given to commanders of large elephant units

Mulaṭṭifah. A short informal letter or note that summarizes the main points of essence of a matter

Mulk. Literally, something possessed; thus, a realm, territory, or kingdom and what it contains and the authority over it

Mushrif. One of a number of individuals who performed official surveillance for the Ghaznavid *sulṭāns* on their subjects and reported their findings regularly

Nadīm. A boon companion, often used as confidant or personal servant by a ruler, with some degree of intimacy

Namāz. Prayer, especially one of the five formal daily services prescribed by law

Namāz-i ṣubḥ. In the morning, just before dawn

Namāz-i pīshīn. At midday

Namāz-i dīgar. In the afternoon

Namāz-i shām. In the evening, immediately after sunset

Namāz-i khuftan. At night, before going to bed, two hours or more after sunset

Naqīb. Local officer in charge of maintaining records of an ᶜAlid community (the *ashrāf*) of which he was a member; since ᶜAlid descent meant special privileges, a prized position; apparently also an army rank

Pādshāh. King, monarch; applied to great kings of the past and in this text in a generic way, but not as a title, to the Ghaznavid *amīrs*

Palūdah. Thin noodles formed by pressing starch jelly through a strainer; also a sweet beverage made with such noodles

Pardahdār. A chamberlain, porter, or eunuch of the *ḥaram*

Qabā. A man's garment, applied either to a short tunic open in front or to a close long gown

Qaṣīdah. A longish, usually tripartite poem derived from pre-Islāmic oral-poetic forms of the Arabs

Qāẓī. A judge of the *Sharīᶜah* law

Ra'īs. One of the *aᶜyān* or notables (in social status and wealth) of a town singled out by the ruler to represent the town to the central government and to cater to the central government's needs therein

Rakᶜah. A unit of praying in which there are three postures: standing, genuflection, prostration; the daily cycle of five prayers includes seventeen *rakᶜahs*—two in the morning, four at noon and in the afternoon, three at sunset, and four later in the evening

Riᶜāyah. The herd or flock; thus the term applied by some Muslim rulers, including the Ghaznavids, to all subjects not part of the court or army or ruling elite and symbolically indicating their status and needs

Rishtah. A kind of paste; also the name of soup made from such

Rishtah and *lāgūshtah.* Thick soup with *rishtah* and meat

Ṣāḥib-i barīd. Official in charge of imperial communications and spy network maintained by a ruler and essential to his authority

Sarāy. In general, a word for house, but here a household of a well-to-do individual, including extended family and other dependents and retainers

Sarhang. A commander of an army (unit)

Sharᶜ. Acceptable to, or prescribed by, *sharīᶜah*

Sharīᶜah. The official law of Muslim territories, containing principles, norms, and prescriptions derived from revelation and the exemplary behavior of Muḥammad and his Companions

Sipāhdār. See *sipāhsālār*

Sipāhsālār. A commander of an army, particularly of a provincial one

Sulṭān. An Arabic term having to do with the exercise of authority that produces security; adopted as a title by most Turkic rulers, including the later Ghaznavids

Ṭāram (ṭārum, ṭāramī): Generally, a (wooden) building with a dome or vault; or a portico, veranda, or balustrade around a garden; in the case of the Ghaznavid palaces, apparently some kind of rotunda off which were audience rooms of the *sulṭān* or in which audience was held

Ta'rīkh. Literally, the act of arranging things of the past in chronological order; thus, the genre of writing history according to that format, and a common title for a book of that sort, as well as a term for material arranged in narrative, chronological form

ᶜUlamā'. Plural of *ᶜālim;* learned man, particularly those learned in the *ᶜulūm* or branches of religious studies

Ustād. A general word, honorific in nature, for teacher in the sense of mentor or master (of apprentices); sometimes used as master in the general sense

Vazīr. Originally the term for a minister of the *khalīfah,* sometimes the chief minister or adviser; in this text often used in place of *Ḥājib-i Buzurg*

Zindīq. In early ᶜAbbāssid times (late eighth century) a word that tended to be applied to Manicheans; later a generic word for an individual with unacceptable beliefs

Bibliography

Editions and Translations of "Ta'rikh-i Bayhaqi"

Bayhaqī, Abū'l-Fażl. *The Tārīkh-i Baihaki containing the life of Massaud, son of Sultan Mahmud of Ghaznīn, being the 7th, 8th, 9th, and part of the 6th and 10th vols. of the Tārīkh-i al-i Saboktakeen by Abu'l Fazl al-Baihaki*. Trans. W. H. Morley. Bibliotheca Indica, Vol. 59. Calcutta: Asiatic Society of Bengal, 1862.

______. *Ta'rīkh-i Bayhaqī*. Ed. Said Nafisi. Tehrān: n.p., 1305–7/1887–89. (Lithographed.)

______, *Ta'rīkh-i Bayhaqī*. Ed. Said Nafisi. 3 vols. Tehrān: n.p., 1365–73/1945–53.

______. *Ta'rīkh-i Bayhaqī*. Ed. Qāsim Ghanī and ᶜAlī Akbar Fayyāẑ. Tehrān: Bānk Millī Press, 1324/1946.

______. *Ta'rīkh al- Bayhaqī*. Trans. into Arabic by Ŝādiq Nash'āt and Yahyā' al-Khashāb. Cairo: Dār al-Ṫibāᶜah al-Ĥadīthah, 1380/1960.

______. *Istoriia Masᶜūda* (1030–41). Trans. into Russian by A. K. Arends. Pamiatniki pis-mennosti vostoka, Vol. 22. 2d aug. ed. Moscow: Nauka, 1969.

______. *Ta'rīkh-i Bayhaqī*. Ed. ᶜAlī Akbar Fayyāẑ. Mashhad: Mashhad University Press, 1391/1971.

Other Arabic and Persian
Sources in the Original or in Translation

"Adab al-sulṫānah wa'l-wizārah." *Chrestomathie persane*. Ed. C. Schefer. Paris: Société des langues orientales, 1883. Pp. 10–28.

Bahār, Mālik al-Shuᶜarā'. *Sabk Shināsī*. 3 vols. Tehrān: Mahfūẑ Press, n.d.

Bayhaqī, Ibrāhīm ibn Muĥammad. *Al-Mahāŝin wa'l-Masāwi*. Ed. Muĥammad Abū'l-Fażl Ibrāhīm. 2 vols. Cairo: Mâtbaᶜah Nahẑah Misr̂, n.d.

Gardīzī, Abū Saᶜīd ᶜAbdū'l-Ĥayy ibn al-D̂ahhak ibn Maĥmūd. *Kitāb Zaynu'l-*

Akhbār. Ed. Muhammad Nāzim. E. G. Browne Memorial Series, Vol. 1. London: Luzac and Company, 1928.

Ghazālī, Abū Hamīd. *Ghazālī's Book of Counsel for Kings (Nasīhat al-mulūk)*. Trans. F. R. C. Bagley. London: Oxford University Press, 1964.

Ibn Funduq, ᶜAlī ibn Zayd Bayhaqī. *Ta'rīkh-i Bayhaqī*. Ed. Ahmad Bahmānyār. 2d ed. Tehrān: Islāmiyyah Press, 1385/1968.

Ibn Miskawayh, Abū ᶜAlī Ahmad ibn Muhammad. *The Eclipse of the ᶜAbbasid Caliphate: Original Chronicles of the Fourth Islamic Century (Tajārib al-umam)*. Trans. and ed. D. S. Margoliouth. London: Basil Blackwell, 1921, Vol. 4.

Jāhiz [real author unknown]. *La livre de la couronne (Kitāb al-tāj)*. Trans. Charles Pellat. Paris: Société d'édition "les belles lettres," 1954.

Juzjanī, Abū ᶜUmar Minhāj al-dīn ᶜUthmān Sirāj al-Din. *The Tabakāt-i-Nāsirī*. Trans. Major H. G. Raverty. 2 vols. Reprint ed. New Delhi: Oriental Books Reprint Corporation, 1970.

Kay Kaᶜūs ibn Iskandār. *A Mirror for Princes (Qābūsnāmah)*. Trans. Reuben Levy. New York: E. P. Dutton and Co., 1951.

Mardān-farūkh. "Sikand-gumanik Vigar." *Pahlavi Texts*, Part III: *Dina-i Mainog-i Khirad; Sikand-qumanik Vigar; Sad Dar*. Trans. E. W. West. *The Sacred Books of the East*, Vol. 24. Ed. Max Mueller. 32 vols. Oxford: Clarendon Press, 1885. Pp. 115–251.

Mashhad University. Faculty of Arts and Letters. *Yādnāmah-yi Abū'l-Fazl-i Bayhaqī*. Mashhad: Mashhad University Press, 1350/1971.

Masᶜūdī. *El-Masᶜudi's Historical Encyclopedia, entitled "Meadows of Gold and Mines of Gems" (Murūj al-Dhahab)*. Trans. Aloys Sprenger. Oriental Translation Fund, London; Oriental Publications, Vols. 54–56. 3 vols. London: Oriental Translation Fund of Great Britain and Ireland, 1841.

Mawardī. *Les statuts gouvernmentaux (Al-Ahkām al-Sultāniyyah)*. Trans. E. Fagnan. Algiers: n.p., 1915.

Nafisi, Said. *Dar Pīrāmūn-i Ta'rīkh-i Bayhaqī*. 2 vols. Tehrān: Furūghī Mahfūz, 1342/1923.

Nizām al-mulk. *The Book of Government or Rules for Kings (Siyāsatnāmah)*. Trans. Hubert Darke. London: Routledge and Kegan Paul, 1960.

Sūlī, Abū Bakr. *Kitāb Awrāq al-Sūlī*. Ed. J. Heyworth Dunne. Cairo: n.p., 1355/1936.

Tabarī, Abū Jaᶜfar Muhammad ibn Jarīr. *Abū Jaᶜfar Muhammad b. Jarīr al-Tabarī's The Reign of al-Muᶜtasim (833–842) (Ta'rīkh al-rusul wa'l-mulūk)*. American Oriental Series, Vol. 35. New Haven, Conn.: American Oriental Society, 1951.

———. "The Death of ᶜUthmān." *Introduction to Islamic Civilization*. Trans. and ed. Marshall G. S. Hodgson. Chicago: University of Chicago Press, 1964, 1 (revised): 9–37.

Tanūkhī, Abū ᶜAlā' al-Muhassin. *The Table Talk of a Mesopotamian Judge (Nishwār al-muhādharah)*. Trans. and ed. D. S. Margoliouth. London: Royal Asiatic Society, 1922.

Ta'rīkh-i Sīstān. Ed. Mālik al-Shuᶜarā' Bahār. Tehrān: Zavvār Publishing House, 1312/1894.

Usāmah ibn Munqidh. *Memoirs of an Arab-Syrian Gentleman*. Trans. Philip K. Hitti. New York: Columbia University Press, 1929.

Books in European Languages

Ahmed, Munir-ud-Din. *Muslim Education and the Scholars' Social Status up to the*

5th Century Muslim Era (11th Century Christian Era) in Light of Ta'rīkh Bāghdād. Zürich: Verlag "Der Islam," 1968.

Arkoun, Mohammed. *Contribution à l'étude de l'humanisme arabe au IVe/Xe siècle: Miskawayh Philosophe et Historien. Études musulmanes*, Vol. 12. Paris: Librairie philosophique J. Vrin, 1970.

Arberry, Arthur J. *Classical Persian Literature*. London: George Allen and Unwin, 1958.

Barlow, Frank. *Edward the Confessor*. Berkeley: University of California Press, 1970.

Barthold, W. *Turkestan down to the Mongol Invasion*. E. J. W. Gibb Memorial Series, New Series, Vol. 5. 3d ed. London: Luzac and Co., 1928.

Bloch, Marc. *The Historian's Craft*. New York: Vintage Books, 1953.

Bombaci, Alessio. *The Kūfic Inscription in Persian Verses in the Court of the Royal Palace of the Mas^c ud III at Ghazni*. Rome: Instituto Italiano per il Medio ed Estremo Oriente, Centro Studi e Scavi Archeologici in Asia, 1966.

Bosworth, Clifford Edmund. *The Ghaznavids: Their Empire in Afghanistan and Eastern Iran 994:1040*. Edinburgh: Edinburgh University Press, 1963.

———, ed. *Iran and Islam in Memory of the Late Vladimir Minorsky*. Edinburgh: Edinburgh University Press, 1971.

———. *The Islamic Dynasties*. Islamic Surveys, No. 5. Edinburgh: Edinburgh University Press, 1967.

———. *Sīstān Under the Arabs*. Reports and Memoirs of the Instituto Italiano per il Medio ed Estremo Oriente, Centro Studi e Scavi Archeologici in Asia, Vol. 11. Rome: Instituto Italiano per il Medio ed Estremo Oriente, Centro Studi e Scavi Archeologici in Asia, 1968.

Browne, Edward G. *A Literary History of Persia*. 4 vols. Cambridge: At the University Press, 1902.

Bulliett, Richard W. *The Patricians of Nīshāpūr: A Study in Medieval Islamic Social History*. Cambridge, Mass: Harvard University Press, 1973.

Cantor, Norman F., and Richard I. Schneider. *How to Study History*. New York: Thomas Y. Crowell, 1967.

Christensen, Arthur. *Le premier homme et le premier roi dans l'histoire légendaire des Iraniens*. Archives d'Etudes Orientales, Vols. 14 and 14:2. 2 vols. Upsala: Appelbergs Boktyckeri Aktiebolag, 1918.

Clive, John. *Macaulay: The Shaping of the Historian*. New York: Alfred A. Knopf, 1973.

Cole, Peter, and Jerry L. Morgan, eds. *Syntax and Semantics*. Vol. 3: *Speech Acts*. New York: Academic Press, 1975.

Doyle, Arthur Conan. *The Complete Sherlock Holmes*. Garden City, N.Y.: Doubleday and Co., n.d.

Eco, Umberto. *A Theory of Semiotics*. Bloomington: Indiana University Press, 1976.

Fischel, Walter J. *Ibn Khaldūn in Egypt*. Berkeley: University of California Press, 1967.

Freeman-Grenville, G. S. P. *The Muslim and Christian Calendars*. London: Oxford University Press, 1963.

Frye, Northrop. *Anatomy of Criticism*. Princeton: Princeton University Press, 1957.

Gay, Peter. *Style in History*. New York: Basic Books, 1974.

Gerhardt, Mia I. *The Art of Story-telling: A Literary Study of the Thousand and One Nights*. Leiden: E. J. Brill, 1963.

Gombrich, Ernst H. *Art and Illusion: A Study in the Psychology of Pictorial Presentation*. Princeton: Princeton University Press, 1961.

Grabar, Oleg. *The Formation of Islamic Art*. New Haven, Conn.: Yale University Press, 1973.

Grunebaum, Gustave E. von. *Classical Islam*. Chicago: Aldine Press, 1970.

Haarmann, Ullrich. *Quellenstudien zur Früher Mamlukenzeit*. Freiburg im Breisgau: U. Schwarz, 1970.

Habib, Mohammad. *Sultan Mahmud of Ghaznine*. 2d ed. Aligarh: Cosmopolitan Publishers, 1951.

Hardy, Peter. *Historians of Medieval India*. London: Luzac and Co., 1960.

Hodgson, Marshall G. S. *The Venture of Islam*. Chicago: University of Chicago Press, 1974. 3 vols.

Hodīvālā, Shāhpūrshāh Hormasjī. *Studies in Indo-Muslim History: A Critical Commentary on Elliot and Dowson's History of India as Told by its Own Historians*. 2 vols. Bombay: n.p., 1939.

Hourani, Albert. *Arabic Thought in the Liberal Age*. London: Oxford University Press, 1970.

Hughes, H. Stuart. *History as Art and as Science*. New York: Harper and Row, 1964.

Huseini, Ishaq Musa. *The Life and Works of Ibn Qutayba*. Beirut: American Press, 1950.

Izutsu, Toshihiko. *Ethico-Religious Concepts in the Qur'an*. Montreal: McGill University Press, 1966.

Khalidi, Tarif. *Islamic Historiography*. Albany: State University of New York Press, 1975.

Lambton, A. K. S. *Persian Grammar*. Student's edition. Cambridge: At the University Press, 1963.

Lane-Poole, Stanley. *The Mohammadan Dynasties*. New York: Frederick Ungar Publishing Co., 1965.

Levin, David. *In Defense of Historical Literature*. New York: Hill and Wang, 1967.

Levy, Reuben. *An Introduction to Persian Literature*. UNESCO Introductions to Asian Literatures, Vol. 1. New York: Columbia University Press, 1969.

Lewis, Bernard, and Peter M. Holt, eds. *Historians of the Middle East*. Historical Writings on the Peoples of Asia. London: Oxford University Press, 1962.

Little, Donald. *Introduction to Mamluk Historiography*. Wiesbaden: F. Steiner, 1970.

Mahdi, Muhsin. *Ibn Khaldūn's Philosophy of History; A Study in the Philosophic Foundation of the Science of Culture*. Chicago: University of Chicago Press, 1964.

Melon, M. *Mahmoud le Gasnevide*. Paris: n.p., 1732.

Margoliouth, D. S. *Lectures on Arab Historians*. Calcutta: University of Calcutta Press, 1930.

Minorsky, Vladimir. *Iranica; Twenty Articles*. Publications of the University of Tehrān, Vol. 775. N.p.: n.p., 1964.

Nāẑim, Muhammad. *The Life and Times of Sultān Mahmūd of Ghazna*. Cambridge: At the University Press, 1931.

Nicholson, Reynold. *A Literary History of the Arabs*. Cambridge: At the University Press, 1969.

Pratt, Mary Louise. *Toward a Speech Act Theory of Literary Discourse*. Bloomington, Indiana: Indiana University Press, 1977.

Richter, Gustav. *Studien zur Geschichte der Älteren Arabischen Fürstenspiegel*. Lepziger Semitistische Studien, n.s., Vol. 3. Leipzig: Zentralantiquariat der DDR, 1968.

Rosenthal, E. I. J. *Political Thought in Medieval Islam*. Cambridge: At the University Press, 1962.

Rosenthal, Franz. *A History of Muslim Historiography*. Leiden: E. J. Brill, 1952.

Scholes, Robert. *Structuralism in Literature*. New Haven, Conn.: Yale University Press, 1974.

Spuler, Bertold, ed., *Handbuch der Orientalistik*. Vol. 4: *Iranistik*. Leiden: E. J. Brill, 1968.

Steingass, Francis Joseph. *A Comprehensive Persian-English Dictionary*. London: Routledge and Kegan Paul, 1963.

Waardenburg, J.-J. *L'Islam dans le miroir de l'Occident*. Paris: Mouton, 1963.

White, Hayden. *Metahistory*. Baltimore: Johns Hopkins Press, 1973.

Zarrīnkūb, A. H. *History of Persia in the Islāmic Period*. Tehrān: n.p., 1385/1965. ''Introduction.''

Articles

Barthold, W. ''Al-Baihakī.'' *Encyclopedia of Islam*, 1:752–53.

Bosworth, Clifford Edmund. ''The Imperial Policy of the Early Ghaznavids.'' *Islamic Studies* 1 (1962): 49–82.

______. ''Maḥmūd of Ghazna in Contemporary Eyes and in Later Persian Literature.'' *Iran* 4 (1966): 85–92.

______. ''The Ṭāhirids and Arabic Culture.'' *Journal of Semitic Studies* 14 (1969): 45–79.

______. ''The Titulature of the Early Ghaznavids.'' *Oriens* 15 (1962): 210–33.

Boyle, J. A. ''Introduction.'' Juvaynī, *The History of the World Conqueror (Ta'rīkh-i Jahāngushay)*. Trans. J. A. Boyle. Manchester: Manchester University Press, 1954.

Burgess, Anthony. ''Permissiveness, with Misgivings.'' *New York Times Magazine*, 1 July 1973, p. 20.

Gibb, H. A. R. ''An Interpretation of Islamic History.'' H. A. R. Gibb, *Studies on the Civilization of Islam*. Ed. Stanford J. Shaw and William R. Polk. Boston: Beacon Press, 1962. Pp. 151–65.

______. ''Al-Mawardī's Theory of the Caliphate.'' H. A. R. Gibb, *Studies on the Civilization of Islam*. Ed. Stanford J. Shaw and William R. Polk. Boston: Beacon Press, 1962. Pp. 151–65.

______. ''Tarīkh.'' H. A. R. Gibb, *Studies on the Civilization of Islam*. Ed. Stanford J. Shaw and William R. Polk. Boston: Beacon Press, 1962. Pp. 108–40.

Goitein, S. D. ''Introduction.'' Balādhurī, *The Ansāb al-Ashrāf of al-Balādhurī (Kitāb Ansāb al-Ashrāf)*. Ed. and trans. S. D. Goitein. Jerusalem: ha-Hevraȟ le-hotsa'at sefarim 'al-yede ha-universitah ha'writ, 1936. Vol. 5.

Haarmann, Ullrich. ''Auflösung und Bewahrung der Klassischen Formen Arabische Geschichts-schreibung in der Zeit der Mamluken.'' *Zeitschrift der Morgenlandisches Gesellschaft* 121 (1971): 46–60.

Hashmī, Yūsuf ᶜAbbās. ''Society and Religion under the Ghaznawids.'' *Journal of the Pakistan Historical Society* 6 (1958): 254–68.

Hodgson, Marshall G. S. ''Two Pre-Modern Muslim Historians: Pitfalls and Opportunities in Presenting them to Moderns.'' *Towards World Community*. Ed. John U. Nef. World Academy of Arts and Sciences Publications, Vol. 5. The Hague: Dr. W. Junk N.V. Publishers, 1968. Pp. 53–68.

Holt, Peter M. ''Al-Jabartī's Introduction to the History of Ottoman Egypt.'' *Bulletin of the School of Oriental and African Studies* 25 (1962): 38–51.

Hourani, Albert. ''Islam and the Philosophers of History.'' *Middle Eastern Studies* 3 (1967): 206–68.

Khū'ī, ᶜAbbās Zaryāb. ''Taᶜrīkh nigarī-yi Bayhaqī.'' *Revue de la Faculté des Lettres et Sciences Humaines de Meched* 4 (1972): 760–71.

Lambton, A. K. S. "An Account of the Tarikhi Qumm." *Bulletin of the School of Oriental and African Studies* 12 (1947–48): 586–96.

———. "Persian Biographical Literature." *Historians of the Middle East*. Ed. Bernard Lewis and Peter M. Holt. Historical Writings on the Peoples of Asia. London: Oxford University Press, 1962. Pp. 141–51.

Lazard, G. "Les emprunts arabes dans la prose persane du Xe au XIIe siècle: aperçu statistique." *Revue de l École Nationale des Langues Orientales* 2 (1965): 53–67.

Little, Donald P. "The Historical and Historiographical Significance of the Detention of Ibn Taymiyya." *International Journal of Middle Eastern Studies* 4 (1973): 311–27.

Minovi, Mujtaba. "The Persian Historian Bayhaqī." *Historians of the Middle East*. Ed. Bernard Lewis and Peter M. Holt. Historical Writings on the Peoples of Asia. London: Oxford University Press, 1962. Pp. 138–40.

Nafisi, Said. "Al-Bayhakī." *Encyclopedia of Islam*. 2d ed. 1:1130–31.

Riggs, Çharles T. "Introduction." Kritovoulos. *History of Mehmed the Conqueror*. Trans. Charles T. Riggs. Princeton: Princeton University Press, 1954.

Shaban, M. A. "Khurāsān at the Time of the Arab Conquest." *Iran and Islam in Memory of the Late Vladimir Minorsky*. Ed. Clifford Edmund Bosworth. Edinburgh: Edinburgh University Press, 1971. Pp. 479–90.

Spuler, Bertold. "Die historische und geographische Literatur in persischer Sprache." *Handbuch der Orientalistik*. Vol. 4: *Iranistik*. Ed. Bertold Spuler. Leiden: E. J. Brill, 1968. Pp. 100–67.

———. "The Evolution of Persian Historiography." *Historians of the Middle East*. Ed. Bernard Lewis and Peter M. Holt. Historical Writings on the Peoples of Asia. London: Oxford University Press, 1962. Pp. 126–32.

———. "Ghaznawids." *Encyclopedia of Islam*. 2d ed. 3:1050–53.

———. "Trade in the Eastern Islamic Countries in the Early Centuries." *Islam and the Trade of Asia*. Ed. D. S. Richards. Papers on Islamic History, Vol. 2. Philadelphia: University of Pennsylvania Press, 1970. Pp. 11–20.

Stern, S. M. "Ya^{c}qūb the Coppersmith and Persian National Sentiment." *Iran and Islam in Memory of the Late Vladimir Minorsky*. Ed. Clifford Edmund Bosworth. Edinburgh: Edinburgh University Press, 1971. Pp. 535–55.

Unpublished Materials

Gelpke, R. "Sulṭan Mas^{c}ūd I. von Gazna." Ph. D. dissertation, University of Basel, 1957.

Hashmī, Yūsuf ^{c}Abbās. "Political, Cultural and Administrative History under the Latter Ghaznavids." Ph.D. dissertation, University of Hamburg, 1956.

Luther, K. Allin. "The Literary Analysis of *Inshā'* Texts." Paper presented at the Middle East Studies Association Annual Meeting, Los Angeles, November, 1976.

McNeill, William Hardy. "Herodotus and Thucydides: A Consideration of the Structure of Their Histories." M.A. thesis, University of Chicago, 1939.

Index

^cAbbāsids: as models for Bayhaqī, 98
^cAbd al-Ghaffār: as source for *TB*, 55, 161–64
^cAbd al-Raḥmān Quvvāl: as source for *TB*, 148–52
^cAbdallāh ibn Zubayr: *fitnah* against Umayyads by 173–75
^cAbdūs: as source for *TB*, 168
Abū'l-Alā Ṣā^cid: as source for *TB*, 55
Abū'l-Muẓaffar: as source for *TB*, 55
Adab: in Irān, 36; nature of, 36; as related to Bayhaqī, 60 ff.; as source for *TB*, 69 ff., 91
Alexander the Great: as portrayed in *TB*, 100, 153–54
Alptigīn: as father-in-law of Sabuktigīn, 31
Altūntāsh: quoted by Bayhaqī, 102
Amīr: meaning of term, 48 n. 9
Arab humanism: Arkoun's idea of, 127 ff.; Bayhaqī's relationship to, 127 ff.
Arkoun, M., 127 ff.
Ardashīr: as portrayed in *TB*, 100, 154
Aryāruq: fall of, 180–86; as portrayed in *TB*, 114
Asāftigīn Ghāzī: involvement of, with Aryāruq, 180–82
Awrāq al-Ṣūlī: as source for *TB*, 69

Bal^camī: as translator of Ṭabarī, 38; as Vazīr of Sāmānids, 159–60
Barīd: as seen by Bayhaqī, 89–90; as seen by Niẓām al-Mulk, 89; under Maḥmūd, 90, 164–66; under Mas^cūd, 188; under Saljūqs, 89
Bayhaqī, al-, Abū'l-Fażl: apprenticeship of, 39; attitude of, to caliphate, 98; biography of, 39–48; birth of, 39; character of, 43–44; choice of topics by, 52; claims to impartiality of, 96, 166 ff.; composition of history by, 41 ff.; concern of, for reputation, 94; connection of, with Persian prose style, 16; death of, 43; defensiveness of, 53, 55, 62, 153, 167; diary of, 56, 183; dualism of, 87–88; effect of aging on, 94; ethical values of, 91–93; evaluation of, as stylist, 104–5; experiences of, 41, 43; full names, 27; historical method of, 12; impact of, as stylist, 118, 125; interest of, in communication, 65; moral views of, 86–94; motivations of, 47; object of study of, 4; place of, in Persian historiography, 124–25; relationship of, to Arab humanism, 127 ff.; religious orientation of, 88–89; retirement of, 42; standards of evidence of, 57 ff., 71–72; style of, compared with others, 111, 121–125; summary evaluation of, 131–33; use of direct speech by, 65–68; view of causation of, 94–95; view of, on consultation, 103 ff., 159–60, 169, 182; view of death of, 93–95; view of evil of, 92–93; view of Ghaznavids of, 82; view of government of, 98; view of history of, 58–59; 196–97; view of kingship of, 81–82, 84–85, 99–103, 152–60; view of Sāmānids of, 82; view of self-knowledge of, 92–93; 156–57; view of, on succession, 105; writings of, 44–48

Bilingualism: at Ghaznavid court, 112; in *TB*, 111–12
Bilkātigīn: Bayhaqī's evaluation of, 92
Bīrūnī, al-: as source for *TB*, 69, 196, 197
Bloch, Marc: views of, on historical evidence, 139–40
Bosworth, C. E., 4, 89
Bū Naŝr-i Mushkān: as head of Ghaznavid chancery, 40; as quoted in *TB*, 102; mother of, as quoted in *TB*, 104; skills of, 112; as source for *TB*, 55, 97, 168–69
Bū Sahl-i Zawzanī: as antagonist of Ĥasanak, 167–69; as described by Bayhaqī, 92, 96–97; personality of, 167, 170, 171, 173; as successor of Bū Naŝr-i Mushkān, 42
Būyids: as models for Bayhaqī, 98
Buzurgmihr: execution of, 191–94; as portrayed in *TB*, 103–4, 134

Causation: in *TB*, 95–96
Cooperative principle: applied to *TB*, 136–37; features of, 135–36

Dabīrī: as focus of *TB*, 63–65; importance of, 180; as way of life, 40–41; as source of Bayhaqī's values, 91
Dār al-Islām: meaning of, 48 n.2
Didacticism, 9–10
Display text: applied to *TB*, 133–38; as concept applied to history, 18–20, 133
Dīvān-i risālat: Bayhaqī as member of, 39; functions of, 41
Drunkenness: as portrayed in *TB*, 113–14, 184, 195–96

Esotericism. *See Taqiyyah*
Evidence: in Bayhaqī's view, 57 ff., 71–72; in historical narrative, 139–41; levels of, 140–41

Farābī, al-: and Persian culture, 35
Farrukhzād (Ghaznavid Amīr): eulogy of, 56–57, 99, 102; reign of, 33
Fictivity, 19
Frame stories: in *TB*, 101, 176

Galen: as quoted by Bayhaqī, 158
Gardīzī, al-: as author of *Zayn al-Akhbār*, 45; compared with Bayhaqī, 121–24
Genre, 14–16
Ghazālī, al-: confessions of, 15; compared wi Bayhaqī, 98
Ghaznavids: cultural policy of, 35; features of, as rulers, 30; historiography of, 4; history of, 30–35; protocol of, 163, 189; relationship of, with caliphate, 168, 171; rise of, in Bayhaqī's view; statecraft of, 34
Gibb, Hamilton: view of, on Islamicate historiography, 125 ff.
Grice, H. Paul. *See* Cooperative principle

Ĥadīth: and historiography, 37–38
Harūn al-Rashīd: division of kingdom by, 105; execution of Ja^{c}far al-Barmakī by, 175–76; as similar to Maĥmūd, 31, 74; as similar to Mas^{c}ūd, 167
Ĥasan ibn Thābit: story about, in *TB*, 113
Ĥasanak-i Vazīr: charges of Qarmatianism to, 168–69; execution of, 93–94, 101, 166–73; mother of, as quoted in *TB*, 101, 116, 173
Historical narrative, general: and context, 19; didacticism in, 9; as "display text," 18–19; as evidence, 139–40; and fictivity, 19; and literary criticism, 18; and literature, 16–18; nature of, 3, 139–40
Historical narrative, Islamicate: anachronism in, 11–12; didacticism in, 9–10, 126–27; esotericism in, 10–12; nature of, 6–16, 22; plagiarism in, 15; problems of, 54; role of context in, 6–9; role of genre for, 14–16
Historiography, Ghaznavid: nature of, 4, 22 n.6; studies of, 22 n.9.
Historiography, Islamicate: effect of philosophy on, 37–38; as evaluated by Gibb, 125 ff.; future of, 141; history of, to tenth century, 37–38; nature of, 5, 6; nature of, in tenth century, 38; new approaches to, 6, 23 n.17; role of context in, 6–9; secularization of, 125–27
Hodgson, Marshall: study of T̂abarī by, 13–14
Hughes, H. Stuart: evaluation of Marc Bloch by, 139
Ĥuṭayah: as portrayed in *TB*, 113; as source for *TB*, 101

^{c}Ibar (^{c}Ibrah): as used by Bayhaqī, 60–61; as used by Ibn Khaldūn, 12
Ibn Funduq: as biographer of Bayhaqī, 39 ff., 41–43
Ibn Khaldūn: difference of, from Bayhaqī, 74; focus on and study of, 5; similarity of, to Bayhaqī, 58–59; use of *^{c}ibar* by, 12
Ibn Miskawayh: similarity of, to Bayhaqī, 52; study of, 5
Ibn al-Muqaffa^{c}, as source for *TB*, 69, 85, 159
Ibn Qutaybah: difference of, from Bayhaqī, 98
Ibn T̂āhir: Muĥammad's overthrow of, 187
Irān: in tenth century, 30
Islāmic renaissance: meaning of term, 125
Islamicate: meaning of term, 21
Islamicate world: in tenth century, 27

Ja^cfar al-Barmakī: chancery skills of, 194; execution of, 175–76; as Vazīr of Harūn al-Rashīd, 167, 194
Juzjānī: compared with Bayhaqī, 121–4

Khurāsān: cultural history of, in tenth century, 34; religious orientations in, 35–36; in tenth century, 30
Khûtbah: examples of, from *TB*, 152–60, 196–97; use of, in *TB*, 57 ff., 80–86
Kingship: dangers of anger for, 85 ff., 157–60; nature of, in *TB*, 84–85, 99–103, 152–60; relationship of, to consultation, 103 ff.
Kitāb al-tājī: as source for *TB*, 62, 69

Luther, K. Allin: explaining style of *TB*, 67–68

Maĥmūd (Ghaznavid Amīr): biographies of, 22 n.7; division of kingdom by, 104; as employer of Bayhaqī, 39; evaluation of, by Bū Naŝr-i Mushkān, 102; focus on, 4; reign of, 31; relationship of, with son, 164–66; use of Barīd by, 104
Maĥmūd Varrāq: as source for *TB*, 55
Maĥmūdīyān: plotting of, 180–81
Maqāmah: as genre, 36
Maqāmāt-i Abū Naŝr-i Mushkān: as source for *TB*, 55. *See also* Bayhaqī: writings of
Mas^cūd (Ghaznavid Amīr), attitude of, to Amīr Muĥammad, 147–49; Bayhaqī's evaluation of, 97–98, 101–2; behavior of, in youth, 90, 113, 161, 164–66; Bū Naŝr-i Mushkān's evaluation of, 102; as heir apparent, 90; as king in *TB*, 100; overthrow of Muĥammad by, 105, 146–47; reign of, 33; relationship of, with father, 164–66
Mas^cūdī, al-: effect of philosophy on, 5; similarity of, to Bayhaqī, 52; study of, 5
Maymandī, al-, Aĥmad ibn Ĥasan: death of, 94
Military patronage state: as describing Ghaznavid state, 34; origin of term, 49 n.11; as political form, 34
Mirrors for Princes: and Adab, 36; and Bayhaqī, 98–99, 100; and political theory, 34
Moses: compared with Sabuktigīn, 179; as portrayed in *TB*, 101, 179
Muĥammad (Ghaznavid Amīr), confinement of, 146–52; overthrow of, 105, 116; reign of, 33
Mukhtaŝar Ŝa^cidī: as source for *TB*, 5
Mulk: as concept in *TB*, 86; transfer of, in *TB*, 154
Musāmarah Khvārazm: as source for *TB*, 69. *See also* Bīrūnī

Mu^ctazilah: in Bayhaqī's view, 59, 155; in Khurāsān, 35–36

Narrative. *See* Historical narrative; Natural narrative
Naŝr ibn Aĥmad (Sāmānid ruler): as character in *TB*, 85–86; 159–60
Natural narrative: applied to *TB*, 134–37; example of in *TB*, 134–35; features of, 133–34
Niẑām al-Mulk: attitude of, to Barīd, 89, 91
Nūĥ II (Sāmānid ruler): fostering of Sabuktigīn by, 31
Nūshīrvān: as portrayed in *TB*, 103–4, 134, 191–94; quoted by Bayhaqī, 100

Persian language: origins of, 35
Pidārīyān. *See* Maĥmūdīyān
Pratt, Mary Louise: view of, on display text, 18–20, 133
Protocol: at Ghaznavid court, 163, 189, 195; at Sāmānid court, 177

Qarmatianism: and Ĥasanak-i Vazīr, 168–69

Rashīd al-Dīn: effect of genre on, 15
Rāshidūn: story from, in *TB*, 98

Ŝābī, al-, Abū Isĥaq: as similar to Bayhaqī, 52; as source for *TB*, 69
Sabuktigīn: as character in *TB*, 101; division of kingdom by, 105; dreams of, 176–79; as founder of Ghaznavids, 31; origins of, 176–77
Sāmānids: cultural policy of, 35; as models for Bayhaqī, 98; protocol of, 177; roots of Ghaznavids in, 31, 153; in view of Bayhaqī, 82, 95
Speech act theory: and history, 18–20, 135–36
Ŝūfism: in *TB*, 84, 104, 125, 193–94; in tenth-century Irān, 84
Ŝūlī, al-: as source for *TB*, 69
Sulṫān: meaning of term, 48 n.9

Ṫabaqāt-i Nāŝirī. *See* Juzjānī
Ṫabarī, al-, Muĥammad ibn Jarīr: account of Battle of Siffīn by, 12; account of ^cUthmān's death by, 11–12; arrangement in work of, 13–14; difference of, from Bayhaqī, 98; and *ĥadīth* method, 37; and Persian culture, 35; study of, by Marshall Hodgson, 13–14
Tabbānīyan: relations of, with Ghaznavids, 101
Ṫanūkhī, al-: similarity of, to Bayhaqī, 59–60; standards of evidence of, 59–60

Taqiyyah (dissimulation), in historical narrative, 10–11; in *TB*, 73 ff., 83, 95, 102, 104
Ta'rīkh-i Bayhaqī (or *Mas^{c}ūdī*): arrangement in, 13; accuracy of, 105–6; audience for, 47; bilingualism in, 111–12; collections of materials in, 46–47; contemporary histories in, 45; contents of, 63–71; conveying of emotion in, 95, 115–16, 171; coverage of, 44–45; dissimulation in, 73 ff., 83, 95, 104; dream interpretation in, 163–64, 176–79; drunkenness in, 113–14; editions of, 45, 50 n.49; extant parts of, 46; figures of speech in, 114–15; flashbacks in, 53 ff.; focus on chancery practice in, 63—65; focus on diplomacy in, 64; frame stories in, 101, 176; graphic imagery in, 115, 170; humor in, 113; interpolations of, 53 ff., 68–75; *khuṭbahs* in, 57 ff., 81, 80–86, 152–60, 196–97; narrative problems in, 53; pace of, 56–57; patterning in, 66, 71–73, 102, 105; political theory in, 128 ff.; relationship of style and content of, 112–18; scope of, 48; sources for, 52, 54–57, 59 ff.; 101, 148–52, 168, 196; structure in, 51 ff.; style in, 109–19; Ṣūfism in, 84, 94, 104, 125, 193–94; suspense in, 113; syntax of, 116–17; themes in, 79–106; theology in, 83; time of writing of, 46; translations of, 119 n.4, 145–97; use of analogical reasoning in, 73 ff., 187; use of cliches in, 114; use of detail in, 61–62; use of documents in, 55–57, 146–48; use of idioms in, 114; use of naming in, 66–67; use of poetry in, 151, 152, 157, 173, 174, 175, 176; use of vernacular in, 113, 114; vocabulary of, 116; volume names of, 45–46
Ta'rīkh-i Mulūk-i ^{c}Ajam (Khudāynāmah): as source for *TB*, 69, 85, 158–59
Ta'rīkh-i Sīstān: compared with *TB*, 121–24; as contemporary with *TB*, 45
Thucydides: as compared with Bayhaqī, 129 n.16, 141 n.1
Tughril al-^{c} Āżdī: as beloved of Yūsuf, 114, 115; as betrayer of Yūsuf, 90–91, 188–89

^{c}Umar ibn al-Khattāb: as portrayed in *TB*, 100–101, 113
Usāmah ibn Munqidh: compared with Bayhaqī, 113
^{c}Utbī, al-: as author of *Kitāb al-Yamīnī*, 15, 45; as source for *TB*, 55
^{c}Uthmān, ibn Affān: as described by Ṭabarī, 11–12

Women: in *TB*, 102, 104, 162–63, 173, 174, 188

Ya^{c}qūb ibn Layth: compared with Mas^{c}ūd, 187; conquest of Ṭāhirids by, 187
Yūsuf, Abū Ya^{c}qūb: betrayed by Tughril, 90–91; love of, for Tughril, 114–15, 190–91; partisanship of, 187–88; seizure of, by Mas^{c}ūd, 186–90

Zayn al-Akhbār. *See* Gardīzī
Zibriqān: story about, in *TB*, 113
Zīnat al-Kuttāb. *See* Bayhaqī: writings of